Chloe Jenkins

CW00429773

PEARSON BACCALAUREATE

WORLD HISTORY

Authoritarian States

2nd Edition

EUNICE PRICE • DANIELA SENÉS

Supporting every learner across the IB continuum

Published by Pearson Education Limited, 80 Strand, London, WC2R 0RL.

www.pearsonglobalschools.com

Text © Pearson Education Limited 2015
Edited by Sze Kiu Yeung
Proofread by Sze Kiu Yeung
Designed by Astwood Design
Typeset by Phoenix Photosetting, Chatham, Kent
Original illustrations © Pearson Education 2015
Illustrated by Tech-Set Ltd and Phoenix Photosetting
Cover design by Pearson Education Limited

The rights of Eunice Price and Daniela Senés to be identified as authors of this work have been asserted by them in accordance with the Copyright, Designs and Patents Act 1988.

First published 2015

20 19 18 17
IMP 10 9 8 7 6 5 4 3 2

British Library Cataloguing in Publication Data
A catalogue record for this book is available from the British Library

ISBN 978 1 292 102573
eBook only ISBN 978 1 292 102580

Copyright notice
All rights reserved. No part of this publication may be reproduced in any form or by any means (including photocopying or storing it in any medium by electronic means and whether or not transiently or incidentally to some other use of this publication) without the written permission of the copyright owner, except in accordance with the provisions of the Copyright, Designs and Patents Act 1988 or under the terms of a licence issued by the Copyright Licensing Agency, Barnard's Inn, 86 Fetter Lane, London EC4A 1EN (www.cla.co.uk). Applications for the copyright owner's written permission should be addressed to the publisher.

Printed in Slovakia by Neografia

Acknowledgements
The authors and publisher would like to thank Tom Buchanan for his invaluable help with and feedback on this title, and Malcolm Price for his expert help in the structuring and writing of the Theory of Knowledge section in this book.

The authors and publisher would like to thank the following individuals and organisations for permission to reproduce photographs:

(Key: b-bottom; c-centre; l-left; r-right; t-top)

Alamy Images: Alex Fairweather 145, Glasshouse Images 202, J Marshall - Tribaleye Images 255b, John Frost Newspapers 200, Julio Etchart 255tl, Peter Horree 192l, Pictorial Press Ltd 95, The Art Archive 183, 188bl, 196, theodore liasi 240; **Camera Press Ltd:** Charles Paynter 156, Gamma 12bc, German Gallego / Digital Press 10; **Corbis:** 121br, Bettmann 7, 60tr, 121bl, 230, Bob Krist 9, Hulton-Deutsch Collection 60tc, 60bl, 60bc, 65tl, Leemage 192r, Lester Cole 12tl, Lucien Aigner 91bl, Owen Franken 45, Underwood & Underwood 60tl; **Getty Images:** AFP 158, Alan Oxley 26, Bentley Archive / Popperfoto 206, Bob Thomas / Popperfoto 191, Carl Mydans / The LIFE Picture Collection 127, ChinaFotoPress 248cr, De Agostini Picture Library 189t, DEA / A. DAGLI ORTI 188br, Ed Clark / The LIFE Picture Collection 91br, Fox Photos 90, 128, Galerie Bilderwelt 99, Grey Villet / The LIFE Picture Collection 244r, Heritage Images 52, Hulton Archive 211b, Joseph Scherschel 12bl, Keystone 164, Keystone France / Gamma-Keystone 225, Keystone-France / Gamma-Keystone 189b, 201, 225, 248tl, Kirby 60br, Michael Ochs Archives / Earl Leaf 124, Mondadori 185, 203, MPI 42t, Paul Popper / Popperfoto 130, 188tl, Photo 12 17, PhotoQuest 254, Popperfoto 65b, Print Collector 110, Rolls Press / Popperfoto 65b, STR / AFP 153t, Ted Thai 78l, ullstein bild 76b, 248b, Universal History Archive 91t, UniversalImages Group 176, VANO SHLAMOV / AFP 258; **Jim Fitzpatrick:** 2010. Creative Commons Fair Use allowed. www.jimfitzpatrick.com 255tr; **Magnum Photos Ltd:** Rene Burri 11; **Mei Xian Qiu:** 253; **N&S Syndication and Licensing:** 231; **Photoshot Holdings Limited:** AISA / World Illustrated 78r, UPPA 55, 106; **Punch Cartoon Library:** 114; **Solo Syndication / Associated Newspapers Ltd:** 237t, 237b; **Stefan R Landsberger Collection/ http://chineseposters.net:** 137l, 137r, 154, International Institute of Social History, Amsterdam 28, 42b; **TopFoto:** 2003 Topham Picturepoint 244l, 12tr, 36, RIA Novosti 65tr, 234, Roger-Viollet 2, 12br, 33t, 33b, 180, The Granger Collection 76t, 123, 171, Topham / AP 246, ullsteinbild 12tc, 213, World History Archive 94; **Universal Uclick:** OLIPHANT copyright 1971. Reprinted with permission. All rights reserved 159

Cover images: *Front:* **Getty Images:** Tanuki Photography

Inside front cover: **Shutterstock.com:** Dmitry Lobanov

All other images © Pearson Education

We are grateful to the following for permission to reproduce copyright material:

Tables
Table on page 70 from *The Soviet Union 1917–1991(Longman History of Russia)*, 2 ed., Routledge (McCauley, M); Tables on page 71 from *An Economic History of the USSR, 1917–1991 (Penguin economics)*, Revised ed., Penguin Books Ltd (Nove, A); Table on page 73 from *The Economic Transformation of the Soviet Union 1913–1945*, First ed., Cambridge University Press (R.W. Davies, M. Harrison and S.G. Wheatcroft); Tables on page 136, pages 139–141, from *The Search for Modern China*, New ed., W. W. Norton & Company (Spence, J). Copyright © 1990 by Jonathan D Spence. Used by permission of W.W. Norton & Company, Inc.; Tables on pages 146–7 from *The Penguin History of Modern China: The Fall and Rise of a Great Power, 1850 to the Present*, Second Ed., Penguin (Jonathan Fenby) p.345.

Text
Extract on page 8 from *Cuba: A Short History (Cambridge History of Latin America)*, Cambridge University Press (Bethell, L); Extract on page 14 from *Cuba: Anatomy of a Revolution*, Revised ed., Vintage Books (Huberman, L and Sweezy, P). Reproduced with permission of Monthly Review Press in the format Republish in a book via Copyright Clearance Center; Extract on page 17 from *Cuba: Between Reform and Revolution*, 5 ed., OUP USA (Louis A. Pérez Jr) p.249; Extracts on pages 17–18 from *Castro (Profiles In Power)*, 3 ed., Routledge (Balfour, S), reproduced by permission of Taylor & Francis Books UK; Extract on page 19 from *Cuba: Between Reform and Revolution*, 5 ed., OUP USA (Louis A. Pérez Jr) p.256,; Extract on page 26 from *Socialism and Man in Cuba*, 3rd ed., Pathfinder Press (Ernesto 'Che' Guevara and Fidel Castro). Copyright © 1989, 2009 by Pathfinder Press. Reprinted by permission.; Extract on page 30 from *Inside the Revolution: Everyday Life in Socialist Cuba*, First Printing ed., Cornell University Press (Rosendahl, M). Reproduced with permission of CORNELL UNIVERSITY PRESS in the format Book via Copyright Clearance Center; Extract on page 36 from *Culture and Customs of Cuba*, Greenwood Press (Luis, W); Extract on page 41 from *Fidel Castro*, New ed., W. W. Norton & Company; (Quirk, RE). Used by permission of W. W. Norton & Company, Inc.; Quote on page 47 from a speech by Nelson Mandela in Matanzas, Cuba, on the anniversary of the Moncada attack, 1991, Nelson Mandela Foundation with permission; Extract on page 48 from *Cuba. A Short History*, 1 ed., Cambridge University Press (Bethell, L) p.145; Extract on page 50 from *Cuba in Revolution: A History Since the Fifties (Contemporary Worlds)*, Reaktion Books (Kapcia, A) with permission from the publisher; Extract on page 50 from *Castro (Profiles In Power)*, 3 ed., Routledge (Balfour, S), reproduced by permission of Taylor & Francis Books UK ; Extract on page 50 from *The Cuban Revolution: Origins, Course and Legacy*, 3 ed., Oxford University Press, USA (Pérez-Stable, M) 07/12/2011; Extract on page 58 from *Stalinism (Studies in European History)*, 2nd ed., Palgrave Macmillan (Gill, G); Extracts on page 65, page 87 from *Comrades: Communism: A World History*, Unabridged ed., Pan (Service, R), Copyright © Robert Service, 2007; Extracts on page 70, page 71 from *The Whisperers: Private Life in Stalin's Russia*, Reprint ed., Penguin (Figes, O), by permission of Taylor & Francis Books UK; Extracts on page 77, page 79 from *A History of the Soviet Union 1917– 1991*, 3Rev Ed., Fontana Press (Geoffrey Hosking). Reprinted by permission of HarperCollins Publishers Ltd © Geoffrey Hosking and David Higham Associates Limited; Extract on page 80 from *A History of Modern Russia: From Nicholas II to Putin*, 2 Rev ed., Penguin (Service, R), (Allen Lane 1997, Penguin Books 1998, 2003, 2009). Copyright © Robert Service, 1997, 2003, 2009; Extracts on page 83 from *Soviet Politics 1917–1991*, Reprint ed., Oxford Paperbacks (McAuley, M); Extracts on page 83, page 84 from *The Whisperers: Private Life in Stalin's Russia*, Reprint ed., Penguin (Figes, O); Extract on page 87 from *The Road to Terror: Stalin and the Self-Destruction of the Bolsheviks, 1932– 1939 (Annals of Communism Series)*, Updated and abridged ed., Yale University Press (J. Arch Getty and Oleg V. Naumov); Extract on page 91 from *The Battle for Spain: The Spanish Civil War 1936–1939*, New ed., W&N (Beevor, B) p.239, Hachette Books with permission, copyright © 1982 by Antony Beevor, © 2006 by Ocito Ltd. Used by permission of Penguin Books, an imprint of Penguin Publishing Group, a division of Penguin Random House LLC., and by permission of Andrew Nurnberg Associates; Extract on page 92 from *The War of the World: History's Age of Hatred*, Penguin (Ferguson, N 2006), copyright ©2006 by Niall Ferguson. Used by permission of Penguin Press, an imprint of Penguin Publishing Group, a division of Penguin Random House LLC, copyright © Niall Ferguson, 2006; Extract on page 96 from *The War of the World: History's Age of Hatred*, Penguin (Ferguson, N 2006) copyright © 2006 by Niall Ferguson. Used by permission of Penguin Press, an imprint of Penguin Publishing Group, a division of Penguin Random House LLC, copyright © Niall Ferguson, 2006; Extract on page 104 from *The Soviet Union 1917–1991(Longman History of Russia)*, 2 ed., Routledge (McCauley, M); Extract on page 115 from *The Rise of Modern China*, 3rd Revised ed., Oxford University Press Inc (Hsu, I 1983); Extract on page 119 from *Modern China*, 3 ed., Routledge (Moise, EE) p.73, copyright © Routledge, reproduced by permission of Taylor & Francis Books UK; Extract on page 124 from *The Penguin History of Modern China: The Fall and Rise of a Great Power, 1850 to the Present*, Second Ed., Penguin (Jonathan Fenby) p.309; Extract on page 125 from *Modern China*, 3 ed., Routledge (Moise, EE); Extracts on pages 125–26

from *The Rise of Modern China*, 3rd Revised ed., Oxford University Press Inc (Hsu, I 1983); Extracts on page 125, page 126, page 153, page 161 from *The Penguin History of Modern China: The Fall and Rise of a Great Power, 1850 to the Present*, Second Ed., Penguin (Jonathan Fenby); Extracts on page 128, page 145 from *The Search for Modern China*, New ed., W. W. Norton & Company (Spence, J), copyright © 1990 by Jonathan D Spence. Used by permission of W. W. Norton & Company, Inc.; Extract on page 128 from *Stilwell's letter to his wife just before his recall, 1944 The Stilwell Papers, Joseph Warren. Theodore H. White (Ed.)* New ed., Da Capo (Stilwell 1962) copyright © Mar 22, 1991, Theodore H. White. Reprinted by permission of Da Capo Press, a member of the Perseus Books Group; Extracts on page 130 from *Access to History: China: from Empire to People's Republic 1900–49*, 2 ed., Hodder Education (Michael Lynch 1996); Extract on page 133 from *Modern China*, 3 ed., Routledge (Moise, EE); Extracts on page 133, page 134 from *The Rise of Modern China*, 3rd Revised ed., Oxford University Press Inc (Hsu, I 1983); Extracts on page 135, from *Modern China*, 3 ed., Routledge (Moise, EE); Extract on page 138 from *The Rise of Modern China*, 3rd Revised ed., Oxford University Press Inc (Hsu, I 1983); Extract on page 142 from *Mao: A Reinterpretation*, Reprint ed., Ivan R Dee, Inc (Feigon, L). Reproduced with permission of Ivan R. Dee Publisher in the format Book via Copyright Clearance Center; Extract on page 144 from *Mao: The Unknown Story*, Vintage (Chang J and Halliday J), The Random House Group, copyright, © 2005 by Globalflair Ltd. Used by permission of Alfred A. Knopf, an imprint of the Knopf, Doubleday Publishing Group, a division of Penguin Random House LLC. All rights reserved; Poetry on page 146 from *The Origins of the Cultural Revolution Volume 1, 1959*, Columbia University Press (MacFarquhar, R), with permission from the publisher; Extract on page 160 from *China without Mao*, 2 ed., Oxford University Press (Hsu, I); Extract on page 160 from *China without Mao*, Oxford University Press Inc (Hsu, I 1982) p154; Extract on page 160 from The Maoist Legacy and China's New Industrialization Strategy, *The China Quarterly*, September (Kueh 1989), Cambridge University Press with permission; Extract on page 161 from *The Rise of Modern China*, 3rd Revised ed., Oxford University Press Inc (Hsu, I 1983) p.780; Extract on page 161 from *Modern China*, 3 ed., Routledge (Moise, EE; Extract on page 168–69 from *Mussolini in the First World War: The Journalist, the Soldier, the Fascist*, Bloomsbury (O'Brien, P) pp.31–32, , Bloomsbury Publishing Group with permission; Extract on page 172 from Payne, Stanley. A History Of Fascism, 1914–1945. © 1995 by the Board of Regents of the University of Wisconsin System. Reproduced by the permission of the University of Wisconsin Press.; Extract on page 172 from *Liberal and Fascist Italy: 1900–1945 (Short Oxford History of Italy)*, OUP Oxford (ed. Adrian Lyttelton); Extract on page 173 from *The European Dictatorships: Hitler, Stalin, Mussolini (Cambridge Perspectives in History)*, Cambridge University Press (Todd, A); Extracts on page 173, page 174 from *The History of Italy*, Westport, CT: Greenwood Press (Charles L. Killinger 2002), The History of Italy by KILLINGER, CHARLES L. Reproduced with permission of Greenwood Publishing Group, Incorporated in the format Republish in a book via Copyright Clearance Center; Extract on page 176 from *Benito Mussolini, My Autobiography*, Dover Publications Inc (Mussolini, B) p. 130; Extract on page 180 from *The Seizure of Power: Fascism in Italy, 1919–1929*, Revised ed., Routledge (Lyttelton, A), by permission of Taylor & Francis Books UK; Extract on page 180 from *Italy from Within*, 1st ed, The Macmillan Company (Massock, RG 1943); Extract on page 182 from *Fascist Voices: An Intimate History of Mussolini's Italy*, Vintage (Christopher Duggan). Reprinted by permission of The Random House Group Limited; Extract on page 183 from *The European Dictatorships: Hitler, Stalin, Mussolini (Cambridge Perspectives in History)*, Cambridge University Press (Todd, A) p.119; Extract on page 183 from *Mussolini*, Chicago University Press (Fermi, L 1966); Extract on page 185 from *Mussolini's Italy*, 1st ed., Macmillan Publishing (Gallo, M); Extract on page 190 from *Fascist Voices: An Intimate History of Mussolini's Italy*, Vintage (Christopher Duggan 2012) Published by Bodley Head. Reprinted by permission of The Random House Group Limited; Article on page 190 from Thomas Meakin Asks to What Extent Italian Fascism Represented a Triumph of Style over Substance, *History Review*, no. 59 (Meakin, T 2007), Thomas Meakin, Mussolini's Fascism: St Hugh's College, Oxford, in Association with History Review: Julia Wood Prize, Used by permission of the publisher, History Today; Extract on page 190 from *The Seizure of Power: Fascism in Italy, 1919–1929*, Revised ed., Routledge (Lyttelton, A) p.402, by permission of Taylor & Francis Books UK; Extract on page 191 from *Football and Fascism: The National Game under Mussolini*, Berg (Martin, S), Bloomsbury Publishing Group; Extract on page 194 from *Uncertain Refuge: Italy and the Jews during the Holocaust*, trans. Florette Rechnitz Koffler and Richard Koffler, University of Illinois Press (Caracciolo, N); Extract on page 195 from *How Fascism Ruled Women. Italy 1922–1945*, Reprint ed., University of California Press (Victoria de Grazia), How fascism ruled women: Italy, 1922–1945 by De Grazia, Victoria. Reproduced with permission of University of California Press in the format Republish in a book via Copyright Clearance Center; Extract on page 195 from *Contradiction and the Role of the 'Floating Signifier': Identity and the 'New Woman' in Italian Cartoons During Fascism*, University of Essex (Mascha, E 2010). Journal of International Women's Studies, 11(4), 128–142; Available at: http://vc.bridgew.edu/jiws/vol11/iss4/9; Extract on

page 200 from *Hitler, Stalin, and Mussolini: Totalitarianism in the Twentieth Century*, 4th ed., John Wiley & Sons (Pauley, BF). Reproduced with permission of Harlan Davidson in the format Republish in a book via Copyright Clearance Center; Extract on page 203 from *The Fall of Mussolini: Italy, the Italians, and the Second World War*, Reprint ed, OUP Oxford (Morgan, M); Extract on page 205 from *The Origins of the Second World War*, Penguin (A. J. P. Taylor), (Hamish Hamilton 1961, Penguin Books 1964, 1987, 1991) Copyright © A J P Taylor, 1961, 1963; Extracts on page 212, page 216, page 221, page 230, page 232, page 233 from *Nasser*, Simon & Schuster (Stephens, R), Reprinted with the permission of Simon & Schuster, Inc. Copyright © 1971 Robert Stephens.; Extract on page 238 from *A History of the Middle East*, Re-issue ed., Penguin (Mansfield, P) reprinted by permission of Peters Fraser & Dunlop (www.petersfraserdunlop.com) on behalf of the Estate of Peter Mansfield; Extract on page 239–40 from *Nasser: The Last Arab* (Said Aburish 2004), Duckworth Publishers and Co. Ltd; Extract on page 244 from *Nasser*, Simon & Schuster (Stephens, R) . Reprinted with the permission of Simon & Schuster, Inc. Copyright © 1971 Robert Stephens; Extract on page 244 from *Nasser: The Last Arab* (Said Aburish 2004), Duckworth Publishers and Co. Ltd; Extract on page 244 from *The State of Africa: A History of the Continent Since Independence*, Simon & Schuster Ltd (Meredith, M), with permission from Simon & Schuster UK Ltd and with permission from the author; Extract on page 245 from *Nasser: The Last Arab* (Said Aburish 2004), Duckworth Publishers and Co. Ltd; Extract on page 253 from *A Bitter Revolution: China's Struggle with the Modern World (Making of the Modern World)*, New ed. OUP Oxford (Mitter, R) p.210; Extract on page 253 from *Modern China*, 3 ed, Routledge (Moise, EE) pp. 166–67; Extract on page 254 from *Nasser: The Last Arab*, Gerald Duckworth & Co Ltd (Aburish, S) p.311, with permission of the publisher; Extract on page 256 from Winston Churchill, in a letter to Mussolini, after a visit to Rome (1927). Reproduced with permission of Curtis Brown, London on behalf of the Estate of Winston S. Churchill Copyright © The Estate of Winston S. Churchill; Lyric on page 256 from *You are the top* from the 1934 musical *Anything Goes*, Lyrics written by P.G. Wodehouse for a London production of *Anything Goes*, J. Peter Lobbenberg & Co with permission; Extract on page 258 from *Comrades: Communism: A World History*, Unabridged ed., Pan (Service, R) p.180. Copyright © Robert Service, 2007; Extract on page 258 from *Inside the Stalin Archives*, Atlas & Co (Brent, J) p. 231, with permission from the author, Professor Jonathan Brent.

Every effort has been made to contact copyright holders of material reproduced in this book.

The assessment objectives have been reproduced from IBO documents. Our thanks go to the International Baccalaureate for permission to reproduce its intellectual copyright.

This material has been developed independently by the publisher and the content is in no way connected with or endorsed by the International Baccalaureate (IB).

International Baccalaureate® is a registered trademark of the International Baccalaureate Organization.

There are links to relevant websites in this book. In order to ensure that the links are up to date and that the links work we have made the links available on our website at www.pearsonhotlinks.com. Search for this title or ISBN 9781292102573.

Contents

Introduction

How will this book help you in your IB examination?

This book will help you prepare for Paper 2 in the International Baccalaureate History exam by equipping you with the knowledge and skills you need to demonstrate in your examination. It focuses on *World history topic 10: Authoritarian states (20th century)*, one of the 12 topics in Paper 2. It addresses five states that feature as suggested examples in the History Guide and covers all aspects of Diploma Programme History. These case studies also constitute relevant material for the different Higher Level regional options.

Notes on the second edition

Included in the book are chapters on each of the selected states. All aspects of the prescribed content under the three topics outlined in the IB History Guide for *World history topic 10: Authoritarian states (20th century) – Emergence of authoritarian states, Consolidation and maintenance of power, Aims and results of policies* – are covered within each chapter, though not necessarily in that order. Instead, the sections in each chapter have been carefully structured in a way that is most logical and beneficial to your understanding of the subject matter.

There is also a chapter on how to approach Paper 2 questions, offering essay-writing techniques, and a fully updated chapter on history and Theory of Knowledge (ToK). Furthermore, this edition includes a chapter on making comparisons between leaders and states from different regions to help you answer comparative questions. By working through these chapters, you will gain an understanding of the aims of the IB History course, as well as the key concepts and skills that are reflected in the structure and assessment objectives of Paper 2. There are a number of new features in this edition (explained in more detail later in the Introduction), including *Challenge yourself* questions to extend learning and boxes addressing international mindedness.

Key concepts

At the start of each chapter, you will see six concepts outlined with suggestions of how you can consider them as you work your way through the material. These should assist you to think critically about the topics that are covered in each chapter. See page vi for more information.

Approaches to learning

You will notice that every Activity addresses a number of approaches to teaching and learning (ATL) skills. For example, a certain question may ask you to do some research on Stalin's policies and then to make a presentation to your classmates, telling them what you found out. In this way, you would be developing not only your research skills but also how to communicate historical knowledge. So, the ATLs give you an idea of what kind of skills you will be practising when you complete certain tasks.

Comparisons

A chapter on comparisons and contrasts is included to help you to think about the similarities and differences between the authoritarian leaders in terms of their rise to power, their policies, and their maintenance of power. This chapter is both useful and important as it is likely that exam questions will ask you to compare and contrast the leaders you study.

What this book includes

This book addresses one of the 12 topics in Paper 2. You are required to prepare for two topics and answer one question from each of these selected topics. This book provides you with detailed information on all the areas you need to study for each of the state leaders included here. It will also be useful to those of you taking the Higher Level regional option Paper 3, as the selected states covered by this book are relevant to the history of their respective regions. In addition, the material included in each chapter can be used to assist you in choosing and researching suitable topics for the Internal Assessment (IA – Historical Investigation) or the History Extended Essays (EE).

Each chapter includes:

- a list of the key themes and topics covered in the chapter
- specific focus on each of the six key concepts for DP History: continuity, change, causation, consequence, perspective, significance (understanding and applying these concepts are central to planning and writing focused answers in your essays)
- timelines of events for each leader
- analysis of the emergence, consolidation, and maintenance of power of each of the leaders included, as well as focus on the aims and results of both domestic and foreign policies
- primary and secondary sources, including reference to historiographical approaches relevant to each major theme
- examples of students' responses to help you reflect on a variety of approaches used by students in tackling exam questions
- examiner's comments to explain the strengths and weaknesses of students' responses, and recommendations on how these answers could be improved
- a review section to help you reflect on your learning and revise key topics.

Important terms used in each chapter are **emboldened** in the text; their definitions can be found in the glossary at the back of the book.

eBook

In the eBook you will find the following:

- Additional worksheets containing student activities
- An interactive glossary
- Practice examination quizzes
- Revision quizzes
- Biographies of key figures covered in the book
- Links to relevant Internet sites
- Enlargeable photos of useful resources, such as maps and source cartoons.

For more details about your eBook, see pages x–xi.

How this book works

In addition to the main text, there are a number of coloured boxes in every chapter, each with a distinctive icon. The boxes provide different information and stimulus:

Interesting facts

These boxes contain interesting information that will add to your wider knowledge, but which does not fit within the main body of the text.

Afro-Cuban religions

These faiths are based on the religious beliefs of former West African slaves, and they have incorporated some aspects of Catholicism. As they were forced to adopt Catholicism during the Spanish rule of Cuba, these slaves hid their religious secrets inside the imagery of their masters' saints. *Santería*, or 'the way of the Saints', is the term slave owners used to refer to their slaves' worship.

International mindedness

These are activities that invite you to explore, for example, the similarities and differences between different states, or to reflect on how your knowledge contributes to a better understanding of the world we live in today.

 **(ATL) Research and thinking skills**

Historians have compared Egyptian involvement in Yemen to the United States' involvement in the Vietnam War. How would you support such an assertion? Can you think of other civil wars that have been compared to the Vietnam War?

Challenge yourself

These boxes invite you to carry out additional research on an aspect discussed in the chapter.

....

CHALLENGE YOURSELF

(ATL) Social, research, communication, and thinking skills

In groups, carry out research on the history of the *Granma* newspaper. Find out information about its relationship with the Cuban state. Also, discuss why you think the PCC formed a youth branch and a children's organization.

....

Hints for success

These boxes can be found alongside questions, exercises, and worked examples. They provide insight into how to answer a question in order to achieve the highest marks in an examination. They also identify common pitfalls when answering such questions and suggest approaches that examiners like to see.

It is not sufficient to show that you know which methods Castro used in his rise to power. You also need to explain *how* they contributed to his rise. A paragraph explaining the events of the Moncada assault will not be an effective way to address how Castro came to power. You will need to explain the significance of the event in Castro's road to power by explaining, for example, how the use of force in Moncada enabled the Cuban population to identify Castro as a leader of the opposition, who was prepared to act in order to change the situation.

Weblinks

At the end of each chapter, you will find the URL for the Pearson hotlinks website in the weblinks box. To access websites relevant to a particular chapter, go to www.pearsonhotlinks.com, search for the book title or ISBN, and click on the relevant chapter number.

 To access websites relevant to this chapter, go to www.pearsonhotlinks.com, search for the book title or ISBN, and click on 'Chapter 2'.

Relevant websites for each chapter can also be found in the Further Reading section at the end of the book. These websites contain video material and additional information to support the topic you are studying.

Theory of Knowledge

There are also Theory of Knowledge (ToK) boxes throughout the book – see page viii for more information about these.

IB History aims and assessment objectives

Whether you are studying history at Higher or Standard Level, you need to take a broad view of how past events have brought us to where we are today. The awareness of how events separated by both time and space are nevertheless linked together in cause and effect is one of the most important skills to be developed during the IB History course. For example, you need to understand what circumstances and methods brought a particular leader to power, and analyse the part played by similar factors in the rise of leaders from other regions.

Although this book is essentially designed as a textbook to accompany Paper 2, Topic 10 (Authoritarian States – 20th century), as you work through it you will be learning and practising the skills that are necessary for different papers. This book also covers the assessment objectives relevant to Paper 2 – specifically, the assessment objectives focusing on the following skills:

Assessment objective 1: Knowledge and understanding

You will learn to recall and select relevant historical knowledge, and demonstrate detailed and in-depth understanding of processes of cause–effect and continuity–change.

Assessment objective 2: Application and interpretation

You will learn to apply historical knowledge as evidence and show awareness of different approaches to, and interpretations of, historical issues and events.

Assessment objective 3: Synthesis and evaluation

You will learn to evaluate and appreciate the reasons and ways in which opinions and interpretations differ, and to synthesize these using evidence.

Assessment objective 4: Use and application of appropriate skills

You will develop the ability to structure an essay answer, using evidence to support relevant, balanced, and focused historical arguments.

IB learner profile

When the IB set out a course curriculum, they have in mind certain qualities that they want a student to develop. These are not abstract ideas; everything you learn and do as part of the IB programme contributes to the development of these qualities. These objectives apply to the study of history.

Through the study of the topics in this book, you will become more knowledgeable about the world around you, become a critical inquirer, and make connections between events and across regions. You will be encouraged to take an investigative approach, gathering and analysing evidence, and producing logical, well-argued answers. Be prepared to change your mind; if you hold a particular opinion about an issue, find out about different points of view. It is useful to reflect on how the material you have learned and the skills you have acquired are relevant to areas other than history, and how they help you deal with your understanding, for example, of global issues.

Theory of Knowledge

History is a Group 3 subject in the IB Diploma. It is an 'area of knowledge' that considers individuals and societies. In the subject of IB History, many different ways of obtaining knowledge are used.

When working through this book you should reflect on the methods used not only by professional historians, but also by yourself, as a student of history, to gain knowledge. The methods used by historians are important to highlight, as it will be necessary to compare and contrast these with the other 'areas of knowledge', such as the Human Sciences and the Group 4 Sciences (Physics, Chemistry, and Biology). You should think about the role of individuals in history, the difference between bias and selection, and the role played by the historian. You will reflect in detail on these types of question in the final section of your Internal Assessment.

Theory of Knowledge boxes

There are ToK boxes throughout the book. These boxes will enable you to consider ToK issues as they arise and in context. Often they will just contain a question to stimulate your thoughts and discussion.

> At the time of writing this book, Fidel Castro had transferred power to his brother Raúl, but has continued to be a leading voice in Cuban affairs. What, if anything, do you know about Raúl Castro? Can you find any recent information in the newspapers about Cuba? To what extent do you think your previous knowledge and opinions of Castro and Cuba can influence your study of this chapter?
>
> **TOK**

We have also included a chapter on Theory of Knowledge, which has been updated for the latest

ToK curriculum with the help of ToK expert Malcolm Price. In it, you will be encouraged to reflect on the methods used by historians by thinking about questions such as:

- What is the role of the historian?
- What methods do historians use to gain knowledge?

- Who decides which events are historically significant?

These types of questions require you to reflect on and engage with how historians work, and will help you with the reflection section of the Internal Assessment.

How to use your enhanced eBook

Jump to any page

Switch from single- to double-page view

Highlight parts of the text

Create notes

Search the whole book

Zoom

Browse   My Searches   Search...   Gc

Page 74   107%

Images

Select the icon to enlarge the image

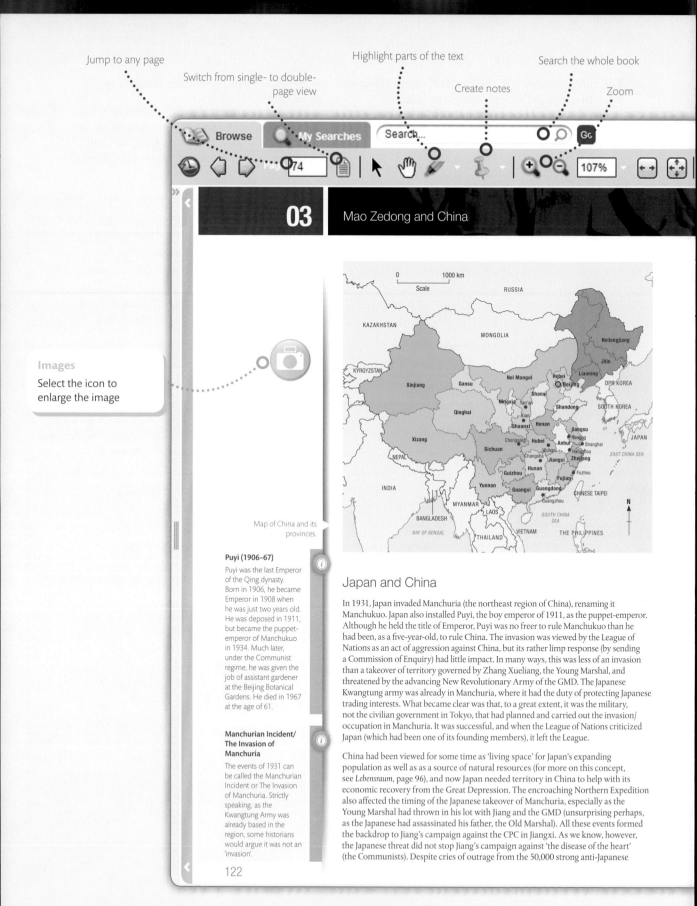

03   Mao Zedong and China

Map of China and its provinces.

Puyi (1906–67)

Puyi was the last Emperor of the Qing dynasty. Born in 1906, he became Emperor in 1908 when he was just two years old. He was deposed in 1911, but became the puppet-emperor of Manchukuo in 1934. Much later, under the Communist regime, he was given the job of assistant gardener at the Beijing Botanical Gardens. He died in 1967 at the age of 61.

Manchurian Incident/ The Invasion of Manchuria

The events of 1931 can be called the Manchurian Incident or The Invasion of Manchuria. Strictly speaking, as the Kwangtung Army was already based in the region, some historians would argue it was not an 'invasion'.

122

Japan and China

In 1931, Japan invaded Manchuria (the northeast region of China), renaming it Manchukuo. Japan also installed Puyi, the boy emperor of 1911, as the puppet-emperor. Although he held the title of Emperor, Puyi was no freer to rule Manchukuo than he had been, as a five-year-old, to rule China. The invasion was viewed by the League of Nations as an act of aggression against China, but its rather limp response (by sending a Commission of Enquiry) had little impact. In many ways, this was less of an invasion than a takeover of territory governed by Zhang Xueliang, the Young Marshal, and threatened by the advancing New Revolutionary Army of the GMD. The Japanese Kwangtung army was already in Manchuria, where it had the duty of protecting Japanese trading interests. What became clear was that, to a great extent, it was the military, not the civilian government in Tokyo, that had planned and carried out the invasion/ occupation in Manchuria. It was successful, and when the League of Nations criticized Japan (which had been one of its founding members), it left the League.

China had been viewed for some time as 'living space' for Japan's expanding population as well as as a source of natural resources (for more on this concept, see *Lebensraum*, page 96), and now Japan needed territory in China to help with its economic recovery from the Great Depression. The encroaching Northern Expedition also affected the timing of the Japanese takeover of Manchuria, especially as the Young Marshal had thrown in his lot with Jiang and the GMD (unsurprising perhaps, as the Japanese had assassinated his father, the Old Marshal). All these events formed the backdrop to Jiang's campaign against the CPC in Jiangxi. As we know, however, the Japanese threat did not stop Jiang's campaign against 'the disease of the heart' (the Communists). Despite cries of outrage from the 50,000 strong anti-Japanese

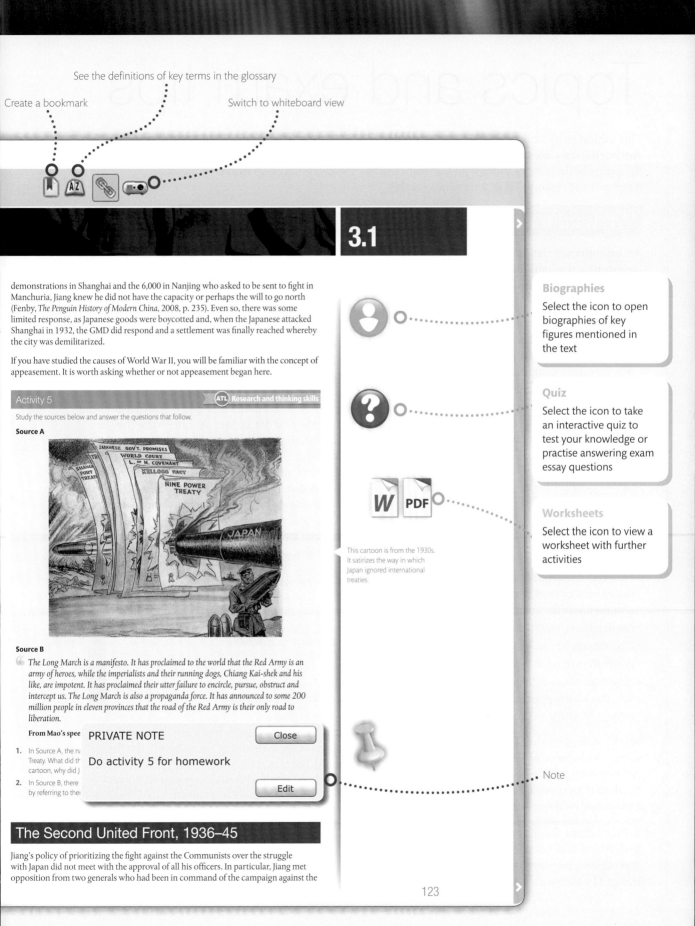

Create a bookmark

See the definitions of key terms in the glossary

Switch to whiteboard view

3.1

demonstrations in Shanghai and the 6,000 in Nanjing who asked to be sent to fight in Manchuria, Jiang knew he did not have the capacity or perhaps the will to go north (Fenby, *The Penguin History of Modern China*, 2008, p. 235). Even so, there was some limited response, as Japanese goods were boycotted and, when the Japanese attacked Shanghai in 1932, the GMD did respond and a settlement was finally reached whereby the city was demilitarized.

If you have studied the causes of World War II, you will be familiar with the concept of appeasement. It is worth asking whether or not appeasement began here.

Activity 5 (ATL) Research and thinking skills

Study the sources below and answer the questions that follow.

Source A

JAPANESE GOV'T. PROMISES
WORLD COURT
L. OF N. COVENANT
KELLOGG PACT
NINE POWER TREATY
SHANGHAI PORT TREATY
JAPAN

This cartoon is from the 1930s. It satirizes the way in which Japan ignored international treaties.

Source B

❝ The Long March is a manifesto. It has proclaimed to the world that the Red Army is an army of heroes, while the imperialists and their running dogs, Chiang Kai-shek and his like, are impotent. It has proclaimed their utter failure to encircle, pursue, obstruct and intercept us. The Long March is also a propaganda force. It has announced to some 200 million people in eleven provinces that the road of the Red Army is their only road to liberation.

From Mao's spee

1. In Source A, the n
   Treaty. What did th
   cartoon, why did J

2. In Source B, there
   by referring to thei

PRIVATE NOTE   Close

Do activity 5 for homework

Edit

Biographies
Select the icon to open biographies of key figures mentioned in the text

Quiz
Select the icon to take an interactive quiz to test your knowledge or practise answering exam essay questions

W PDF

Worksheets
Select the icon to view a worksheet with further activities

Note

The Second United Front, 1936–45

Jiang's policy of prioritizing the fight against the Communists over the struggle with Japan did not meet with the approval of all his officers. In particular, Jiang met opposition from two generals who had been in command of the campaign against the

123

Topics and exam tips

This section introduces **World history topic 10: Authoritarian states (20th century)**. It examines the nature of these states, along with the major topics listed in the IB History Guide. It then looks at the structure of the exam and the kind of questions that you may be asked, before giving advice on how to write a good essay answer in the exam.

What constitutes an authoritarian state?

An authoritarian state is defined as a system of government that puts order and obedience to the regime above the personal freedoms of its citizens.

To be classed as authoritarian, a state has to have:

- either only one legal political party, or it limits the existence of other parties by not allowing them to play any significant role in political life
- a government that is not constitutionally responsible to the people and exercises political power arbitrarily
- a leader often chosen by/from the military following a coup.

In general, authoritarian states have the following characteristics in common:

- Little or no freedom of speech
- No freedom of assembly (unable to hold meetings without the approval of the government)
- No freedom of movement – often, individuals need documents or even internal passports to move around inside the country
- No freedom to travel abroad
- No independent judicial system
- All sources of information are censored
- Any opposition to the regime is harshly punished
- A leader whose popularity is reinforced by a personality cult.

Not all such states have these characteristics and some may be more or less oppressive than others. All, however, will exercise strict control over the freedom of the people and will use a variety of methods to hold on to power.

In many states, the age of Kings and Emperors ended with World War I, and short-lived experiments with democracy gave way to a new kind of all-powerful leader. The authoritarian states and leaders that you

study will be examples taken from the 20th century. This century was one of the most bloody in history, and included two major world wars and ideologies that subordinated the needs of the individual to the needs of the state.

Twentieth-century ideologies include **Fascism** in Italy and Nazism in Germany. They emerged in very similar circumstances. In Germany there was despair associated with defeat in World War I; in Italy, the perception of a 'mutilated victory' that had not been worth the cost of that war. Although they began with **socialist** programmes intended to appeal to the lower classes (the workers, small farmers, and skilled craftsmen), both ideologies became more conservative as they sought the support of the middle classes. Inevitably, enemies were treated harshly and dissent was not tolerated. Under Hitler, the racial aspects of his ideology led to the attempted extermination of the Jews in Europe.

Italian Fascism

Name given by Mussolini to the movement he led in Italy from 1922. The term is commonly used to identify other right-wing regimes such as German Nazism and Spanish Falangism. It is characterized by extreme nationalism, hostility to democracy, respect for collective organizations, the cult of the leader, and army-like discipline. Fascism is also anti-communist and anti-liberal.

Juan Perón in Argentina and General Francisco Franco in Spain do not fit so easily into the 'fascist' mould, but they were strongly nationalistic and considered communism to be a serious threat.

One of the most widespread ideologies of the 20th century was **communism**. It was born out of industrialization in the 19th century and based upon the writings of Karl Marx and Friedrich Engels. This ideology promised a society in which all people were equal and in which the state would 'wither away', as it had no need to control or to legislate when there was no private property to protect. Under Lenin and Stalin, the Soviet Union created a template for all other communist states in the 20th century. Neither leader claimed to have reached the goal of communism, or 'Great Harmony' as it was called by Mao Zedong. Yet the road to this 'paradise on earth' was a difficult one and so, they believed, justified the application of harsh measures.

There were significant variations in the nature of authoritarian states. They ranged from the violent and complete dictatorship of Stalin to that of Gamal Nasser of Egypt, who was vehemently anti-communist and followed an ideology tempered with **capitalism**.

One characteristic all these leaders had in common, regardless of their ideology, was their belief that they alone had the knowledge and the will to bring about the ideal state. Note also that, apart from Italy under Mussolini, most of the examples of authoritarian states in the 20th century were republics, for example: Portugal under Salazar, Hungary under Bela Kun, Spain under Franco, and so on. Many of the authoritarian states were created in the post-monarchical vacuum after a strong leader had been overthrown or had abdicated.

Socialism

The roots of socialism and communism were very similar. The Social Democratic Parties of Germany and Russia, for example, were originally based on the writings of Karl Marx, with the more radical members splitting off at a later stage to form communist parties. What did develop in Europe, especially after World War II, was what may be called modern socialism. This had the following characteristics:

- The redistribution of wealth through taxation
- The state ownership of major industries such as steel and coal
- The state ownership of 'monopolies' such as transport, communications, water, etc.
- Free health care and free education for all.

In many countries, these criteria became known as the 'welfare state' based on the belief that the government should ensure a basic standard of living for all its citizens.

The stages of communism according to Marxist theory

The classic Marxist interpretation of history can be broken down into distinct stages determined by which class owned the wealth of the state and the 'means of production'.

These stages can be seen as:

1. **Primitive communism**: meaning the prehistoric hunter-gatherer communities in which there was no monopoly over the means of production. In other words, people worked together to find food and shared their resources. This was viewed by Marx as some kind of early communism.

2. **Feudalism**: this stage came about when settled, agricultural-based communities developed into kingdoms, and powerful rulers took ownership of the land and the people who farmed it.

3. **Capitalism**: commercial activities such as trading in manufactured goods became a greater source of wealth than land, especially after the Industrial Revolution. The powerful merchant/business/bourgeoisie class came into being and political systems became more democratic.

4. **Communism**: Marx predicted that the workers (proletariat) would rise up against the capitalist owners of the means of production (factories and businesses), and would replace the democracy of capitalism with the true democracy of the workers' state. In this state, private property would no longer exist and the people would contribute their skills, taking only what they needed. This situation would then lead to a 'withering away of the state', as there would be no need for laws to protect wealth and property as all would be communally owned.

Lenin knew that the establishment of a communist state in the Soviet Union would not be achieved quickly and he was prepared to fail and try again (as when he abandoned War Communism and replaced it with the NEP in 1921). It was expected that there would be a series of attempts and the maxim would be 'try, fail, fail better'. Lenin also considered the stage between 'post-capitalism' and the achievement of communism to be 'socialism'. Khrushchev predicted that communism would be achieved by 1980, although Brezhnev settled for calling the Soviet Union a 'developed socialist state'.

What topics should you study?

The IB History Guide outlines three major topics for *Authoritarian states*:

1. Emergence of authoritarian states

This topic asks you to look at the rise to power of authoritarian leaders or the emergence of authoritarian states. In order to cover the prescribed content, you need to consider what kind of circumstances made it possible for this to happen and what kind of methods were used by the leader to take power.

2. Consolidation and maintenance of power

This topic asks you to look at the leader or the state once power has been assumed and other political parties or groups have been suppressed. In order to cover the prescribed content, you need to consider how power was maintained, probably through the use of popular policies and/or terror. You also need to assess whether the foreign policy of the authoritarian state contributed to (or hindered) its leader's maintenance of power.

3. Aims and results of policies

This topic asks you to look at the way a state was actually structured and what kinds of policies were carried out. In order to cover the prescribed content, you need to consider what kind of programme was put into practice, as well as how economic and social policies were created and implemented. You will also need to know something about the role of women (always an interesting aspect of regimes that took power when women had fewer rights than men), attitudes towards religion, and the kind of culture that developed inside the state. By the end, you should be able to discuss the extent to which each leader was able to achieve authoritarian control of his people.

How is the exam structured?

The paper

The exam for Paper 2 consists of 12 topics, each with two questions. You have to answer two questions, each taken from a different topic.

The questions

All questions in each topic will be 'open-ended' or general questions. This means that you can choose any suitable example that you have studied. For example:

> **Examine how and why one leader of an authoritarian state was able to make a successful bid for power.**

Some questions may ask you to consider authoritarian states from different regions. For example:

> **Discuss the role and status of women in two authoritarian states, each chosen from a different region.**

Command terms

At the start of each question, there will be a 'command term'. This refers to the way the question is asked. A comprehensive list of command terms, with explanations, is given in the IB History Guide. For example:

Compare and contrast: Give an account of similarities and differences between two (or more) items or situations, referring to both (all) of them throughout.

Discuss: Offer a considered and balanced review that includes a range of arguments, factors, or hypotheses. Opinions or conclusions should be presented clearly and supported by appropriate evidence.

Evaluate: Make an appraisal by weighing up the strengths and limitations.

Examine: Consider an argument or concept in a way that uncovers the assumptions and interrelationships of the issue.

To what extent: Consider the merits or otherwise of an argument or concept. Opinions and conclusions should be presented clearly and supported with appropriate evidence and sound argument.

(All definitions taken from the IB History Guide © IBO, 2015)

Doing the exam

Preparation

If you are planning to answer a question from *World history topic 10: Authoritarian states (20th century)*, it is best to revise a minimum of three leaders from at least two regions and, if possible, different ideologies as these would often influence their aims and policies. The leaders may be selected from the list of suggested examples in the Guide but you may also study any other appropriate authoritarian leader that you find interesting. Please note that questions will not ask on specific leaders but will focus on the topics and prescribed content.

Make sure you know enough to be able to answer questions that may come up on any of the three topics listed under *Authoritarian states* in the IB History Guide. If you choose a leader that is not on the example list in the Guide, check that there is material to cover the prescribed content in each topic.

Writing an exam essay

Choosing the question

You will have five minutes of reading time before the exam officially begins. You may not write during this time, but you can read the questions and think about how you could answer them. Read the questions carefully and choose the two that are best suited to the material you have revised. Make sure they are from different topics. Take your time and, if you need to discuss more than one leader, see if you can choose appropriate examples. If a question asks you, 'To what extent do you agree…' see if you can challenge the assertion.

Timing

You have probably had plenty of practice at writing history essays, and so you can use the same technique in the exam. The only difference is that you will only have 90 minutes for two essays, or 45 minutes per essay.

Planning

No matter how desperately you want to start writing, always take five minutes of your time to plan your answer. This can make a huge difference to the quality of your answer and help you to know where you will end up before you start to write! A good plan or outline is more than just a list of facts that you can recall. It should help you to organize your ideas and to think through arguments.

For example, how would you plan your answer to this question?

> *Compare and contrast the social and economic policies of two authoritarian leaders, each chosen from a different region.*

Take a look at these student samples and see if you agree with the examiner's comments.

Student plan 1 – Sally

Examples: Mao and Stalin

Mao – Land reform, Five-Year Plans, Cooperatives, Collectives, Communes, Backyard furnaces, Hundred Flowers, Antis, Cultural Revolution.

Stalin – Collectivization, Five-Year Plans, Industry, Purges, Terror, Culture.

Examiner's comments

This is not much of a plan, but more of a brainstorm. Sally has jotted down all the policies she can think of and will use the lists as a reminder to mention all these points. She has not made it clear to herself how she will compare and contrast the two leaders she has chosen.

Student plan 2 – Peter

Examples: Mao and Stalin

For comparison:

* Both wanted rapid industrialization and based this on a planned economy (give examples... refer to Five-Year Plans)
* Both had largely agricultural economies and a population that worked on the land – land reform was followed by collectivization in both cases
* Both had huge labour resources – big populations
* Both wanted more education – literacy campaigns in both states
* Both wanted more women in the workforce
* Both used terror to ensure the policies were carried out (but terror is not 'a domestic policy')
* Both used propaganda campaigns to get the population working with them e.g. speak bitterness, 100 flowers, antis

For contrast:

* Mao wanted to develop the countryside and the town together in the Great Leap Forward (GLF); Stalin wanted the countryside to finance the industrialization of the USSR; link to different interpretations of Marxism
* Stalin wanted to urbanize, to create a proletariat; Mao wanted to 'walk on two legs' (a reference to the GLF)
* Stalin wanted to rearm (Plan #3); less important for Mao
* Stalin was isolated; Mao had the help of the USSR to train his workers
* Stalin wanted to do away with the role of the Orthodox Church, especially in the countryside; religion was less important for Mao except for Christian missionaries, who were associated with imperialism

Examiner's comments

Peter has a much better plan. He has not simply jotted down a lot of key facts, but has focused on answering the question and using a comparative structure. He has also been careful to include only social and economic policies. Stalin and Mao make a good choice, because they have similar policies, so there is a lot to compare, but also less to contrast. Don't worry too much about this; the examiner will be looking for a nicely structured answer that is reasonably balanced (so not only comparison or not only contrast), but don't feel that if you have five comparisons you must also have five contrasts.

Of course, your plan could be even shorter than Peter's, and you could use your own abbreviations to save time (but, please, not in your exam essay answer!). Similarly, you may prefer to draw a spidergram or a mind map. Whatever helps you to plot your journey through to the conclusion is fine, as long as you figure it out before you start to write.

How to structure your essay – and some dos and don'ts

An exam essay is really no different from a class or a homework essay, except that you have to write it without access to sources and within a given time period.

Dos:

* Do read the question very carefully and make sure that you can answer it. If a specific time period is mentioned, do you have enough material to cover it all? If the question asks about social and economic policies, do you know enough about both?
* Do answer the question that is asked on the exam paper and not a similar one you prepared earlier!
* Do plan your answer and include this plan in your exam answer booklet.
* Do begin with an introduction and always refer to the question in the introduction. Name the leaders you will use to answer the question here.
* Do define any key words such as 'totalitarian' or 'authoritarian' if the question mentions these.
* Do use a comparative structure if the question asks you to compare and contrast. (Look at Peter's plan; he will be writing about both Mao and Stalin at the same time and not simply listing Stalin's policies and then listing those of Mao.)
* Do include DATES! When you are writing about why something happens, you will usually need to refer to what came before (cause and effect), and so knowing the order in which events happen is very important.
* Do refer to the question in each paragraph, to make sure that your answer stays focused.
* Do finish with a conclusion that sums up your arguments.

- Do include some reference to different historical interpretations, if this is appropriate.

Don'ts:

- Don't write down everything you know about a topic; you need to select only relevant material.
- Don't leave out facts and dates. Your arguments need to be supported, so saying that Castro used guerrilla tactics to come to power is fine, but you need to support this statement with evidence of how he did this.
- Don't just state what historians say about a topic; use **historiography** to support, not replace, your arguments.
- Don't use quotations to replace your arguments. If you use quotations, explain why and link them to your arguments.
- Don't use 'I think…' or 'In my opinion…' but instead write 'It is clear that…' or 'Given the evidence, it can be seen that…' Try to keep an academic tone to your writing.

Introductions and conclusions – don't neglect these!

Introduction

There is no formula for a good introduction. While some students will state very clearly how they will structure their answers, others may simply give some relevant background and their thoughts on the question. Examiners will want to know that you have understood the question and have grasped its implications. Think of it as a 'first impression', leading the examiner to think 'Good, they are on the right track'. Introduce the leaders you will use to answer the question. Also, if you are answering an open-ended question that asks, for example, about the rise to power of a leader, then you can state here what time period you will focus on. In the case of Nasser, for instance, would you begin in 1952, 1948, or even earlier? Also, are there terms that need to be defined? If so, it is a good idea to do this in the introduction.

Conclusion

Here is your chance to make a 'lasting impression'. You will need to summarize your arguments concisely, but not by repeating them one by one – this is tedious and doesn't add much to your answer. If you have a nice quotation that is relevant (make sure it is!) and sums up your argument, then use it in the conclusion. It may spark the examiner's interest and leave a good impression. For example, if you were writing about Nasser, it may be relevant to mention that Zhou Enlai said Nasser had died of a 'broken heart' (see Chapter 5 on Nasser).

Plan ahead!

See if you can get access to previous examination papers so that you can become familiar with the kind of questions that will be asked. Then, think about how you would answer them. Work in a group and come up with plans for typical questions.

01

Fidel Castro and Cuba

This chapter examines Castro's rise to power and his rule of Cuba until 2006. It focuses on:

- the conditions and methods that led to Castro's rise to power
- the methods Castro used to consolidate power after the success of the Cuban Revolution
- the aims and impact of Castro's social, political, economic, and foreign policies
- the extent to which Castro was able to deal with opposition and establish an authoritarian state.

This photograph shows Fidel Castro talking to Cuban peasants in Sierra Maestra. The interest he took in their problems and the promises of an agrarian reform made the 26th of July Movement very popular among the peasants.

Key concepts:

As you work through this chapter, bear in mind the key concepts we use when studying history.

- **Change**: Think about the ways in which the lives of Cuban citizens changed as a result of Castro's rise and rule.

- **Continuity**: To what extent do you think the rule of Castro shared some of the characteristics of the regime he overthrew? Consider, for example, the treatment of his opposition.

- **Causation**: Consider the reasons that can help explain why Castro has been able to maintain himself in power in Cuba for so long.

- **Consequence**: Events related to the Cold War had an important impact on Cuba. What consequences did events such as the Cuban Missile Crisis of 1962, or the fall of the Soviet Union in 1991, have on Cuba? To what extent were they turning points for Castro and the revolution?

- **Significance**: As you read through the chapter, reflect on how important Castro's ideology was to his rise to power. For example: When did he make his ideology more explicit? To what was this decision a response? In his rule, how far have his policies been consistent with his ideology?

- **Perspective**: When reading different perspectives of Castro's rule, consider the issues that may have influenced the way events were recorded and explained. For example, do you think the fact that many Cuban historians write from outside the country has an impact on how they perceive the events they are writing about? In what ways could their perceptions be different from those of historians writing from inside Cuba? Can you think of some reasons?

Cuba is one of the few countries in the world that remain communist in their ideology. Ever since 1959, historians have tried to explain the reasons why Fidel Castro was able to rise and maintain himself in power for so long, in spite of often adverse domestic and international circumstances.

A Spanish colony until 1898, and a republic strongly linked to the United States after its independence in 1902, Cuba did not seem to offer the conditions for a successful communist revolution. Other countries in the region suffered deeper political, social, and economic problems. Yet events between 1953 and 1959 contributed to the rise of Fidel Castro and his 26th of July Movement.

This chapter deals with the rise to power and the rule of Fidel Alejandro Castro Ruz (b. 1926) in Cuba. It focuses on the conditions against which he came to power, addresses the methods used in his rise, and analyses domestic and foreign policies up to 2006.

Timeline of events – 1926–2006

1926	Fidel Alejandro Castro Ruz is born in Biran, south-eastern Cuba.
1933	President Gerardo Machado is overthrown by the head of the army, Fulgencio Batista.
1934–44	Fulgencio Batista controls the country through puppet governments.
1934	The Platt Amendment is abolished. The United States retains a naval base in Guantánamo Bay and trade agreements between the nations remain in place.
1940	Batista becomes president. A new constitution is adopted.
1944–48	Authentic Party (*Partido Auténtico*) leader, Ramón Grau San Martín, becomes president.
1948–52	Authentic Party leader Carlos Prío Socarrás rules Cuba.
1952	Batista seizes power in a coup against Prío Socarrás.
1953	Castro leads the Moncada assault against a military garrison. He is sentenced to 15 years in prison.
1955	Castro is granted amnesty and leaves Cuba.
1956	Castro returns from Mexico, leading the *Granma* expedition. He launches a military campaign against Batista in the Sierra Maestra mountains.
1958	The United States withdraws assistance to President Batista. Batista's final offensive against the rebels ends in failure.
1959	Batista flees the country. Castro's troops enter Havana and a provisional government is set up. Fidel Castro becomes prime minister in February. Expropriation and nationalization of businesses begins.
1960	Castro nationalizes foreign companies. The United States abolishes Cuban sugar quota and begins an economic blockade. Castro establishes diplomatic and commercial relations with the Soviet Union.
1961	The Bay of Pigs invasion is repelled. The United States breaks diplomatic ties with Cuba, and Castro announces the socialist character of the revolution.
1962	Cuban Missile Crisis. The United States imposes a trade embargo on Cuba.
1963	Castro makes his first visit to the Soviet Union.
1967	Ernesto 'Che' Guevara is killed in Bolivia.
1968	Castro announces the Revolutionary Offensive.
1970	The 'Ten Million Zafra' programme fails to achieve its target.
1975–91	Cuba becomes engaged in Angola and Ethiopia.
1976	Under a new constitution, Castro assumes the title of President of the State Council, and becomes head of state, head of government, and commander-in-chief of the armed forces.
1980	Massive Cuban emigration of approximately 125,000 people to the United States from the Mariel port.
1991	Cuba begins 'Special Period in Times of Peace' programme following the end of Soviet aid to Cuba.
1995	Castro visits China for the first time.
1998	Castro welcomes Pope John Paul II in the pontiff's historic visit to Cuba.
2006	Castro announces a temporary transfer of power to his brother, Raúl Castro.

Sierra Maestra
Mountain range in the south-east of Cuba, in the Oriente province.

TOK

At the time of writing this book, Fidel Castro had transferred power to his brother Raúl, but has continued to be a leading voice in Cuban affairs. What, if anything, do you know about Raúl Castro? Can you find any recent information in the newspapers about Cuba? To what extent do you think your previous knowledge and opinions of Castro and Cuba can influence your study of this chapter?

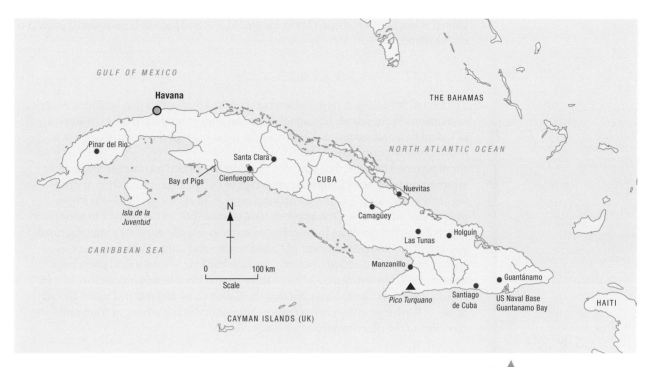

▲
Map of Cuba.

The emergence of an authoritarian state

No doubt Fidel Castro played a large part in the success of the Cuban Revolution in 1959, and in retaining power for over 50 years. It is also true, however, that particular historical conditions created the background against which Castro became an appealing option to many and an indisputable force to others.

This section aims at analysing the contributions of Fidel Castro to the success of the Cuban Revolution in January 1959, as well as the part played by the historical, political, and economic circumstances against which he rose to power.

Conditions in which Castro emerged – Cuba before the revolution

Cuban independence

After many years of struggle, and following US intervention, Cuba shook off Spanish rule in what became known as the Spanish–American War (1898). The Treaty of Paris (1898) between Spain and the United States granted the territories of Puerto Rico, Guam, and the Philippines to the United States in exchange for money. Spain also lost sovereignty over Cuba, which was placed under military occupation by the United States for five years. In 1902, the Republic of Cuba was declared. Yet Cuba was not fully sovereign. By the Platt Amendment, which was annexed to the Cuban constitution, the United States kept the right to intervene in Cuba's finances and foreign relations. The Platt Amendment not only aimed at preventing the influence of third-party countries in Cuba, but also at guaranteeing US control of Cuban affairs. In the following years, until its abolition in 1934, the Platt Amendment was used on several occasions by the

⚠ Exam questions in Paper 2 may ask about the emergence or consolidation of power of authoritarian leaders. Because they are now open questions (no leader will be named), it is very important that you select the examples carefully. In this case, don't just choose Castro on the grounds of how much you know about him; make sure Castro is an appropriate example for the specific question asked. When reading this chapter, identify specific areas and policies for which Castro would be a good choice to answer a question in Paper 2.

United States to intervene in Cuban internal affairs and protect US economic interests on the island.

Economic and social factors

The United States' interests in Cuba were protected by policies that benefited American investments in the island. US capital played an important part in the exploitation of Cuban national resources. Known as 'the sugar bowl of the world', Cuba was a **monoculture economy**. Although it also produced tobacco, coffee, and rice, it was the production of sugar that provided the most important income for the republic. Washington bought a significant percentage of Cuban sugar production at prices higher than those set by the international market. In exchange, Cuba was to give preferential access to American products. Cuba was not an industrialized nation and depended on the revenues from exported sugar to buy the necessary manufactured goods and oil. The development of Cuban service and utility industries, such as gas, electricity, communications, railways, and the banking system, relied upon large amounts of US investment. Although there were economic advantages for Cuba in these agreements, they also meant that the Cuban economy was tied to the United States. If Washington decided to reduce the quantity of sugar bought from Cuba, the economy of the island would be seriously affected.

Cuban workers enjoyed a better standard of living than workers in other regions of the continent, but there were many social and economic problems that affected them. The living conditions for workers were precarious. Wages were low; housing was limited; access to health and education was not available to all. Few rural areas possessed running water or electricity. Illiteracy was widespread, reaching 50 per cent in certain parts of the countryside. Sugar workers were seasonal – this meant there were months when they did not have steady employment. The ownership of land and of the sugar mills was largely concentrated in the hands of the upper class and foreign companies.

CHALLENGE YOURSELF

ATL **Research, communication, and social skills**

To understand the social and economic situations against which Castro rose to power, it is important that you are familiar with the role played by foreign companies as well as with the importance of sugar to the Cuban economy.

In groups, find information about some of the different foreign companies operating in Cuba before the revolution. For example, which countries invested in Cuba? Consider the economic activities on which these companies focused. What was the relationship between the foreign employers and the Cuban workers? What were the living and working conditions like? Research the importance of sugar before the revolution and the reasons why it began to lose economic value throughout the 20th century.

Weakness of the political system

Between independence and revolution, Cuba was led by a series of governments that showed high levels of corruption and limited success in solving economic problems and social inequality. By 1934, the armed forces under the command of General Fulgencio Batista controlled the nation by the appointment of puppet presidents. In 1940, Batista himself became president of Cuba and ruled until 1944.

Between 1944 and 1952 there was a return to democracy, but corruption continued to dominate every branch of the government, while Cuba faced inflation and unemployment. On 10 March 1952, Batista returned to the political stage and overthrew President Carlos Prío Socarrás. He suspended the constitution to rule as a dictator.

The rule of Fulgencio Batista, 1952–59

During Batista's period as president, political corruption continued to reign, and at shocking levels. As economic problems worsened, social and political unrest developed. Batista moved from making concessions to using repression to maintain control of the country.

One of the reasons why the Cuban economy worsened was the decline in sugar prices on the international sugar market. As the price of sugar dropped, Cuba found it more expensive to purchase the goods it did not produce at home. This situation is known as the 'deterioration of the **terms of trade**'. However, because of its international obligations with the United States, Cuba could not successfully develop an industry to substitute its imports, a measure many Latin American countries had taken by the end of World War II. The rise in the cost of imports led to shortages and inflation. Furthermore, the rise in the price of oil affected transportation and the operation of sugar mills, increasing unemployment to an alarming 17 per cent during the late 1950s, to be combined with a 13-per-cent level of underemployment and low wages for those who were employed.

▲ Fulgencio Batista

Under these circumstances, opposition to Batista's dictatorship intensified. The rural workers, poorly housed and under-educated, did not support the regime. Urban workers were affected by the economic problems of inflation and unemployment, and student unions demanded freedom and democracy. The higher social classes, who were losing their purchasing power and whose businesses were being affected by the atmosphere of economic uncertainty, were another source of opposition to Batista. Opposition, however, was not organized and had not yet found a leading figure.

The rise of opposition to Batista

One of the factors that contributed to the rise of Castro was the fact that the Cuban political parties did not seem to offer a genuine alternative to the existing order. The Authentic Party (*Partido Auténtico*) and the Orthodox Party (*Partido Ortodoxo*) were the two main political parties in Cuba before the revolution. The communists were represented by the Popular Socialist Party (PSP).

Authentic Party (full name: *Partido Revolucionario Cubano*; Cuban Revolutionary Party)

Founded in 1934, this party's platform had socialist and nationalist elements. It defended the rights of workers to be represented by trade unions. Nationalism was expressed in its motto 'Cuba for the Cubans'. However, Presidents Ramón Grau San Martín (1944–48) and Carlos Prío Socarrás (1948–52) were Authentic Party leaders who ruled during one of the most corrupt and undemocratic periods in Cuban history.

Orthodox Party (full name: *Partido del Pueblo Cubano*; Cuban People's Party)

Born from a split of the Authentic Party, this party was founded in 1948 by Eduardo Chibás, who coined the party's motto 'Integrity against Money'. It played an important role in the denunciation of the corruption in Cuban politics. Its aims were to end government corruption and to nationalize US-owned companies. Orthodox leader Chibás was considered to be a solid presidential candidate, but he committed suicide in 1951. Fidel Castro was a member of the party until he formed his own organization, the 26th of July Movement.

Popular Socialist Party (full name: *Partido Socialista Popular*; PSP)

The PSP was Cuba's communist party. Founded in 1925, it suffered persecution and was banned from participating in elections several times. In 1953, Batista banned the PSP again. In 1965, it was renamed the Cuban Communist Party (*Partido Comunista Cubano*, PCC)

CHALLENGE YOURSELF

Research and thinking skills

Find information on Eduardo Chibás's ideas and roles. Explain how and why he decided to end his life.

Read the source below and answer the question that follows.

> The Auténtico and Ortodoxo parties proved incapable of responding effectively to Batista's seizure of power. The Orthodox were leaderless and the Auténticos could not lead. After 1952 Cuba's two principal parties became irrelevant to a solution of the political crises. Both parties, to be sure, condemned the violation of the 1940 Constitution, but neither party responded to the army usurpation with either a comprehensive program or compelling plan of action.
>
> **From Louis Perez Jr, 'Cuba c. 1930–1959' in Leslie Bethell (ed.), *Cuba: A Short History*, Cambridge University Press, 1993**

1. Why, according to the above source, was opposition to Batista ineffective?

The greatest challenge for the government would not come from any of the more traditional Cuban parties. It would come instead from the rise of Fidel Castro as leader of a totally new movement.

The Cuban Revolution and the emergence of Fidel Castro

Fidel Alejandro Castro Ruz was born in 1926 in the eastern province of Oriente. His father, an immigrant from Spanish Galicia, owned sugar plantations in the region. In 1945, Castro enrolled in law school in Havana and soon joined the Orthodox Party. He was an outstanding orator, who had an exceptional memory for everything he read and heard; he was also a fine athlete. All of these factors helped him gain popularity and support within the party. In 1952, Castro planned to run for a seat in Congress, but elections were never held as a result of Batista's **coup** against Prío Socarrás. From the very beginning Castro showed his opposition to the rule of Batista and in 1953 he tried to depose him for the first time.

When analysing the role played by Fidel Castro in the Cuban Revolution, three stages must be taken into consideration:

1. The attack against the Moncada Barracks (1953), which provided him with an opportunity to be known by fellow citizens and launch the 26th of July Movement.
2. The landing of the *Granma* expedition (1956), which marked the beginning of the armed struggle at a national level.
3. The campaign in the Sierra Maestra (1956–59), which ended with his Rebel Army's victorious entry into Havana city in January 1959.

If you were to write a biography of Fidel Castro, what would you include? Would your choice be affected by the context in which you would be using the biography? For example, is there a history of Castro the leader that is different to a history of, for example, Castro the family man? Explain your answer fully.

When you need to find the biography of a historical character, where do you go? Do you go to Wikipedia? Evaluate the usefulness of the entry for Fidel Castro in Wikipedia.

Is knowledge that is collectively produced in any sense 'better' than a biography written by one person? How much of a person's knowledge depends on interaction with other knowers?

The Moncada Barracks.

The Moncada assault (1953) and the emergence of the 26th of July Movement

On 26 July 1953, a group of approximately 140 men dressed in military uniforms attacked a military garrison in Cuba known as the Moncada Barracks. Most of them were members of the Orthodox Party; they were led by Fidel Castro, his brother Raúl, and Abel Santamaría. Moncada is situated in Santiago de Cuba, in the Oriente province, and was chosen for several reasons. It was the second-largest military garrison in the country and had large supplies of ammunition that Castro hoped to seize. Also, Oriente was one of the regions with the greatest social unrest, which Castro thought would provide popular support for the attack. Moreover, the distance between Santiago de Cuba and Havana (see map on page 5) ensured that if Batista's troops were sent from the capital to defend the building, there would be enough time to complete the takeover. Finally, the timing of the attack coincided with a popular celebration in the streets of Santiago, so Castro hoped to find fewer soldiers in the garrison.

The aim of the operation was to obtain weapons that would help spark a general insurrection against Batista. Castro believed that if the attack was successful and his men acquired weapons, they would gather massive popular support for the uprising.

The attack had been carefully planned, but several last-minute problems complicated the work of the rebels. Although the surprise factor was intended to play in the rebels' favour, the army managed to defend the building successfully. Almost half of the rebels who participated in the attack were killed; many were captured and tortured to death, including Abel Santamaría. Fidel and Raúl Castro managed to escape, but were soon captured by Batista's forces and imprisoned.

Batista decided to make the trial of the rebels a great show of strength. He wanted the Cubans to see how determined he was to crush any opposition to the regime, in the hope that it would work as a deterrent. Fidel Castro, a lawyer, decided to defend himself at the trial. Although Castro's own trial took place in a separate room and attendance was restricted, his speech 'History will absolve me' became not only his defence but also a programme for the political and social reform of the country. In his speech, Castro promised to deal with Cuba's most pressing problems – namely housing, the lack of industrialization, and the poor education system.

Abel Santamaría (1927–53)

A member of the Orthodox Party, Santamaría met Castro in 1952 and, like him, rejected Batista's coup. He was captured and tortured to death by Batista's forces after the Moncada raid.

'History will absolve me' speech

When asked about the 'History will absolve me' speech, Castro claimed that he had written the speech while in prison waiting for his trial. He said that he had used lime juice to make it invisible to others and had inserted it between the lines of ordinary letters, so that it could be smuggled out of prison for printing and distribution in 1954.

José Martí (1853–95)

Known as 'The Apostle', Martí is a hero of the War of Independence. His political writings had a large influence on Cuban politicians, including Fidel Castro. He died in combat in 1895, becoming a martyr of the independence struggle.

Consequences of the Moncada assault

The Moncada assault marked the foundation of Castro's political movement '26th of July', named after the day of the attack. The rebels became known as the 'Generation of the Centenary', as 1953 marked the hundredth anniversary of the birth of Cuban hero José Martí.

Fidel Castro became the only political leader who not only complained about Batista's dictatorship, but who was also ready to do something about it. Although the rebels were the aggressors, Batista's excesses in repression, torture, and persecution affected his image, and allowed Castro and his men to emerge as martyrs of the dictatorship.

In 1954, in an attempt to legitimize his rule, Batista held elections and ran as presidential candidate. With Castro in prison, the PSP banned, and no effective opposition to his candidature, Batista used the elections to claim that he had been rightfully chosen by the people. The following year, among some other concessions made to appear democratic, Batista allowed political parties to regroup and released many political prisoners, including the leaders of the Moncada raid. Fidel Castro was now a free man and went into exile in Mexico to prepare the revolution.

Despite Batista's efforts to appear democratic, demonstrations in Cuba grew in size and led to armed clashes in towns and cities. Different revolutionary organizations spread through the countryside, promoting rural insurgence, sabotaging property across the island, and organizing **guerrilla** groups. Communications and the delivery of food to towns and cities were often disrupted. Sugar production dropped as a consequence of acts of sabotage against sugar mills, oil refineries, and railroads. Political parties – with the exception of the 26th of July Movement, which believed change in Cuba would only come after the use of force to overthrow Batista – demanded elections but Batista refused to hold them.

On 2 December 1956, Fidel Castro returned to Cuba and launched the next stage of the struggle that would take him to power.

Fidel Castro and other prisoners leave prison after Batista's amnesty.

The *Granma* expedition (1956)

Rebels disembarking from *Granma*.

In 1956, Fidel and Raúl Castro returned from exile aboard the overcrowded and poorly equipped yacht *Granma*. They landed on the southern coast of Oriente with some 80 rebels who had been recruited in Mexico.

The voyage was rough, as *Granma* was heavily laden with men, weapons, and supplies of additional oil to enable it to reach the shores of Cuba. The radio failed and the engines were poor, so *Granma* reached Cuba two days behind schedule. The urban arm of the 26th of July Movement, under the command of Frank País, had prepared a strike in Santiago de Cuba in support of the landing, but coordination was affected by the delay in *Granma*'s arrival. Castro also failed to make contact with those who had prepared land support for the operation. Spotted by government forces, Castro and his men landed in a swamp and were forced to leave supplies and ammunition behind. They were ambushed at Alegría del Pío and those surviving (only 12 of the original 82-man crew) dispersed and hid in the Sierra Maestra to regroup and emerge as the Rebel Army.

Anti-government rebellions led by several groups in the cities continued throughout 1957 and 1958, and included an attempt to seize the presidential palace and murder Batista. Although it failed, it showed the president how difficult it had become to maintain himself in power. Batista struggled desperately to control the situation, but his response was so violent that it embittered the people against him.

The cast of characters

Although Castro was the leading figure, many men and women contributed to the success of the 26th of July Movement. Some of them played an important part in the struggle for power; others continued to work in the revolutionary government. Study these photographs and biographical details carefully. You will find reference to these characters throughout the chapter.

Frank País (1934–57)

Student leader who fought against Batista since the 1952 coup and who joined the 26th of July Movement. He led the movement while Castro was in exile. His brutal murder in 1957 at the age of 23 led to one of the largest general strikes in Cuba.

▲ Raúl Castro   ▲ Vilma Espín   ▲ Camilo Cienfuegos

▲ Ernesto 'Che' Guevara   ▲ Haydée Santamaría   ▲ Celia Sánchez

'Che' Guevara (1928–67)

'Che' is an interjection widely used by Argentines when speaking. Guevara's use of it in conversations earned him the nickname of 'El Che'. Che Guevara believed in the need to expand the revolution to other areas of the world. In 1966, he arrived in Bolivia hoping to make the revolution succeed and to export it to neighbouring Argentina, Chile, Peru, Brazil, and Paraguay. The Bolivian government asked the United States for help and CIA agents were sent to Bolivia to search for Guevara and his men. Guevara was captured on 8 October 1967 and was executed the following day.

Raúl Castro Fidel's younger brother Raúl took part in the attack on the Moncada Barracks, was imprisoned with Fidel, and later exiled to Mexico, from where he helped prepare the *Granma* expedition. Since 1959, he has acted as Fidel's right-hand man and has served in many key positions, such as head of the Cuban Communist Party, minister of defence, and vice-president of the Council of State. He was appointed president in 2008 after his brother resigned for health reasons.

Vilma Espín Wife of Raúl Castro, she took part in urban uprisings in support of the *Granma* expedition. After the revolution, she founded the Cuban Women's Federation (*Federación de Mujeres Cubanas*, FMC) and became a member of several government organizations until her death in 2007.

Camilo Cienfuegos A survivor of the *Granma* expedition, Cienfuegos was responsible for many of the victories of the guerrillas in the Sierra Maestra. With the success of the revolution, he became head of the armed forces but died in an aeroplane accident in 1959.

Ernesto 'Che' Guevara A medical doctor born in Argentina, Guevara travelled throughout Latin America widely and became convinced that the region needed a solution to its poverty and corruption. He met the Castro brothers in Mexico and joined the *Granma* expedition. He was a leading figure in the Sierra Maestra fighting and became an icon of the revolution. After the revolution, he was responsible for the purges of the **batistianos** and other opponents. He also acted as head of the Bank of Cuba and minister of industry. Persuaded of the need to spread the revolution worldwide, he travelled to Congo in 1965 in support of a revolution, which ended in failure. In 1967 he was killed in Bolivia.

Haydée Santamaría   A member of the 26th of July Movement and sister to Abel. Together with her friend Melba Hernandez, she was one of the few women to participate in the Moncada assault. She then became responsible for distributing copies of Castro's 'History will absolve me' speech. Her role in the development of a Cuban culture after the revolution was fundamental. In 1959 she founded Casa de las Américas, a key literary institution of Cuba, which was visited by leading intellectuals and artists from all over the world. She committed suicide on 26 July 1980.

Celia Sánchez   A close friend of Fidel and an early member of the 26th of July Movement, she was responsible for providing land support for the *Granma* expedition. Once in Sierra Maestra, she contributed to the founding of the female 'Mariana Grajales' army. She occupied different government positions until her death in 1980.

Haydée Santamaría's suicide

Her suicide on an anniversary of the Moncada assault has been explained by the fact that she had never been able to overcome the suffering she endured that day. After her brother had been tortured and refused to give any information, his eyes were pulled out of their sockets and taken to Haydée on a tray. Her boyfriend also died as a consequence of torture after the assault.

Activity 2	**Communication and thinking skills**

Study the source below and answer the questions that follow.

> *Bombs exploded in the capital. Two stores were attacked and in the exchange between police and the assailants, three uniformed men were killed and several wounded. Twenty civilians died. On interurban and rural transportation lines, drivers of trucks and buses, as well as automobile passengers, were attacked and killed. When the strike failed, the terrorists sabotaged the electric companies and plants, throwing many rural cities into darkness. For three days a section of Old Havana had no lights. To make repairs more difficult, the aggressors blew up one of the main outlets which used special cables not found in the Cuban market.*

From Fulgencio Batista, *Cuba Betrayed*, Vantage Press, 1962

1. According to source above, which methods did the rebels use to fight?
2. With reference to its origins and purpose, assess the value and limitations of the source to a historian studying the nature of the Cuban Revolution.

 TOK

In the source opposite, Batista used the word 'terrorists'. How far could it be said that the term is being used as a value judgement? To what extent does the choice of words affect the way we view and understand historical events?

In the Sierra Maestra mountains, 1956–59

Support for Castro and the rebels by the people from the Sierra Maestra increased with time, and varied from supplying the army with food and shelter to joining the rebels. There were several reasons why people all across Cuba felt attracted to the 26th of July Movement. First, peasants got to know a totally different type of army to the national army Batista had often used to suppress unrest. Castro's forces did not steal from the peasants and always paid for the food they were given. They respected women, put their medical doctors at the service of the peasants, taught them to read and write, and even helped in the household chores. Any soldier breaking this code was sentenced to death. Peasants received more from the Rebel Army than they had ever received from the Cuban government.

Another factor that contributed to the popularity of and support for the Rebel Army was that their leaders explained what they were fighting for and what kind of new society they were hoping to achieve. The most important element in the new programme was the Agrarian Reform. The 26th of July Movement promised peasants an end to the ownership of large estates by a small sector of society or companies, and committed themselves to a fairer distribution of the land.

The rebels made use of the radio to spread their message and news about events in the Sierra. Radio Rebelde ('Rebel Radio') began to broadcast from 'the territory of Free Cuba in the Sierra' in 1958. People tuned in because they relied more on the news from

Radio Rebelde than on the government media. Castro himself addressed the people on Radio Rebelde in a style that everyone understood. He also made sure people found out what government censorship was hiding from them about the fight against Batista.

News about the progress made in the Sierra Maestra encouraged urban support for the revolution. Workers in towns and cities joined the revolution underground. They printed leaflets in support of the rebels and condemning Batista. They planted homemade bombs to blow up government installations, railways, and public buildings, and sabotaged telephone lines, electricity stations, and gas services. They assassinated those they believed to be enemies of the revolution.

Activity 3   **Thinking and communication skills**

Study the source below and answer the questions that follow.

> " In the two-year period from Christmas, 1956, when the twelve men were alone on the mountain top until Batista fled and his army surrendered on January 1, 1959, nearly all classes of the population had identified themselves, in varying degrees, with the July 26th Movement. Some became an integral part of it because they believed in its revolutionary program; others made common cause with it because it had become the most effective force in the struggle to overthrow Batista.
>
> To offset this overwhelming superiority in men and weapons, the revolutionary army had three advantages: (1) the battle was to be on its home grounds, a terrain of rugged mountains and treacherous jungle made to order for guerrilla warfare and defensive fighting; (2) unlike the government soldiers, the rebel soldiers weren't paid for fighting – they fought for something they believed in; (3) their leaders were men of outstanding ability – inspiring, humane, and master strategists in guerrilla warfare.
>
> The rebel leaders' humanity – and excellent strategy – were illustrated in the order to the revolutionary army that captured soldiers were to be treated with kindness, their wounded given medical attention.

From Leo Huberman and Paul Sweezy, *Cuba: Anatomy of a Revolution*, Vintage Books, 1960

1. What light does the source above throw on the reasons why the 26th of July Movement and the Rebel Army gained support across the country?
2. What other reasons can you provide to explain the success of the Rebel Army?

Fighting in itself did not guarantee the success of the revolution. The 26th of July Movement also needed to make alliances with other political parties and define the future of Cuba after the fall of Batista. Castro, aware of such needs, made contact with leaders from different political parties. By 1958, under the Pact of Caracas, the vast majority of the opposition recognized the leadership of Fidel Castro in the struggle to overthrow Batista. The Pact of Caracas included all the main political parties and organizations, even the communist PSP, which had remained critical of the Moncada attack and Castro's leadership until then. The pact was a heavy blow to Batista, as it openly exposed his political isolation.

To what extent did Batista contribute to the success of the revolution and the emergence of Castro?

The success of the guerrilla war was due in part to the excesses of Batista's regime. The police and the army imprisoned and tortured anyone they suspected of being a rebel or having helped rebels. This policy led to the death and imprisonment of many innocent men and women. To reduce support for the rebels, Batista ordered peasants to evacuate whole areas of the countryside, and those who remained behind were treated as traitors. In an attempt to wipe out rebels who could not be seen in the thick jungle, entire plantations were set on fire, causing the peasants to lose their crops. The government wanted to frighten citizens so that they would not help the rebels, but instead people were drawn to the rebels, in hatred of the government. Batista not only pushed people away from him, but also away from more moderate opposition into the arms of Fidel Castro, the 26th of July Movement, and the Rebel Army.

Batista launched a major attack against the guerrillas in the Sierras in July 1958, involving over 12,000 soldiers, but the campaign Operacion Verano (Summer Offensive) failed. Soldiers, fearful of the guerrilla forces and often isolated from relief, deserted in massive numbers or surrendered to the rebels without firing a shot. The weapons and equipment left behind by deserting soldiers were used by the resistance.

Elections were held in 1958 but Batista's candidate, Andrés Rivero, was fixed to win. This outcome disappointed the few who still hoped for a democratic solution to the conflict. For the same reasons, Rivero did not obtain US backing. In disagreement with Batista's violent actions, the United States imposed an arms **embargo** on Cuba in March 1958. The US position complicated government access to weapons and ammunitions, and had a demoralizing effect on the army.

Batista still refused to negotiate. He rejected a proposal from the United States for him to capitulate to a caretaker government, to which the United States could give military and diplomatic support in order to prevent Fidel Castro coming to power. US officials feared Castro might turn to communism.

Activity 4

 Social, thinking, and communication skills

Group discussion

You have now read about the reasons why support for Castro grew and about Batista's mistakes and miscalculations. In groups, discuss the relative importance you think each factor had in contributing to the fall of Batista and the rise of Castro.

Now, consider the following question:

Why and how did Fidel Castro come to power in Cuba?

In the first part of the question – under *why* (reasons) – you are being asked about the conditions that contributed to Castro's rise. These could include an analysis of the economic and social problems in Cuba before 1959; the failure of previous governments to address these issues and the consequences of that failure; the greed and corruption prevailing in society; the suspension of the 1940 constitution after 1952; the part played by Batista; and the reasons why Castro was appealing to different sectors of the Cuban population, among other relevant factors. Be careful not to produce a narrative of the historical background; you should focus on the links between Castro's rise and each condition you select. You may want to briefly go back to the period before 1953 (for example, to explain the economic problems of Cuba), but the focus should remain on Castro and the events from 1953.

The second part of the question asks you to explain *how* Castro came to power – that is, the methods he used. These need to be clearly linked to how these methods aimed at making use of the existing conditions to help Castro's rise.

Read the following paragraph on how Castro came to power:

This is a two-part question. It asks you to explain why (reasons) and how (methods) Castro came to power. Both aspects of the question must be addressed and you need to show clear knowledge and understanding of both conditions and methods.

It is not sufficient to show that you know which methods Castro used in his rise to power. You also need to explain *how* they contributed to his rise. A paragraph explaining the events of the Moncada assault will not be an effective way to address how Castro came to power. You will need to explain the significance of the event in Castro's road to power by explaining, for example, how the use of force in Moncada enabled the Cuban population to identify Castro as a leader of the opposition, who was prepared to act in order to change the situation.

Student answer – Antonio

Fidel Castro was seen as someone who could bring genuine change to Cuban society. His promises to end corruption in the government and to produce a fairer society were of great importance to gain him the support of peasants in the Sierras. The fact that his soldiers helped with the harvest and taught the peasants to read and write also showed that they meant to bring about genuine change in society. Castro was seen as a hero and that helped his rise.

Examiner's comments

This paragraph focuses on a specific example of Castro's methods – his popular appeal. The candidate shows he understands how the conditions against which Castro rose were used to present his movement as one prepared to bring about genuine change, explaining how Castro's men related to the peasants and using specific examples to prove a point. However, this response could offer a deeper level of analysis. For example: Why were the promises to end corruption and bring about justice of such importance? To whom? Castro was certainly not the only opponent to the government who believed in the need for such change, so what made him different? Was it perhaps the fact that he had dared act upon his beliefs in the Moncada assault? Who saw Castro as a hero? Why did this contribute to his rise?

Activity 5

 Thinking and communication skills

Revision activity

Make a list of the methods used by Fidel Castro. Can you think of specific examples for each of the methods listed?

The triumph of the revolution

After the success against Batista's forces in the Sierra, Castro believed the time had come to spread the war to the other Cuban provinces. He trusted Camilo Cienfuegos, Raúl Castro, and Che Guevara to lead the campaigns. As they moved around, they were joined by more volunteers, marching at night or under the rain to hide from Batista's planes. By Christmas 1958, the city of Santa Clara, capital of the province of Las Villas, had been taken. Raúl and Fidel Castro marched towards Santiago de Cuba, while in Havana rebel leaders increased their acts of sabotage and their attacks against army installations. Politically isolated and unable to control the situation, Batista fled Cuba on 1 January 1959. The army refused to continue fighting against the rebels and an immediate ceasefire was ordered. Soon after, Fidel Castro and his *barbudos* ('bearded men') entered Havana and established a provisional government.

One explanation for Fidel Castro's rise to power can be found in his charisma. In an attempt to explain the sources of authority (i.e. why a leader was obeyed by the people), sociologist Max Weber defined the characteristics of charismatic leadership. He considers authority to come from the fact that the leader is set apart from the rest of the people because of his exceptional personal qualities or his exemplary actions, which inspire loyalty among his followers. Even in the years in Sierra Maestra, Castro showed his charisma by inspiring the peasants. Take a look at the photograph at the beginning of this chapter, for example. In what ways does it show a charismatic aspect of Castro? How does it contribute to inspire loyalty?

Eric Selbin in *Modern Latin American Revolutions* analyses the part played by charisma in revolutions. He states that charismatic leaders promote and make the revolutionary process possible by their ability to represent the people's needs and aspirations in a vision of the future. Charismatic figures represent the potential for rejecting an old order, creating attractive future possibilities for the people.

 Charismatic leaders are good communicators. They appeal to people's feelings and needs. In the next sections, you will study some of Fidel Castro's speeches. When you do, pay attention to the elements in the speech that relate to the ideas above.

Activity 6

 Thinking and communication skills

Analyse the following sources and answer the questions below each.

Source A

Photograph taken at a speech given by Fidel Castro in January, 1959. The man beside Castro is Camilo Cienfuegos.

1. What do you think is the message in Source A?

Source B

66 *Revolutionary leaders reached ascendancy in spectacular fashion, and en route were endowed with proportions larger than life. Already in 1959 the leaders of the revolution had become the stuff of legends and lore, the subjects of books and songs, of poems and films. Revolutionaries were celebrities, folk heroes, and the hope of the hopeful.*

Extract from Louis A. Pérez Jr, *Cuba: Between Reform and Revolution*, Oxford University Press, 1988, p. 249

2. Why do you think that, according to Source B, the leaders of the revolution were the 'hope of the hopeful'?

Source C

66 *Castro thus stepped into a power vacuum that was not entirely of his making. He had skilfully seized the opportunities offered by a conjunction of historical conditions that were unique to Cuba. His success, moreover, owed as much to his imaginative use of the mass*

Thinking and research skills

How does Castro's rise compare to that of other leaders you have studied? Did they come to power by the use of force? Were they elected by the people? Did they, like Castro, come to power as a consequence of a fight against a dictatorial system?

media as to the guerrilla campaign… By 1959 Castro had become the repository of many disparate [different] hopes for Cuba's regeneration. As he had made his slow triumphal way by road from Santiago to Havana, he was treated as the last in the long line of Cuban heroes – the last, because, unlike the others, he had survived and prevailed.

From Sebastian Balfour, *Castro*, 3rd ed., Routledge, 2008

3. Explain the meaning of 'Castro had become the repository of many disparate hopes for Cuba's regeneration'?

4. Which opportunities do you think had been 'skilfully seized' by Castro?

5. Discuss the part played by the use of the mass media and the guerrilla campaign in Castro's success in the revolution. Explain your answer fully.

1.2 Consolidation and maintenance of power

Fidel Castro came to power certain that Cuba needed not only a new government but also a new order. This new order had to be based on Cuba's economic independence. The influence of the United States on Cuban affairs had brought, in Castro's view, many of the economic and social problems affecting the nation. It was not enough to have put an end to Batista's corrupt dictatorship. Just as the Cubans wanted their political rights back, they also wanted better living conditions. Redistribution of land, improved working conditions, and better wages were only a few of the demands people expected Castro and his men to address. Living standards needed to be raised; health and education made accessible to all. The question was how to meet these demands in the shortest period of time.

This section explains how and why Fidel Castro moved from being a member of the provisional government to becoming the undisputed leader of Cuba.

The consolidation of power, 1959–62

In order to consolidate the revolution, Castro made use of several methods between1959 and 1962. First, he removed the people associated with Batista's regime. Next, he consolidated the position of the 26th of July Movement within the provisional government. Third, he launched reforms to show that the revolution lived up to its promises, and to gain support. Finally, he exploited the idea that Cuba was threatened by the United States and appealed to the people's sense of nationalism.

Citizens who had served in the Batista government and armed forces were now imprisoned, their properties confiscated as they were brought to trial. They were either executed or given long prison sentences. The trials took place with little time to assess the real participation in the Batista regime of each of the people involved, and they did not conform to the standards of justice. As such, they were criticized not only in Cuba but also in the United States for not offering human rights guarantees to the prisoners. Those who believed justice had not been done were told that the revolution was endangered by these people and that 'immediate justice' was more necessary than a fair trial.

The provisional government established in January 1959 was formed by a significant number of liberals. They hoped to moderate the left-wing elements, which included the rebels of the 26th of July Movement as well as members of the PSP. The government was led by moderates Manuel Urrutia as president, and José Miró Cardona as his prime minister. Castro set up an office outside the presidential palace, at the Havana Hilton hotel, as commander of Cuban armed forces.

In spite of the provisional government representing many political sectors, real authority was in the hands of Fidel Castro from the very start. He was seen everywhere and heard by everyone. His almost-daily speeches appealed to people's hopes for a new Cuba, based on the grand ideas of the leaders of the independence and on the ideals of social justice, economic security, and political freedom. He approached people in a way that Cuba had never experienced before, going out into the streets and travelling across the country to meet them face to face. It was not uncommon to see Castro spending an afternoon in a rural village discussing who should repair tractors or fixing refrigerators for the people.

Six weeks after the provisional government took over, Prime Minister Cardona unexpectedly resigned. Fidel Castro stepped in as prime minister. Next, in July 1959, President Urrutia resigned because he was opposed to the increasing influence of communists in the government, as well as to Castro's refusal to hold elections. He was replaced by Osvaldo Dorticós, who remained president until the 1976 constitution was passed.

Castro's appointment as prime minister enabled the revolution to move quickly, implementing reforms that led to the transformation of the country into a communist state by the end of 1961. He was supported in this move to the left by the members of the PSP.

Activity 7
 Thinking and communication skills

Study the source below and answer the questions that follow.

> Personal turnovers in the government, in part voluntary, in part forced, increased quickly thereafter. Liberals and moderates resigned, or were forced out, their places taken by loyal fidelistas and members of the PSP. At the time, senior administrative positions in the Ministry of Labour were filled by the PSP. The presence of the PSP in the armed forces was also increased. Party members received teaching appointments at various Rebel Army posts in Havana and Las Villas. The appearance of the PSP in the armed forces, in turn, led to wholesale resignation and, in some cases, arrest of anti-communist officers. In October, Raúl Castro assumed charge of the Ministry of the Revolutionary Armed Forces (MINFAR), and forthwith launched a thorough reorganization of the military, distributing key commands to only trustworthy officers. By the end of the year, anti-communism had become synonymous with counter-revolution.

From Louis A. Pérez Jr, *Cuba: Between Reform and Revolution*, Oxford University Press, 1988, p. 256

1. With reference to the above source and your own knowledge, account for the increasing influence of the PSP in the revolutionary government.
2. What is the significance of the policies implemented by Raúl Castro?
3. What are the implications of 'by the end of the year, anti-communism had become synonymous with counter-revolution'?

Castro and his supporters introduced dramatic changes in the organization of the political parties in Cuba. In 1961, various revolutionary organizations that had acted against Batista were unified under the Integrated Revolutionary Organizations (ORI), which aimed to provide the government with a political party of its own. The ORI was formed by the 26th of July Movement (led by Castro), the PSP, and the Revolutionary Directorate (*Directorio Revolucionario*), a revolutionary student organization. The following year, ORI became the United Party of the Socialist Revolution of Cuba (*Partido Unido de la Revolución Socialista de Cuba*) under Castro's leadership.

CHALLENGE YOURSELF

 ATL Social, research, communication, and thinking skills

In groups, carry out research on the history of the *Granma* newspaper. Find out information about its relationship with the Cuban state. Also, discuss why you think the PCC formed a youth branch and a children's organization.

Huber Matos (1918–2014)

A former teacher and member of the Orthodox Party who joined the Rebel Army against Batista. Matos played a leading part in the Sierra Maestra days in the taking of Santiago de Cuba. In the early stages of the revolution, he was appointed commander of the army in the province of Camagüey.

Soon after that, Matos began to express his opposition to the radicalization of the revolution and was arrested by Castro. He spent 20 years in prison and was subjected to physical and psychological tortures. When released in 1979, he fled to Costa Rica, then to Miami where he became a leading voice of Cuban dissidence and published his memoirs, *How the Night Came*.

In 1965, the party was renamed Cuban Communist Party (*Partido Comunista Cubano*, PCC).

The PCC remains the only officially authorized political party in Cuba and has ruled since 1965, as other existing political parties in Cuba cannot participate in elections. The PCC began to publish its own newspaper, *Granma*, and developed its youth branch (Young Communist League) and children's organization (the José Martí Pioneers).

Activity 8 **ATL** Thinking and communication skills

Study the source below and answer the questions that follow.

> ❝ *Since we feel that we have already reached a stage in which all types of labels and things that distinguish some revolutionaries from others must disappear once and for all and forever and that we have already reached the fortunate point in the history of our revolutionary process in which we can say that there is only one type of revolutionary, and since it is necessary that the name of our party says, not what we were yesterday, but what we are today and what we will be tomorrow, what, in your opinion, is the name our party should have? The Communist Party of Cuba! Well, that is the name that the revolutionary conscience of its members, and the objectives of our revolution, our first central committee adopted yesterday, and that is quite proper.*

From a speech by Fidel Castro at the inaugural meeting of the PCC, 1965

1. What reasons does Fidel Castro give in the source above for the foundation of the PCC?
2. What other reasons can you suggest to explain the foundation of this party?

The growing influence of the PCC and of communist ideas in the government was looked at with some suspicion, even within Castro's inner circle. While men like Raúl Castro and Che Guevara welcomed the revolution's turn to the left, not everyone supported this shift.

One of the people who opposed the turn to the left was Huber Matos, a leader of the 26th of July Movement. He decided to resign as Military Chief of Camagüey – where he enjoyed immense popularity – because he opposed the increasing influence of communist ideas in the revolution and also objected to Castro's refusal to set a date for elections in Cuba. The resignation of someone who had played a leading role in the revolution would have been a great embarrassment for Castro. Also, there was fear that Matos' attitude could encourage more dissidence within the movement. After failing to persuade Matos not to resign, Castro ordered Camilo Cienfuegos to travel to Camagüey, to inform Matos that he was under arrest and would be tried for conspiracy and treason against the revolution.

Shortly after his visit to Camagüey, Cienfuegos' plane disappeared in an accident. The bodies of the passengers and the remains of the aircraft were never found. There are several theories that propose that Castro had Cienfuegos eliminated. One claims that Cienfuegos had also expressed his concerns about the communist nature of the reforms. Another theory claims that what disturbed Castro above all was Cienfuegos' popularity. The Cuban government has always explained these events as an accident. Matos was accused of treason and sentenced to 20 years' imprisonment. He was released after he fulfilled his sentence and left Cuba in 1979.

Use of legal methods – the reforms of 1959–62

Study the source below and answer the questions that follow.

> We will not forget our peasants in the Sierra Maestra and those in the interior of the country… I will never forget those country people and as soon as I have a free moment we will see about building the first school city with seats for 20,000 children. We will do it with the help of the people and the rebels will work with them there. We will ask each citizen for a bag of cement and a trowel. I know we will have the help of our industry and of business and we will not forget any of the sectors of our population.
>
> There will be freedom for all men because we have achieved freedom for all men. We shall never feel offended; we shall always defend ourselves and we shall follow a single precept, that of respect for the rights and feelings of others.

From a speech by Fidel Castro in Santiago de Cuba, 3 January 1959

1. What, according to the speech, were Castro's aims?
2. How did he plan to achieve them?
3. In your view, to whom is the speech addressed? Explain your answers fully.

The speech in the activity above was one of many of similar tone delivered by Castro immediately after the overthrow of Batista, focusing on the challenges ahead and the proposed solutions. If you refer to a complete version of the 'History will absolve me' speech, you will be able to identify many similarities with this speech. Castro offered every sector of society what they needed to improve their living standards: work for the unemployed, land for rural workers, improved working conditions for the urban workers. The middle class were promised they would be able to become professionals; women that they would be able to work in equal conditions to men. Castro concentrated on his role as a man of action, designing policies to bring about these changes.

The most significant of the measures in this period was the Agrarian Reform Act, which aimed at making the distribution of land more equitable, agriculture more efficient, and Cuba less dependent on sugar. The act, which had been promised by the rebels in the Sierra Maestra days, restricted the land that could be owned; anyone owning above the established limit had their extra part **expropriated** and received **bonds** as compensation. Expropriated land was to be organized in **cooperatives**. The act also nationalized the land in foreign hands and ended both Cuban and foreign ownership of large estates, while still allowing private medium- and small-sized farms. These would be the targets of the second (1963) and third (1968) Agrarian Reform laws.

The act was opposed by property owners affected by the reform, and was widely criticized in the Cuban press. It also raised alarm in the United States, as the companies affected saw it as a confiscatory measure and refused to settle for the compensation in Cuban bonds that was offered. Washington began to consider cutting the sugar quota in retaliation.

Other reforms included an increase in wages and the reduction of rents. These created great enthusiasm amongst the lower classes but, again, antagonized the middle and upper classes. Foreign-owned companies began to face waves of strikes as workers took advantage of a more favourable political situation to demand increases in wages and improved working conditions. They found support in the new government, which

The detailed study of an authoritarian leader requires considering the links between the conditions that contributed to his rise, the promises made in response, and the eventual policies implemented. Paper 2 questions may ask you to assess the aims and impact of different policies. You should be able to evaluate the extent to which the promises made addressed the problems of the country, and whether the policies implemented were effective in fulfilling those promises.

Self-management skills

Once you have completed the table for Castro, produce another one for a different authoritarian leader you have studied.

intervened in many of the conflicts, often in favour of the workers. Some foreign companies were threatened with expropriation, accused of representing countries that had provided Batista with weapons.

Import taxes were imposed on 'luxury goods' with several aims. Making these goods more expensive aimed at reducing their imports so that Cubans spent less money on them. But also, with the money raised with these taxes, the government hoped to invest in industrialization and the diversification of the economy (i.e. break with the sugar monoculture). This again affected the United States, which saw its sales to Cuba decrease by as much as 35 per cent.

To improve the living conditions, the government began to work on education and health reforms. Later in this chapter, you will be offered a detailed analysis of the literacy campaign of 1961.

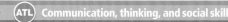

Activity 10 — Communication, thinking, and social skills

You have now examined the conditions of why and how Castro came to power. You have also analysed the promises he made to the Cuban population and some of the reforms implemented in the period 1959–62.

1. Copy and complete the following table to help you establish the links between these three factors. Some suggestions have already been inserted to help you get started; add as many rows as you consider necessary until you have addressed as many aspects as you can. Compare your table with others in your group.

Condition	Promise	Policies
		Agrarian reform
Illiteracy		
	Economic independence	

The impact of the reforms, 1959–62

The reforms announced between 1959 and 1962 had several results. First, they allowed Castro and the PSP to become more popular among many sectors of society and to consolidate their position in the government. Many Cubans therefore became less concerned about when Castro would call for elections and restore the constitution. They seemed to accept the idea that it was first necessary to dismantle the old political, social, and economic systems.

Yet there was a certain level of resistance to the changes, as small groups opposed the pace of the revolution and took up arms in some parts of the country. Local opposition was controlled by the government and did not lead to major crises, particularly because at this stage Castro still allowed those against the revolution to leave the country. Between January 1959 and October 1962, approximately 250,000 people left Cuba, including former *batistianos*, middle-class citizens who feared the radicalization of the revolution, and members of religious congregations who disliked the communist nature of the reforms.

Castro was less successful in dealing with opposition from the United States. Relations between Havana and Washington deteriorated dramatically between 1959 and 1962. Two major international incidents involving Cuba developed in these years, the Bay of Pigs Invasion (1961) and the Cuban Missile Crisis (1962).

The impact of foreign policy on Castro's consolidation of power, 1959–62

Even before 1959, Fidel Castro had made it clear that he believed Cuba needed to develop its economy outside the shadow of the United States. When US interests began to be affected by Cuban policies, Washington pressed other countries to prevent economic aid from reaching the island. Castro then ordered the expropriation of US property in Cuba. In turn, President Dwight D. Eisenhower cancelled the sugar quota, a measure which extended into an economic embargo that was intensified in October 1960, after all US banks in Cuba had been confiscated.

While tensions between the United States and Cuba increased, Cuban relations with the Soviet Union improved. Probably encouraged by the direction of the early reforms, in May 1960 the Soviets established formal diplomatic relations between the two countries. (Previously, relations between Cuba and the Soviet Union had been severed as a consequence of Batista's coup in 1952.) Trade agreements were signed and Cuba found a new market for its sugar production. The Soviet Union also granted Castro loans to purchase industrial equipment and weapons. It was not long before the Soviet Union promised to help Cuba 'prevent an armed United States intervention against Cuba'.

The Bay of Pigs Invasion, 1961

While Cuba was cementing its relationship with Moscow, Washington contemplated a plan for the invasion of the island. The plan aimed at using Cuban exiles, trained as a paramilitary force, to return to Cuba and overthrow Castro. This was the origin of the Bay of Pigs Invasion of April 1961.

President J.F. Kennedy (1961 63) had promised a tough attitude against the penetration of Marxism in Latin America. He approved the plan, which had been devised during President Eisenhower's administration (1953–61). Cuban exiles trained in Guatemala and Nicaragua in preparation to invade Cuba and start a popular uprising against Castro. US troops were not to be directly involved in the invasion. The Cuban Revolutionary Council, an anti-Castro group led by former prime minister Miró Cardona (now exiled in the United States), was ready to take over and form a provisional government after the fall of Castro.

The operation was a failure on many levels. When the troops landed in Bay of Pigs (Playa Girón), Cuban forces led by Castro himself defeated them and imprisoned more than 1,000 participants. The hope that the invasion would spark spontaneous uprisings against Castro revealed that the significance of his reforms had not been fully understood by Washington.

Fidel Castro emerged from Bay of Pigs more powerful than before. The victory against the United States made Cubans conclude that Castro was definitely making Cuba a stronger country, and the credibility of the revolution was reinforced. The image of Castro leading the resistance against the invasion added a new dimension to his hero-worship and reinforced Cuban nationalism. In addition, the Bay of Pigs episode gave Castro what he needed to demand increasing commitment to the revolution: a visible enemy. In the face of this, Cubans needed to remain united and accept the leadership of Castro in preparation for another attack. A final implication of the Bay of Pigs incident was that it tempted the Soviet Union to establish stronger military ties with Cuba, and a military presence within Cuba itself.

The Cuban Missile Crisis, 1962

The next incident between Cuba and the United States came with the Cuban Missile Crisis of October 1962, when Washington and Moscow confronted each other over the Soviet placement of nuclear missiles on the island. The crisis took the world to the brink of nuclear war. After 13 days of tense negotiations, the Soviets removed the missiles and dismantled the sites in Cuba. In exchange, the United States removed its own nuclear missiles from Turkey and made a promise that it would not invade the island. Although this pledge was good news for Cuba, Castro was faced with the disappointment that the Soviets would no longer defend his island.

By 1962, Fidel Castro had freed himself from the *batistianos* and the liberals in government. He had also extinguished revolts in the provinces and implemented revolutionary domestic policies. No other figure from the revolution seemed to be in a condition to dispute his authority. Furthermore, he emerged from this period with a more radical position by accepting Soviet assistance, and also making public that he was a Marxist–Leninist. In December 1961, for example, he declared 'I am a Marxist–Leninist and shall be one until the end of my life.'

If a Paper 2 question asks you to discuss issues relating to the consolidation of power, answers on Castro should only include events up to 1962.

Activity 11

 Thinking skills

1. Consider the following question: In what ways did the Bay of Pigs Invasion (1961) and the Cuban Missile Crisis (1962) contribute to Castro's consolidation of power?

Activity 12

 Social, research, communication, and thinking skills

Class discussion

With your class, discuss whether the Bay of Pigs incident and the Cuban Missile Crisis strengthened or weakened Castro's position in Cuba. Find material to support your views. This could include treatment of these events in the Cuban press, public speeches, popular songs, etc.

CHALLENGE YOURSELF

 Research and thinking skills

Find information to help you understand the context against which the Bay of Pigs Invasion and the Cuban Missile Crisis took place. What do you know about the Cold War? How was Cuba affected by this conflict?

The role of ideology

It is often discussed whether Castro had always intended to align the revolution with Marxism, or whether this was the product of US policies that pushed Cuba into the arms of the Soviet Union. It was not clear in 1959 that Cuba would soon adopt a communist ideology. The inclusion of liberals in the provisional government, for example, seemed to indicate that all the revolution was hoping to change was tyranny for democracy. Also, in 1959 Castro seemed little inclined to commit himself to any specific ideology or detailed programme, and he publicly denied any relation between the 26th of July Movement and the communists. He refused to answer questions about which global political ideology matched his own. Any observance of a fixed set of principles, such as communism, would have restricted the methods at Castro's disposal.

Activity 13

Study the source below and answer the question that follows.

> The 26 July movement which is a truly revolutionary movement, which wants to establish the economy of the country on a just basis, which is a revolutionary movement and at the same time a democratic movement with broad human content, was established in Cuba, its ranks were swelled by many people who previously had no political alternative and who inclined toward parties with radical ideas. The 26 July movement is one with radical ideas, but it is not a communist movement, and it differs basically from communism on a whole series of basic points. And those in the 26 July movement, both Raúl and Guevara, like all the others, are men who agree very closely with my political thinking, which is not communist thinking. The thinking of the 26 July movement is not communist thinking.

From a transcript of a press conference given by Fidel Castro at Havana Presidential Palace on 27 February 1959

1. What does the source above reveal about Castro's political ideology in 1959?

CHALLENGE YOURSELF

In groups, find additional information to help you discuss the following questions:

1. Why did Castro change his views about communism by December 1961?
2. To what extent did the more radical members of his movement, such as Che Guevara and Raúl Castro, contribute to this change?
3. How far do you consider the US policies towards Cuba may have influenced Castro's turn to the left?
4. Can you think of other elements that played a part in the shift towards a Marxist–Leninist society?
5. Once your group has collected sufficient evidence, discuss with the rest of the class the strengths and limitations of the different arguments which explain Cuba's shift to the left.
6. Assess the role played by the policies implemented between 1959 and 1962 in the consolidation of power of Fidel Castro.

This question here does not ask you to evaluate the successes and failures of the policies in themselves, but *the extent to which* they enabled Castro to consolidate his position by 1962. In other words, you need to analyse how far the policies contributed to making Castro an undisputed leader.

1.3 Aims and results of Castro's policies

Aims and results of economic policies

Fidel Castro aimed to make Cuba an economically independent and industrialized nation. However, the Cuban economy was to remain linked to the decisions and policies of other nations. The US embargo, the economic dependence on the Soviets, and the impact of the subsequent collapse of the Soviet Union on Cuba helped shape Castro's different economic policies. Although these policies were claimed to uphold the aims of the revolution, Cuba responded to the internal and international challenges with different – and at times contradictory – instruments.

This section analyses the economic policies adopted by Cuba after 1962 in order to assess their levels of success in achieving the revolutionary aims.

The embargo on Cuba

The US commercial and financial embargo upon Cuba reached 55 years' duration in 2015. Its stated aim is to bring democracy to Cuba by forcing the collapse of Castro's regime. However, the embargo has been criticized for humanitarian reasons, as it affects the living conditions of the Cuban population in a negative way. Another source of criticism comes from the fact that the embargo placed on Cuba has actually given Fidel Castro a scapegoat on which to blame all the economic and social problems, proof of which is the fact that, in 55 years, the embargo has not reached its aim of democratizing Cuba. In 2014, negotiations between the United States and Cuba to re-establish diplomatic relations, and to relax travel and economic policies began. Negotiations aimed at lifting the embargo began in 2015.

Paper 2 questions may ask about the economic policies of leaders. In your answers, you will be expected to provide sufficient detail to support your views. The following section will equip you with detailed material on some of Castro's economic policies, so that you are able to provide specific evidence when assessing, for example, whether they have been successful. You can also find additional information about any of these policies and share your findings with the group.

The influence of Che Guevara – moral incentives and voluntarism

A revolutionary who played an important part in the design of Cuba's economic policies was Che Guevara. He occupied the positions of president of the National Bank of Cuba and, later, minister of industries. With the revolution in power, Guevara believed it was time to leave capitalism behind and adopt communism. He favoured a **centrally planned economy,** with an emphasis on moral incentives and self-sacrifice. By this he meant that people should work for the ideals and values of the revolution rather than for personal gains. Moral incentives included party membership and state recognition, amongst others. All workers were to receive equal pay; overtime would not be paid for, as workers were expected to cover it voluntarily as their personal contribution to the revolution.

Guevara aimed at creating a new consciousness, and with it a 'new man' prepared to sacrifice himself for a higher good – a society ruled by the principles of the revolution.

Activity 14 **Thinking, communication, and social skills**

Source analysis

Study the following sources and answer the questions that follow.

Source A

 We are doing everything possible to give labour this new status of social duty and to link it on the one side with the development of a technology which will create the conditions for greater freedom, and on the other side with voluntary work based on a Marxist appreciation of the fact that man truly reaches a full human condition when he produces without being driven by the physical need to sell his labour as a commodity.

This is not a matter of how many pounds of meat one might be able to eat, nor of how many times a year someone can go to the beach, nor how many ornaments from abroad you might be able to buy with present salaries. What is really involved is that the individual feels more complete, with much more internal richness and much more responsibility.

From Ernesto Che Guevara, *Socialism and Man in Cuba*, Pathfinder Press, 2009

Source B

▲ Ernesto 'Che' Guevara at work with Cuban locals.

1. What, according to Source A, were the aims of the revolution?

2. What is the message of Source B? How do you think this photograph relates to Source A?

3. In groups, discuss the ideas presented by Guevara in 'Socialism and Man in Cuba'. Can you identify any source of inspiration for Guevara's ideas? Who do you think they were appealing to and who might have opposed to them? Justify your answers.

The push to transform the Cuban economy into a communist one continued after 1961. In 1962, Cuba changed the national currency and anyone caught with their savings in banks that did not belong to the state lost them overnight. In the cities, rents – which had been reduced by 50 per cent in 1959 – were abolished. This meant that those people living in a property that they did not own virtually became property owners overnight. In 1963, a second Agrarian Law reduced again the amount of land that could be owned by a single person or entity, to prevent the existence of 'rich' peasants. After 1963, the state owned 70 per cent of the land, the rest being small farms, which were expropriated in 1968.

But the economic plans to increase productivity met several obstacles. First of all, Cuba faced a lack of specialized personnel and technicians, many of whom had left the country since the revolution. This deficit meant that the assessment of problems and the implementation of solutions were limited. Also, moral incentives were not efficient in raising productivity levels or in tackling poor-quality work and absenteeism. Farmers in collective farms were forced to sell their product to the state at very low prices. They consequently lost motivation to produce more than what they needed to survive. As a result, sugar production levels were very low and government plans to diversify away from the cultivation of sugar did not compensate for the drop in those levels.

Determined to advance the industrialization programme, the government continued to buy machinery from the Soviet Union and Eastern European nations and to increase its debt. Cuba was again trapped in trade relations of subsidized sugar in exchange for goods and, by 1964, it had to return to intensive sugar production to reduce debt.

The Revolutionary Offensive, 1968

In March 1968, Castro launched the 'Revolutionary Offensive' to move Cuba further towards a communist state and remove the last vestiges of capitalism from the island. The offensive emphasized the ideas of Guevara's 'new man', in which work was a social duty rather than a way to achieve personal aims. Under the Revolutionary Offensive, Castro ordered the expropriation of all remaining privately owned enterprises, such as family stores, restaurants, handicraft stores, grocers, service shops, and street vendors. All of these were to be owned and managed by the state and put at the service of a centrally planned economy. Farmers' markets were eliminated. Self-employment was banned, as it was seen as pursuing individualist aims.

The offensive did not achieve an increase in productivity, but instead produced administrative chaos as the number of government agencies needed to organize the different fields of production and sales grew exponentially. Also, the return to the policy of moral incentives was met with high levels of absenteeism and vagrancy.

The 'Year of the Ten Million', 1970

In order to solve the problems left by the Revolutionary Offensive in 1969, Castro announced that he intended Cuba to break its previous sugar production record and reach a 10-million-ton output in 1970. The campaign aimed to obtain from the harvest enough money to pay off Cuban debts to the Soviet Union and, by selling surplus sugar, make investments to achieve economic diversification. In Castro's words, it was 'a liberation campaign'.

With 1970 becoming the 'Year of the Ten Million', the *zafra* (sugar season) became another battle for Cuban pride. It was intended to show those who remained sceptical about the revolution that it could attain its dreams. The campaign became a crusade that mobilized the entire population and became a political test for Castro.

In order to achieve the 10-million-ton target, and aware that the appeal to voluntarism and solidarity had not guaranteed results in the past, Castro appealed for the 'militarization' of labour (organized and disciplined like an army). Students, conscripts, law breakers, emigrants awaiting their turn to leave the island – all worked cutting cane side by side as 'volunteers'. The armed forces occupied the sugar-producing regions and were put in charge of the sugar mills. Castro himself was seen cutting cane in street posters to motivate people to work. To increase productivity, bars and theatres were closed – even Christmas and New Year celebrations were cancelled.

Activity 15   (ATL)   Thinking and communication skills

Study the poster below and answer the questions that follow.

Propaganda poster used in 1970. It reads 'And where shall we be on January 2? AT THE SUGAR CANE!'

1. What is the message of this poster?
2. What do you think was the purpose of the poster?
3. How does it help you understand the nature of the campaign?

Despite the fact that the entire nation had been put at the service of the campaign, and that a record harvest of 8.5 million tons was reached, Castro was forced to admit that they had been unable to reach the 10-million-ton target. Deep harm had been inflicted on the economy. The agricultural machines had been over-used; agricultural production of crops other than sugar had suffered; other economic areas such as forestry and fishing had seen important losses. Rather than raise the morale of Cubans, the campaign had exhausted them and made them sceptical. The soldiers, for example, who had been mobilized to oversee operations, had felt their status diminished – they had been asked to cut cane when they had been trained to defend the nation. Because the campaign had been given so much importance, its failure was a terrible blow for Castro not only at an economic but also at a political level. In an address to the nation on 26 July 1970, he admitted that the campaign's failure was due to the administrative apparatus rather than the ordinary citizens' commitment. In doing so, and by offering his resignation to a crowd that cheered his name, Fidel Castro managed to survive the political effects of the failure. The price he had to pay was the abandonment of Guevara's ideas of solidarity, voluntarism, and self-sacrifice, and the acceptance of a greater economic dependency on the Soviet Union.

Farmers' markets were reinstated. State-owned companies were given enough autonomy to take some daily decisions without having to go through the state bureaucracy. Material incentives, such as pay for overtime work, were introduced. However, Cuba continued to suffer similar economic problems.

The end of the 1970s brought new levels of recession. Cuba was badly hit by the international economic situation as the Soviet Union cut the price it paid for Cuban sugar. Unemployment, debt, and policies that limited consumption led to increased discontent, which contributed to the 1980 Mariel exodus, when 125,000 abandoned Cuba for the United States.

The Rectification Campaign, 1986

In 1986, Castro blamed the more liberal measures that had been adopted in the past for the present economic problems. He consequently advocated a return to the values of solidarity and voluntarism under the 'Rectification Campaign'. The aim was to 'rectify errors and negative tendencies' linked to the relaxation of communist principles after 1970.

Under the Rectification Campaign, farmers' markets were again banned; bonuses and extra pay were abolished, and self-employment was discouraged. Farm cooperatives were given new emphasis as, under a new Agrarian Reform Act, the percentage of land managed by independent farmers dropped to 2 per cent. Labour discipline was enforced and the workers lost many union rights.

The economic results of the Rectification Campaign were poor. Productivity fell; absenteeism at work increased. Reduced supplies of milk, oil, textiles, and sugar led to an increase in their prices. Parallel or black markets reappeared to offer goods that were difficult to obtain, or that had been added to the list of rationed products. Transport and electricity rates also increased and affected the population's living standards. But Cuba had not yet seen the worst.

The Special Period, 1991

The dissolution of the Soviet Union in 1991 was, in Castro's words, 'the most unfavourable international economic juncture ever faced by the Cuban economy in the entire history of the Revolution'. The 30-year period in which the Soviet Union had become central to Cuba's economy and social development ended suddenly and unexpectedly. Soviet technicians left Cuba as hundreds of projects were abandoned. Subsidized goods, oil, access to international loans, and everything the Soviet Union had provided to Cuba were finished.

As a result, Castro announced Cuba had entered a 'special period in peacetime'. Cubans faced new levels of rationing as basic goods disappeared from the market.

Mariel

One of Cuba's emigration ports. Built between 1762 and 1768 on the Mariel Bay in the province of Pinar del Río, it soon became an important deep-water port and integral to the country's economy. For more information, see page 44.

With Soviet oil gone, the need to save energy limited the working hours of the population, imposed long blackouts, and restricted public transport.

Activity 16   **Thinking and communication skills**

Study the source below and answer the questions that follow.

> *Large cuts had been made in food rations, and gasoline, electricity and other goods and services were in short supply. Food was scarce. People were not starving, but they could definitely not eat as much as they had before and they complained that there was no lard or cooking oil and that the food therefore had no taste. A disease was spreading that affected the eyes and the legs of many people and that was later diagnosed as caused by the drastic drop in food intake.*

From Mona Rosendahl, *Inside the Revolution: Everyday Life in Socialist Cuba*, Cornell University Press, 1997

1. What does the source above reveal about the state of the Cuban economy during the Special Period?
2. To what extent can it be argued that the Special Period demonstrated that the Cuban Revolution had failed in its economic aims?

In order to adjust to the new scenario, and in response to growing unrest at home, new policies were implemented:

- A large percentage of state-owned farms began to be run as worker-managed cooperatives in an attempt to increase levels of productivity.
- In an effort to attract capital and diversify economic activities, Cuba was opened to international business. Foreigners were invited to join the state in the development of certain areas of the economy, such as tourism, mining, and energy. Tourism in particular developed positively.
- In 1993 it was made legal for Cubans to buy and sell US dollars in an attempt to attract dollars from the relatives of Cubans overseas. The fact that Cubans could now buy and sell dollars freely had a positive impact on the demand for goods and contributed to the reactivation of the economy.
- Farmers' and handicraft markets reappeared and some level of self-employment and private businesses was allowed. The state aimed at saving money by reducing some subsidies and increasing taxes.

Partly as a response to growing tension with Cuba, but also to the rise of foreign investment in the island, the United States passed the Cuban Liberty and Solidarity Act (Helms–Burton Act) in 1996. Among other economic measures that tightened the embargo, Helms–Burton restricted entry into the United States for international travellers doing business with Cuba. Aimed at promoting 'a peaceful transition to a representative democracy and market economy', the act stated the United States would eliminate sanctions against Cuba only if both Fidel and Raúl Castro were out of office and free elections took place.

However, Cuban politics did not become more democratic after the act was implemented. If anything – like with the embargo itself – the Helms–Burton Act contributed to increase economic hardships for Cuban citizens while providing Castro with an excuse for the failures of the economy.

Activity 17 ATL **Thinking and communication skills**

1. Fill in the following chart by identifying the aims of the different economic programmes you have studied in this section and listing their successes and failures. It will be useful revision before you approach the next exercises.

Policy	Aims	Achievements	Failures

2. Consider the following question:

Fidel Castro's government tried to promote economic development, but his policies did not succeed. To what extent do you agree with this view?

Now read the following introduction to the question above:

> An effective approach to this question requires that you first show that the revolutionary government sought to generate economic growth. Because the question does not ask you to focus on a specific period, it would be a good idea to decide, before you start writing, which specific policies you plan to address. For each of the selected policies, you should show how the government hoped it would produce economic growth and then decide the extent to which this was achieved.

Student answer – Jenna

Fidel Castro came to power in Cuba in 1959 with the aim of making radical changes to the country. He promised to end inequality, corruption and the economic dependency on the USA. With these aims, he implemented economic policies to generate economic growth. These policies included the nationalization of industries and banks, the passing of an Agrarian Reform Act and the development of national industries. However, they did not bring about economic growth. Castro's attempt to increase the production of sugar to pay for the industrialization of the country did not succeed, as shown by the failure to reach the target of the 10 million tons of sugar in 1970. Also, after the revolution Cuba began to depend on the USSR and, with the collapse of that state, Cuba entered a very difficult economic period.

Examiner's comments

This introduction shows specific knowledge of the aims and policies of Castro's economy, and the candidate is aware of the need to assess them. More could have been done to show explicitly which period/policies are treated in the essay and the attempt to assess the 10-million-ton sugar campaign could have been left for the essay itself.

Now read the following conclusion to the question above:

Student answer – Jenna

The Cuban Revolution did not produce the promised economic growth. Under Fidel Castro, Cuba continued to experience the problems caused by economic dependence and the consequences of the collapse of the USSR on the island were devastating. Castro was equally unable to develop a national industry that would make Cuba more self-sufficient and the country was never really able to reduce the influence of the sugar market on the national economy. Economic policies increased the shortage of goods, which made the living standards of the population drop, as seen during the Rectification Campaign. Although the Cuban population gained access to land to work and houses to live in, the levels of economic recession were very high at different times, as shown by the analysis of the late 1970s. All in all, the economic policies of Cuba never brought economic growth.

This question requires a more specific treatment of the aims of the revolution and you will need to identify them early in your essay.

Examiner's comments

This conclusion is clearly focused on the demands of the question. It also makes reference to specific arguments, which, presumably, have been developed throughout the essay. Make sure you do not introduce new arguments and new evidence in your conclusion because there will be no time for you to develop the ideas. Use the conclusion to round up the supporting arguments you have presented in the essay with a clear focus on how they have helped answer the question before you.

3. Now read the following question:

   To what extent were the economic aims of the revolution achieved by Fidel Castro's government by 1990?

   • In what ways is this question similar/different to the previous one?
   • How would you approach it?
   • Think of the arguments you could develop and which examples you would be using to illustrate each point made.

The aims and impact of social policies

The revolution aimed to introduce social justice and allow all sectors of society to have equal opportunities. Reforms in health, education, and the treatment of women and of minorities were implemented, among other areas. Some of these reforms clashed with Cuban traditions and culture. Therefore, the arts played a fundamental role in designing a new Cuban culture in which, for example, the role of women as workers was promoted.

The following section analyses two significant areas of social policy: the status of women and education. It evaluates the parts played by the FMC and the literacy campaign to change the status of women and promote education. It analyses the relationship between the Cuban government and the arts to understand the attempt to transform Cuban culture through revolutionary values. It also addresses the relationship between the revolution and religious and racial groups.

The impact of policies on women

The status of women in Cuba by 1959 was different from that in many Latin American countries. Women were given the right to vote as early as 1934. The 1940 constitution also granted them equality before the law; women could not be discriminated against at work and were to receive equal pay for equal work. Yet, although women were allowed to vote, study, work, and even sue for divorce, pre-revolutionary Cuba remained in many ways a traditional society. Only a few occupations, such as teaching and nursing, were considered to be appropriate for women in the pre-revolutionary years. Women often faced discrimination at work, as the jobs with greater responsibility went to men. In the middle and upper classes, men preferred women to stay at home to look after their families rather than join the workforce.

The defence of the rights of women at work was largely a response to Cuba's economic needs. To achieve modernization, and in order to produce record harvests, women needed to become an active part of the workforce. This implied having to fight against two main problems: discrimination against women at work, and finding how to make women's role in the workforce and the household compatible.

To address the first problem, new legislation was passed reinforcing the equal rights of men and women to access all types of jobs. Women were offered training at technical and professional levels to prepare themselves for posts with greater responsibility. They entered fields that had so far been almost exclusively all-male, such as construction, biotechnology, and IT. In the rural areas, the Agrarian Reform acts opened the opportunity for women to work in areas that had also been limited to men, such as driving and repairing tractors. In the towns and cities, an increasing number of day-care centres for working mothers were made available so that women could become part of the workforce.

Under Castro, women were expected to leave their families and homes for long periods and work in 'Agricultural Legions', cutting cane and harvesting coffee and other crops. There was pressure on women to be efficient workers, participate in political life, volunteer to serve the revolution while at the same time fulfil their responsibilities as wives, mothers, and housewives.

Activity 18

(ATL) Thinking and communication skills

Study the sources below and answer the question that follows.

Source A

Photograph showing a peasant woman ready for work.

Source B

A group of Cuban women enjoy a music class, c. 1965.

1.   Explain the message of Source A and Source B. To what extent do you consider the sources a reflection of the change in the role of women in Cuba?

Cuba nevertheless remained a very patriarchal society. Women were expected to fulfil their roles as housewives, but men refused to share household responsibilities or live with potentially economically independent women. This conflict proved difficult to manage and resulted in many women giving up work and in entire families leaving Cuba.

In the 1970s, a new 'Family Code' was put in place. It stipulated equality of sexes both at home and at work. Men were to share in the household duties and the education of children; not doing so was seen as the exploitation of women. The presence of women in the workforce, however, remained lower than government expectations, a fact that even Castro was forced to admit.

Case study: The Cuban Women's Federation (FMC)

The FMC was created by Vilma Espín (wife of Raúl Castro) in 1960 with the aim of helping women integrate into the revolution. It trained women to take up new jobs in farming, construction, and teaching, among others. The FMC also organized many aspects of the campaign against illiteracy, and created and ran successful health programmes. FMC women joined 'Sanitary Brigades' that travelled to the rural areas to deliver vaccination campaigns, and they also served as social workers. The FMC worked with the Ministry of Education in the design of new textbooks to be used in revolutionary Cuba. In them, women were portrayed as committed workers and soldiers. Former domestic workers were trained to work as seamstresses or cooks, and they received education in history, geography, and the new laws of revolutionary Cuba. Housewives were also taught in FMC headquarters so that they could complete their schooling.

Assessment

The policies aimed towards encouraging the equality of women seem to have been more geared towards increasing the size of the Cuban workforce than towards gender equality. More than 600,000 Cubans, many of whom were middle-class professionals, left the island in the 1960s. In order to fill up these vacancies, Cuban women trained for jobs and professions that had been denied to them in the past, and women played an important role in the success of literacy and health campaigns.

Yet despite the work of the FMC, the government could not achieve the levels of female employment it had hoped for. Furthermore, the low number of women in decision-making positions and in the higher levels of the PCC leads us to question whether the government really intended equality between the sexes, or if it was merely creating policies to reach its economic goals.

Activity 19 **Research, social, and communication skills**

Group activity

In previous sections of this chapter, you have read about women who contributed to Castro's rise to power, such as Celia Sánchez, Haydée Santamaría, and Vilma Espín. Split into groups, with each group choosing one of these women and researching her role after 1959. Share the information with the other groups and discuss their importance in the revolutionary government. Why did they become role models?

'Authoritarian states allowed women to play a fuller role in society.' With reference to one authoritarian state, assess the validity of this claim.

Read the following introduction.

> ### Student answer – Chang
>
> Castro's Cuba aimed at making a significant change in the lives of women. It expected to incorporate women into the revolution and the workforce. Several women played important roles in the government, such as Celia Sánchez and Vilma Espín. The latter founded the Federation of Cuban Women, which was the institution that led the policies for women in Cuba. Although Castro tried to limit the traditions which demanded women to be mothers and wives above all, he did not succeed and Cuban women were forced to be housewives, mothers, workers and party members, so they were not truly liberated by the revolution.

Examiner's comments

Paper 2 questions will not name specific authoritarian states and leaders, so you are free to choose which examples to use. It is very important that you let the examiner know in your introduction what your examples are and show an understanding of the question. Chang has missed the opportunity to define what is meant by a 'fuller role'. He has an implicit understanding, however, of the idea that women had to play multiple roles and seemed to be worse off. Perhaps this introduction would be clearer if he had tried to establish the context: What is meant by a 'fuller role'? What was the situation of women at the time of the revolution? In general terms, in which areas were women allowed to play a fuller role and where were they limited by the revolution?

> **!** In order to answer this question, you should start by explaining what you understand by 'a fuller role in society'. It is not only about whether more women were allowed in the workforce, but also about what their role was in that workforce. You could also use the information from your research into the important women of the revolution in your discussion on whether the fact they seemed to have played a 'fuller role' was the exception or the rule in Castro's Cuba.

Education

Cuba's access to education in the pre-revolutionary years varied significantly across geographical regions, becoming more restricted in the rural areas. It was also limited by economic status. Cuba had one of the highest illiteracy rates in Latin America. It reached 24 per cent among children under 10 and was high in the adult population as well. Public education was poor, while access to university was limited to those who could afford it and lived near one of the few universities on the island.

Case study: The literacy campaign

As he rose to power, Castro had promised Cubans improvements in education. During the years in Sierra Maestra, the Rebel Army taught children and adults alike to read and write.

Under the slogan 'If you do not know, learn; if you know, teach', 1961 was declared 'The Year of Education' and Castro promised to end illiteracy within the year. To achieve this aim, he needed to solve two initial problems: the lack of schools and the lack of teachers. To solve the shortage of buildings, military barracks were turned into educational complexes, while new schools were built all across the country, particularly in the rural areas. Between 1959, when Castro began his policy of school expansion, and 1962, more schools were built than in the previous 58 years of Cuban history.

To produce more educators for the literacy campaign, Castro implemented a training programme for 271,000 teachers. To reach all areas, they were sent across the country to teach people in their homes. Literate citizens were expected to act as 'literacy volunteers' in their free time. They were dressed in an olive-green uniform and were also sent to the countryside to teach the peasants. These *brigadistas*, as they were known, lived with rural families during the campaign.

The Year of Education brought the entire Cuban population into a joint patriotic effort. By1962, illiteracy had dropped to 4 per cent. The success of the campaign was spectacular and, as such, it increased the hopes in the revolution.

The aims of the literacy campaign had been twofold. First, it sought to fight illiteracy among the poor. Second, it also aimed to make the middle-class literate youth familiarize themselves with the living conditions and hardships of the poor, and to act in response to the values of the revolution: service and self-sacrifice. Their work in the literacy campaign opened their eyes to the 'other Cuba', and thousands of volunteers emerged from the experience totally transformed. The illiterate peasants, in turn, learned what the revolution could do for them and were given another reason to support it.

Activity 21   ATL   Thinking and communication skills

Study the sources below and answer the questions that follow.

Source A

Female soldiers of the Cuban armed forces seen here marching on parade.

Source B

❝ In the case of Cuba, we have the one Latin American country that has overcome the lockstep of school failure, the absence of educational opportunity, and poverty. Cuba has gone a long way toward fulfilling the educational needs of children at all school levels and has adopted broad measures to provide sound health care and proper nutrition, indispensable ingredients in a comprehensive effort to achieve victory over a history of neglect.

From William Luis, *Culture and Customs of Cuba*, Greenwood Press, 2001

1. What is the message of Source A?
2. What, according to source B, were the educational achievements of Castro's Cuba?
3. 'Authoritarian states use education to obtain support rather than to instil knowledge.' How far do you agree with this statement?

For Question 3, opposite, Fidel Castro would certainly be an appropriate example to use in discussing the quotation. In the treatment of Castro's educational policies you will find material to both agree and disagree with the statement. Discuss all views before you come up with a conclusion.

Impact on schools, teachers, and students

The shift towards communism in 1961 affected education. That year, all private schools were nationalized, boarding schools opened, and a large scholarship programme for gifted and committed students was established. Participants were selected by the government who often decided the subject areas in which particular students should specialize. Free time had to be used in 'intellectually valuable choices', such as volunteer work.

Teachers who did not support the revolution lost their jobs, and the new ones who came to replace them soon realized students acted as spies. On the other hand, teachers who supported the regime were rewarded with training in the Soviet Union and Eastern Europe, where communist values were reinforced. New textbooks were adopted and teaching focused on the history of the revolution and the lives of heroes: Fidel, Che, and Camilo (on first-name terms). Libraries were purged of what was considered to be inappropriate material. In Castro's words: 'The task of the schools… is the ideological formation of revolutionaries, and then, by means of the revolutionaries, the ideological formation of the rest of the people.'

Activity 22	(ATL) Thinking and communication skills

Read the source below and answer the questions that follow.

> It doesn't take me long to discover that despite my initial reservations, I am going to enjoy school after all. We sit at our uncomfortable wooden desks learning to recite an alphabet where the F is for Fidel, the R for rifles and the Y is for the Yankees. Learning about Fidel and rifles and why we should hate the Americans can sometimes take up a fair amount of the school day, even in primary school. As we get older, more and more time is taken out for what my parents describe with growing alarm as indoctrination.

From Luis M. Garcia, *Child of the Revolution: Growing Up in Castro's Cuba*, 2006

1. According to the source above, what were students expected to learn?
2. Explain the message in 'the F is for Fidel, the R is for rifles and the Y is for the Yankees'.
3. Explain the meaning of 'what my parents describe with growing alarm as indoctrination'.
4. To what extent does the source above support Castro's view that schools had to provide the 'ideological formation of revolutionaries'?

Treatment of religious groups and minorities

Cuba is considered a Catholic country. However, along with Catholicism, Afro-Cuban religions also have a great influence. There are also minorities of Protestants and Jews.

The relationship between religious congregations and the revolutionary government has been a complex one. When the revolution triumphed in 1959, some sectors of the Catholic Church welcomed the opportunity to achieve social justice. Others looked at it with suspicion, particularly as the revolution began to move to the left. Castro thought many of the congregations in Cuba represented foreign interests, as their members were Americans or Spaniards. Whenever bishops criticized the policies of the revolution, Castro accused them of abandoning their pastoral duties and getting involved in politics. The nationalization of schools following the Bay of Pigs incident, and the government's decision that religious education could only take place in churches, increased tension between the state and many religious leaders. Many congregations lived in what historian Antoni Kapcia called 'internal exile', that is, as invisible groups with limited or no influence. Some pastors, however, thought that the only way to attract people back to their churches was to participate in the campaigns of the revolution as volunteers, so they joined the *zafra*, health campaigns, and other forms of voluntary labour.

Afro-Cuban religions
These faiths are based on the religious beliefs of former West African slaves, and they have incorporated some aspects of Catholicism. As they were forced to adopt Catholicism during the Spanish rule of Cuba, these slaves hid their religious secrets inside the imagery of their masters' saints. *Santería*, or 'the way of the Saints', is the term slave owners used to refer to their slaves' worship.

In an attempt to show there was no room for putting religious beliefs before the revolution, the constitution of 1976 stated that 'It is illegal and punishable by law to oppose one's faith or religious belief to the Revolution, education or the fulfilment of the duty to work, defend the homeland with arms, show reverence for its symbols and other duties established by the constitution.'

The hardships experienced during the Special Period – which seemed to augur the end of the revolution – strengthened attendance of people in their churches. In 1998, Pope John Paul II paid a historic visit to Cuba. A strong anti-communist, the pope addressed the lack of political freedom in Cuba but he also criticized the US economic embargo. As a sign of improved relations, the government modified the PCC statute and allowed religious people to join. The separation between state and Church, however, continued to exist, and religious education remained forbidden in all schools.

As for racial relations, in the years before the revolution Afro-Cubans (approximately 50 per cent of the population) were discriminated against in education, work opportunities, shops, and restaurants. Supporters of the revolution in Cuba claim it has eradicated racial discrimination. Those who disagree maintain that the revolution raised the living standards of the poor – which happened to include a significant number of non-whites – but that inequality between the races continues to exist. Evidence of this is found in the limited number of non-whites who occupy positions of power within the PCC or decision-making posts in the Cuban government. During the Special Period, racial tensions resurfaced. Remittances in dollars sent by Cubans overseas to their families in Cuba improved the status of white Cubans more than that of black Cubans. This is because about 85 per cent of Cubans overseas were white. Also, the growth of tourism in this period provided white Cubans with new employment opportunities. This can be explained by the fact that whites had more access to remittances in dollars, which enabled them to open small businesses to cater for the needs of tourists.

Activity 23 **Thinking and communication skills**

1. Assess the role of social policies as factors explaining the consolidation and maintenance of power of one authoritarian leader.

This section has provided you with information about Castro's social policies. It has addressed the status of women, education, religion, and the treatment of minorities. Castro is an appropriate example to use to answer questions on social policies: there is an opportunity to asses their contribution to his rise and consolidation of power, as well as looking at continuity and change in Cuban society.

For this question, you should focus on how social policies helped (or hindered) his consolidation and maintenance of power, so starting after 1962 would be appropriate. Because you have approximately 50 minutes to answer this question, there will be no time to include everything you have studied. Spend a few minutes planning your answer and thinking which specific examples you will use to illustrate your arguments.

The aims and impact of cultural policies

The revolution's new order aimed to change Cuban culture. Castro believed that Cuban culture before the revolution had been marked by foreign influence, and that truly nationalist values had not been established. He therefore founded many organizations aimed at developing a Cuban culture based on nationalist and revolutionary values. These organizations coordinated the different policies to ensure the arts reflected and encouraged these values.

Popular culture and the arts

Among the early measures taken to end foreign influence was the translation of English terms into Spanish, such as on all wrappers and labels. Terms such as 'struggle', 'battle', 'victory', and 'enemy' were used to explain different events, from the campaign against illiteracy to the harvest season. Visual images of what constituted the ideal man and the ideal woman were based on the revolutionary heroes of the wars against Spain, as well as the revolutionary war against Batista.

The National Ballet and the Cuban Institute of Arts and Cinema Industry (*Instituto Cubano de Arte e Industria Cinematográficos*) were created in 1959. Two years later, the Union of Artists and Writers of Cuba (*Unión de Escritores y Artistas de Cuba*, UNEAC) was formed. Its declaration stated that '[the] writer must contribute to the revolution through his work, and this involves conceiving of literature as a means of combat, a weapon against weaknesses and the problems that, directly or indirectly, could hinder this advance.'

Case study: The *PM* affair and 'Words to the intellectuals'

PM (1961) was a short film documenting Afro-Cubans dancing and enjoying themselves. It was considered to show a decadent aspect of Cuba, so was accused of being counter-revolutionary and was eventually censored. The censorship of *PM*, a truly apolitical film, angered many Cuban writers and artists who had been enthusiastic supporters of the revolution. They feared that the government, and particularly Castro, would direct culture by dictating the themes and content of their work. In response to these concerns, Castro organized the First Congress of Cuban Writers and Artists, from which UNEAC emerged.

At this congress, Castro gave a speech that has become an essential document in the study of the history of the arts in the revolution. His objective was to enforce revolutionary discipline and to mobilize support for the regime. This speech, known as 'Words to the intellectuals', defined the responsibilities of artists in times of revolution when Cuba was being threatened by the enemy (the Bay of Pigs Invasion had taken place earlier that year). The intellectuals were no longer free to create what they wanted; they were at the service of the revolution and had to work to strengthen its values.

In this speech, Castro made another point very clear. Art had a purpose, and its purpose was dictated by the needs of the revolution. An artist had to be a revolutionary first; he could not paint or write about what he wanted, he had to do it in such a way that the masses – the focus of the revolution – would receive a clear message. In other words, inspiration had to come from what the revolution demanded of the artist.

TOK

'Language shapes the way we see the world.' By making reference to the emergence of a revolutionary culture, discuss the extent to which you agree with this quotation.

Activity 24   **Thinking and communication skills**

Study the source below and answer the questions that follow.

> *The Revolution should maintain a majority, not only of revolutionaries, but also of all honest citizens. The Revolution should only turn away those who are incorrigible counter-revolutionaries. And, the Revolution must have a policy for that part of the population so that everyone in that sector of artists and intellectuals who are not genuinely revolutionary may find that they have a space to work and to create within the Revolution; and that their creative spirit will have the freedom to express itself. This means that within the Revolution, everything; against the Revolution, nothing. This is a general principle for all citizens; it is a fundamental principle of the Revolution.*

From Fidel Castro, 'Words to the intellectuals', 30 June 1961

1. What is the significance of 'This means that within the Revolution, everything; against the Revolution, nothing'?
2. To what extent is Castro's speech consistent with his policies? Explain your answer fully.

In the light of these new directives, the arts were to promote revolutionary values. Poets wrote to encourage people to work in the *zafra* or the coffee harvest; novels described women who were role models at work and at home; films highlighted the achievements of the revolution, such as Manuel Herrera's *Girón*, which represented the Bay of Pigs incident, or Jorge Fraga's *Me hice maestro* (*I Became a Teacher*).

The arts came under even closer supervision after the Revolutionary Offensive was launched in 1968. The economic problems, the demoralizing effect of the death of Che Guevara, and the need to stimulate people to achieve the 10-million-ton sugar target demanded an even greater control of intellectuals and artists.

The Padilla affair and the 'grey period', 1971

In 1971, conflict between the writers and the government broke out again over the work of poet Heberto Padilla, who had become disappointed with the revolution. In 1968, Padilla was awarded the UNEAC poetry prize for his work *Fuera del juego* (*Out of the Game*), which contained poems critical of the revolution. These appeared at a very sensitive time in Cuba, since the 10-million-ton harvest programme had just failed and Castro was prepared to be far less tolerant towards dissent. Padilla was put under arrest and tortured. He was given a confession he had to learn and deliver in a staged public trial. In his 'confession', Padilla admitted to the charges of being an enemy of the revolution, and he was made to accuse his wife and friends of being counter-revolutionaries.

Padilla's detention and trial had an enormous impact not only in Cuba but also among intellectuals worldwide who had supported the revolution. Numerous artists intervened on Padilla's behalf and asked Castro to respect freedom of expression. Many of them broke away from the revolution.

The Padilla affair was followed by what became known as the 'grey period', in which artists were afraid to produce anything that could be interpreted as counter-revolutionary. Closer surveillance of their actions and work was carried out by the state and extended to other forms of academic and scientific activities.

The 1976 constitution established that 'there is freedom of artistic creation as long as its content is not contrary to the revolution', echoing Castro's 'Words to the intellectuals' speech. (For more on the 1976 constitution, see page 43.) Although there have been times when censorship appeared to loosen, most Cuban writers who

TOK

In groups, discuss the following questions in relation to policies towards the arts under Fidel Castro:

- To what extent can art change the way we understand the world?
- Should art be politically subversive? Should it serve the interests of the community, the state, the patron, or the funding organization?

dissented from the revolution found the only way of publishing their work was to have it smuggled out of the island. In 1998, Castro again accused filmmakers who criticized Cuba's social and economic conditions of being counter-revolutionaries.

Propaganda

Previous sections in this chapter have made reference to the use of propaganda in Castro's rise, consolidation, and maintenance in power. Propaganda was used to mythologize the revolution and to create the cult of Castro. Ever since the founding of Radio Rebelde, Castro used Cuban radio and, later on, television to make the revolution a permanent presence in Cuban homes. Magazines such as *Bohemia* and newspapers like *Granma* were used to raise awareness of the ideals and actions of the government, and to increase commitment to its policies. Given educational levels had increased so much in Cuba, written propaganda was a very effective tool.

Castro relied on his skills as a speaker to create the image of an engaged leader – one who fought for the ideals of the revolution in the Sierras, on the shores of Bay of Pigs, and at international and diplomatic conferences. His nationalistic speech, together with his appeal to the idea that Cuba's integrity was threatened by imperialism and that it was essential for Cubans to remain united and follow the directives of the government, were fundamental in shaping the political system with which Castro has remained in power since 1959.

| Activity 25 | **ATL** **Thinking and communication skills** |

Study the sources below and answer the questions that follow.

Source A

66 *He lectured to soldiers on military matters, schoolteachers on education, physicians on medicine, agronomists on plant cultivation, coaches on athletics, filmmakers on the art of the cinema, master chess players on the best opening gambits, poets and novelists on the guidelines of acceptable writing. These speeches served various purposes. He instructed, explaining the workings of the revolution to the Cuban people. He responded to some crisis, announced a new policy. He spoke almost daily, and on some days more than once. Each assembly provided an opportunity to 'mobilize the masses,' to assure popular support for him and for the revolution. He marked important landmarks in the history of his revolution – the landing of the Granma, the defeat of Batista…, the attack on the Moncada barracks…*

From Robert E. Quirk, *Fidel Castro*, W.W. Norton & Company, 1993

Propaganda was also used to rally support for new policies or to emphasize the successes of the regime by the use of posters like these:

Source B

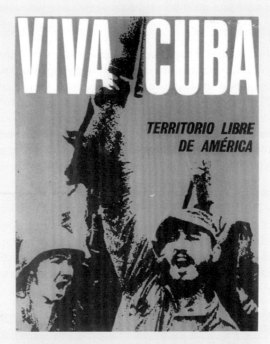

This poster reads: 'Long live Cuba. Territory free of America.'

Source C

This 1961 poster reads: 'We have accomplished it! Everyone to greet the victorious brigades!'

1. What, according to Source A, was the purpose of Castro's public addresses?
2. Explain the message in Source B.
3. What event does Source C make reference to? What message does it convey?

Aims and impact of political policies and treatment of opposition

Previous sections have addressed how Fidel Castro consolidated his political power between 1959 and 1962 by a combination of legal methods and use of force. From 1962, Castro continued to use this combination of methods to maintain himself in power. This section analyses the structure of the government administration and Castro's policies for dealing with the opposition.

Impact of the 1976 constitution

When Fidel Castro overthrew Fulgencio Batista, he said that elections would be held at the appropriate time, after Cuba had successfully replaced Batista's dictatorial system with the revolution. However, it was not until the year 1976 that a new constitution was given to the people of Cuba and elections were held for the first time. The constitution, which is still in effect at the time of writing, is communist in nature and explicitly recognizes the influence of the political and social ideas of Marx, Engels, and Lenin. It establishes the importance of the PCC in the administrative structure of the country by stating that 'it is the highest leading force of society and of the state, which organizes and guides the common effort towards the goals of the construction of socialism and the progress toward a communist society.'

Elections in 1976 were the first ones to take place since the revolution, but the only party allowed to campaign was the PCC, and all nominees to elections at any level had to be chosen by the party. Under the new constitution, Fidel Castro became head of state, replacing Dorticós. He was also head of the government, president of the Executive Committee of the Council of Ministers, first secretary of the Central Committee of the PCC, and commander-in-chief of the armed forces. As in the period before 1976, Castro remained personally involved in all governmental decisions. Although a legislative body – the National Assembly – was created, and elected provincial and municipal authorities were established, the 1976 constitution brought little change in practice. The National Assembly only met twice a year for a period of four to five days.

The economic crisis of the Special Period led to a re-examination of Cuba's political institutions, which had to adapt to the new policies resulting from the opening of the economy. In 1992, the constitution was revised. References to Cuba as a member of the socialist community were removed from the document as the country invited foreign investment. The first direct elections for deputies to the National Assembly were held, where Cubans were allowed to choose from a list of party candidates approved by the government. Also, freedom of religion became a constitutional right. Cubans were no longer required to be atheists or agnostics in order to be members of the party or to be elected. This encouraged a religious revival in the country.

However, the new constitution brought limited political change. Cuba continued to be an authoritarian single-party state. Castro held emergency powers that enabled him to suspend the constitution. Freedom of association to protest against government policies was not granted. All mass media has been controlled by the state since the 1960s.

Another characteristic of the Cuban government that has prevailed over time is the excessive level of bureaucratization. The different social, political, and economic plans launched in Cuba led to the creation of a large public sector that employs a vast proportion of the workforce in an inefficient bureaucracy – as seen with the implementation of policies such as the Revolutionary Offensive. However, civil servants constitute an important sector of the economy, and the state is the largest employer on the island. Even if this state bureaucracy may not have been efficient, its existence serves the purpose of maintaining employment levels.

The nature, extent, and treatment of opposition

Previous sections have addressed policies implemented to control opposition, such as the use of show trials (the Padilla affair) or the restrictions placed on people's freedom to express their views. The role played by the Committees for the Defence of the Revolution (*Comités de Defensa de la Revolución*, CDR), set up in 1960 to 'defend the revolution', is also significant for understanding how Castro has treated opposition. The committees were responsible for some social projects, but their primary role was to report counter-revolutionary activity. There were CDRs in operation in every workplace, street block, and inside residential buildings. Members were instructed to identify 'enemies of the revolution' and report on their activities. By the end of its first year, the CDR had more than 800,000 members and had become an important tool in government surveillance. By 1963, one third of the Cuban population worked for a CDR. It meant that the level of peer surveillance was very high, which intimidated people. Many Cubans, however, felt that being members of a CDR was a way to contribute to the goals of the revolution and to ensure that what they had gained by it would not be lost.

The use of force to control and repress opposition was clearly illustrated in the creation of the Military Units to Aid Production (*Unidad Militar de Ayuda a la Producción*, UMAP). Between 1965 and 1968, about 25,000 young men were sent to UMAP labour camps. Anyone opposing military service on whatever grounds was sent to these camps, together with a variety of other 'offenders': children of political prisoners, youngsters imitating American dress codes and tastes, homosexuals, and political dissenters. All were sent to the labour camps to be 're-educated through the liberating effects of collective work'. The camps were finally closed in 1968 as a result of domestic and international pressure on Castro, although he continued to claim that he had made that decision himself.

One of the distinguishing features of Fidel Castro in his treatment of opposition is that he has, at different times, allowed the exodus of Cubans from the island. You have already seen in an earlier section of this chapter how this policy helped him consolidate his power between 1959 and 1962. That was not the only time when Castro tolerated, and to some extent encouraged, the opposition to leave the island.

Case study: The Peruvian embassy and the Mariel boatlift

Economic problems in Cuba made 1980 a year of political challenge for Castro's leadership. In April that year, a bus full of Cubans wishing to seek **asylum** crashed the gates outside the Peruvian embassy in Havana. In the incident, a Cuban guard was shot. In response to the Peruvian embassy's refusal to hand over these asylum seekers, Castro withdrew all guards from the embassy. Soon after, more than 10,000 Cubans forced themselves into the building, demanding asylum.

'Let them all go!' shouted Castro at a rally in his support in Havana. The Cuban press treated the asylum seekers with disdain, and hundreds of supporters of Castro and the PCC staged demonstrations outside the Peruvian embassy to express their rejection of those seeking asylum, referring to them as 'scum'. Castro announced that anyone was free to leave the island if they wanted to. Soon after that, hundreds of boats of all sizes, rented by Cubans living in Florida, arrived to assist in the emigration of 125,000 Cubans in the Mariel boatlift. These *marielitos*, as they became known, were not only

CHALLENGE YOURSELF

Research and social skills

In groups, find out about Operation Peter Pan, the children's exodus to the United States. What caused the operation and what were the results? Look for different sources that analyse the events. How do they differ in their explanations? What are the values and limitations of the sources you have found?

opponents to Castro or people wanting to be reunited with their relatives; thousands of prisoners and mentally ill people were released by the government and forced to board the arriving boats.

The Mariel boatlift showed levels of discontent that had been unheard of in Cuba before. Despite demonstrations in support of Castro, it put into question the level of commitment of the people towards the revolution and its very legitimacy. It seemed the readiness to tolerate hardship in the name of the revolution was coming to an end. The relaxation of the legislation that allowed Cubans living overseas to return to visit their relatives had exposed thousands of Cubans to, at times exaggerated, stories of success and accomplishment of their visiting relatives. This contributed to creating a feeling of disillusion at the revolution and its gains.

This crisis was also unique in other aspects. This was not the first time Castro had used emigration as a valve to defuse conflict. In the early days of the revolution, thousands of Cubans, mostly middle class and professionals, left the island as the early manifestations of what would become a communist state appeared. But unlike these previous migration waves, the people leaving in 1980 were economic rather than political emigrants.

Activity 26

 Thinking and social skills

Study the sources below and answer the questions that follow.

Source A

Cuban refugees sailing out from Mariel port towards the United States. Overcrowding on many of the refugee boats made the trip extremely perilous.

Source B

❝ *Of course, at first they took the refined bourgeois, the well-dressed landowner. And then they took the physician, the professional. And remember they took half of our country's doctors… Now it is very difficult, very difficult to take a doctor away, because the ones that stayed behind were the best ones, and doctors who trained along other lines, with a solidarity and human spirit, doctors who are not money-minded.*

From a speech by Fidel Castro in Havana on 1 May 1980

1. With reference to their origins and purpose, assess the values and limitations of the two sources to a historian studying the 1980 Mariel boatlift.

2. In pairs, find information about other times when Castro used emigration as a method to control or reduce opposition. How effective do you consider this method has been?

45

The economic hardships of the Special Period led to rising political discontent in the 1990s. Dissident groups protested in demand of political freedom, the release of other political prisoners, freer markets, and more ownership rights. The government responded with more repression and arrests.

The impact of foreign policy on Castro's maintenance of power

Previous sections in this chapter, for example on the Bay of Pigs incident (1961) and the Cuban Missile Crisis (1962), focused on the impact of Castro's foreign policy on his *consolidation* of power. We will now consider the ways in which Castro's foreign policy contributed to his *maintenance* of power.

With the economy suffering from the US embargo, Castro understood the importance of new commercial and political partners. To this end, he strengthened ties with the Soviet Union and also became actively involved in global affairs.

The strengthening of relations with the Soviet Union in the 1960s and 1970s provided Castro with access to military equipment and training for his armed forces. The Soviet Union also subsidized Cuban sugar and nickel, provided oil, and granted essential financial assistance. Relations with the Soviet Union became essential to Cuba's economy and, in that way, to Castro's maintenance of power.

Fidel Castro made it an aim of his foreign policy to support **national liberation movements** worldwide. He believed that one way of protecting Cuba was by assisting leftist revolutions in other nations against the United States' attempts to curb them. After his success in 1959, Castro believed his country was able to support the expansion of revolution worldwide because Cuba had a military force and that it was defending an ideology of liberation. In doing this, he didn't always see eye to eye with the Soviet Union. The Soviet Union was not prepared to allow an escalation of Cold War tensions as a result of Castro's foreign policy, and restricted economic assistance when it considered Castro had gone beyond the limits. At other times, Cuban intervention served the Soviet purposes, as shown in the following case study on Angola.

Map of Southern Africa in the 1970s.

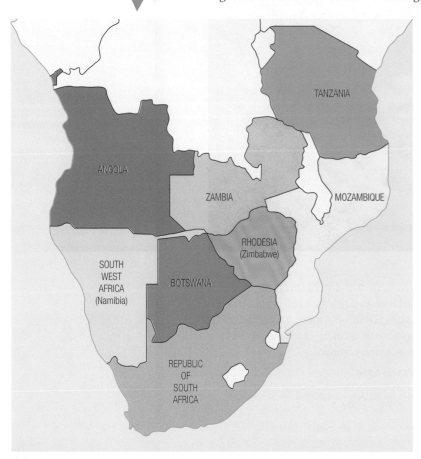

Case study: The Angolan Civil War, 1975–1991

Between the 1970s and 1980s, Cuba supplied thousands of troops, doctors, teachers, and advisors to as many as 17 African countries that were gaining independence from European nations, amidst political and social unrest. Cuba's involvement in Angola – extending from 1975 to 1991 – was by far its largest in the African continent. Although intervention in Angola would not have been possible without Soviet assistance, Cuban forces were largely responsible for the ensuing results.

Although Angola won independence from Portugal in 1975, civil war soon broke out between rebel factions for control of the country. As part of Operation Carlota, Castro deployed troops to help the left-wing Movement for the Liberation of Angola (MPLA) to gain control of the whole country and remain in power. At the time, the MPLA – also supported by the Soviet Union – was threatened by other armed groups, such as the National Union for the Total Independence of Angola (UNITA), that were assisted by both South Africa and the United States. As a result, war in Angola escalated and the country became another scenario for Cold War confrontation.

Castro explained the intervention in Angola as a moral duty of Cuba. He claimed he was fighting for the 'most beautiful cause' – the struggle against **apartheid**. Also, he emphasized the African origins of a large part of the Cuban population, and described the war as an opportunity to repay the injustices of slavery.

As news of progress in the war in Angola reached Cuba, it contributed to Castro's popularity and a rise in national pride among Cuban citizens. However, Castro's Angolan intervention was also responsible for the loss of many Cuban lives and had caused an economic drain in the country: by 1988, Cuba had deployed over 50,000 soldiers in Angola; official figures quoted 2,000 Cuban war victims but unofficial ones claimed it was at least double that.

In 1988, after intense fighting, both sides agreed to end South African and Cuban military presence in Angola. However, civil war between Angolan factions continued until 2002. Castro believed that South African forces stationed in South-West Africa (now Namibia) could attempt to destabilize the MPLA and pressed for the withdrawal of South African troops from the territory. This contributed in turn to the independence of Namibia from South Africa in 1990.

Castro's contribution to the maintenance of power of the MPLA in Angola, his support for the independence of Namibia, and for the end of apartheid showed him as a statesman who had played an influential role in the region.

> **South-West Africa (now Namibia)**
>
> South-West Africa was the name for modern Namibia when it was ruled by the German Empire during the late 19th century, and later by South Africa for much of the 20th century. The country gained independence from South Africa on 21 March 1990, following the Namibian War of Independence.

Activity 27 — (ATL) Thinking and communication skills

Study the sources below and answer the questions that follow.

Source A

> *The Cuban people hold a special place in the hearts of the people of Africa […] From its earliest days the Cuban Revolution has itself been a source of inspiration to all freedom-loving people […] In particular we are moved by your affirmation of the historical connection to the continent and people of Africa [...]*
>
> *How many countries of the world benefit from Cuban health workers or educationists? How many of these are in Africa?… How many countries under threat from imperialism or struggling for national liberation have been able to count on Cuban support?…*

From a speech by Nelson Mandela in Matanzas, Cuba, on the anniversary of the Moncada attack, 1991

Source B

> Cuba's foreign policy succeeded in ensuring the survival of revolutionary rule and obtaining resources from the Soviet Union. [...] Its leaders commanded world attention; its policies had to be monitored by statesmen everywhere; its people could be found throughout the globe. The stage of the Cuban Revolution had become universal and its concerns and policies impinged on millions of its friends and foes in many countries.

From Leslie Bethell (ed.), *Cuba: A Short History*, Cambridge University Press, 1993

1. According to Source A, what is the significance of Nelson Mandela's speech in Cuba for Castro?
2. To what extent do you agree with the view expressed in Source B, which states that 'the Cuban Revolution had become universal'?
3. 'Foreign policy plays a significant role in the maintenance of power of authoritarian leaders.' With reference to one authoritarian leader, examine the validity of this claim.

CHALLENGE YOURSELF

(ATL) Thinking and communication skills

The following map shows some of the countries where Cuba had intervened between the 1960s and early 1990. Some of these conflicts involved military intervention; others included sending doctors, teachers, advisors, and workers.

Some areas of Cuban intervention around the world, between the 1960s and the early 1990s.

In groups, find out about the role of Fidel Castro in one conflict in a country other than Angola. Why did Cuba become involved in that particular conflict? What role did it play? What was the result of the intervention for both the country of your choice and Cuba? What impact did it have on both the conflict in question, and on Cuba and Fidel Castro?

Previous sections of this book have focused on the strained relations between Cuba and the United States. Looking at the map above, assess the extent to which the United States felt threatened by Cuba's foreign policy under Fidel Castro. How legitimate do you consider these fears to be?

Castro's foreign policy after the collapse of the Soviet Union

The collapse of the Soviet Union had a major impact on Castro's foreign policy. Having lost Soviet assistance, Cuba was unable to support revolutionary movements with either material or ideological resources. The strengthening of the US embargo made matters worse. In an attempt to address these issues, Castro looked for new partners. This required moving away from ideological principles to opening the economy of the country. We have looked at some of the measures taken to this end earlier in this chapter.

The 1990s brought a number of foreign-investment opportunities. Canada, Spain, and China became some of Cuba's most important partners in the fields of tourism, energy, and communications. This helped Castro mitigate some of Cuba's crises, as foreign investments created new employment opportunities and provided the government with profits.

At the same time, several Latin America countries saw the rise to power of democratically elected leftist parties. Relations between these countries and Cuba improved, but it was particularly with Chavez's election in Venezuela in 1998 that Castro gained a political and economic ally of significance. Trade between the two countries intensified and various cooperation agreements were signed. Chavez aided the Cuban economy by supplying it with much-needed oil in exchange for Cuban health and educational support. The two countries also became diplomatic allies, expressing their opposition to US foreign policy.

The extent to which Castro achieved authoritarian control

The question of why Fidel Castro was able to remain in power for so long is one that has fascinated historians. They agree on the fact that a combination of factors has made Castro's rule the longest personal dictatorship in the history of Latin America, but they differ in the relative importance given to each.

Some studies emphasize Castro's appeal to Cuban history and to the belief that the revolution was the continuation of the war for Cuban independence. They analyse the use of events, such as the Sierra Maestra campaign or the defeat of the United States at the Bay of Pigs, to appeal to nationalism and unite the country behind him. Other researchers claim what helped Castro most were his policies to promote social justice and equality of opportunities, which guaranteed him a significant level of support to overcome the crises that followed. There are also historians who claim the figure of Castro himself is the truth of the matter. His charisma, political skills, and capacity to turn defeat into success are some of the qualities mentioned.

If you would like to use different historiographical interpretations when answering a question, it is important that you analyse the ways in which they help you answer the specific question asked. Examiners will not be impressed by the fact that you can remember the names of historians, but might place your answer in a higher mark band if you make use of their interpretations to offer different explanations.

For question 3, the first task is to determine to what extent you consider the Cuban economy a 'successful one'. If you consider that the economic successes experienced by some sectors of Cuban society are not a sufficient explanation as to why Castro remained in power for so long, then you will need to explain the reasons for your position. Only after you have shown why a successful economic policy is not the explanation for Castro's maintenance in power, can you offer alternative explanations, such as social policies, propaganda, the use of the party, or any other elements you consider to be a more appropriate explanation for Castro's longevity in power.

Activity 28

 ATL Social and communication skills

Group activity

Study the following sources and answer the questions that follow.

Source A

❝ Yet Castro has also been an astute politician, playing world politics as easily as playing the domestic scene. Within Cuba he has often demonstrated a clever ability to read the popular mood, occasionally, as in 1970 in his criticisms of the disastrous zafra, acting as his own opposition, but also, in the early 1960s, recognising the popular demand for rapid social reform and mobilisation.

From Antoni Kapcia, *Cuba in Revolution: A History Since the Fifties*, Reaktion Books, 2008

Source B

❝ The main source of the inspiration and legitimacy of Castro's revolution, however, has been the Cuban nationalist tradition in its more radical version. Castro saw his movement as a culmination of a time-honoured struggle for independence and development stretching from the first revolt against colonial rule in 1868 to the student rebellion of the thirties. His own supreme self-confidence was based on the conviction that he embodied that struggle.

From Sebastian Balfour, *Castro*, 3rd ed., Routledge, 2008

Source C

❝ Nonetheless the Cuban government retained an undetermined level of popular support. For many citizens, breaking with the government meant breaking with their lives: they had grown up or were young adults during the 1960s when the social revolution engulfed Cuban society, and they had committed themselves to a new Cuba. Many others – particularly poor and non-white Cubans – remembered their plight before the revolution and feared a post-socialist Cuba that would disregard their welfare.

From Marifeli Pérez-Stable, *The Cuban Revolution: Origins, Course and Legacy*, Oxford University Press, 1993

1. In groups, discuss the views from the sources above on why Castro maintained himself in power for so long. Look for examples that could be used to support each of the views presented above. Choose one of the views and present it to the other groups using relevant examples. Listen to others' arguments for alternative explanations.

2. Can you think of other explanations as to why Fidel Castro was able to remain in power for so long? How would you illustrate your views?

3. Now read the hints for success opposite, then answer the question below.

   'A successful economic policy is the most important factor for an authoritarian ruler to remain in power.' To what extent does the rule of Fidel Castro support this view?

Activity 29

Revision activity

Look back at the chapter breakdown on page 3. Do you feel confident that you could answer an examination question on all of these topics? Pick your weakest topic and spend some time revising it, then try out one of the practice questions contained in this chapter. Go to the chapter titled 'Comparing and contrasting authoritarian states', and compare Castro or Cuba with another leader or region. There are lots of ideas in that chapter to help you draw out relevant points for comparison.

 To access websites relevant to this chapter, go to www.pearsonhotlinks. com, search for the book title or ISBN, and click on 'Chapter 1'.

02

Josef Stalin and the Soviet Union

This chapter examines the rise to power and rule of Stalin as the leader of the Soviet Union. In particular, it focuses on:

- how, after the death of Lenin, Stalin rose to power through the hierarchy of the Communist Party
- the methods Stalin used to achieve his aim to industrialize the Soviet Union and to consolidate his control of the Communist Party
- the social and economic policies that were carried out under Stalin's leadership
- the methods used by Stalin to deal with opposition within the Soviet Union
- Stalin's foreign policy
- Stalin's leadership of the Soviet Union during and after World War II until his death in 1953.

Josef Stalin photographed when he was a captain in the Red Army during the Russian civil war. He became General Secretary of the Communist Party of the Soviet Union in 1922 and, by 1929, had emerged as its leader.

> ### Key concepts:
>
> As you work through this chapter, bear in mind the key concepts we use when studying history.
>
> - **Change**: Think about the ways in which the Soviet Union changed when Stalin established himself as Lenin's successor.
>
> - **Continuity**: What stayed the same in the Soviet Union? Did the daily lives of ordinary people remain more or less the same, despite the change during Stalin's time in power?
>
> - **Causation**: Consider the reasons for Stalin's rise to power; what events were important for this to happen?
>
> - **Consequence**: Consequences can be both intentional and unintentional. What were the consequences of the Great Terror? Did Stalin intend them to be like this? How can we tell?
>
> - **Significance**: As you read through the chapter, think about whether some reasons were more important than others for Stalin's maintenance of power.
>
> - **Perspective**: Are there different perspectives about Stalin's rule? Is he viewed differently today? Do historians' opinions vary according to their nationality or their political beliefs?

One of the most important leaders of the Soviet Union during the 20th century, Josef Stalin established the political and economic structure that remained in place until the collapse of the Soviet Union in 1991. This chapter will cover Stalin's rise to power and how he was able to consolidate his control of the Soviet Union both before and after World War II.

The Soviet Union (USSR)

Known in 1918 as the Russian Socialist Federation of Soviet Republics (or Soviet Russia), the name was changed to the Union of Soviet Socialist Republics (USSR, or the Soviet Union, for short) in 1922. Lenin wanted each republic to be equal and also to have the right to secede if they chose to do so. In practice, power lay in Moscow and secession was not allowed, certainly not after Stalin took over. In 1936, the number of republics was increased to 11: Russia, Ukraine, Belorussia, Georgia, Armenia, Azerbaijan, Kazakhstan, Kirgizia, Uzbekistan, Turkmenistan, and Tadzikhistan.

Timeline – 1878–1953

1878	Stalin is born on 18 December in the town of Gori in Georgia. In 1929, he changed his date of birth to 21 December 1879 probably so that his birthday celebrations would be for a more significant 50th (and not 51st) birthday.
1894	Stalin enters Tiflis Theological Seminary.
1898	The Russian Social Democratic Labour Party (RSDLP) is established.

1899	Stalin is expelled from Tiflis Seminary.
1902	Stalin is involved in illegal political activity; he is arrested and exiled to Siberia.
1903	The RSDLP splits into Bolsheviks and Mensheviks.
1905	Revolution breaks out in Russia.
1914	World War I breaks out.
1917	The March Revolution takes place in Russia; Tsar Nicholas II abdicates; Lenin returns to Petrograd in April; Stalin arrives in Petrograd and becomes one of the editors of *Pravda*. The Bolshevik Revolution takes place in October; Stalin is appointed commissar for nationalities.
1918	The Treaty of Brest–Litovsk is signed with Germany; civil war breaks out in Russia; Stalin is placed in charge of Red Army forces in Tsaritsyn.
1921	The New Economic Policy is introduced.
1922	The Union of Soviet Socialist Republics (USSR or the Soviet Union for short) is founded; Stalin is appointed General Secretary of the Communist Party.
1924	Lenin dies in January.
1925–29	Stalin consolidates his control over the Politburo and removes rivals.
1929	Stalin begins collectivization. The First Five-Year Plan is officially approved.
1930	Stalin's 'Dizzy with Success' speech is published in *Pravda*.
1932–33	There is famine in the Soviet Union.
1934	Stalin's close friend and comrade Sergei Kirov is murdered.
1936	The show trial of Zinoviev and Kamenev takes place and both are executed; Tomsky commits suicide.
1937	Stalin purges the military; the 'Great Terror' begins.
1938	The show trial of Bukharin and Rykov takes place; both are executed.
1939	The Great Terror draws to a close; the Nazi–Soviet Pact is signed; World War II breaks out in Europe.
1940	Trotsky is assassinated in Mexico in August.
1941	Operation Barbarossa begins on 22 June.
1943	This year is seen as the turning point of the war, as Germans are defeated at Stalingrad. Stalin meets with Churchill and Roosevelt in Tehran.
1945	Stalin meets with Churchill and Roosevelt in February at Yalta; war ends in Europe in May; meeting in July at Potsdam with Attlee and Truman; the Red Army occupies much of Central and Eastern Europe; the atomic bomb is dropped on Hiroshima and Nagasaki in August; the war in the Pacific ends in September.
1948	The Berlin Blockade is put in place.
1949	The People's Republic of China is established.
1950	The Korean War breaks out in June.
1953	Stalin dies on 5 March.

Josef Stalin

2.1   The emergence of an authoritarian state

Stalin's background and role in the emergence of an authoritarian state in Russia

Josef Stalin was not primarily responsible for the establishment of an authoritarian state in Russia. He was a **Bolshevik** and a member of the political party that carried out the October Revolution, but it was Vladimir Ilyich Ulyanov (Lenin) who set up the structure of what became known as the Soviet Union. Stalin, however, is associated with the consolidation of the Soviet Union and it was his policies that became the model for all communist states in the 20th century.

Stalin before the Bolshevik Revolution

One of the most notorious authoritarian leaders of the 20th century, Josef Vissarionovich Dzhugashvili (Stalin) was born in 1878 in Gori, Georgia. Although part of the Russian Empire, Georgians had their own language and culture and, for Stalin, Russian was a second language that he always spoke with a heavy accent. Rebellious at school, he later attended a theological seminary; this was not an unusual path for intelligent but impoverished young men who wanted an education. Stalin became influenced, however, by Messame Dassy, a revolutionary socialist group that

Bolsheviks and Mensheviks

In 1903, at a conference held in London, there was a disagreement among the leaders of the Russian Social Democratic Labour Party between those who favoured a broadly based mass party (Mensheviks) and those who wanted a small, 'vanguard' party that would lead the workers towards a revolution (known as the Bolsheviks).

There are different accounts of when Stalin first met Lenin. The most likely one claims that they met in London in 1903 at the Fifth Party Congress. Helen Rappaport mentions that Stalin stayed at 33 Jubilee Road under a pseudonym – Mr Ivanovich – and that he developed a liking for toffee sweets (*Conspirator: Lenin In Exile*, 2010, p.144).

wanted to secure Georgia's independence from Russia. Through this organization, he met socialists whose ideology was based on **Marxism**. Stalin was expelled from the seminary in 1899 and in 1901 he joined the **Russian Social Democratic Labour Party (RSDLP)** and became a professional revolutionary.

Marxism and the ideology of the Communist Party

Based upon the writings of Karl Marx and Friedrich Engels, Marxism formed the basis of the political ideology of the Communist Party. Central to this ideology is the belief that, whoever owns the means of the production of wealth also controls all aspects of society. In feudal times, when agricultural production was paramount, whoever owned the land controlled wealth and power, and structured society to benefit them. When wealth shifted to those who owned the means of industrial production (the bourgeois or middle classes), social and political power also shifted to the middle classes. Marx predicted that the workers (the proletariat), whose labour was exploited by the bourgeois, would rise up to seize power and establish the 'dictatorship of the proletariat'. This would lead to the final stage of communism when there would be no private property and resources would be shared.

Unlike leaders such as Lenin, Stalin did not go abroad into exile, but stayed behind in Russia and became involved in organizing strikes among factory workers. Arrested for this in 1902, Stalin was sent into exile in Siberia, although he escaped in 1904.

Stalin was arrested several times by the Tsar's secret police before being sentenced to exile for life in 1913. He remained in Siberia until 1917, when the overthrow of the Romanov dynasty led to the establishment of the Provisional Government and the subsequent release of all political prisoners.

Stalin's role in the 1917 revolutions

Stalin returned to Petrograd (known today as St Petersburg) in 1917 when he joined the editorial board of *Pravda*, a post he had previously held in 1913. He was also elected to the Central Committee of the Bolshevik Party.

The Bolsheviks were a minority party in the early months of 1917, but Lenin's leadership and events over the summer gave it publicity and a reputation for being the only party to consistently oppose Russia's involvement in World War I. Lenin also strongly opposed any collaboration between the Petrograd soviet and the Provisional Government.

'Land, Peace, and Bread' and 'All Power to the Soviets' became the slogans of the Bolsheviks, but these also signified a departure from the policies adopted before Lenin returned to Petrograd. As one of the editors of *Pravda*, Stalin was caught up in a struggle within the Bolshevik Party. Lenin now criticized editorials that had supported the war and even accused Stalin of being a 'betrayer of socialism'. Stalin was quickly persuaded to change his approach, to abandon support for the Provisional Government and the war, and to work towards the revolution. Despite his rather senior position within the party, Stalin did not take a leading role in planning the October Revolution, as this was mostly the work of Trotsky and Lenin.

Pravda

This was the newspaper of the Central Committee of the Communist Party. Its name means 'The Truth'.

Petrograd soviet

The Petrograd soviet was a council composed of representatives elected by the soldiers stationed in Petrograd and by ordinary workers. It was intended to represent the views of the proletariat. During the February/ March (depending on the calendar) Revolution of 1917, the Duma refused to disband when asked to do so by the Tsar. Demonstrations in Petrograd, a mutiny by the army, and growing discontent with the rule of Tsar Nicholas II led to his abdication. The Duma became the Provisional Government and it shared power with the Petrograd soviet that was set up in March 1917.

Leon Trotsky (real name Lev Bronstein) (1879-1940)

Lev Bronstein was a Marxist who became the first chairman of the St Petersburg soviet in 1905. This was quickly suppressed by the Tsar, but Trotsky (the pseudonym used by Bronstein) took up journalism and reported on the Balkan Wars of 1912–13. He was in New York when the February Revolution took place in 1917 and returned to Petrograd to hover on the edges of the Bolshevik Party, although he did not join until the summer. A brilliant strategist, he planned the October Revolution and became a close comrade of Lenin. By 1923, it was widely expected that he would also be Lenin's successor.

Activity 1  ATL Thinking skills

Study the source below and answer the questions that follow.

> In the days of the upheaval, Stalin was not among its main actors. Even more than usual, he remained in the shadow, a fact that was to cause embarrassment to his official biographers and perhaps justified Trotsky in saying that 'the greater the sweep of events the smaller was Stalin's place in it'… But in spite of their best intentions and indubitable zeal, the official Soviet historians have not been able to write Stalin's name or anyone else's into the blanks left by the deletion of Trotsky's.

From Isaac Deutscher, *Stalin: A Political Biography*, Oxford University Press, 1966

1. What does the source above tell you about Deutscher's views on Stalin?
2. What does he mean by 'official Soviet historians'?
3. What is significant about the date when this was first published?

The Bolshevik Revolution

The October Revolution of 1917 marked the seizure of power by the Bolshevik Party. The traditional Soviet view of the events of October 1917 was that it was a popular uprising expertly led by Lenin and his supporters. Other interpretations suggest it was a *coup d'état* by a small group of determined revolutionaries with limited popular support. More recently, historians who have now had access to the archives of the Soviet Union have leaned more towards interpreting the revolution as popular unrest combined with dynamic leadership from the Bolsheviks. This party of revolutionaries was able to harness enough support to get into power and to stay there long enough to build the structure of an authoritarian state, after which popular support was no longer so important. Soon after the October Revolution, the Decree for Land and the Decree for Peace were issued in response to popular demand. Also issued was the Decree on the Rights of the Peoples of Russia, while the Congress established **Sovnarkom** to run the country.

Decree for Land

Although, according to Marxist doctrine, land would be held communally (no one would own it but all would share it), peasants had already taken over privately owned land and divided it up. Lenin saw this as a done deal and, rather than try to rule against it, he made the land seizures legal by stating that, in theory, there would be no private ownership of land and that it would be 'held in common' by the people who farmed it. In practice, this meant that land owned by landlords (people who rented out their land to small farmers) and the Church would be taken away without compensation being paid for it. The land would then be divided among the peasants.

Decree for Peace

Russia would pull out of the war and begin negotiations for peace with Germany. It also stated that no more secret diplomacy would be conducted.

Decree on the Rights of the Peoples of Russia

This decree set up the structure for a federal state (in which different regions or republics would have their own independent rights over domestic policy); it was followed by another decree in January 1918 that said any state wanting to leave (to secede from) the Soviet Union could do so.

While in Finland, where he had been hiding before the October Revolution, Lenin had written an important book, *The State and Revolution*. In it, he outlined his plans for a post-revolutionary Russia and indicated that he did not intend to share power with other parties. For Lenin, only one party knew how to proceed towards communism and it was up to the Bolsheviks to lead the way, to be the 'vanguard of the revolution'.

Lenin knew that elections for the Constituent Assembly had been promised by the Provisional Government and that these were expected to take place, although he considered the Soviets to be more democratic than a parliament. Elections were held in November 1917, but the Bolsheviks did not gain enough seats to form a majority. Although Lenin did not prevent the Constituent Assembly from meeting in January 1918, he promptly closed it down. The Soviet Union had not turned into an authoritarian state yet, but liberal parties were banned, and then, gradually, the more leftist parties were excluded from the Central Executive Committee after the Soviet elections in May 1919. By 1921 all opposition was officially banned.

In his book *Stalinism* (1998) Professor Graeme Gill states that:

> ❝ *...the closure of the Constituent Assembly, the suppression of other political parties, the elimination of press freedom and the establishment of party control over the soviets all occurred in the early years of Bolshevik rule. These moves effectively limited popular access to the political sphere ... and by 1920 had rendered any notion of unfettered competitive politics impossible.*

From *Stalinism*, 2nd ed., Palgrave Macmillan, 1998

Activity 2   **(ATL) Research and thinking skills**

1. Find out what is meant by 'pluralism' in politics and discuss to what extent Lenin had decided by 1918 that this would not be put into practice in the Bolshevik state.
2. How far, do you think, was this rejection of pluralism a reflection of how the Bolsheviks believed that they were the party to lead the people towards communism?

The Treaty of Brest–Litovsk signed with Germany in March 1918 gave the people the peace they craved, but the price paid was very high and added to the discontent that was growing among opponents of the Communist Party. Three years of brutal civil war followed and this led to radical policies being imposed in areas controlled by the Red Army. What mattered the most now was that the revolution was secured, and the White and Green armies were defeated. Meanwhile, the Tsar and his family were held under guard in Yekaterinburg where they were executed in July 1918.

Stalin after the Bolshevik Revolution

In 1917, Stalin, now a well-established member of the Communist Party leadership, was appointed commissar for nationalities. Unlike Lev Kamenev and Grigory Zinoviev, two other leading members of the party, Stalin had not openly opposed the decision to take power in October and, unlike Trotsky, had been a long-standing member of the Bolshevik Party.

It was as commissar for nationalities, however, that Stalin had his first major disagreement with Lenin. Lenin believed that the republics of the former Russian Empire would support a communist revolution and could be trusted to bind themselves willingly to the Soviet Union. Stalin took a more pragmatic view, however, and wanted to ensure that all the republics were tightly bound to the centre and to the Bolshevik Party. In *The Soviet Century* (2005), Moshe Lewin explains that Lenin wanted a federation of fairly autonomous states but Stalin, influenced by his own experience as a Georgian and also by his experiences during the civil war, was convinced that the republics had to be ruled from a strong centre and with strict discipline.

Treaty of Brest–Litovsk

A very harsh peace treaty with Germany in which Russia (now the Russian Soviet Federated Socialist Republic) lost 32 per cent of its arable land, 26 per cent of its railways, 33 per cent of its factories, 75 per cent of its iron and coal mines, and 62 million of its total population. (McCauley, *The Soviet Union 1917–1991*, 1993)

White and Green armies

The White armies were composed of forces opposed to the Bolsheviks. These were not united in their aims, and ranged from social revolutionaries to fervent monarchists who wanted the return of the Romanov dynasty. The Green armies were composed mostly of peasants and were especially active in the Ukraine. They were nationalistic and fought for regional independence.

For the most part, the Greens would oppose both the Red and the White armies but, when required to choose a side, would more often side with the Reds, who had redistributed land to the peasants.

Activity 3   **ATL** Thinking skills

Read the source below and answer the questions that follow.

> *In four years of Civil War, we were obliged to display liberalism towards the republics. As a result, we helped to form hard-line 'social-independentists' among them, who regard the Central Committee's decisions as simply being Moscow's. If we do not transform them into 'autonomies' immediately, the unity of the soviet republics is a lost cause. We are now busy bothering about how not to offend these nationalities. But if we carry on like this, in a year's time we'll be verging on the break-up of the party.*

Stalin quoted in Moshe Lewin, *The Soviet Century*, Verso Books, 2005

1. What did Stalin mean by suggesting the republics considered the Central Committee's decisions as 'simply being Moscow's', according to the source above?
2. What does this source tell you about how Stalin behaved as commissar for nationalities?

In 1922, the 'Georgian Question' brought this conflict to the surface. Georgia wanted to join the Soviet Union as an independent republic, and the Georgian Central Committee of the Communist Party complained they were limited in their autonomy and always overruled by the Transcaucasian Committee. According to Martin McCauley, Lenin had two irreconcilable aims because he wanted the republics to be independent but party organizations within them to be absolutely loyal to Moscow. Lenin suspected that Stalin wanted to restore centralized control that resembled Tsarist imperial ideology, and when the Treaty of the Union finally came into being in January 1924, Georgia did indeed enter as a member of the Transcaucasian Federation.

The Resolution on Party Unity, also known as 'the ban on factions', passed at the 10th Party Congress in 1921, tightened control over the party at all levels from the state down to the local branches. Stalin was to use this increasing control to good effect, as we shall see.

In 1922, he was appointed Party General Secretary. He was now a member of the Politburo, the Orgburo, and the Secretariat, the only leading member of the party to be in all three. This gave him a unique overview of the everyday running of the most powerful institutions in the Soviet Union.

10th Party Congress of 1921

At the 10th Party Congress that met in 1921, Lenin proposed the Resolution on Party Unity. This established that issues could be discussed at the level of the Central Committee, but once a decision had been made there could be no further discussion or disagreement. To pursue a different policy or to criticize party policy would be considered 'factionalism'. This method of imposing party unity is also referred to as **'democratic centralism'**.

The Politburo, Orgburo, and Secretariat

The Politburo was a group of seven officials elected from the Central Committee of the Communist Party. These officials decided on policies and so were extremely influential. The Politburo met regularly and was chaired by Lenin. After his death, it formed a 'collective leadership', although it was thought that Trotsky would probably succeed Lenin as its chairman and leader. Both the Orgburo and the Secretariat dealt with the more practical but rather mundane aspects of the day-to-day running of the party, such as the election of representatives at a local level, the promotion of members within the party, and so on. It is likely that the other leading Bolsheviks did not care for the rather humdrum work this involved. As the importance of the party grew, however, Stalin was now well placed to ensure that he controlled its membership at all levels.

Exam questions will sometimes ask you to analyse the rise to power of an authoritarian leader. If you want to use Stalin as an example, you could refer to events as far back as the October Revolution. Or, you could begin with the death of Lenin in 1924, referring briefly to Stalin's appointments as commissar for nationalities and general secretary. Don't forget, you should focus on Stalin and not Lenin! Also, if you are asked to compare and contrast certain aspects of the rise to power of two authoritarian leaders, it may be useful to think of another leader who was part of a revolution, but like Stalin, was not the first head of an authoritarian state.

The death of Lenin; Stalin's rise to power

The cast of characters

Grigory Zinoviev

Lev Kamenev

Leon Trotsky

Nikolai Bukharin

Alexei Rykov

Mikhail Tomsky

St Petersburg, Petrograd or Leningrad?

In 1914, St Petersburg had its name changed to the more Russian- (and less German-) sounding Petrograd. This remained the name until the death of Lenin in 1924 when, in his honour, it was renamed Leningrad. The name was changed back to St Petersburg in 1991, after the fall of the Soviet Union.

Grigory Zinoviev   A Bolshevik since 1903 and a close comrade of Lenin. He was a member of the Politburo, the leader of the Leningrad (Petrograd) city and regional government. He was appointed the first chairman of **Comintern** in 1919. Tried and executed in 1936.

Lev Kamenev   A Bolshevik since 1903 and a close confidant of Lenin. He was a member of the Politburo and chairman of the Moscow Party. Tried and executed in 1936.

Leon Trotsky   A Bolshevik only since 1917, he was a brilliant orator and strategist. Planned the revolution in October 1917 and led the Red Army to victory in the civil war. Commissar for foreign affairs and then appointed commissar for military and naval affairs. On Stalin's orders, Trotsky was assassinated in Mexico in 1940.

Nikolai Bukharin   A Bolshevik since 1906, he was the editor of *Pravda*. He was in the Politburo and also on the committee of Comintern. Tried and executed in 1938.

Alexei Rykov   A Bolshevik since 1903, deputy chairman of Sovnarkom, chairman of **Gosplan**. He was a moderate who favoured Lenin's New Economic Policy (NEP; see below). Tried and executed in 1938.

Mikhail Tomsky   A trade union leader who joined the Bolsheviks in 1906. A moderate who favoured the NEP, he was elected to the Politburo in 1927. In 1936, he openly criticized Stalin and then committed suicide.

These six staunch Communists were to play a very important role in Stalin's rise to power.

What methods did Stalin use to take power?

Like a number of other authoritarian leaders, Stalin took over an already established authoritarian state. Lenin's health had not been good since he suffered an assassination attempt by Fanya Kaplan in August 1918. He never fully recovered and, in his early 50s, he suffered a number of debilitating strokes in 1922 and 1923. Moshe Lewin considers Lenin's ill health to have been crucial to Stalin's readiness to challenge him and suggests that, without it, Stalin would not have dared scheme against Lenin too openly. As General Secretary of the Party, 'Stalin was charged by the Central Committee with supervising Lenin's medical treatment' and so was kept closely informed about Lenin's health (see Lewin, *The Soviet Century*, 2005).

Lenin reversed his most controversial economic policy, War Communism, in 1921 and replaced it with the NEP. War Communism had provoked a lot of opposition from the peasants, but also from the soldiers and sailors of the Kronstadt naval base (an important source of support for the Bolsheviks in 1917). The so-called Kronstadt Uprising in March 1921 was harshly suppressed, but it made Lenin realize that he needed to turn back to a more moderate economic policy, the NEP.

The NEP was what Lenin referred to as 'one step back', meaning that War Communism had not only failed to introduce a communist economy into the Soviet Union but had plunged the country into economic chaos. A less radical and more moderate solution had to be found and so a 'step back' into capitalism was taken. The NEP retained state control of what were called the 'commanding heights', meaning heavy industry, transportation and so on, but small businesses could be privately owned. Peasant farmers who had suffered greatly under the grain requisitioning policies of the civil war were now allowed to keep any surplus produce after they had paid taxes in kind (in goods). Later, they were allowed to pay tax in cash and so to keep or sell their goods as they wished.

This proved controversial, but Lenin succeeded in putting the new Soviet state on a more stable economic footing. In this way, economic factors were very important in the emergence of Stalin as the leader. Yet the switch to the NEP was so controversial that Lenin had to propose the Resolution on Party Unity to halt further discussion and opposition. Within the Politburo, Trotsky had been vocally opposed to the NEP, believing that it led away from, rather than towards, the development of a socialist state.

War Communism

During the civil war, Lenin wanted to ensure that food grown in the countryside was delivered to the cities to feed the workers and to the army to feed the soldiers. In order to do this, he ordered the requisitioning of grain. In other words, peasants had to hand over the food they produced. Often, they were left with nothing, leading to widespread famine. Lenin extended this policy to introduce a system of barter to eliminate the need for cash. There was rationing, a ban on the private purchase and sale of goods, and major industries were nationalized. He thought these measures would serve two purposes, to win the war and also to proceed quickly towards a communist society.

CHALLENGE YOURSELF

 Research, communication, self-management, and social skills

In this section, the focus is on the establishment of a communist state but, during the late 1970s and 1980s, due to economic difficulties, both the Soviet Union and China had to introduce reforms.

Find out more about these reforms (*Perestroika* in the Soviet Union and *The Four Modernizations* in China) and consider how far they resemble the 'mixed economy' system of the NEP.

Then make a presentation about this to your class.

By 1923, it was apparent that the NEP suited the peasants, as agricultural production (severely hampered by the war and War Communism) had recovered. Industrial growth was much slower to recover, however, and there was a disparity between the cost of agricultural goods (cheap) and industrial goods (expensive). As a result, farmers had less incentive to produce more food. Trotsky suspected that the peasants were turning back to the old ways of producing food for profit and so, in effect, holding the state to ransom, although Bukharin thought it was an economic trend that would be resolved once industrial production speeded up, providing cheaper, more affordable goods. This was referred to as the 'Scissors Crisis' because, on a graph, the decline in the cost of food and the increase in the cost of industrial goods intersected to look like an open pair of scissors.

Lenin's control of the Politburo weakened as his health deteriorated and he was less able to keep the Soviet Union on the course he had planned. By 1923, the leading Bolsheviks were divided over whether or not to support the NEP. Meanwhile, after a debilitating stroke, Lenin had lost the power of speech and was less able to persuade the Politburo to follow his policies.

Lenin's health continued to worsen; he died in January 1924. Although he had led a modest existence as the head of the Soviet Union, Lenin's funeral turned into many days of official mourning and an elaborate ceremony was organized to commemorate his leadership. Lenin's body was embalmed and displayed in a mausoleum, which was to become a place of pilgrimage for the Soviet people. Lenin's widow, Nadezhda Krupskaya, complained that he would not have wanted this, but her objections were brushed aside by Stalin, who set about turning Lenin into a god-like figure and himself into the closest and dearest disciple.

When you read about Stalin's rise to power, it is tempting to see it all as inevitable. It can read like a story with Stalin as the schemer who plots the downfall of Trotsky, his arrogant rival; how he astutely supports popular economic policies (NEP), moving almost seamlessly from the Right (with Bukharin) to the Left (against Bukharin); how he accuses enemies of 'factionalism', fills the Politburo with supporters; and how, by 1929, he is in sole charge of the Soviet Union.

Could it all have been so easy? Beware of what is called '20/20 hindsight'! Sometimes we look back at events that seem, inevitably, to lead to one conclusion. Did Stalin really plan it all so successfully? Luck probably played a part, but so did events over which he had no control, such as the War Scare of 1927 and popular unrest over the results of the NEP. To what extent did Stalin rise to power, not only because of what he did, but also because of what happened in the Soviet Union?

As you read through the following sections, consider how Stalin both created and took advantage of opportunities to accumulate power. It is important to distinguish between 'methods' and 'conditions' associated with the rise to power of authoritarian leaders. With Stalin, 'conditions' refer to factors such as the rivalry among members of the Politburo or the death of Lenin, while 'methods' would refer to ways in which Stalin took advantage of such conditions by fermenting distrust among the other members of the Politburo, for example, or by creating the cult of Lenin.

Method 1: Stalin and Lenin

By 1923, Lenin was getting angry with Stalin's boorish behaviour towards his wife Krupskaya and this convinced Lenin that Stalin was 'too rude' to continue as General Secretary of the Party. Due to his ill health, however, Lenin was unable to do anything other than to express his reservations about Stalin (and others) in his Testament, a series of memoranda written between 1922 and 1923 outlining his impressions of those in the leadership of the Communist Party likely to be his successors. The Testament was to be read at the 12th Party Congress in 1924, but Trotsky and Zinoviev decided not to publish it because it was clearly quite critical of Stalin, and they had wanted to spare Stalin's feelings. Another reason for withholding the Testament was because it was felt that the leadership had to appear united after Lenin's death. (The Testament was mentioned by Nikita Khrushchev in his secret speech in 1956.)

Lenin also had concerns about Stalin's Russian chauvinism in his role as commissar for nationalities, and was intending to act on these when he suffered a major stroke in March 1923. After this, Lenin was more or less incapable of directing the Politburo, and Stalin became alert for opportunities to assert his influence. Much has been written about this period from 1923 to 1924, and it seems that Stalin was aware of how much was at stake and was able to take advantage of the power vacuum far more effectively than any of his rivals. For example, although Trotsky was expected to give the speech (the oration) at Lenin's funeral, this very important role was given to Stalin. Trotsky was absent and according to Issac Deutscher, Trotsky claimed that '…he failed to return for the funeral in Moscow because Stalin had misinformed him about the date'. (*Stalin*, 1996, p. 270).

After Lenin's death, Stalin, as general secretary, proposed an expansion of the party membership as a way to honour Lenin. This was known as the 'Lenin Enrolment' and helped to build the cult of personality dedicated to Lenin. However, it was also very useful for Stalin as it changed the composition of the party. The Bolshevik Party had quite deliberately limited its membership to a core of dedicated revolutionaries whose task it would be to guide the masses. Now it was encouraging the masses to join its ranks. Stalin understood, perhaps better than the other Bolsheviks, that the new membership would elect representatives to the Central Committee and that he could influence them. Unlike the founding members of the party who had argued with Lenin over interpretations of Marxism, the new membership would have a ready-made explanation of party policy in *The Foundations of Leninism*, written by Stalin and published in 1924.

Method 2: Stalin and the removal of his rivals

Trotsky

Trotsky – with his legacy as the strategist of the October Revolution, his brilliant leadership of the Red Army during the civil war, and his considerable oratorical skills – was best placed to succeed Lenin in 1924. However, he appeared to lack the will for a political fight and was unsure that, as a Jew, he would have the support necessary to lead the Soviet Union. Also, Trotsky failed to forge strong ties with his fellow members of the Politburo, and made enemies by attacking the NEP and by advocating military-style leadership for the economy.

Neither Zinoviev nor Kamenev would support Trotsky, and both saw him as arrogant and overbearing. Along with Stalin, Kamenev and Zinoviev formed a *troika* (group of three) that planned to take over the leadership of the party once Trotsky had been removed. Trotsky now lost support because of his opposition to the NEP and his advocacy of 'permanent revolution', and resigned as commissar for military and naval affairs in 1925. He remained in the Politburo, but was no longer considered a potential leader for the party.

Permanent revolution

Trotsky (and Lenin) had believed that the Russian Revolution would soon be followed by revolutions elsewhere. Support would then be given by the more industrialized countries (e.g. Germany) to help modernize the Soviet Union. Meanwhile, within the Soviet Union harsh methods would have to be used to push it towards communism. Military discipline would be required to organize workers, and peasants would be forced to accept collectivization.

Some of this material is useful for showing how Stalin created the cult of Lenin. Do be careful, however, not to over-emphasize this if you are discussing Stalin's rise to power. Stalin could not rewrite the history of the party and the revolution, for example, when he was not yet in full control, when so many of his colleagues would have challenged his version of events.

Zinoviev and Kamenev – the Left Opposition

In 1925 there was considerable debate over whether or not to continue with the NEP. Did it favour the peasants over the workers? Kamenev and Zinoviev argued that it did and so should be discontinued. Perhaps it is not surprising that the two leaders whose support lay in the two major cities of Moscow and Leningrad should have sympathized with the workers rather than the peasants. Bukharin, however, argued that the NEP was working effectively to develop the economy of the Soviet Union and should be continued. At the 14th Party Congress in 1925, Kamenev attacked not only the NEP but also Stalin's policy of 'Socialism in One Country'. The Central Committee was now being filled with supporters of Stalin, however, and a vote was taken to remove Kamenev from the Politburo.

The Left Opposition became the United Opposition in 1926 when Kamenev and Zinoviev were joined by Trotsky. They were branded by Stalin as 'factionalists' (see page 59 for a definition), and were expelled from the Central Committee and the Party. Trotsky was exiled to Alma-Ata (known today as Almaty) in Kazakhstan. Kamenev and Zinoviev, knowing when they were defeated, repented and were allowed back into the Party.

Socialism in One Country

Stalin pointed out that the communist revolution had not succeeded elsewhere (by the end of the 1920s, Mongolia was the only other communist country) and it was unlikely to succeed in Germany or France, for example, in the near future. The Soviet Union, therefore, had to depend upon its own resources and to focus on building socialism at home, an idea known as 'Socialism in One Country'. The methods Stalin would use to achieve this, however, were rather similar to the methods Trotsky proposed to achieve permanent revolution.

ATL Social, self-management, research, and thinking skills

Working in a group, compare and contrast what is happening in the Soviet Union and China between 1924 and 1930. In both countries, a leader dies and another replaces him. There is also a struggle to impose one ideology. Don't forget that these two countries are neighbours.

Bukharin, Rykov, and Tomsky – the Right Deviationists

Stalin changed his mind in 1927 and began to criticize the NEP, advocating a harsher policy towards the peasants. The War Scare had led to peasants hoarding grain in case of war and this caused food prices to rise. Stalin was not prepared to tolerate this and spoke of the need both to industrialize and to bring agriculture under the control of the state. This was contrary to Bukharin's opinion that the NEP worked effectively as it gave peasants an incentive to increase production. By 1928, Stalin had started a policy of grain requisitioning, and it was clear that he no longer tolerated the NEP or its supporters; Bukharin, Rykov, and Tomsky were voted off the Politburo.

By 1929, Stalin had established his position as the most powerful member of the Politburo. He had undermined the authority of the Bolsheviks who had risen to power alongside him after the October Revolution. Among the new members of the Politburo were Voroshilov, Mikoyan, and Molotov, three comrades who were to remain alive (quite an achievement) and stay close to Stalin for the rest of his life.

The War Scare

This was the name given to a period of tension following alleged interference by the Soviet Union in the British General Strike of 1926 and the general election of 1927. The following events gave the impression that the Soviet Union had many enemies and so had to prepare for the eventuality of war: In 1927, Britain broke off diplomatic relations after a police raid on the Soviet trade delegation in London; in China, Jiang Jieshi (the leader of the Guomindang in China) had turned against his former communist allies in what was known as the White Terror; in Poland, Voikov, the Soviet envoy to Warsaw, was assassinated.

Stalin (left) and Voroshilov

Anastas Mikoyan

Molotov (right) and Stalin

> *Stalin was the most violent of leading Bolsheviks. His terror campaigns in the civil war were gruesome. He adopted a military style tunic and knee-length black boots, and his soup-strainer moustache indicated a pugnacious man. At tactics and conspiracy he was masterful. He had reached dominance in the party before Trotsky, Zinoviev, Kamenev and Bukharin knew what had happened. There was no keeping a bad man down in the politics of the Soviet Union.*

From Robert Service, *Comrades: Communism: A World History*, Pan, 2008

Activity 4   (ATL) Self-management, communication, and thinking skills

1. Look at the list below and write a few lines about each of these points to make sure you understand what each one means. Then, sort the list into two columns: one under the heading 'Conditions' and the other under the heading 'Methods'.

   - Lenin's early death
   - Lenin's Testament is kept secret
   - Disagreements over the NEP
   - The Lenin Enrolment
   - *The Foundations of Leninism*
   - Lenin doesn't seem to have a clear successor
   - Trotsky seems easily outwitted by Stalin
   - Permanent revolution vs. Socialism in One State
   - Changing membership of the Politburo
   - The War Scare of 1927
   - The Scissors Crisis

   You may find it rather difficult to decide where to place some of these bullet points. How, for instance, do you choose where to put the War Scare of 1927? Was this a 'method' thought up and used by Stalin or a 'condition' that he used to his advantage?

2. Now consider the following question:

   Evaluate the causes of Stalin's rise to power as the leader of the Soviet Union by 1929.

> When you consider how authoritarian leaders rise to power, there are several factors to bear in mind. For example, what conditions allow leaders to centralize power? (In other words, what opportunities are there to enable leaders to seize power?) What kind of methods do they use to get their hands on power?

Essay introductions

The introductory paragraph is an important part of your essay. This is where you can immediately show you understand what the question is asking and explain how you will answer it.

Here are some samples of introductions for the essay question from the previous page.

Student answer A – Patrick

Josef Dzhugashvili (named Stalin), was born in Georgia in 1879, he was the son of a shoemaker and the grandson of serfs. He soon became Marxist and in 1904 he joined the Bolshevik Party. He climbed up the ladder of the party and in 1917 he was the editor of *Pravda*. He became Commissar for Nationalities and was one of the main artisans of the creation of the Soviet Union. He was also General Secretary of the Party's Central Committee since 1922 (a position considered as boring bureaucratic work by the other Revolutionaries) and a member of the Politburo. Before 1924, he was not a public figure but his internal influence was important.

Examiner's comments

This introduction is rather short and has too much narrative content. It does mention Stalin and give some context to his emergence as leader, but it makes no mention of the essay question. It is a good idea to refer to the question in your opening paragraph. In this way, you will show the examiner that you are focused and that you will be answering the question. It also reminds you not to be too narrative in your approach.

Student answer B – Clara

Lenin was for sure the strong commander of Russia till 1922, when he suffered his first stroke. After that, his leadership began to weaken, until his death on the 12th of January 1924. Before he died, though, it was clear to him that there would almost certainly be a struggle for power after he was gone. For this reason he wrote his Testament, in which he gave short portraits of his most probable successors, and their faults. He recognized five possible candidates: Trotsky, Zinoviev, Kamenev, Bukharin and Josef Stalin. Of these, it was Stalin who climbed to the top and became the main leader by 1929. Lenin had warned that although Stalin had great practical abilities, these were offset by his roughness and lack of consideration for his colleagues. Stalin, Lenin said, was 'too rude' and should be removed from his post as General Secretary of the Communist Party. Not only did Stalin manage to keep this quiet, he also managed to outmanoeuvre the other likely candidates for leader. How far, however, was his rise to the top a result of conditions that Stalin was able to exploit or of Stalin's own political skills? This essay will evaluate the causes of Stalin's rise to power and so consider their relative significance.

Examiner's comments

Clara's introduction is quite a lot better than Patrick's. She begins with a reference to Lenin and gives some relevant background before moving on to mention the essay question. This introduction makes a good impression by indicating that Clara will select relevant material and focus on Stalin's rise to power. Furthermore, she has defined the command term 'evaluate' and so has shown that she understands the task.

How you end your essay is also important! A good conclusion should sum up your arguments and, again, focus on answering the question.

Student answer C – Joanna

Among the important causes of Stalin's rise to power were his political skills as well as his pragmatism, his populism, and his patience. Also important was his astute use of propaganda, especially the 'Cult of Lenin'. Propaganda led the new, less educated base of the party to Stalin's cause, marginalizing his opponents. Stalin also benefited from the many errors of his opponent, particularly about Lenin's Testament. Stalin's rise to power left him in a position of entire control. He would soon become a strong authoritarian leader.

Examiner's comments

This is a rather short conclusion, but it does summarize the main points. It would be a good idea to say a little more about Lenin's Testament, however, as it needs to be made clear here why it was so important (was it more important than the accusations of 'factionalism', for instance?). Mentioning 'authoritarian' in the last sentence – thus introducing an entirely new term at such a late stage – is perhaps not such a good idea.

Student answer D – Chris

There is a great deal of controversy regarding how Stalin rose to power as many causes needed to be considered. Stalin was lucky, benefiting from factors such as the premature death of Lenin and his rivals' weaknesses. In addition to this, Stalin benefited from circumstances such as the economic situation in the Soviet Union as well as the failure of revolution abroad. However, Stalin's triumph was not due just to good fortune and accidental circumstances. Indeed, it is not to be forgotten that Stalin's emergence as the single leader of the Soviet Union would not have been possible without his own ruthless political ability and his skill to take advantage of all the previously mentioned circumstances. As Bukharin once said, Stalin was 'an unprincipled intriguer who changed his theories at will in order to get rid of whomever he wished'.

Examiner's comments

This is a much better conclusion. It mentions both methods and conditions, but adds another factor, which is Stalin's political skill. It also ends nicely with an appropriate quotation.

Other aspects of Stalin's rise to power

Were his methods to gain power legal or illegal?

In some cases, authoritarian leaders use a combination of legal and illegal methods to come to power. For Stalin, what he did was entirely legal. He was an elected member of the Politburo, he was appointed to be General Secretary of the Communist Party and to the Orgburo. He had considerable power available to him because he held high office and when he accused his rivals of 'factionalism', he was using Lenin's resolution that had been accepted by the 10th Congress of the Supreme Soviet in 1921. When his rivals were expelled from the Politburo, they were voted off by the majority of the members. So, you could argue that, whatever his motivations, Stalin's actions were quite legal within the framework of the government of the Soviet Union.

Did Stalin respond to popular opinion?

Historians consider Stalin's ability to gauge public opinion and understand what people wanted to be one of the ways in which he established himself in power. Of course, clever use of propaganda can also be used to tell people what they want, and Stalin was able to use this very effectively.

Since 1917, workers had looked for greater participation in the running of factories and an improved standard of living. The civil war had brought great hardship, but many workers felt the NEP's reintroduction of the right to own small businesses and to hire labour as a betrayal of the revolution. The growth in the number of 'NEPmen' further angered workers, who saw these entrepreneurs, or 'middle men', as exploiters of the working class. Stalin ceased to support the NEP once he had got rid of the Left Opposition and, in doing so, he also seemed to respond to the grievances of the workers.

2.2 Aims and results of Stalin's policies

Stalin's economic policies

Throughout his time in power, Stalin's aim was to establish a powerful, state-controlled economy in the Soviet Union. Ever since the defeat of Russia in the Crimean War, rulers of Russia/Soviet Union sought economic modernization. However, it was the ruthless determination of Stalin that achieved the most spectacular growth in industrialization and urbanization. How did he achieve this?

The Five-Year Plans – 'the turn to the left'

In 1927, Stalin began work on the first of the Five-Year Plans. This was a model of economic planning that would eventually be adopted in almost every communist country during the 20th century.

A measure of central planning had been put in place by Lenin, and Gosplan was set up in 1921 to control the 'commanding heights' of industry that were to be nationalized under the NEP. Another organization that supervised nationalized industry was **Vesenkha**, set up in 1917.

Stalin believed that only strict centralized control would enable the Soviet Union to achieve the level of production it needed to industrialize and urbanize. Since 1855, Russia had been attempting to achieve these twin aims, but with only limited success. Where the Tsars had failed, Stalin was determined to succeed.

The Soviet economy was based on agriculture and it was agricultural exports that underpinned its prosperity. In order to industrialize, new technology needed to be imported from abroad; and to afford it, an increase in agricultural exports was required. In other words, the Five-Year Plan would be financed by agriculture; the peasants, always unreliable in the eyes of the Bolsheviks, would have to work in the interests of the state. To achieve this, farms would have to be collectivized – this became one of Stalin's main aims.

The collectivization of agriculture

The peasants were a force to be reckoned with, as they constituted more than 80 per cent of the population of the Soviet Union, but they were also a force to be harnessed and bent to the will of the state. Bukharin had maintained that financial incentives would encourage peasants to increase production, but Stalin did not want to do this. He wanted to be sure that land and food production was under the full control of the state. Collectivization was also considered to be an important way to instil 'communalism' (people living and working together) and also to provide a workforce for the industrial cities.

In 1929, *kolkhozi*, or collective farms, were established to replace the individual plots owned by the peasants. Those who disagreed or refused to go along with the orders of the party were branded **kulaks** and were severely punished. Norman Lowe states, 'it was probably in September, 1929 that Stalin was converted to total collectivisation' (*Mastering Twentieth Century Russian History*, 2002). Approximately 25 million small peasant farms were consolidated into 200,000 *kolkhozi*, and hundreds of thousands of peasants became paid labourers on *sovkhozi* (state farms). By 1936, 90 per cent of all peasant households in the Soviet Union had been collectivized and so we can conclude that Stalin had achieved his aim.

For Stalin, there were several advantages to collectivization:

- The Soviet Union had an agrarian economy as most of its people lived in the countryside and worked the land, so collectivization gave the state control to the main source of national wealth.
- Agriculture would fund industry and cheap food would feed the workers in the cities, and would be exported to finance the purchase of machinery from abroad.
- The authority of the Communist Party would be extended over the countryside and peasants. Machine Tractor Stations were set up for each group of *kolkhozi*: tractors and other machinery could be hired from these stations; party officials were also based here to check that party policies were being carried out.
- Food production would be made more efficient; working on larger fields meant it made more sense for the workers to use machinery.
- Not all the peasants needed or wanted to stay in a collectivized countryside, so the 'surplus labour' would be encouraged to look for work in the cities.
- Collectivization would ensure state control over the production of food and this would be centrally planned like the rest of the economy.

Collectivization was not a popular policy and, in 1930, a very poor harvest led Stalin to write an article for *Pravda*, entitled 'Dizzy with Success', in which he called for a temporary halt to forced collectivization.

Stalin also sent a small army of party activists known as the '25,000ers' to the countryside to encourage the peasants to follow party directives.

In the end, Stalin dealt harshly with any resistance – even when people were starving because of severe shortages, he did not slow the pace of collectivization. One consequence was the disastrous famine of 1932–33 that killed as many as 5 to 8 million people, mostly in the Ukraine, where famine is known as the **Holodomor**. Although many historians would argue that the Holodomor was a 'genocide', Robert Service challenges this allegation by pointing out that the requisitioning quotas were cut three times during 1932 in response to evidence of widespread starvation. He also maintains that Stalin needed Ukrainian labour as much as he needed labour from elsewhere, and that a deliberate policy of starvation would not have made economic

Dizzy with Success

This is a reference to an article by Stalin published in *Pravda* in March 1930 that suggested collectivization had been pushed ahead too quickly by party officials who were 'dizzy with success'. The pace needed to be slowed down and so houses, small plots, and animals would no longer be collectivized. Peasants left the collective farms at an alarming rate and planted the spring wheat. Once this had taken place, Stalin resumed collectivization.

sense (*A History of Modern Russia*, 2003). Grain requisitioning was, nevertheless, a brutal policy carried out regardless of the human cost.

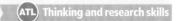
The famine of 1932–33 was terrible with thousands of people dying from starvation. It was kept secret and, if you lived in another region of the Soviet Union, there was every chance you would not have known about it. Could this happen today? Can you think of any countries where famines have occurred, or where we think they have occurred, in the last 10 years? What is the usual international response to a famine?

Activity 5  **ATL** Thinking skills

Study the source below and answer the question that follows.

> Collectivization was the great turning point in Soviet history. It destroyed a way of life that had developed over many centuries – a life based on the family farm, the ancient peasant commune, the independent village and its church and the rural market, all of which were seen by the Bolsheviks as obstacles to socialist industrialization. Millions of people were uprooted from their homes and dispersed across the Soviet Union… This nomadic population became the main labour force of Stalin's industrial revolution, filling the cities and the industrial building sites, the labour camps and 'special settlements' of the Gulag.
>
> The First Five-Year Plan, which set this pattern of forced development, launched a new type of social revolution (a 'revolution from above') that consolidated the Stalinist regime: old ties and loyalties were broken down, morality dissolved and new ('Soviet') values and identities imposed, as the whole population was subordinated to the state and forced to depend on it for almost everything – housing, schooling, jobs and food – controlled by the planned economy.

From Orlando Figes, The Whisperers: Private Life in Stalin's Russia, Penguin, 2008

1. What does the source above tell you about the impact of Stalin's policies upon society in the Soviet Union?

Activity 6 **ATL** Thinking and research skills

Study the tables of statistics below and answer the questions that follow.

Source A

Table of statistics for grain production and procurement 1929–34 (millions of metric tons)

	Grain production	Grain procurement	Procurement as a % of production
1929	66.8	10.8	(16.2%)
1930	71.0	16.0	(22.5%)
1931	65.0	22.1	(34.0%)
1932	65.0	23.7	(36.5%)
1933	71.0	23.3	(32.8%)
1934	77.5	28.4	(36.6%)

Source: Martin McCauley, The Soviet Union 1917–1991, 2nd ed., Routledge, 1993

Source B

Table of statistics for grain production (millions of metric tons) and grain export 1929–33

	Grain production	Grain export %
1929	71.7	0.18
1930	83.5	4.76
1931	69.5	5.06
1932	69.6	1.73
1933	68.4	1.69

Source: Alec Nove, *An Economic History of the USSR*, Penguin Books, 1969

Source C

Table of statistics for numbers of farm animals 1929–34 (million head)

	1929	1930	1931	1932	1933	1934
Cattle	67.1	52.3	47.9	40.1	38.4	42.4
Pigs	20.4	13.6	14.4	11.6	12.1	17.4
Sheep and goats	147.0	108.8	77.7	52.1	50.2	51.9

Source: Alec Nove, *An Economic History of the USSR*, Penguin Books, 1969

1. What do these tables tell you about the rate at which the state procured grain from the peasants?
2. Is there a decrease in the level of procurement? Why did this take place, do you think?
3. What happens to the numbers of farm animals? Why does this happen?
4. If you look at the statistics for the levels of grain production in the two tables, you will see they are different. Why, do you think, is this so? (Think about the reliability of statistics as sources for historians, especially when they are released by authoritarian states.)

Peasants to proletariat

British historian Orlando Figes has written extensively on the political, social, and cultural history of Russia and the Soviet Union. In particular, he has focused on the history of ordinary people and how their lives were impacted by the Bolshevik Revolution and its aftermath. According to Figes,

> *[for] every thirty peasants who entered the kolkhozi, ten would leave the countryside altogether, mostly to become wage labourers in industry. By the early months of 1932, there were several million people on the move, crowding railway stations, desperately trying to escape the famine areas. The cities could not cope with this human flood. Diseases spread and pressure grew on housing, on food and on fuel supplies, which encouraged people to move from town to town in search of better conditions. Frightened that its industrial strongholds would be overrun by famine-stricken and rebellious peasants, the Politburo introduced a system of internal passports to limit the immigration to the towns.*

From Orlando Figes, *The Whisperers: Private Life in Stalin's Russia*, Penguin, 2008

Figes then goes on to describe how internal passports were used to get rid of 'socially dangerous elements' that might rise up against the government. He also states that for many of the dispossessed, having no passport made them move often, seeking work illegally. In this mass movement, children were often abandoned. They were also

The reliability of *The Whisperers* was questioned by two US academics, Professor Peter Reddaway and Professor Stephen F. Cohen, in an article published in *The Nation* in May 2012. They argued that Figes' presentation of research carried out by Memorial (see p. 83) included 'misrepresentations' and 'factual inaccuracies'. Furthermore, they argued that *The Whisperers* was not banned in Russia for political reasons, as Figes claimed, but because the numerous errors it contained caused publishers to cancel publication. Figes responded to the article by admitting there were some errors due to translation and other difficulties, but that many of the other allegations were inaccurate. The controversy continues to this day.

TOK

Slavoj Zizek, a Slovene philosopher, argues that the Soviet Union was different from the German Third Reich because in the Nazi regime the enemies of the state were clearly identified as communists or Jews. In this way, there was a horrible rationale to the death camps, whereas in the Soviet Union, no one knew who would be executed or sent to the gulags.

Those who say that Nazism was worse would argue that at least communism had a utopian vision to fulfil, one that intended to establish a more egalitarian society. Is this an acceptable argument, do you think? If a leader is responsible for the deaths of thousands or even millions of people, can this be justified if it is for the good of the majority?

CHALLENGE YOURSELF

 Thinking and research skills

Now is a good time to reflect on how much change and continuity there was between the Soviet Union of the early 1920s (maybe we can call it 'Lenin's Soviet Union') and that of the 1930s when Stalin's policies were put into practice.

abandoned by parents exiled to **gulags** who wanted to spare their children the same fate and, during the famine, by parents who could not feed them. 'They roamed the streets, rummaging through rubbish for unwanted food. They scraped a living from begging, petty theft and prostitution' (*The Whisperers*, 2007).

According to Figes, police figures showed that between 1934 and 1935, more than 840,000 homeless children were brought to the 'reception centres' and then sent to orphanages or the camps. In December 1934, Stalin passed a law stating that children over 12 could be treated as criminals and subject to the same punishments as adults, including execution. Figes states that between 1935 and 1940, more than 100,000 children between 12 and 16 were convicted of criminal offences.

The dark side of the Soviet Union during the 1930s is very bleak indeed, with both Figes and the British novelist Martin Amis, in his book *Koba the Dread*, emphasizing the brutality of a system determined to forge a new utopia. It is claimed Stalin once said that 'to make an omelette, you must break eggs', and that 'if a man is a problem, no man, no problem'. His callousness is demonstrated over and over again, as well as that of his henchmen, who arrested, tortured, imprisoned, and executed victims. These victims were often innocent people plucked at random for having the wrong name, being in the wrong place, or because they had powerful enemies. This 'randomness' was terrifying and meant that no one was safe.

The First, Second, and Third Five-Year Plans

The Five-Year Plans were Stalin's answer to the economic challenges faced by the Soviet Union. Only by taking full state control of the resources and the labour of the Soviet Union would industrialization be achieved. For Stalin, this policy would result not only in economic growth and economic self-sufficiency, but would also increase state control (party control) over the Soviet Union and create a disciplined **proletariat**. The theory of Marxism would be put into practice not from the bottom up but from the top down, which is why it is sometimes called the 'revolution from above' or 'the second revolution'. The Bolshevik Revolution had occurred in 1917, but the conditions for a Marxist state would now be put in place.

The First Five-Year Plan, 1928/29 to 1932

The First Five-Year Plan was officially adopted in 1929, although, unofficially, it had started in late 1928. It called for a massive increase in industrial output; this was highly ambitious for a country that did not have a workforce with the necessary skills. Stalin now set out to create a proletariat by moving large numbers of peasants from the countryside to the cities, or in some cases, to areas where cities would be built.

The aim of this plan was to 'increase the production of the means of production', in other words, to build iron and steel manufacturing plants, electric power stations, infrastructure such as railways, and to increase the production of coal and oil. This would be the basis for industrialization.

Listed here are some of the problems that Stalin faced with the Five-Year Plan, along with the solutions that he came up with.

Problem	Solution
To access the necessary skills	Encourage skilled technicians and engineers to come from abroad on fixed-term contracts
To import the necessary technology	Pay for it by accumulating foreign exchange from the sale of grain
To persuade peasants to adapt to the discipline necessary for working in a factory, for example, getting to work on time	Introduce harsh labour laws to punish offenders
To prevent workers from leaving jobs they found too demanding and looking for work elsewhere	Introduce internal passports that prevented workers from changing jobs
To explain why the targets set by the Five-Year Plans were not achieved	Change the statistics or blame the 'foreign experts'

Activity 7 Research, communication, and social skills

Research activity

Go through the 'problems and solutions' table listed above. See what you can find out about when some of these measures were introduced. Discuss your answers with the class.

The Second (1932–37) and Third Five-Year Plan (1937–)

The focus of these two Five-Year Plans shifted to the production of heavy industrial goods. Iron and steel plants were now in production, and the electric power stations were functioning, but the country still needed trains, trucks, and tractors. You can pause here to think about the European context at this time, when Hitler was rearming Germany, and many Central and Eastern European countries were governed by right-wing authoritarian governments opposed to communism and the Soviet Union. For these reasons, Stalin wanted to ensure that the Soviet Union would have the resources to rearm, and this was an important aspect of both the Second and Third Five-Year Plans. (Note that the German invasion of the Soviet Union in 1941 interrupted the Third Five-Year Plan.)

Activity 8 ATL Research, communication, self-management, thinking, and social skills

Study the table below and answer the questions that follow.

Industrial production during the First and Second Five-Year Plans

	1928	1932	1933	1936
Electric power (billion kWh)	5.0	13.5	16.4	32.8
Coal (million tons)	35.5	64.4	76.3	126.8
Pig iron (million tons)	3.3	6.2	7.1	14.4
Rolled steel (million tons)	3.4	4.4	5.1	12.5
Quality steel (million tons)	0.09	0.68	0.89	2.06
Cement (million tons)	1.85	3.48	2.71	5.87
Locomotives (standard units)	478	828	941	1566
Tractors (thousand 15hp units)	1.8	50.8	79.9	173.2
Lorries (thousands)	0.7	23.7	39.1	131.5
Woollen fabrics (million linear metres)	101	89	86	102

Source: R.W. Davies, M. Harrison, and S.G. Wheatcroft (eds), *The Economic Transformation of the Soviet Union 1913–1945,* **Cambridge University Press, 1994**

1. Why does the rate of growth in the production of goods increase quite slowly at first but quite significantly by 1936?
2. Why was the number of tractors produced so significant?
3. Look at what is listed in the table. Why are these goods so important to the Soviet Union during the 1930s? What kind of progress do they indicate?
4. What happens to the production of woollen fabric? What would this be used for? What does it suggest about what is not given importance in the Five-Year Plans?
5. Working in a group, see if you can find similar statistics for another country during the same time period. How do they compare with those of the Soviet Union?

If you choose to write about Stalin in an essay question that asks about the success or failure of the economic policies of an authoritarian leader, it is a good idea to support your argument with statistical evidence. You wouldn't need to use all the statistics in the table in Activity 8, but you could perhaps show the increase in the production of coal or the output of electricity.

How did Stalin carry out the Five-Year Plans?

Labour discipline

Many of the workers who came to the cities were peasants who were used to working from sunrise to sunset, and working harder in the summer than in the winter. They now needed to adjust to the strict routine of factory life, arriving on time and staying to the end of their shift. Harsh laws were introduced to punish workers who were late or absent. It was a crime to break machinery or to take anything from the workplace. In the most extreme cases, these crimes were punished with execution. Early on during the First Five-Year Plan, workers would move from one factory to the next looking for easier work or higher wages, but this ended when workers had workbooks as a form of internal passport, which tied them to their workplace. Losing a job meant losing the right to accommodation and food rations.

Managers were held responsible for meeting targets given to them by the state. If they failed to do so, they could be charged with 'sabotage' and accused of deliberately preventing the fulfilment of the Five-Year Plan. This was a capital crime, so managers would be sure to meet targets.

Slave labour

It was during the 1930s that many of the gulags were built. These were the labour camps where the kulaks who opposed collectivization were sent and where hundreds of thousands of political prisoners were shipped to during the 'purges' (see Section 2.3, page 81). Conditions in the gulags were so harsh that many prisoners would die, often in their first year of captivity. Many of the gulags were located in the most inhospitable areas of the Soviet Union, where winter temperatures fell as low as minus 50 degrees Celsius. They were remote from areas of habitation so escape was difficult. Often, these locations were chosen because they were rich in resources such as gold, uranium, and coal. Free citizens would not have wanted to work in such places, but prisoners had no choice. When the growth of the Soviet economy during the Five-Year Plans is measured, the forced labour of the gulag prisoners has to be included as part of the terrible human cost.

Enthusiasm

There was enthusiasm among the workers for many of Stalin's ambitious policies, although Robert Service maintains that the enthusiasts were in a minority. Even so, many people believed in the importance of what they were achieving and were ready to endure extremely difficult conditions. Those who toiled to build Magnitogorsk, for example, endured conditions hardly better than those in the gulags. Machinery was scarce but astonishing feats were achieved with man- (and woman-) power alone. Enthusiasts maintained that they were working for the country's future and so this was not the 'alienated' labour that Marx had written about, but the labour of people building a new world for themselves and for future generations.

Rewards

Workers were given different rewards or incentives for their efforts:

- Posters and party directives extolled the virtues of Stakhanovites, and workers were encouraged to emulate Stakhanov's success. They could receive food that was in short supply, or even a motorbike for doubling or tripling their work quotas.
- League tables were published in all the factories, publicizing what each worker had produced in a week.
- Wages differentiated between skilled and unskilled workers.
- A good work record and party membership could lead to promotion for workers who had little formal education.

Propaganda

Stalin's speeches about the successes of the Five-Year Plans were printed in *Pravda*. Yet the workers who actually built huge factories and electric power plants could see with their own eyes that the Soviet Union was industrializing, and would have found it credible that it was catching up with capitalist countries. Workers were told that the living and working conditions in these western states were dire; during the Great Depression, these claims could be supported by newspaper photographs of food lines in New York and hunger marches in Britain. What Stalin did not tell Soviet citizens was that in the Soviet Union prison camps were overflowing with people put there for no other reason than that their names had been added to a list. Like everything else, there were quotas to be filled with political prisoners.

For ideological indoctrination, Stalin's *History of the All-Union Communist Party (Bolsheviks): Short Course* was published in 1938 and, like *The Foundations of Leninism*, served as an introduction to the history and the ideology of the Soviet Union.

TOK

If you were asked to work hard or to put up with difficult circumstances so that conditions could be better for future generations, how, do you think, would you react? Would you do so willingly?

Consider the question of climate change, when we are asked to reduce energy consumption – or even to become vegetarians – in order to secure the future of the planet at a time when we may not even be alive. What arguments can you think of to support and also to reject such a proposal?

Stakhanovites

Alexei Stakhanov was a coal miner who mined 106 tons of coal or 14 times his quota during a single shift in 1935. A movement was named after him to encourage all workers in the Soviet Union to work harder. It was very popular, with many workers attracted by the rewards such as extra rations, medals, or even a motorcycle.

Activity 9 **Research, thinking, communication, and self-management skills**

Consider the following essay question:

Examine the successes and failures of Stalin's economic policies.

In this kind of essay question, you would need to refer to the Five-Year Plans.

You would also need to use statistics to support your arguments. To help you put these statistics in perspective, you should consider the levels of economic growth in the Soviet Union against other countries. For comparison, check the GDP (Gross Domestic Product) of the United States, China, and Nazi Germany between 1929 and 1937, as they might be useful to provide a comparison or a contrast.

Don't forget that, before you can assess the 'successes', you must first consider the aims. For example, when you consider the success of a leader's policies, you need to ask what their intentions were. Then, you can look at the evidence and determine if they achieved their goals. Also, it's worth looking more holistically at the notion of 'success'. Was the policy successful for the citizens of the country concerned? Was the human cost of 'success' too much to bear?

Stalin's social and cultural policies

How did Stalin change the role of women in the Soviet Union?

The role of women did change after the revolution, with new career opportunities – such as engineers and doctors – opening up, which were professions traditionally seen as the preserve of men. Even so, the upper echelons of the Communist Party did not have many women in its ranks and none appeared in the Politburo. Furthermore, by 1930, Stalin wanted to restore more conservative values and this shift backwards became known as 'The Great Retreat': the family once again became the central unit of society; the social freedoms afforded by the revolution had to be reined in. During the revolution, easy divorce had led to the abandonment of many children, and the availability of abortion threatened to halt population growth – although other reasons for this halt included poor nutrition, shortage of accommodation, and exhaustion from hard work. In order to encourage population growth, abortion was made illegal in 1936, divorce was discouraged, and women were rewarded with medals for giving birth to 10 or more children. Moshe Lewin notes that, officially, there was a slight improvement in the birth rate in 1937, but that it fell again in 1939.

As well as being mothers and homemakers, women also had to play their part in the expansion of the Russian economy. This was especially important during and after World War II, when men were drafted into the Red Army and millions did not return from the war. On collective farms, women were expected to do most of the work in the fields. In factories, women had to do the work of men and to take part in construction brigades, which helped to rebuild war-torn cities after 1945. In the military, women were trained as pilots during the war and, unlike their counterparts in the United States and in Britain, they also saw combat duties.

This poster shows women on a collective farm. The woman in the foreground is gathering corn and the women behind her are also working. Notice that the supervisors, however, are men. ▼

Russian women fighter pilots of World War II. Women had been trained as engineers and technicians during the 1930s, and it is not surprising that they were expected to be on active duty during the war. Of course, the majority stayed at home to be a vital part of the workforce in factories and on collective farms.

The women pilots who flew in the 58th Night Bomber Regiment during World War II were called Night Witches (*Nachthexen*) by the German soldiers whom they attacked. They flew lightweight Polikarpov-Po 2 biplanes and turned off their engines as they approached, making a whooshing sound like a broomstick. Altogether, they numbered around 115 and about 30 were killed in action. See if you can find out more about the Night Witches.

Religion

The Russian Orthodox Church had for centuries been a strongly nationalist mainstay of Russian society. Under Lenin, it was frowned upon to attend church services. Churches were destroyed, bells hauled away to be melted down, and priests were driven out along with the kulaks. Geoffrey Hosking maintains, however, that centuries of religious worship could hardly be eradicated so easily and that many 'underground' churches were formed where people met secretly (*A History of the Soviet Union, 1917–1991*, 1992). In areas where Islam was the dominant religion, most mosques closed and imams suffered the same fate as priests. Such practices as the veiling of women, fasting during Ramadan, polygamy, and travelling to Mecca on the Hajj were forbidden. As with the Christian communities, however, official prohibitions did not end religious belief but, rather, drove it underground.

When World War II broke out, Stalin used the Church to gather support from the people for the war effort. Religion was, once again, linked to patriotism and Soviet efforts to halt a German invasion.

Art and culture

Stephen Lee suggests that music in the Soviet Union underwent something of a renaissance during the 1930s. The compositions of Prokofiev and Shostakovich, in particular, gained critical acclaim and may be considered among the finest music of the 20th century. No other dictatorship is associated with the composition of so much fine music. Stalin himself did not understand music but, clearly, he did not fear it either, although in the post-war period his taste grew more conservative, and even Prokofiev and Shostakovich fell out of favour.

As summed up by Robert Service, 'above all, the arts had to be optimistic' (*A History of Modern Russia*, 2003). The art movement known as socialist realism produced paintings that resembled propaganda posters intended both to entertain and educate the masses. In literature, the writer Maxim Gorky returned to the Soviet Union in 1928. He was feted by Stalin and was provided with a large house in which to live. In 1934, he was instrumental in establishing the First All-Union Congress of Soviet Writers to 'unite all writers supporting the platform of Soviet power and aspiring to participate in the building of socialism' (Hosking, *A History of the Soviet Union, 1917–1991*, 1992). In other words, the aim was to capture socialist realism in literature. Geoffrey Hosking explains how a number of novels from this period revolved around a hero 'who appears from among the people, … guided and matured by the party … and then leads his comrades and followers to great victories over enemies and natural obstacles in the name of the wonderful future that the party is building' (*A History of the Soviet Union 1917–1991*, 1992). *How the Steel Was Tempered* (1934), an autobiographical novel by Nikolai Alexeevich Ostrovsky, was of this genre and glorified the workers of the new Soviet Union. Another famous novel, called *And Quiet Flows the Don*, was written by Mikhail Sholokhov. It focused on the heroic years of the revolution and civil war, gaining an international reputation when Sholokhov was awarded the Nobel Prize for Literature in 1965.

Writers who found favour with the regime were well looked after and led lives of privilege. Not all writers followed Party guidelines, however; Isaac Babel, Oscar Mandelstam, and Anna Akhmatova chose what Babel called 'the genre of silence'.

Sergei Eisenstein, the famous film-maker, had produced epics recalling Russia's great leaders, such as *Ivan the Terrible*. The sequel to this film, however, was interpreted as being critical of Stalin. Eisenstein was criticized and dismissed from his post as the head of the Moscow Film School.

Sergei Eisenstein (1898–1948)

Best known for his film of the mutiny on the battleship *Potemkin*, and for *October*, his account of the 1917 revolution, Eisenstein was one of the leading film-makers in the Soviet Union. He experienced mixed fortunes under Stalin. He was praised both for *Alexander Nevsky* (1938) and *Ivan the Terrible – Part One* (1943), both of which were strongly nationalistic. *Ivan the Terrible – Part Two* (1946), however, depicted the Tsar as a ruthless tyrant, and Eisenstein was strongly criticized. The film was banned and scenes that had been filmed for *Ivan the Terrible – Part Three* were destroyed.

When criticizing *Ivan the Terrible* with Molotov, Stalin said, 'you need to show historical figures correctly in their style. So, for instance, in the first part, it's wrong that Ivan the Terrible spent so long kissing his wife. In those days that wasn't allowed.... Ivan the Terrible was very cruel. You can show that he was cruel but you have to show why it was essential to be cruel...' (Jonathen Brent, *Inside Stalin's Archives*, 2008).

Here are examples of the kinds of art that were encouraged and discouraged under Stalin's rule. On the left we have an example of socialist realism; on the right, an example of the work of Kazimir Malevich.

Why, do you think, did Stalin encourage socialist realism? Which painting would be critically acclaimed today? Justify your answers.

Education and social mobility

One of the dilemmas that faced the revolutionaries in their efforts to transform the Soviet Union into a socialist state was how to address education. The children of the better-educated were more likely to go on to higher education, but this would also perpetuate an elitist system. The difficulty lay in how to get more people from poorer backgrounds into higher education. Under Lenin, there was an attempt to make education more accessible, although the actual curriculum in schools did not change much. In 1928, it was pronounced that 65 per cent of those entering higher technical education had to be of working-class origin; by 1929 this figure was raised to 70 per cent, and 14 per cent of students had to be women. The percentage of working-class students in higher education went up from 30 per cent in 1928–29 to 58 per cent in 1932–33, and an effort was made to get rid of non-party lecturers and professors.

By 1931, the Central Committee was determined that the Soviet youth needed to be literate and to understand basic science. By the mid 1930s, there were officially prescribed textbooks; tests and exams were restored; the teaching of history had to focus on political events and great men; school uniforms were compulsory (including pigtails for girls); and fees were imposed for the three upper forms of secondary school.

But education was not just about reading books and preparing for exams. During the late 1920s, reforms took place to create closer links between education and work experience. As Geoffrey Hosking explains, 'the upper forms of middle schools were reclassified as *tekhnikuny*, or vocational training colleges, and by the end of 1930 all schools were required to attach themselves to an enterprise… The proportion of political instruction was also increased' (*A History of the Soviet Union 1917–1991*, 1992). Hosking mentions some of the side-effects of these reforms, with children as young as 11 working in coal mines or picking cotton for weeks on end. In other cases, factory managers found the attendance of children to be disruptive. Undoubtedly, the dismissal of schoolteachers who were either not party members or had been educated before the revolution opened up opportunities for social mobility as younger 'red specialists' were given teaching posts. The party also realized it needed future leaders from factories, mines, and state farms to study at technical institutes.

'According to Sheila Fitzpatrick, during the first Five-Year Plan, some 110,000 communist adult workers and some 40,000 non-party ones entered higher educational institutions in this way' (Hosking, *A History of the Soviet Union 1917–1991*, 1992). Even so, there were problems, and the quota system imposed in 1929 was abolished in 1935 as it is estimated that '70 per cent failed to complete their course' (McCauley, *The Soviet Union 1917–1991*, 1993).

Urbanization and more access to education often resulted in increased social mobility as young people grasped opportunities they could hardly have previously imagined. As the Soviet Union made economic progress, it needed more managers and technicians. Former peasants moved to cities, where at least a few could become managers and could rise within the ranks of the party to lead privileged lives. By the end of the 1920s, the importance of coming from the 'correct' class meant that a humble background was advantageous.

 TOK Stalin considered himself to be an 'engineer of human souls'. He believed that it was possible to 'fill' an individual with the correct ideology and to create a society of like-minded individuals. For example, if you put a young child in a school that teaches everything according to a set of beliefs or a particular ideology, do you that think that the child will grow up believing and following everything he or she is taught, or is human nature resistant to that kind of control? Even if someone said he or she believed in it, would it necessarily be true?

! This essay question asks how much social and cultural policies really changed people's lives. Do consider, however, how far lives were changed and how far they remained the same. Try to support your answer with good evidence. It is difficult to know what people really felt about propaganda, for example, but, on the other hand, there is quite a lot of evidence to show that women's lives changed. If you are discussing culture, mention the names of artists or musicians, and show that you know something about their music or books.

Activity 10 **(ATL) Research, communication, thinking, and self-management skills**

Evaluate the impact of Stalin's social and cultural policies on the Soviet Union up to 1941.

Here are some extracts from student essays where they discuss the impact of cultural change.

Student answer A – Leo

Stalin also wanted to change Soviet culture. He liked art to be used for propaganda and preferred paintings that showed him with Lenin or surrounded by children, but he did not like modern art. He wanted people to read his books such as *The History of the Communist Party* and not novels and poetry. Stalin did like to attend the ballet and composers like Shostakovich were very popular. As long as artists and composers did what they were told to do, they were able to survive and they often lived in large apartments and were part of the elite of Soviet society.

Examiner's comments

Leo mentions art and literature as well as music. His paragraph is rather descriptive though. He mentions a composer, but what about writers, poets, or artists? There is not much supporting evidence here for his arguments.

Also, he does not mention if there was a change of policy or whether it had any impact on the Soviet Union.

It may be that Leo has left his analysis of 'change' for the conclusion, in which case, he will not score very well. It is important to refer to the question as you go along.

Student answer B – Susan

Another area in which there was change in Soviet culture was in the arts. Stalin understood the importance of music, literature and art and how these could be used to create a 'proletarian culture'. He approved of the music of Prokofiev and Shostakovich and encouraged their compositions. It is not very clear if these composers changed Soviet society in any way, but their music was considered to be very good, even outside the USSR. Also, concert tickets were cheap and everyone was encouraged to appreciate Russian composers, so it was also linked to encouraging nationalism. In literature, the works of Mikhail Sholokhov were available because he wrote about the civil war and the revolution. Stalin did not like the poetry of Oscar Mandelstam, though, because his verses spoke about the Terror. By censoring such poetry, Stalin wanted to limit opposition. Stalin liked the people of the USSR to read novels and to look at paintings that were about the lives of workers and peasants, and the Writers' Union, for example, made sure that novelists knew what they had to produce.

Examiner's comments

Susan has written a much fuller paragraph about culture. She has also included the names of several composers and writers, so there is some supporting evidence. Furthermore, there is an attempt at analysis as she tries to assess the impact on Soviet society. She could have said more about censorship and how this helped to control the kind of culture that was made available, but she has kept a focus on the question.

Activity 11   **(ATL) Thinking skills**

Study the source below and answer the questions that follow.

> Stalin put the matter vividly in 1931: 'To lower the tempo means to lag behind. And laggards [lazy people] are beaten. But we don't want to be beaten. No, we don't want it! The history of old Russia consisted, amongst other things, in her being beaten continually for her backwardness. She was beaten by the Mongol khans. She was beaten by the Turkish beys. She was beaten by the Swedish feudal lords. She was beaten by the Polish-Lithuanian nobles. She was beaten by the Anglo-French capitalists. She was beaten by the Japanese barons. She was beaten by all of them for her backwardness.'

From Robert Service, *A History of Modern Russia: From Nicholas II to Putin*, 2nd ed., Penguin, 2003

In the source above, Stalin makes many references to Russian history. He does not mention communism at all. What does this suggest to you about how Stalin viewed the Soviet Union? Was it a new, revolutionary state, do you think, or the latest manifestation of the Russian Empire? How would you support your answer?

TOK

Stalin said, 'The death of one man is a tragedy, the death of millions is a statistic.'

Consider how this statement may or may not be valid today. Newspapers, the internet, and television carry news stories that cover tragic events on a daily basis. Does the way news is communicated to us reflect Stalin's statement? Is this how we react to the news of a suicide bombing or a train crash?

2.3   Consolidation and maintenance of power

What methods did Stalin use to maintain power?

Like many authoritarian leaders, Stalin did not tolerate dissent and used a number of methods to ensure that his policies were carried out.

The use of force

Securing his own position as the leader of the party and the state, Stalin had removed his rivals from the Politburo by the end of the 1920s. This did not mean that he was in complete control, however, and criticism from Martemian Riutin and associates in 1932 showed that Stalin's policies were not always popular with the Central Committee of the Communist Party. Although the 17th Party Congress in 1934 was named the Congress of the Victors, Stalin knew that the Second Five-Year Plan had huge difficulties in meeting its targets and the human cost of collectivization was devastating for the countryside. More importantly, others knew this too and were not afraid to voice their concerns.

Meanwhile, punishment was meted out to peasants who resisted collectivization; to factory workers who did not work hard enough; to managers who did not meet targets; and to party members who were considered too passive.

For Stalin, terror was one of his methods of ruling the Soviet Union. It made people afraid, and people who were frightened were more likely to be obedient. If instilling fear was his aim, he certainly achieved it. Even those who were not afraid of Stalin would be frightened of the dangers he told them existed. These included the fear of invasion, the fear of a counter-revolution, and the fear of Stalin being removed from power by his enemies. The terror grew as Stalin became more powerful and surrounded himself with supporters in the Politburo and the Central Committee of the party. During the early 1930s, he still had to be cautious, and his recommendation in 1933 that Riutin be executed was opposed by Sergei Kirov. Events such as Kirov's murder in 1934 gave Stalin opportunities to purge the Leningrad Party, to introduce legal changes such as the possibility of a death sentence being sanctioned for children over 12, and the removal of the right to appeal so that a death sentence could be carried out immediately.

The following is a brief list of the purges that were carried out during the 1930s:

- The purge of engineers and managers included the Shakhty Trials. The aim was to instil labour discipline and punish anyone accused of failing to meet targets.
- The purge of the Communist Party to ensure that all members were loyal to Stalin. The purging of the party began after Riutin's criticisms of Stalin's leadership.
- The purge of the leadership of the party that followed the death of Sergei Kirov.
- The purge of the military in 1937 that targeted the officers of the armed forces.
- Random quotas issued to local party branches with instructions that 'counter-revolutionaries', kulaks, and 'Trotskyites' be imprisoned or executed. Party branches would receive orders to arrest a specific number of enemies of the state, whether these existed or not.

An exam question may ask you to consider the extent of opposition to an authoritarian leader. If you choose to write about Stalin, it is worth considering whether it really was so extensive. Certainly, there was opposition from the kulaks, for example, and from some political opponents. But surely, much of it was imagined by Stalin and so it was not so extensive as he claimed. You might argue that Stalin's purges and mass deportations to the gulags were ways in which he prevented the rise of opposition.

Martemian Ivanovich Riutin (1890–1937)

Riutin criticized Stalin's overthrow of the collective leadership of the party, saying that this had led to ordinary people's disillusionment with socialism. The radical nature of collectivization had also contributed to Stalin's unpopularity with some leading cadres. Riutin was expelled from the party in 1930 and his associates were expelled in 1932, accused of trying to restore capitalism and of being kulaks. It is claimed that Stalin wanted the death penalty for Riutin, but that Kirov intervened. Riutin was sentenced to 10 years' solitary confinement, but was shot in 1937.

Sergei Kirov (1886–1934)

A close friend of Stalin, Kirov had taken over the administration of the Leningrad Party after the demotion of Zinoviev. A popular member of the leadership, Kirov had gained more votes than Stalin in the elections to the Central Committee in 1934. Soon after, he was murdered by Leonid Nikolaev who, it was alleged, was jealous because his wife had an affair with Kirov. The circumstances surrounding the murder were mysterious and there has always been a suspicion that Stalin ordered the murder, although no proof for this accusation has ever been found. He did use the opportunity, however, to purge the Leningrad Party and to arrest Kamenev and Zinoviev.

The Shakhty Trials

Named after the town in the Donbass coal-mining region where they took place, these were trials of 'foreign experts' and 'class elements' blamed for breaking machinery and sabotaging the Five-Year Plan. Most likely, the breakage was the fault of unskilled workers, but 'experts' were convenient scapegoats. Public trials were held and 11 death sentences handed down, of which five were carried out.

The purge of the military

The purge of the military in 1937 cut a swathe through the officer ranks of the armed forces. In his unrelenting hunt for career officers who could not be trusted, Stalin executed thousands and put thousands more in prison. This was to lead to problems in 1941, when the early successes of the German invasion were partly due to the absence of experienced officers. It also influenced Britain's reluctance to seriously pursue an alliance with the Soviet Union in 1939.

The Great Terror, as this period became known, affected every aspect of Soviet society. It was one of the most important methods by which Stalin enforced loyalty and by which any opposition was suppressed.

In June 1936, Zinoviev and Kamenev, who had been accused of having plotted Kirov's murder, were tried and executed. Stalin was now targeting influential Bolsheviks who had been members of the party leadership. Genrikh Yagoda, the head of the People's Commissariat for Internal Affairs (NKVD, the internal security police), objected to the execution of party leaders and was criticized by Stalin for having started the terror four years too late (Lewin, *The Soviet Century*, 2005). In September 1936, Yagoda was replaced by Nikolai Yezhov, a great admirer of Stalin, who followed instructions to prise out enemies within the party. According to Robert Service, 681,692 people were executed between 1936 and 1938 (*A History of Modern Russia*, 2003). Bukharin and Rykov were put on trial in 1938 and executed, having confessed to betraying the party. Service considers this period of unbridled terror to have had a negative impact upon the Soviet Union's economy and its military, and that even Stalin recognized that events had gone beyond his control by 1938. Slowly, the 'quotas' were reduced and, finally, Yezhov was demoted, imprisoned, and executed in February 1939. It is not clear why Stalin slowed down the process of disposing of imagined enemies, but it is possible that the worsening situation in Europe meant that he had to shift his attention to foreign policy. Yezhov was accused of having been over-zealous in carrying out purges, with the Great Terror being described as the period of *Yezhovchina*.

Historians have argued over the numbers killed as well as the motivation that sparked the process. A study of the documents in the Russian archives released in the 1990s confirms that the numbers arrested and executed started to go up as Stalin consolidated his grip on power. In 1929, for example, 162,726 were arrested and this increased to 331,544 in 1930 and 505,256 in 1933. In 1937, 936,750 were arrested, 779,056 of these for counter-revolutionary crimes and 353,074 were shot (Jonathan Brent, *Inside the Stalin Archives*, 2008). Brent argues, 'no thinking person could have believed that all 936,750 people arrested in 1937 were Trotskyists or wreckers… During the terror, there is little evidence that Stalin or his closest colleagues ever suffered such delusions or fully believed the objective charges they brought against those they persecuted. Often they didn't even know the names of their victims' (*Inside the Stalin Archives*, 2008 p. 164).

Mary McAuley, meanwhile, notes the difficulty of assessing the impact of the terror when the statistics were so unreliable. She also considers the difficulty of accumulating eyewitness memoirs when most people who wrote about their experiences were intellectuals. What, she asks, 'of the peasants and workers and the criminals' who were also imprisoned (*Soviet Politics 1917–1991*, 1992)? McAuley notes that Solzhenitsyn argued that the purges were symptomatic of Bolshevik ideology:

> *Solzhenitsyn argues … if one believes that class origin determines behaviour and consciousness, if one believes that individuals' actions and ideas are determined by their social origins and that therefore members of the bourgeoisie cannot but act in a particular way, it is only logical to argue that they should be eliminated … the belief that revolutionary justice should be administered by those with a proper proletarian consciousness, and little else, allowed the riff-raff and sadists of society to staff the penal institutions.*

McAuley also quotes Stanislaw Swianiewicz, a Polish economist:

> *[Stanislaw Swianiewicz] offers us a materialist explanation… Economic development necessitates the finding of resources for investment, for holding back consumption. How could this be done? One way to reduce consumption was to withdraw consumers from the market, place them in labour camps where they worked and consumed almost nothing… The labour camps, Swianiewicz argues, had an economic rationale.*

Both sources from Mary McAuley, *Soviet Politics 1917–1991*, Oxford University Press, 1992

Another historian, Orlando Figes, has researched the 1930s in depth, accessing the archive of memoirs collected 'in collaboration with the Memorial Society organized in the late 1980s to represent and commemorate the victims of Soviet repression' (*The Whisperers*, 2008). He estimates that '25 million people were repressed by the Soviet regime between 1928 … and 1953. These 25 million – people shot by execution squads, Gulag prisoners, "kulaks" sent to "special settlements", slave labourers of various kinds and members of deported nationalities – represent about one-eighth of the Soviet population…'.

Figes also comments on how, inevitably, in a regime that was so repressive, one survival method was for people to identify so strongly with Stalin that even their punishment could not shake their belief in his righteousness. Read Sources A and B in Activity 12 for more on Figes's views.

Memorial Society

Set up during the period of *perestroika* and *glasnost* in the 1980s, this society tried to ensure that the victims of Stalin's purges were not forgotten. For example, it recorded the recollections of people who had survived the purges. In recent times, Memorial has been subject to harassment by government officials. However it continues to exist and to gather and preserve historical sources on the Soviet era.

Activity 12

ATL Research and thinking skills

Study the sources below and answer the questions that follow.

Source A

> *Immersion in the Soviet system was a means of survival for most people, including many victims of the Stalinist regime, a necessary way of silencing their doubts and fears, which, if voiced, could make their lives impossible. Believing and collaborating in the Soviet project was a way to make sense of their suffering, which without this higher purpose might reduce them to despair. In the words of (another) 'kulak' child, a man exiled for many years as an 'enemy of the people' who nonetheless remained a convinced Stalinist throughout his life, 'believing in the justice of Stalin … made it easier for us to accept our punishments, and it took away our fear'.*

From Orlando Figes, *The Whisperers: Private Life in Stalin's Russia*, Penguin, 2008

Source B

 '… a true Bolshevik will readily cast out from his mind ideas in which he has believed for years. A true Bolshevik has submerged his personality in the collectivity, 'the Party', to such an extent that he can make the necessary effort to break away from his own opinions and convictions… He would be ready to believe that black was white and white was black, if the Party required it.'

Yuri Piatakov quoted in Orlando Figes, *The Whisperers: Private Life in Stalin's Russia*, Penguin, 2008

1. How could you use Source A to support the argument that Stalin continued to be revered even by those he punished?
2. Why, do you think, did they respond in this way?
3. How could you use Sources A and B to agree/disagree with the following assertion: 'Stalin had total control over the population of the Soviet Union'?

CHALLENGE YOURSELF

 Thinking, self-management, and research skills

In 1956, Nikita Khrushchev – then the General Secretary of the Communist Party – gave a controversial speech in which he criticized Stalin. Investigate this and find out what the impact of his speech was on:

1. the Politburo of the Soviet Union
2. the leadership of the communist parties in Poland and Hungary.

As an additional activity, see if you can find out how the West found out about this 'secret speech'.

Stalin's political policies – the constitution of 1936

In 1936, Stalin revised the constitution of the Soviet Union. On paper, it sounded very democratic, as it guaranteed freedom of the press, freedom of thought, the right to public assembly, and all other basic human rights. It also stated, however, that these rights would be guaranteed only as long as they were in accordance with the interests of the workers. In fact, everything that was not specifically allowed was forbidden. Even so, the constitution gave the impression or illusion that the Soviet Union was a liberal state, at a time when Stalin was increasingly concerned about its image abroad.

Popular policies

Don't forget that many of Stalin's policies were popular: his rejection of the NEP in 1927, for example, appealed to workers who felt that the Soviet Union had slipped back into capitalism. His punishment of kulaks was probably supported by peasants, who resented their richer neighbours. After they had confessed their guilt in the show trials, it is likely that most people did not question the execution of leading Bolsheviks. Also, the population of the cities increased during the 1930s, with more opportunities for education and job promotion. In 1926, only 17.4 per cent of the population lived in cities, but this almost doubled by 1939 (Lewin, *The Soviet Century*, 2005). Social mobility was a fact of life in Stalin's state, and, in a macabre way, the terror brought employment opportunities – even promotion – for those who were not shot or sent to the gulags.

Stalin's cult of personality was important in ensuring that his image and words were familiar to all Soviet citizens. Paintings, photographs, and statues made Stalin recognizable throughout the Soviet Union; his speeches and messages were carried to the people through radio broadcasts and in the pages of *Pravda*.

The use of language was also an integral part of the Stalinist system. Enemies were defined as kulaks even when they were not rich peasants, or as Trotskyites even if they had no connection with Trotsky. What was important was to use these terms to identify people as counter-revolutionaries. Getty and Naumov stress that the same language was used in private as was used in public. Officials '"spoke Stalinist" as a matter of group conformity and even individual survival' (J. Arch Getty and Oleg V. Naumov, *The Road to Terror*, 2010).

The extent to which Stalin achieved authoritarian control

An important question to consider is the degree to which authoritarian leaders controlled every aspect of the state. Even with a secret police to arrest opponents (real or imagined) and strict control over the allocation of economic resources, the monitoring of the movement of the population, and so on, how total could control be in a country as large as the Soviet Union?

Nature, extent, and treatment of opposition

Stalin believed that he encountered a great deal of opposition and once stated that he trusted no one: 'I trust no one, not even myself.' It was also said that he had an inferiority complex and thought he was less educated, less intellectual, and less popular than the other Bolsheviks. It is possible to dismiss Stalin as paranoid, imagining enemies around every corner, but was there real opposition to his bid for power and to his policies?

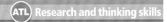

Activity 13

(ATL) Research and thinking skills

1. What was the extent of the opposition that Stalin faced?

Using the following list, consider what kind of opposition Stalin faced and when. Did Stalin respond to opposition or did he create it, do you think?

- Lenin
- Nadezhda Krupskaya (Lenin's wife)
- Trotsky
- Kamenev and Zinoviev
- Bukharin
- Riutin
- Kirov
- Ordinary party members
- Workers
- Peasants

Don't forget to consider 'extent', so think about how much opposition there really was and where it came from.

TOK

Today, when a government censors information that is broadcast by TV stations or published either in newspapers or on the internet, we usually consider it to be rather authoritarian. Are there ever good reasons, do you think, for censoring information or, indeed, literature and films? For instance, would we accept censorship in a time of war? Are there other circumstances when it would be acceptable, or is it always the right of citizens to have free access to all information?

If you are asked to consider the methods that an authoritarian leader used to stay in power (or to consolidate power), you can start your plan by making a list of factors that would apply not only to Stalin but also to other authoritarian leaders you study. Don't forget that you may be asked to compare and contrast two leaders so it is a good idea to plan ahead and to think about which other leaders used, for example, propaganda and terror.

Common factors may include:

- terror
- propaganda
- education and youth groups
- the centralized control of the party
- popular, successful policies.

Once you have done this, include evidence to support your points and some analysis to determine which were the most important.

When planning an answer for this question you probably think of the terror and the gulags. Certainly, these were important methods used by Stalin to deal with his enemies, but don't forget that authoritarian leaders can also be proactive by using propaganda and populist policies to prevent the growth of opposition.

Activity 14  ATL Thinking skills

Another kind of essay question could ask how Stalin actually dealt with opposition, for example:

In what ways and with what success did Stalin deal with internal opposition to his regime?

To answer a question like this, it is a good idea to write a detailed plan, first outlining all the different kinds of opposition to Stalin. These could include:

- opposition from within the party
- opposition from the peasants
- opposition from the workers
- opposition from the Church.

Then consider the methods used to deal with each one and how successful they were.

Also notice that the question has two parts: 'in what ways' and 'with what success'. You need to address both parts so structure your answer accordingly. Begin by mentioning the kinds of opposition Stalin had to deal with and then discuss the 'ways' before ending with an assessment of how successful he was. Alternatively, you can begin by mentioning the different kinds of opposition, then discuss how and with what success he tackled each one.

Form of government and ideology

The Soviet Union followed the left-wing ideology of communism, although both Lenin and Stalin had adapted the ideology according to what they perceived to be the needs of the state. Stalin had become a committed Bolshevik as a young man, and was prepared to break the law for his political beliefs and to spend many years in exile. He had supported the October Revolution and fought to save the revolution during the civil war.

Regarding how the Communist Party planned to run the country, Robert Service mentions that Lazar Kaganovich had produced a pamphlet 'on the party workings' and that, 'already one of Stalin's close associates, (he) spelled out the system of vertical command needed in the party-state if the communists were to enhance their power…' (*Comrades*, 2007).

According to Marxism, the proletariat were meant to rule, but in the Soviet Union this can hardly be said to have been true when the Communist Party had so much control. The excuse given for the 'dictatorship of the party' was that Russia was too backward and the 'dictatorship of the proletariat' could not take place until people had been educated to have the correct values. This policy, of course, would require social engineering. Proletarians would have to be made and made quickly!

Activity 15  ATL Thinking skills

Read the opinions below. They are all about Stalin's political beliefs. Then answer the questions that follow.

- In the secret speech given at the 20th Party Congress in 1956, Nikita Khrushchev said that Stalin was not a 'Marxist'.
- Trotsky referred to Stalin as 'the gravedigger of the revolution'.
- Simon Sebag Montefiore wrote a book about Stalin and called it *The Court of the Red Tsar*.
- Robert Service stated that Stalin 'knew his Marxism and he was a dedicated Leninist' (*Comrades*, 2007).

1. Can you find evidence in this chapter to support and/or oppose each one of the opinions above?
2. To what extent can Stalin be considered a Marxist?
3. To what extent can Stalin be considered a Leninist?
4. Is there a difference between a Marxist and a Leninist? How would you explain the difference?

Activity 16

 Research skills

Read the source below and answer the questions that follow.

> *Robert Service in* Comrades *mentions how Alexander Herzen, a 19th-century Russian essayist, '… expressed fear of bloody revolution in his country. He thought that, if ever the peasantry rose against their masters, they might be led by some "Genghis Khan with the telegraph".' Service goes on to describe the Bolsheviks as 'Jacobins with the telephone and the machine gun'.*

Adapted from Robert Service, *Comrades: Communism: A World History*, Pan, 2008

1. What was meant, do you think, by the phrase, 'Genghis Khan with the telegraph'? (A better way to describe it today, perhaps, would be 'Genghis Khan with a smart phone'!)
2. Do you know who the Jacobins were? Why, do you think, does Service compare the Bolsheviks to them?

The structure and organization of government and administration

The governmental structure of the Soviet Union was established by the constitution of 1922 and amended slightly by the constitution of 1936. In both, the hierarchical structure for both the soviets and the party were outlined. Each republic had a Congress of Soviets, which sent representatives to the Union Congress of Soviets that elected the Central Executive Committee. This body, divided into the Congress of the Union and the Congress of Nationalities, appointed the members of Sovnarkom. Similarly, the Communist Party had local branches that sent representatives to the Central Committee from which the Politburo was elected. It was imperative that members of the soviets, even at a local level, were members of the party and so the party dominated the government. It was the Politburo that was the policy-making organ; Lewin mentions that by the late 1930s, the Politburo had in practice become limited to a 'quintet' of Stalin, Molotov, Mikoyan, Beria, and Malenkov. Although it was often reduced to Stalin and Molotov consulting only each other (Lewin, *The Soviet Century*, 2005).

> **Lavrenti Beria (1899–1953)**
>
> Lavrenti Beria was Stalin's 'hatchet man'. He took over the leadership of the NKVD (the secret police) in 1938 after the dismissal of Yezhov. He remained close to Stalin, becoming a member of the Politburo in 1946. He was arrested and executed after the death of Stalin in 1953.

Activity 17

 Thinking skills

1. What does the above paragraph tell you about the way power was centralized in the Soviet Union under Stalin?

Was Stalin an authoritarian leader?

To be an authoritarian leader implies complete power and control over the state. When Stalin ordered the purges of the party and the military, did he really have complete control over exactly what took place?

> *Although by the end of the decade he was unquestionably the supreme leader, he was never omnipotent, and he always functioned within a matrix of other groups and interests.*

From J. Arch Getty and Oleg V. Naumov, *The Road to Terror: Stalin and the Self-Destruction of the Bolsheviks, 1932–1939*, Yale University Press, Updated and Abridged ed., 2010

Getty and Naumov stress that communication was very difficult when not all the regions of the Soviet Union had a telephone connection. Party messengers had to struggle on motorbikes along poor roads carrying instructions from Moscow. What hope was there, then, of keeping a close eye on what went on across the vastness of the Soviet Union? This argument suggests that Stalin may have had a lot of power but it is difficult to imagine that he had complete control or was able to influence all the decisions made in the most remote areas of the Soviet Union.

> When you consider all these points about Stalin's rule during the 1930s, you can see how he had many methods he used to consolidate his power. The structure of the party, as well as the ideology of Marxism–Leninism, are also important to consider as these also helped Stalin to centralize power.

An overview of Stalin's domestic policy

Now is a good time to think about Stalin's aims, his domestic policies, and the results of these polices.

They have all been mentioned throughout this section of the chapter, and here is a table that you could complete to provide an overview that may be useful for revision. You could start with a table for economic policies, then create different tables for each of the following areas of domestic policy: education, women, religion, culture. For example:

Domestic policy area	Education	Women	Religion	Culture
Aims				
Achievements				
Failures				

Stalin's foreign policy up to 1941

In Stalin's opinion, the Soviet Union was a fragile state. It did not have a well-developed industrialized economy; outside its borders there were many countries that feared the spread of communism. By the early 1930s, Fascism was well established in Italy, and Nazism was on the rise in Germany. Both of these very similar ideologies had their roots in socialism, but were vehemently opposed to communism. In a war, the Soviet Union would need to defend its borders and have a well-trained and well-equipped army.

Timeline – 1930–1941	
1930	Maxim Litvinov is appointed commissar for foreign affairs.
1933	The United States establishes diplomatic relations with the Soviet Union.
1934	The Soviet Union joins the League of Nations.
1935	The Franco-Soviet Pact; Comintern orders cooperation with anti-fascist governments.
1936	The Spanish Civil War begins (1936–39); Germany signs the Anti-Comintern Pact with Japan.
1937	Italy joins the Anti-Comintern Pact.
1938	The Munich Conference; border conflict with Japan begins and ends in 1939.
1939	Molotov replaces Litvinov as foreign minister; the Nazi–Soviet Pact is signed; World War II begins; Poland invaded and divided between Nazi Germany and the Soviet Union; the 'Winter War' with Finland begins in October.
1940	The Katyn Massacre; the 'occupation' of the Baltic States and Bessarabia.
1941	Operation Barbarossa – the German invasion of the Soviet Union – begins.

The 1930s were a decade of great tension in Europe and the Far East. Authoritarian states had emerged across Eastern Europe as well as in Germany, Italy, and Japan, although these three countries also had ambitions to expand into neighbouring (and more distant) countries to acquire empires. Stalin was not unaware of the threat posed by Germany and Japan to the security of the Soviet Union. In particular, Stalin feared a two-front war and this became a greater threat after Germany and Italy signed the Anti-Comintern Pact in 1936.

Stalin and the Spanish Civil War, 1936–39

Having remained rather isolated from events outside of the Soviet Union, in 1936 Stalin was drawn into what is often described as 'the dress rehearsal for World War II'. In Spain, a civil war had broken out after an attempted military coup to overthrow the Popular Front government. The Nationalist or Rebel forces – led by General Francisco Franco – were aided by Hitler and Mussolini who sent arms, planes, and soldiers. The Republican government was made up of representatives from the left (anarchists, socialists, communists, etc.) and the centre-left; it looked to France and Britain for support. Although France was keen to provide arms to its neighbour, it argued in favour of neutrality and proposed the Non-Intervention Committee.

On 25 July 1936, the Republican government of Jose Giral asked Stalin for assistance. At first, Stalin hesitated for the following reasons:

- He did not want to aggravate Hitler into taking action against the Soviet Union.
- He did not want to alienate Britain and France in case he needed their support to fight against Fascism.

As the only communist leader in Europe, however, it was difficult for Stalin to avoid giving aid to a left-wing government.

According to Antony Beevor, Trotsky lost no time in criticizing Stalin's failure to provide assistance as 'betraying the Spanish revolution and aiding the fascists' (*The Battle for Spain*, 2006, p.139) and that this may have 'goaded (Stalin) into action'. For Stalin, an acceptable compromise was to provide just enough aid to show support but not so much as to affect the outcome of the war that was, by 1938, clearly moving towards a Nationalist victory.

What aid was sent from the Soviet Union?

In response to Giral's pleas, Stalin sold fuel to Spain at a very favourable price. This was followed by military aid that arrived in October 1936. Meanwhile, the Spanish Communist Party grew rapidly from 38,000 members in 1936 to 300,000 by 1937. Beevor mentions two interpretations of why Soviet aid was sent to Spain:

- It was sent to help establish a pro-Soviet regime.
- It was sent, with no ulterior motive, to help the legal government of Spain.

Beevor says that neither interpretation is completely accurate and that the second (that Stalin had no ulterior motive) is perhaps least likely. Whatever the reason for sending aid, there was a heavy focus in the Soviet Union on propaganda films and newspaper articles to evoke sympathy for Spain. Senior officers were sent as military advisors and Comintern was represented in Spain by Palmiro Togliatti, the exiled leader of the Italian Communist Party. As the situation of the Republican government worsened, Largo Caballero, also known as 'Spain's Lenin', persuaded Stalin to send aid; the Soviet T-26 and BT-5 tanks proved to be better than the German tanks sent by Hitler. In addition, Stalin sent 42 IL-15 biplanes and 31 IL-16 monoplanes. Arms were also sent, but many of the guns predated World War I and the ammunition, of different calibres, often did not fit the guns. The aid sent by Stalin was of some help but it was not enough to win the war.

Non-Intervention Committee

This was established in 1936 to advocate the neutrality of the European powers to prevent the spread of the war into neighbouring countries. A policy was signed by 27 countries including Britain, France, Germany, Italy, and the Soviet Union; in reality, it was a sham: the policy was flagrantly ignored by the three latter powers who were committed to containing the war within Spain and refused to assist either side. Not only did Britain turn a blind eye to repeated (and successful) attempts by Italy to get past naval patrols of Spain's coastline, but along with France it prevented the sale of much-needed arms to the beleaguered government.

Thinking skills

Can you think of other examples when governments gave aid to support one side in a war? For what reasons do governments usually do this? How do they justify the expense to their tax-paying citizens?

Who paid for all this?

It is well known that the gold reserves of Spain (the fourth largest in the world at the time) were transferred to Moscow as a kind of advance payment. According to Beevor, in September 1936, 510 tons of gold and silver, worth $518 million, were shipped to Moscow. Furthermore, 'nothing was free' and 'creative accounting' meant that Moscow presented a bill for $661 million and so Spain, effectively, had spent its entire reserves (*The Battle for Spain*, 2006, p. 154).

The International Brigades and their link to the Soviet Union

The volunteers who came from the rest of Europe and the United States to aid the Republicans were collectively known as the International Brigades; they were recruited by the Comintern. Between 1936 and their departure in October 1938, an estimated 32,000 to 35,000 volunteers from 53 countries joined the Brigades, of whom an estimated 50 per cent were members of the Communist Party. As the Non-Intervention Committee forbade volunteers to fight in Spain, an elaborate travel plan was set up for recruits to travel to Paris, and from there either to be sent by sea to the Spanish coast or on foot across the Pyrenees.

Some of the volunteers had fought in World War I but many were inexperienced recruits, drawn mostly from the ranks of the unemployed and manual workers. Their training was inadequate, and many carried rifles for the first time as they marched to the battlefronts.

Republican soldiers in Barcelona looking at propaganda posters urging women to join the fight to save Spain.

There is evidence to say that, on the Republican side, a civil war was being fought within the civil war. The Workers' Party of Marxist Unification (*Partido Obrero de Unificación Marxista*; **POUM**) and the National Confederation of Labour (*Confederación Nacional del Trabajo*; **CNT**) in particular had their ideological differences with the CNT alleging that Andres Nin, the leader of the POUM, was a Trotskyist. Although this is disputed, Nin's reputation as a one-time friend of Trotsky was enough to spread rumours that he and his followers were fascist sympathisers to be arrested and executed. Both factions were, however, targeted by the Communists in the government and the Communist Party of Catalonia. The May Days of 1937 in Barcelona were an example of how the factions on the left fought bitterly against each other, and how these purges also extended to the International Brigades. In this way, you can see that Stalin extended the reach of his purges into Spain and, according to Beevor, the Spanish Civil War also impacted the intensity of the purges in the Soviet Union. If there were rumours that a Soviet official in Spain was not absolutely loyal to Stalin, they would be executed.

The Spanish Civil War ended in 1939 with the victory of Franco and the Nationalists. By this time, Stalin was already looking for a closer relationship with Nazi Germany. This would result in the Nazi–Soviet Pact signed on 23 August 1939.

In 1998, Welsh rock band the Manic Street Preachers released a track called 'If you tolerate this, your children will be next'. The lyrics were taken from the wording on a Spanish Civil-War poster showing a dead child beneath a flight of bombers. Do some research on this to find out why the band used these lyrics and what they aimed to achieve. Do we run the risk of trivializing tragedy if, as in this case, it is likely that people listening to the song would be unaware of its origins?

The legacy of the Spanish Civil War also inspired the English band the Durutti Column. See what you can find out about the name, the band, and the music they played.

▶ A Republican propaganda poster showing the image of a dead child below planes with swastikas on their wings.

Activity 18

ATL Research and thinking skills

Read the source below and answer the questions that follow.

> ❝ The Spanish Civil War is one of the comparatively few cases when the most widely accepted version of events has been written more persuasively by the losers of the conflict than by the winners. This development was of course decisively influenced by the subsequent defeat of the nationalists' Axis allies.
>
> **From Antony Beevor, *The Battle for Spain: The Spanish Civil War 1936–1939*, Weidenfeld & Nicolson, 2007, p. 239**

1. According to the source, what was Beevor saying about the legacy of the Spanish Civil War?
2. How far, do you think, did the involvement in Spain influence Stalin's rule in the Soviet Union? Did it influence the image of the Soviet Union abroad?
3. Can you think of other examples where the 'losers' won the propaganda war?

A change of course, 1939

Stalin's economic policies were certainly driven in part by his determination to rearm his military forces and to prepare for war. The military leadership was also thoroughly purged, probably because he did not trust his officers and also because executions and imprisonment would instil fear and so guarantee loyalty in the event of war.

▲ Maxim Litvinov

▲ Vyacheslav Molotov

Maxim Litvinov was appointed the commissar for external affairs in 1930, and until his replacement in 1939 he was the architect of Soviet foreign policy. At first glance, Litvinov had many of the characteristics of Stalin's victims: he was an 'old Bolshevik' who had joined the party in 1903; he was well travelled and spoke many languages; he was married to an Englishwoman; he was Jewish. Yet Litvinov survived possibly because his skills were needed in determining foreign policy, which was not an area of expertise for Stalin. It was Litvinov who proposed collective security for the Soviet Union, resulting in its joining the League of Nations in 1934. He also favoured closer cooperation with anti-fascist governments, a policy approved by the Comintern in 1935, after which **popular front** governments were established in France and Spain and the Second United Front was set up in China (for more, see page 123).

The weakness demonstrated by the League of Nations over the Manchurian Crisis of 1931 and the Italian invasion of Abyssinia in 1935 damaged the reputation of 'collective security'. A natural alliance might have been with Britain and France, but Britain, in particular, was reluctant to ally with the Soviet Union. This possibility was also undermined by the events of 1938, when Stalin was not invited to attend the Munich Conference, although the Soviet Union had an alliance with Czechoslovakia.

Activity 19  **(ATL) Thinking skills**

Study the source below and answer the question that follows.

> *Litvinov explicitly told the British delegation to the League [of Nations] that, if the Germans invaded Czechoslovakia, the 'Czechoslovak–Soviet Pact would come into force', and proposed a conference between Britain, France and the Soviet Union to 'show the Germans we mean business'.*

From Niall Ferguson, *The War of the World: History's Age of Hatred*, Penguin, 2006

1. How reliable, do you think, is Litvinov as a source for what the Soviet Union intended if Germany invaded Czechoslovakia?

By 1939, a close alliance with the French and the British looked increasingly unlikely, although in April a poll held in Britain showed that 87 per cent of respondents said they favoured an alliance with France and the Soviet Union (Ferguson, *The War of the World*, 2006). The government of Britain did eventually send a delegation to Moscow in July, but they travelled by sea, suggesting there was no sense of urgency. Turning away from the West, Stalin aimed to foster closer cooperation with Nazi Germany; Litvinov, who would have been an unlikely emissary to Berlin, was replaced as commissar of external affairs by Vyacheslav Molotov.

The Nazi–Soviet Pact

On 23 August 1939, German foreign minister Joachim von Ribbentrop and the Soviet foreign minister Vyacheslav Molotov signed the Nazi–Soviet Pact. This was the result of several months of highly secret negotiations that began in May 1939 with discussions about trade and developed into tentative enquiries made by Molotov about a '**rapprochement** with Germany' (from the Foreign Office Memorandum, June 15, 1939, retrieved from the Avalon Project, Lillian Goldman Law Library).

There were several possible reasons for this dramatic shift in Soviet diplomacy:

- Maxim Litvinov, who had been in favour of closer links with the democracies of Western Europe, was replaced by Molotov as foreign minister in May 1939. Molotov was more flexible and more willing to enter into negotiations with Nazi Germany.

- The Munich Crisis of September 1938 had influenced Stalin's opinion of Britain and France as likely allies, as he considered them to have abandoned Czechoslovakia, as well as being weak and vacillating in their negotiations with Hitler.
- Stalin was concerned about growing tensions with Japan and feared a border conflict. These might be alleviated if he reached out to Germany, Japan's ally in the Anti-Comintern Pact.
- Neither Britain nor France had made any concrete offers of an alliance with the Soviet Union, possibly because Britain feared that such a treaty might antagonize Japan, but also because the show trials and the brutal purges of the Soviet military raised questions about the Soviet Union's capability in the event of war with the Axis Powers.
- There was the question of Poland, which did not want to be part of an alliance that included the Soviet Union.
- An alliance with France and Britain was likely to provoke Nazi Germany into attacking the Soviet Union.
- An alliance with Nazi Germany was intended to ensure a 10-year breathing space, if war did break out, as well as extra territory.

In the preliminary negotiations that took place mostly between Molotov and von der Schulenburg, the German Ambassador in Moscow, it was agreed that foreign policy could be determined regardless of internal ideological convictions. The Anti-Comintern Pact, Stalin was assured, was an alliance formed against Britain and not the Soviet Union.

Possible objections from Italy and Japan, the other members of the Anti-Comintern Pact, were taken into consideration by Germany and assurances given that the security of either partner would not be put at risk.

By July, tentative agreements had been reached on a 10-year non-aggression pact as well as recognition of areas of interest, such as Danzig for Germany and the Baltic States, and Bessarabia for the Soviet Union. The treaty was signed on 23 August and consisted of six articles that outlined the terms of the non-aggression agreement that would last for 10 years and, if no objection were raised, for a further five years. Immediately, a further Secret Protocol was also signed. This related to what was referred to as 'territorial rearrangement'.

Friedrich Werner von der Schulenburg

Von der Schulenburg was German Ambassador to the Soviet Union in 1934 and, in 1939, worked tirelessly to achieve an agreement between the Soviet Union and Germany. When he became aware of Hitler's plans to invade the Soviet Union in June 1941, he tried to obstruct this by exaggerating the strength of the Red Army. When Operation Barbarossa was launched, he left for Turkey and was later appointed to head the Russian Committee in Berlin, although this post had no political influence. In 1944, he participated in the Stauffenberg Plot that attempted to assassinate Hitler. Schulenburg was among the conspirators arrested, tried, and hanged.

Activity 20 **Research, thinking, and self-management skills**

Study the sources below and answer the questions that follow.

Source A

Secret Additional Protocol

On the occasion of the signature of the Nonaggression Pact between the German Reich and the Union of Socialist Soviet Republics the undersigned plenipotentiaries of each of the two parties discussed in strictly confidential conversations the question of the boundary of their respective spheres of influence in Eastern Europe. These conversations led to the following conclusions:

1. In the event of a territorial and political rearrangement in the areas belonging to the Baltic States (Finland, Estonia, Latvia, Lithuania), the northern boundary of Lithuania shall represent the boundary of the spheres of influence of Germany and the U.S.S.R. In this connection the interest of Lithuania in the Vilna area is recognized by each party.

2. In the event of a territorial and political rearrangement of the areas belonging to the Polish state the spheres of influence of Germany and the U.S.S.R. shall be bounded approximately by the line of the rivers Narew, Vistula, and San.

The question of whether the interests of both parties make desirable the maintenance of an independent Polish state and how such a state should be bounded can only be definitely determined in the course of further political developments.

In any event both Governments will resolve this question by means of a friendly agreement.

3. With regard to Southeastern Europe attention is called by the Soviet side to its interest in Bessarabia. The German side declares; its complete political disinterestedness in these areas.

This protocol shall be treated by both parties as strictly secret.

Moscow, August 23, 1939.

For the Government of the German Reich:

V. RIBBENTROP

Plenipotentiary of the Government of the U.S.S.R.:

V. MOLOTOV

Source retrieved from the Avalon Project, Lillian Goldman Law Library

1. What is implied by the phrase 'territorial and political rearrangement' used in the articles of the Secret Protocol in Source A?

2. According to Source A, what fate lies in store for Poland?

3. Find out when the Soviet Union invaded Poland.

4. Find out which territories were taken by Hitler and by Stalin in 1939–40.

The famous (infamous) Nazi–Soviet Pact was signed in August 1939. In a decade that came to be synonymous with messianic ideologies used to justify unspeakable acts of terror, it was truly shocking to see two avowed enemies sign a pact of neutrality that agreed to carve up Poland between them. The following contemporary cartoons reflect some of the disbelief and cynicism that greeted this unexpected alliance. Study them carefully and answer the questions that follow.

Source B

This cartoon from 1940 shows the Balkans being eyed enviously by Adolf Hitler and Josef Stalin.

Source C

WONDER HOW LONG THE HONEYMOON WILL LAST?

This is a cartoon making fun of the Nazi–Soviet Pact of August, 1939.

5. What, do you think, is the message conveyed by Source B?

6. As an extension to your answer to question 5, find out what happened to the 'goldfish' in the bowl in 1940.

7. How does the cartoonist in Source C show that the two ideologies of Nazism and Communism are now united?

8. How long did the 'honeymoon' between Stalin and Hitler last? Why did it end?

9. The caption in Source C reads 'How long will the honeymoon last?' Why were there doubts about this 'marriage'?

War on the Eastern Front

For Stalin, the Nazi–Soviet Pact signed on 23 August 1939 could be seen as a win-win situation. Not only was there a guarantee of 10 years' peace with Germany, the Soviet Union also regained the land it lost in 1918 to Germany and in 1921 to Poland. This must have seemed a far better deal to Stalin than signing a treaty with two reluctant allies (France and Britain), receiving no territory and possibly being dragged into a war against Nazi Germany. Germany invaded Poland on 1 September 1939. After some hesitation from Stalin, but encouragement from Hitler, the Red Army invaded Poland on 17 September. Just over a week later, on 27 September, the Boundary and Friendship Treaty with Germany handed Lithuania over to the Soviet Union in exchange for some of eastern Poland.

Soviet rule over conquered or annexed territories was brutal and Stalin was determined to 'decapitate' Polish society. Niall Ferguson points out how, after experiencing life under Soviet rule, many Poles who had sought refuge in the east now asked to be sent home, believing that life under the Nazis could hardly be worse than under Soviet occupation (*The War of the World*, 2006). For many Poles, however, the choice was between ending up in a concentration camp under the Nazis or a gulag under the Soviets.

Activity 21   **ATL Research, thinking, communication, and social skills**

The source below gives some indication of the nature of the 'terror' that was carried out in Soviet-occupied Poland. Study it and answer the questions that follow.

> *Beginning on the night of February 10th, 1940, the NKVD unleashed a campaign of terror against suspected 'anti-Soviet' elements. The targets identified … were 'those frequently travelling abroad, involved in overseas correspondence or coming into contact with representatives of foreign states; Esperantists; philatelists; those working with the Red Cross; … priests and active members of religious congregations; the nobility, landowners, wealthy merchants, bankers, industrialists, hotel [owners] and restaurant owners.'*

From Niall Ferguson, *The War of the World: History's Age of Hatred*, Penguin, 2006

Look carefully at all the different categories of people targeted in the source above.

1. What, do you think, do the categories of people all have in common?
2. Why were these people seen as a threat to Soviet control?
3. Up until 1939, despite both fearing Germany, Poland and the Soviet Union were unlikely to form an alliance. Why, do you think, was this so? Discuss your answer with the class.

One of the most widely known wartime atrocities carried out by the NKVD was the Katyn Massacre of 1940. More than 4,000 Polish Army officers, as well as police officers, prison guards, government officials, and other 'leaders' of society, were taken into the Katyn forest in Russia, shot and buried in mass graves. Meanwhile, in Estonia, Latvia, and Lithuania, government representatives were required to sign 'defence treaties' and, in 1940, to 'request' that they be incorporated into the Soviet Union.

Stalin was also concerned about security to the north and demanded that Finland relinquish territory to the Soviet Union. When Finland refused, the Winter War broke out in November 1939 and, although some Finnish territory was lost, more than 200,000 Red Army soldiers were killed. The weakness of the post-purge Red Army had been revealed and this was noted by Hitler.

Stalin's foreign policy from 1941

Stalin's wartime foreign policy can be thought of as consisting of two parts. The first part is the alliance with Nazi Germany that began in August 1939 and continued until June 1941; the second part is the alliance with Britain and the United States, a result of each of these countries being at war with Nazi Germany. Two interesting questions to consider as you read through this section are: How far was the latter alliance a temporary one? Did the fundamentally different ideologies mean this was solely a convenient arrangement that would end as soon as the common enemy was defeated?

Operation Barbarossa

Hitler's policy of *Lebensraum* led to the invasion of the Soviet Union and the planned colonization of its territory by the German/Aryan race. Niall Ferguson mentions that the timing of Operation Barbarossa in June 1941 may have been influenced by Hitler's

Lebensraum

This was Hitler's policy of expansion eastwards to find 'living space' for the Aryan race. He believed that the Third Reich should colonize lands to the east such as Poland and the Soviet Union where the Slav people would either be displaced or become slave workers for the Reich.

concern about Stalin's encroachment on Romania and the Balkans. In the summer of 1940, Stalin demanded that Romania hand over northern Bukovina and Bessarabia (known today as Moldova); this demand was followed by a 'promise of security' for Bulgaria. Hitler started to plan the invasion of the Soviet Union at this point, beginning with a meeting of his military chiefs in June 1940. When did Stalin begin to suspect something was afoot? Geoffrey Roberts suggests that when Molotov failed, in 1940, to negotiate an extension to the Nazi–Soviet Pact, Stalin knew that war was likely (quoted in interview with Aaron Leonard in historynewsnetwork.org, 2009). Moreover, Stalin was alerted to German invasion plans: by Richard Sorge, a double agent working in the German embassy in Tokyo; by the British who had cracked the German military ENIGMA code; by German informants who swam across the River Bug (the border between German and Soviet-occupied Poland) but were shot as enemy agents. Ferguson estimates that there were 84 warnings in all sent to Moscow and that Stalin ignored them all. It could be that Stalin still trusted Hitler, and was afraid that any defensive action by the Red Army would be interpreted by the Germans as preparation for an attack, or – and this would not be contradictory – he wanted to do everything possible to delay war for as long as possible.

Stalin as a wartime leader

Stalin knew that the war against Nazi Germany would take a tremendous toll on the people of the Soviet Union and that they would have to accept enormous hardship and sacrifice. It was unlikely they would do so in the name of communism, and Stalin understood that an appeal to nationalism would be far more compelling. Propaganda now turned this into a war to save the Soviet Motherland. It was named the 'Great Patriotic War' and the Orthodox Church was restored to a position of prominence to help rally the people to save their country.

Initially, the German strategy of **blitzkrieg** meant that the **Wehrmacht** made rapid advances but the German divisions were halted at Moscow when Stalin, despite being warned of an offensive from Japan on the eastern border, recalled General Zhukov from Siberia and provided him with whatever was necessary to organize the city's defence. The Wehrmacht now changed strategy and moved towards Stalingrad in 1942.

The Soviet Union and Japan

There had been conflicts on the border between Japanese-occupied Manchuria and the Soviet Union in 1939–40 but these ended when a neutrality pact was signed in April 1941.

Stalingrad could not be sacrificed, in part because its original name, Tsaritsyn, had been changed to Stalingrad in honour of Stalin's defence of the city during the Russian Civil War (today, it is named Volgograd). It also had a strategic importance because, if captured, Soviet oil supplies from the Caucasus to the Red Army force further north would be compromised. The German Army Group B nearly succeeded in capturing the city, but a Soviet counter-offensive encircled, trapped, and destroyed the German Sixth Army and much of the Fourth Army. The German defeat at Stalingrad in early 1943 is seen as the turning point of the war and the beginning of Germany's retreat. Hitler refused permission for General Friedrich von Paulus, the commander of German forces at Stalingrad, to break out from the encirclement in a timely manner, thus consigning hundreds of thousands of men to either death or capture. Dmitri Volkogonov mentions how, although it took time to explain that an encirclement of the German forces was the best strategy – ' Zhukov… had to explain it three times' (*The Rise and Fall of the Soviet Empire*, 1999, p. 119) – Stalin agreed to it, and victory was secured when defeat had been very close. It is an interesting example of how Stalin, unlike Hitler, listened to his generals and heeded their advice.

The German advance during Operation Barbarossa.

The siege of Leningrad, 1941–44

Among the most famous events of World War II on the Eastern Front were the long drawn-out efforts of the Nazi invaders to force the surrender of Leningrad, the cradle of the Bolshevik Revolution as well as the 'Venice of the North'. It was considered imperative that the city be saved, and from 1941 to 1944 its population suffered bombardments and starvation to win through a 900-day siege. It is estimated that more than 600,000 people died out of a population of approximately 2,500,000.

The battle of Moscow, October 1941 to January 1942

Known as Operation Typhoon, the occupation of Moscow was considered by Hitler to be vital to the success of Operation Barbarossa. The defence of Moscow was led by General Zhukov and, aided by extremely harsh winter conditions, he was able to prevent German victory.

The battle of Kursk, 4 July to 23 August 1943

One of the largest land battles of the 20th century, the battle of Kursk was fought between the Red Army fielding 3,600 tanks and 1,300,000 soldiers, and the German Army of 2,700 tanks and 800,000 soldiers. Although the Red Army lost 1,500 tanks and suffered 860,000 casualties, this engagement was their victory and the battle of Kursk led the way to the recovery of the city of Kharkov.

The end of the war

The tide began to turn against Germany in 1943, and over the next two years the Red Army slowly but methodically marched westwards in the wake of the retreating Germans. The Red Army claimed to have 'liberated' the Baltic States, Poland, and

Activity 22 ATL Thinking skills

Study the source below and answer the questions that follow.

A Soviet poster from World War II showing how 'The Big Three will tie the enemy in knots'. The arms of Soviet Russia, Great Britain, and the United States tie a strangling knot around Hitler's neck.

1. What is the message conveyed in the cartoon?
2. What methods did the Big Three use to 'tie the enemy in knots'?

much of Central and Eastern Europe. Post-1989 interpretations in these countries, however, would argue that although the German Army was driven out, what followed was another occupation. As the Red Army marched to Berlin, they had no pity for the German people: an estimated 2 million German women were raped in the areas that were now under Red Army occupation. Rape was both a weapon of war and a revenge for the destruction wreaked on the Soviet Union, when German forces had razed 70,000 villages, killing hundreds of thousands of civilians.

The wartime conferences at Tehran, Moscow, and Yalta discussed the borders of post-war Europe. Stalin was adamant that, in future, any invasion launched against the Soviet Union would be halted in neighbouring countries, which would provide a security zone to protect the Soviet Union. The German surrender took place on 8 May 1945, although the commemorations in the Soviet Union always took place on 9 May. It was not until 9 August that the Soviet Union joined the war on Japan, occupying northern Manchuria, and acquiring the Kurile Islands and South Sakhalin.

Activity 23 ATL Thinking, research, and self-management skills

1. Why did the Red Army defeat Germany?

Reasons for Stalin's victory

Control over resources and strategy

The Soviet Union was already a planned economy in 1941, and it made a seamless transition to '**total war**' conditions in which the government controls the production

 Just as it is a good idea to consider why victorious countries win wars, it is also worth asking why the defeated countries lose. Consider why the Soviet Union, with its purged military and recently industrialized economy, was able to hold off the German invasion. It is also worth asking why a vast landmass where the people had endured so much hardship in the name of 'socialism' would be prepared to wage war to save a regime that was so brutal. Some possible reasons are listed in the following section.

and distribution of resources. Stephen Lee, in *Stalin and the Soviet Union*, mentions however that production levels in the Soviet Union escalated with the loosening of centralized control in 1943, suggesting that local control of production proved more effective than central planning.

The State Committee of Defence (GOKO) was set up on 30 June 1941, with Stalin as its chairman. He was an indefatigable war leader, taking charge of every aspect of the defence of the Soviet Union. He rarely visited the frontline, but he followed the actions of his generals closely and made it clear to them that retreat or defeat in battle was not an option. Order No. 270 of the State Committee of August 1941 decreed that 'those who surrendered to the Germans "should be destroyed by all means available, from the air or from the ground, and their families deprived of all benefits", while deserters should be shot on the spot and their families arrested'.

Stalin used propaganda very effectively during the war. As mentioned earlier, the so-called 'Great Patriotic War' was fought to save the Soviet Motherland rather than an ideological war to save communism. Stalin understood that people would fight to save their country, when they may not have fought so determinedly for an ideology.

A 'racial war'

For Hitler, this war in the East was a racial war against an enemy that was considered to be 'sub-human'. It was to be a war of extermination in keeping with Nazi ideology, but strategically this was a huge error. Initially, there was support for the German forces in areas of the Ukraine and in the Baltic States, as they were often seen as liberators. This mood changed, however, as the death toll of civilians mounted from German policies of extermination and eviction. Even so, an estimated 2 million Soviet citizens fought on the side of the Germans. To prevent any risk of further internal disturbance, Stalin 're-settled' large numbers of Chechens, Karachais, Meskhetians, Crimean Tatars, Balts, Ukrainians, and Cossacks further east. Stephen Lee considers that this had possibly thwarted the risk of more serious rebellion within the Soviet Union (*Stalin and the Soviet Union*, 1999).

The Soviet Union – climate and geography

The *Wehrmacht* made swift progress towards Moscow in the first five months of the war, but stalled just short of the capital city as 'General Winter' brought rain followed by frost and snow. The severe climate may not have been the main reason for the long-term defeat of the German Army, but it contributed to slowing their advance in 1941 and gave the Red Army a breathing space in which to recover. Stalin brought General Zhukov back from the border between Japanese-occupied China and the Soviet Union in order to defend Moscow, a crucial and very successful decision.

The huge expanse of the Soviet Union was also an advantage. The Soviet forces could sacrifice territory to the advancing Germans and retreat eastwards. Also, many factories could be dismantled and the infrastructure, along with the workforce, shipped east of the Urals, reassembled and brought back into production. Geoffrey Hosking mentions that 10 million people were transferred east of the Urals and that by 1945, over half of the metal output of the Soviet Union was produced there, compared with a fifth in 1940 (*A History of the Soviet Union 1917–1991*, 1992, p. 283). This was enormously important as it meant that the Soviet Union was able to keep its factories working.

Allied assistance

External help was also important, as Stalin received very substantial aid, especially trucks and jeeps, from the US Lend-Lease arrangement that was extended to the Soviet Union as early as the summer of 1941. Britain's merchant marine, assisted by the Royal Navy, also shipped vast quantities of equipment to the Soviet Union along the treacherous Arctic passage to Murmansk.

Theatres of war

The end of the siege of Stalingrad came around the same time as the defeat of German forces at El Alamein in North Africa. The Allied invasion of Sicily also took place at the same time as the battle of Kursk, requiring German forces to be diverted to Italy. Although there can be no doubt that the brunt of the fighting in Europe took place on the Eastern Front, some of the more momentous turning points need to be placed within the context of World War II as a whole.

More than 27 million Soviet citizens (of whom at least 20 million were civilians) were killed during World War II. This was a tremendous sacrifice, and made the losses of Britain and the United States seem small by comparison. This fact was not lost on Stalin, who used it to his advantage at meetings with Churchill and Roosevelt.

Stalin's leadership

Stalin's leadership was an important factor in his victory. Historians such as Roberts and Volkogonov assert that Stalin learned from his generals, and his skills as a wartime leader improved over time. He was also ruthless in his willingness to sacrifice troops and tireless in his efforts to keep the war effort going.

Stalin emerged from the Great Patriotic War as the undisputed *vozhd* (leader) of the Soviet Union. It was Stalin who, according to state propaganda, had saved the Soviet Union from the Nazi invaders. Even though Stalin visited the front only once, in 1943, he made a great deal of this theatrical appearance and referred to it in correspondence with Roosevelt. Posters and postcards were produced to herald his commitment to the war effort; statues were raised to praise his role as 'liberator'; articles and books placed Stalin in the pantheon of Great Russian leaders, such as Peter the Great. Less was known inside the Soviet Union of the 'smaller fronts', as they were called, such as the hard-fought battles in the Pacific, North Africa, or Western Europe following the Normandy landings in June 1944.

The Soviet Union came out of World War II with territorial gains that restored land taken in 1919 from the former Russian Empire. Stalin was now a world statesman and the Soviet Union a world superpower. Despite this, its economy was devastated and Stalin lost no time in demanding more sacrifice, more unrelenting hard work, and promising more lean years with no hope yet of a better standard of living for Soviet citizens.

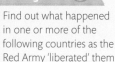

Research and thinking skills **ATL**

Find out what happened in one or more of the following countries as the Red Army 'liberated' them from Nazi rule: Hungary, Bulgaria, Romania. How did the political structure of these countries change as the war came to an end?

Stalin visits the frontline

Stalin made a visit to the Kalinin Front in August 1943. He stayed in the small village of Khoroshevo in the cottage of an old lady. He met with his generals, who travelled many miles to the meeting and who were astonished by the humble surroundings. One whispered to another that the very basic environment was intended to 'resemble the front', and so create a favourable impression for propaganda purposes.

The East–West divide after 1949.

An overview of Stalin's foreign policy in his maintenance of power

Like many authoritarian leaders, Stalin used foreign policy to enhance his control over the Soviet Union. For example, he emphasized the threat from external enemies to justify the very harsh methods used to achieve the rapid industrialization of the Soviet Union. The population had to accept that the very survival of the Soviet Union was imperilled if the Five-Year Plans did not succeed. Also, you may recall that during the purges, managers who failed to meet production quotas were labelled as traitors and spies. In the same way, leading members of the Communist Party, such as Zinoviev, Kamenev, and Bukharin, were accused of being spies and of supporting Fascism. The same accusation was made against Trotsky and those labelled as Trotskyites. In this way, Stalin heightened the fear of war, and convinced the population of the absolute necessity for unity and an unquestioning acceptance of his guidance and leadership.

In the Soviet Union, the use of propaganda to convey foreign policy to the population was very important. The swift turnaround from Nazi Germany being an arch-enemy to being an ally reflects how successful propaganda could be (or was the population too afraid to ask questions?). Similarly, when World War II was over, propaganda showed Britain and the United States as bitter enemies. The fear of another war, this time against former allies, justified the endurance of further hardship to ensure the rapid recovery of the Soviet Union and a policy of anti-cosmopolitanism to enforce isolation from the West.

Activity 24

 **Thinking skills**

This is a good time to reflect on the aims of Stalin's foreign policy up to 1945.

1. Make a list of how there was a) change and b) continuity in Stalin's foreign policy from 1929 to 1939, and again from 1941 to 1945.

2. What were the causes of the changes and the continuity that you mentioned?

2.4 Stalin and the Soviet Union after 1945

The Soviet Union emerged from World War II as a world superpower. The people had suffered enormously and made huge sacrifices, but when the war was finally over, it was evidently clear that the Soviet Union had regained the borders of the former Russian Empire and that its political reach extended into Central and Eastern Europe.

Economic recovery after 1945

The devastation suffered during the war meant that the recovery of the Soviet economy was a gargantuan task. Some indication of the scale of the challenge is given in a book written by John Fischer, a member of the United Nations Relief and Reconstruction Agency (UNRRA) mission to Ukraine in 1946. He wrote about his experiences in *The Scared Men in the Kremlin*, published in 1947. He described daily life both in the cities and in the rural areas that he visited, and repeated many times that he was at liberty to ask any questions he liked and to mix freely with ordinary members of the public as well as party officials.

Fischer's account provides a fascinating insight into post-war Ukraine and he recognizes the enormous hardship experienced in simply finding enough food, clothing, and shelter in a region devastated by war.

> *In Kiev, least damaged of the big cities, each person was supposed to have six square metres of living space. That means a strip of floor about ten feet long and six feet wide – somewhat larger than a grave – on which to sleep, cook, eat and store one's possessions. In Kharkov … the official allocation was 4.8 square metres… If you really want to know how a typical Ukrainian family lives, pick the smallest room in your house or apartment and move your wife*

and children into it. Then pack in the beds, spare clothes, and furniture which you regard as absolutely indispensible. Knock off a few chunks of plaster and most of the paint… Scrap the radiators and cooking range and substitute for both a brick stove which seldom raises the winter temperature much above freezing. Break off the hot water tap in the bathroom, which you will share with several other families. Finally, invite your widowed cousin Sophie and her four youngsters to move in with you.

From John Fischer, *The Scared Men in the Kremlin*, Hamish Hamilton, 1947

John Fischer also wrote of the difficulty faced by ordinary people to find fresh food, beyond the small pieces of meat, limited array of vegetables, or the few eggs brought into markets by peasants who were able to cultivate small private plots. When the Fourth Five-Year Plan was announced in 1946, it called upon the citizens of the Soviet Union, once again, to put aside any hope of increased production of consumer goods and to focus on industrial and agricultural production.

Just how bad this news was did not dawn on the Russians until March 15th 1946, when the government announced the details of the first of its new Five-Year Plans. This document outlined a truly back-breaking task. It called for the restoration of all industries wrecked in the war, plus an increase in output nearly fifty per cent above the pre-war level.

From John Fischer, *The Scared Men in the Kremlin*, Hamish Hamilton, 1947

The losses were so immense that they were almost incalculable: 70,000 villages, 98,000 kolkhozi completely or partly destroyed, 1,876 sovkhozi, 17 million head of cattle and 7 million horses driven away; 65,000 kilometres of railway track, half of all railway bridges in occupied territory, over half all urban living space there, 1.2 million houses destroyed as well as 3.5 million rural homes. And then, there was the greatest loss of all, the 20 million dead, as well as the maimed in body and mind.

From Martin McCauley, *The Soviet Union 1917–1991*, 2nd ed., Routledge, 1993

Despite the enormous task that lay before the Soviet people, and despite the immense difficulties of restoring infrastructure and repairing factories and mines, the official claim was that by 1950 industrial production was 75 per cent higher than in 1940. The rearming of the Red Army remained a priority that increased in importance as the Cold War took hold. Labour and resources were also diverted to the building of the atomic bomb, tested in 1949. Agriculture was far slower to recover and by 1950 the grain harvest amounted to only 40 per cent of that of 1940 (McCauley, *The Soviet Union 1917–1991*, 1993). The recovery of numbers of farm animals was also slow and was hampered by the pseudo-science of Lysenkoism.

Domestic policies after 1945 – aims and results

Stalin continued to push forward his plan for 'Russification', as he wanted to introduce Russian settlers into the Baltic States, to weaken nationalism, and impose the Russian culture and language. This plan extended to Moldova, where the purging of the local population and the 'planting' of ethnic Russians took place. Anti-Semitism also resurfaced with a crackdown on Jewish literature, journalism, and culture, as well as a purging of Jewish officials from the higher levels of the party leadership.

Known as the *Zhdanovshchina*, a campaign was led by Andrei Zhdanov, the Leningrad Party leader, to remove all 'Western' influence from music and literature. Prokofiev and Shostakovich were among the composers whose music was now criticized, along with the poetry of Anna Akhmatova. There was even criticism of Einstein's theory of relativity, which was declared to be 'bourgeois' and 'reactionary'.

Lysenkoism

Named after Trofim Lysenko, this was a popular 'scientific' hypothesis that was based upon the theory of 'inherited characteristics'. Put simply, it was the belief that characteristics (in animals or plants) developed in one generation could be passed on to the next. Such ideas had been popularized by Professor William McDougall who, working at Harvard University, had suggested that rats could learn to negotiate a maze and that this characteristic could be passed on to new generations. Lysenko experimented by freezing wheat grains in snow in the belief that he was developing strains of wheat that would grow in winter. He also thought that breeding cows with high milk yields with those with high beef yields would automatically produce animals with both characteristics. Although they remained popular in the Soviet Union until the 1960s, his ideas were based on faulty genetics.

After Zhdanov's death in 1948, Stalin carried out a purge of the Leningrad Party known as the 'Leningrad Affair'. This was followed by another purge known as the 'Doctor's Plot' in November 1952, when the mostly Jewish doctors in the Kremlin were arrested and accused of killing their patients, including Zhdanov. It was probably Stalin's death in March 1953 that saved the lives of his closest comrades, including Beria, Molotov, Mikoyan, and Malenkov.

Terror and propaganda after 1945

The purges of the 1930s were not repeated on the same scale after 1945, although returning prisoners of war, along with White Russians and Cossacks whom Stalin had insisted be returned to the Soviet Union, were often shot or sent to a distant gulag. Stalin did not want to risk knowledge of the outside world penetrating the walls of the Soviet Union. Norman Lowe notes that an estimated 2.8 million soldiers who had survived imprisonment in German camps returned to the Soviet Union 'to be arrested and interrogated by the NKVD' (*Mastering Twentieth Century Russian History*, 2002). Of these, only around 500,000 (or one-sixth) were allowed to return home.

New labour camps were built mostly to hold 'bandits', the term used to denote nationalists in Ukraine and in the Baltic States. Dmitri Volkogonov in *The Rise and Fall of the Soviet Empire* estimates that more than 90,000 'kulaks and their families, bandits, nationalists and others' were deported from the Baltic States alone. By 1947 there were more than 20 million prisoners in the gulags and 27 additional camps had been built. A law was passed 'imposing twenty years hard labour for anyone attempting to escape from exile' (*The Rise and Fall of the Soviet Empire*, 1999). For most people, however, the Great Terror was a grim memory and few people would have dared to plot against Stalin or even to criticize Soviet rule. Show trials and the purges did take place in Central and Eastern Europe, however, where local communist parties were ruthlessly purged with the same random selection of victims as in the Soviet Union during the 1930s.

Within the Soviet Union, gratitude for victory in the Great Patriotic War boosted Stalin's popularity further, and the suffering undoubtedly led people to believe that whatever hardship came with peace, it did not begin to compare with the suffering endured during the war.

Activity 25 Research, thinking, and communication skills

There is no doubt that the Cold War had a decisive influence on Stalin's decision to push for a rapid recovery for war-torn Soviet Union and to divert resources towards the building of an atomic bomb. He feared the West and galvanized the Soviet population, once again, to rearm and to rebuild the economy.

It is also worth considering where Soviet policy towards Central and Eastern Europe fits in. Is this domestic or foreign policy? Countries such as Poland, Romania, and Hungary are not within the Soviet Union, and so need not be discussed in an answer to an exam question that asks about Stalin's post-war domestic policy. Even so, via **Cominform** and **Comecon** the Soviet Union did have a very significant impact upon the internal policies of these countries and, to a lesser extent, vice versa.

For example, consider the following question:

> *Compare and contrast the successes and failures of the foreign policies of two authoritarian leaders, each chosen from a different region.*

If you chose Stalin as one of your leaders, you could go beyond 1941 (unless the question states otherwise) and you could make a reference to the extension of Soviet influence to Central and Eastern Europe (using some specific examples), linking this to Stalin's concerns about security.

Stalin's role as a world leader

Even before the end of World War II, Stalin was already a recognized world leader and his meetings with Winston Churchill and Franklin Roosevelt to determine post-war arrangements have been well documented. Unlikely allies, the 'Big Three' were in close contact throughout the war and historians have discussed, extensively, the nature of their pre-war, wartime, and post-war relationships. It is still a matter of heated debate at what stage the wartime allies became post-war enemies.

Churchill, Roosevelt, and Stalin meet at Yalta in February 1945.

Activity 26
ATL Thinking, research, and social skills

Along with Tehran (November 1943) and Potsdam (July 1945), Yalta was one of the three wartime conferences.

1. What was discussed at Yalta and what decisions were made about the post-war world?
2. To what extent was Yalta both the end of the wartime alliance and the beginning of the Cold War? Working with a classmate, think of how you would support arguments to both a) agree and b) disagree with this assertion.

How did Stalin influence the Cold War?

There is a great deal of **historiography** concerning the role of Stalin in the outbreak of the Cold War. His actions and motives have been carefully scrutinized by many historians, but the following events are worthy of investigation.

- In 1945, Soviet expansion into Central and Eastern Europe aroused the fears and suspicion of the United States. There was concern that Stalin was intending to extend Soviet influence over the whole of Europe.
- After the Potsdam conference in July 1945, Stalin did not meet again with the Western leaders and this contributed to a climate of suspicion. Unlike Franklin Roosevelt, President Truman did not seem to want to cooperate or compromise with Stalin.
- Stalin's 'election speech' of 1946 suggested that the Soviet Union was, once again, using anti-Western rhetoric and this implied that the post-war peace was fragile.
- Hiroshima and Nagasaki brought in the atomic age and although Stalin had placed Beria in charge of a project to build a Soviet atom bomb, this was not tested until 1949. Meanwhile, the Baruch Plan of 1946 was proposed but rejected by Stalin, who was not content to have UN control over nuclear arms.
- The Marshall Plan of 1947 (European Recovery Programme) was condemned by the Soviet Union as 'dollar imperialism', and Poland and Czechoslovakia were prevented from taking part in this US-led plan for economic recovery. This prompted the communist takeover of Czechoslovakia.
- When the United States and Britain united their zones of Germany in 1946, calling it Bizonia, Stalin objected as he argued that this was contrary to agreements on the administration of occupied Germany. France was persuaded to attach its zone to Bizonia in 1948, making it Trizonia. The Marshall Plan also made it imperative that the economy of the Western zones was placed on a sound footing, leading to the introduction of a new West German currency. Whether or not this could also be introduced into the western sectors of Berlin led to a difference of opinion with the Soviet Union and prompted what became known as the Berlin Blockade of 1948–49. Although Stalin's intention was to push the Western powers out of Berlin, this strategy rebounded on him, and he had to lift the blockade in May 1949.
- In many of the Central and Eastern European states that came under Soviet control, free elections were held in the post-war period. Gradually, however, 'salami tactics' (cutting something slice by slice) enabled the communist parties, which were often part of coalition governments, to control the police or the justice system. Little by little, the communists would end up in power and these countries became known as the 'satellite states'.
- The Cold War turned into a 'hot war' in 1950 with the invasion of South Korea by North Korea. At the time, the United States suspected that this had been instigated by the Soviet Union, although later research showed quite clearly that Kim Il Sung, the leader of communist North Korea, had been the one to approach Stalin to ask for support.

Activity 27 **Self-management, research, communication, and thinking skills**

If you already study the Cold War, then it is likely that you will be familiar with Stalin's very significant contribution to post-war international relations. This belongs to World History: Topic 12, The Cold War, and so will not be discussed in detail here.

The list you have read earlier includes most of the main events that are discussed in relation to the origins of the Cold War. See if you can rewrite each one to reflect the different historiographical interpretations of the Cold War (see Interesting Fact opposite).

For example: 'The United States misread Soviet concerns about security and believed that Stalin intended to expand Soviet influence beyond Central and Eastern Europe.'

Historiography of the Cold War

The three interpretations of the origins of the Cold War include the following:

1. The Orthodox view sees US actions to be a response to the expansionist policies of the Soviet Union.

2. The Revisionist view blames the United States for over-reacting to Soviet concerns about its security.

3. The Post-Revisionist view sees both the United States and the Soviet Union reacting with fear and suspicion towards each other.

The death of Stalin

Stalin ruled the Soviet Union from 1929 until 1953, longer than any other leader. He created the Soviet system of government and was the undisputed leader of world communism during his lifetime. Stalin had not been in good health for several years before his death, and in March 1953 he suffered a serious stroke that killed him. When he died, there was much relief but also anguish about the future of the Soviet Union. Stalin had gathered around him a small group of dedicated supporters who knew that not only their jobs but their lives depended on Stalin's goodwill. He never ceased to tell those most likely to succeed him that when he was gone, the West would challenge the Soviet Union and 'the capitalists will crush you like little kittens.' In fact, the Soviet Union maintained its role as a world superpower, but the legacy of Stalin continued through the all-powerful secret police, the lack of political freedom, and the strictly controlled command economy.

Activity 28

 Thinking, research, and communication skills

This chapter has looked at the rise to power of Stalin and his time as the authoritarian leader of the Soviet Union. Exam questions on authoritarian states/leaders may ask about:

- the rise to power of a ruler or the establishment of an authoritarian state
- the kinds of policies that were introduced, how they were implemented, and how successful they were
- how a leader consolidated his power
- what kind of opposition he faced and the methods used to deal with it.

When you prepare for the exam, be sure to revise these themes. You may also be asked to compare and contrast two authoritarian leaders, for example:

> ***Compare and contrast the methods used to consolidate power by two authoritarian leaders.***

Plan an essay outline that addresses each of the following topics, showing the similarities and the differences in the way they were used by Stalin and one other leader:

- Propaganda (Don't forget to consider how propaganda was communicated as well as what it conveyed.)
- Economic policies (Did they both use a planned economy?)
- Social policies (What was the role of education, the role of women, religion, etc.?)
- The use of terror and the secret police
- Purges of the ruling party

Can you think of any other 'methods' you could add to this list?

 The way we look at the past and the kinds of opinions we have about leaders like Stalin or the origins of the Cold War are influenced by the work of historians. Invariably, historians judge events differently according to their fields of research, their scholarly backgrounds, or their generation. Throughout this chapter, the works of different historians have been mentioned so you can see where the information comes from. It is quite a good idea when you answer an exam question to remember that historians have reached different conclusions about Stalin's purges, for example, and it can be useful to mention one or two historians to show that you are familiar with more than one interpretation. Do be careful, however, not to just list the names and views of different historians without answering the question. Examiners like to see that you are aware of what has been written about a topic, but a list of pre-learned quotations from historians does not make a good response.

Activity 29

Revision activity

Look back at the chapter breakdown on page 53. Do you feel confident that you could answer an examination question on all of these topics? Pick your weakest topic and spend some time revising it, then try out one of the practice questions contained in this chapter. Go to the chapter titled 'Comparing and contrasting authoritarian states', and compare Stalin or the Soviet Union with another leader or region. There are lots of ideas in that chapter to help you draw out relevant points for comparison.

 To access websites relevant to this chapter, go to www.pearsonhotlinks. com, search for the book title or ISBN, and click on 'Chapter 2'.

03

Mao Zedong and China

Spelling systems for transliterating Chinese

There are two systems of transliterating Chinese characters, especially names, into Western text: Wade–Giles and Pinyin. The Wade–Giles system was used by scholars and historians until the late 20th century, when Pinyin became the international standard. This chapter uses the Pinyin method: for example, *Mao Zedong* (Pinyin) not *Mao Tse-Tung* (Wade–Giles); *Guomindang* not *Kuomintang*; *Jiang Jieshi* not *Chiang Kai-shek*. However, depending on when they were written, you will find that some of the sources or names mentioned in the chapter use Wade–Giles spellings.

This chapter examines the rise to power of Mao and his years as the authoritarian leader of the People's Republic of China. It focuses on:

- the conditions of China during the early 20th century and the political influences at work during Mao's early adulthood
- the emergence of the Communist Party of China and how Mao rose to a position of power within it
- the impact of the Second Sino-Japanese War and the Chinese Civil War on Mao's rise to power
- the establishment of the People's Republic of China under the leadership of Mao with reference to his economic, social, and foreign policies
- the kind of opposition that Mao feared would challenge his authority and what methods he used to deal with this
- the Cultural Revolution and the impact this had upon Mao's authority
- the views of different historians on Mao's rule.

Key concepts:

As you work through this chapter, bear in mind the key concepts we use when studying history:

- **Change**: How much did people's lives change in China when Mao established the People's Republic of China in 1949?

- **Continuity**: China had a deeply traditional social system based on the teachings of Confucius. Consider which aspects of this society remained untouched by the Communist Revolution.

- **Causation**: What were the causes of the Cultural Revolution in 1966? When we think about the causes of historical events, how far back should we go?

- **Consequence**: If you had to examine the economic and social consequences of Mao's policies, what kind of information would you need in order to answer the question?

- **Significance**: When you read about Mao's foreign policy, see if you agree that it didn't seem so important inside China but had great significance for the development of the Cold War, even for countries like the United States that, for the most part, were slow to realize that, for example, the Sino-Soviet split had taken place.

- **Perspective**: Mao is still revered in China as a great leader but China is now a very successful economic superpower. Does this change the way Mao is perceived by the Communist Party of China?

This chapter deals with the emergence of Mao Zedong as the authoritarian leader of China, his aims and policies, and how he consolidated and maintained power. Mao Zedong was in power for over 25 years, from 1949 until his death in 1976. During that time, he transformed China into a strongly centralized state dominated by the rule of the **Communist Party of China**.

Timeline of events – 1893–1976

1893	Mao was born in Hunan Province. His father had been a prosperous farmer.
1894–95	The First Sino-Japanese War takes place.
1911	In what becomes known as the Double Tenth Revolution of 10 October 1911, the last emperor of China is removed and a republic is established in 1912.
1921	Mao, a librarian at Peking (Beijing) University, becomes one of the founding members of the Communist Party of China (CPC).
1923	Acting on the Comintern's instructions, members of the CPC also became members of the Guomindang (GMD) to form the United Front.
1925	Following the death of Sun Yixian, Jiang Jieshi becomes leader of the GMD.
1926	The Northern Expedition is launched to rid China of warlordism and to unite the country under the leadership of the GMD.
1926–27	The United Front ends, as the GMD purge the CPC. This leads to the Shanghai Massacre, also known as the White Terror. The First Civil War begins.
1927	The Autumn Harvest Uprising in Hunan province leads Mao to revise his views on Marxism.
1927	Mao goes to Jiangxi province to join other Communists fleeing the White Terror. The First Chinese Civil War ends with the establishment of the Second United Front.
1931	The Jiangxi Soviet is established.
1934–35	The Long March to Yan'an takes place.
1935–45	Mao creates the Yan'an Soviet.
1936–45	The Xi'an Incident leads to the Second United Front against the Japanese.
1937–45	The Second Sino-Japanese War takes place in mainland China.
1946–49	Mao and the CPC defeat Jiang Jieshi and the GMD in the Second Chinese Civil War.
1949	The People's Republic of China (PRC) is founded on 1 October.
1950	The Marriage Reform Law and Agrarian Land Reform Law are enacted. The Korean War begins.
1951–52	The Three Antis and the Five Antis Campaigns are waged against the remnants of capitalism.
1953–57	The First Five-Year Plan, modelled on those of the Soviet Union, is introduced in China.
1956	The Hundred Flowers Campaign is launched.
1957	The Anti-Rightist Movement carries out purges of critics of the regime.
1958–63	The Great Leap Forward begins; the Second Five-Year Plan is introduced.
1961	The Sino-Soviet split begins.
1962–66	The Socialist Education Movement is formed.
1966–76	The Great Proletarian Cultural Revolution takes place.
1971	Lin Biao dies, suspected of having betrayed Mao.
1972	Mao meets Nixon in Beijing.
1976	Zhou Enlai, Zhu De, and Mao Zedong die.

3.1 The emergence of an authoritarian state

This section looks at the conditions in which the Communist Party of China (CPC) was able to establish itself as a revolutionary, ideological force in China. Economic factors were important, because most of the Chinese population was very poor, and this contributed to deep social divisions. After the fall of the **Qing dynasty**, the political system was weak and there was a lack of centralized government control; China faced not only a civil war but also a major war against Japan.

On 1 October 1949, Mao declared the establishment of the People's Republic of China (PRC): this was not seen as an accomplished fact, but rather the first step towards what was realistically seen as a long struggle. According to Maurice Meisner, 'three years of recovery and ten years of development' became the slogan that reflected the importance of having realistic aims and emphasizing stability and unity (*Mao's China and After*, 1999, p. 57). Unlike many other authoritarian rulers, Mao came to power after a long period of conflict that included the First Chinese Civil War (1927–36), the Second Sino-Japanese War (1937–45), and the Second Chinese Civil War (1946–49). During this long wait for power, Mao had many opportunities to put his ideas into practice, for example, in the Jiangxi and Yan'an Soviets. He also had opportunities to think, discuss, and debate how the ideology of Marxism–Leninism could apply to China. We can now proceed to examine the importance of Mao's rise to power and how this long period of waiting in the wings deeply influenced his rule.

Mao's background and role in the establishment of an authoritarian state in China

Like many men who later became authoritarian leaders, Mao's background was one of relative prosperity. His father was a successful peasant farmer, who was able to afford a good, if basic, education for his three sons. Although he did not have a scholarly background, Mao was to become an assistant librarian at Peking (Beijing) University. As a young man, he had already become interested in politics, having been born when the Qing dynasty was in decline and unable to prevent the expansion of foreign influence in China. During the 19th century, China had lost wars to both Britain and Japan, as its military forces were no match for these industrialized states. In addition, China had been forced to agree to a number of treaties (known in China as the unequal treaties) – granting territorial and/or trading concessions – with countries such as Russia, Britain, France, Germany, and the United States. Although China did not become the colonial possession of any country, its independence was compromised and it suffered loss of prestige.

The responses to foreign interference were twofold:

- *The Boxer Rebellion of 1900*: This violent uprising against foreign powers – the rebels themselves encouraged by the Dowager Empress Cixi – took place mostly in the north of China and was centred on Beijing. The failed rebellion (the Boxers were eventually subdued by an international force) came upon the heels of the First Sino-Japanese War of 1894–95 that pitted China against the rapidly modernizing Meiji Empire of Japan. Japan won the war quite swiftly and emerged as one of the dominant powers in East Asia.

- *Sun Yixian and the Three Principles of the People*: A medical doctor by profession, Sun Yixian (commonly known as Sun Yat-sen) was a staunch Chinese patriot despite

The Boxers

These were members of a secret organization called the Society of the Righteous and Harmonious Fists. They were called Boxers by Westerners because the members believed their boxing skills gave them not only physical but also spiritual strength, which would keep them unharmed, even from bullets. Their aim was to rid China of foreign involvement, particularly that of missionaries who tried to convert the poor to Christianity.

dynasty. He believed in the primary importance of the modernization of China and in the introduction of democracy. His 'Three Principles' were Nationalism, Democracy, and the People's Livelihood. Sun called his movement the Alliance League, but, after the 1911 Revolution, changed its name to the **Guomindang (GMD)**, which is translated as the Chinese Nationalist Party.

Having grown up in such tumultuous times, it was not surprising that Mao Zedong should be influenced by these events and, as an 18-year-old, he would have been aware of the 1911 Revolution that overthrew the Qing dynasty. The revolution was not very well organized and grew out of the refusal of troops to suppress an uprising; nevertheless, it ended millennia of imperial rule and laid the foundations for the Republic of China. Sun Yixian was appointed president, despite his having been in the United States at the time of the revolution. He did not remain in this post for long, however, as Yuan Shikai, a military officer, used the army as a bargaining tool to ensure the abdication of Puyi, the five-year-old emperor, as well as to replace Sun as president. The explanation offered to the people was that the Mandate of Heaven had now passed on to the Republic.

The Mandate of Heaven

This was the term used to justify the rule of an emperor who was also the Son of Heaven. According to Immanuel Hsu, an emperor was obliged to be 'moral, virtuous and attentive to the needs of his subjects' (*The Rise of Modern China*, 1995, p.46). Indeed, there was a long list of characteristics that were considered essential for good governance, and if the emperor failed to honour these, then a coup or a rebellion might occur because the emperor would have lost the Mandate of Heaven. You can think of this as a kind of right to rule bestowed upon an emperor who could also lose this right if he did not respect the duties of his office.

CHALLENGE YOURSELF

ATL Thinking, social, communication, and self-management skills

Working with a classmate, do some research on the following topics:

- Emperor Puyi
- the Double Tenth Revolution
- President Yuan Shikai

See if you can find a way to link all three and present your findings to the class.

Activity 1

ATL Thinking and research skills

Cartoon analysis

Study the source below and answer the question that follows.

The 'John' referred to in the caption "Hold on, John!" is John Bull (a symbol of Britain), dressed here as a sailor.

"HOLD ON, JOHN!"

1. Name the countries depicted in the source. What does this cartoon tell you about the relationship that China had with these countries? Can you think of an appropriate caption that would effectively convey the message of the cartoon?

In 1916, Yuan proposed changes to the constitution that would allow him to become Emperor. This was resisted, both by his supporters and his enemies, and his grand schemes came to nothing. Immanuel Hsu suggests that Yuan was 'overcome by his own megalomania … he failed to see the old imperial system could never return' (*The Rise of Modern China*, 1995, p. 480). Yuan Shikai did not live long after he became president. He died in June 1916.

China and World War I

The Anglo-Japanese Alliance 1902

This was a treaty signed by Britain and Japan in 1902 that gave focus to their mutual interests in China and Korea. It was notable for bringing Britain out of its period of 'splendid isolation' and also for influencing the decision by France not to support its ally, Russia, in the Russo-Japanese War of 1904–05. In 1914, Japan adhered to the spirit of this treaty by supporting Britain in World War I.

To place the events you have read about so far in their historical context, it is worth thinking about how World War I influenced events in China at the time. Germany, Britain, France, and Russia all had interests in the Far East, and Japan had been very quick to announce its commitment to the Anglo-Japanese Alliance of 1902.

Japan proceeded to 'look after' British and German interests in China (at the time, Germany had control over the Shandong province). In 1915, Japan issued its **Twenty-one Demands** to the government of China. Yuan Shikai acceded to these demands, giving another reason for the growth of opposition towards him. The demands demonstrated Japan's desire to increase its influence over China and Premier Duan Qirui – partly due to American pressure, partly to benefit from possible loans to help train the army, and partly to defend China against Japanese encroachment – declared war on Germany in 1917. What was most important about World War I's impact on China was that Japan's growing militarism was openly demonstrated, and nationalist tempers rose in response. The May Fourth Movement was one of the main outcomes in China and this, in turn, influenced the emergence of the CPC.

Warlordism

Warlordism is the term used to describe the period of weak government control over China after the death of Yuan Shikai. The warlords were leaders who had their own militias and controlled different regions in the manner of feudal overlords. They fought each other '… for power and self-aggrandisement without any sense, logic or reason' (Hsu, *The Rise of Modern China*, 1995, p. 482).

For Mao, now in Changsha, Hunan, this was a formative period as he witnessed the excesses of one of the most brutal warlords, Zhang 'the Venomous' Jinghui. Zhang was appointed governor of the province in 1917 to replace 'Butcher' Tang (Clements, *Mao Zedong*, 2006, p. 35) – you can imagine what it would have been like to live in a region ruled by someone whose nickname was 'Butcher'! An estimated 21,000 people were executed in Hunan for offences against the regime and Mao became instrumental in organizing a student movement to demand the removal of Zhang.

Whilst Mao was organizing protest movements in Hunan, the May Fourth Movement of 1919 emerged in Beijing. This was a student-led protest that voiced its objection to the terms of the Treaty of Versailles that granted the former German-controlled area of Shandong province to Japan. At least 5,000 protesters called for a general strike and a boycott of Japanese goods. Later on, the terms were changed, but for now Shandong came under Japanese control. According to Hsu, this was the lure to get Japan to agree to join the League of Nations (*The Rise of Modern China*, 1995, p. 505).

Mao's emergence as an activist coincided with what turned out to be a period of disillusionment with the West and a growing interest in the ideas of Marx by the intelligentsia. Mao was particularly drawn to these ideas and Jonathan Clements mentions how Mao was also impressed by the repeal of the unequal treaties of the Tsarist era by the new government of the Soviet Union. Indeed, Mao was so impressed that he briefly tried to learn Russian, although he found the Cyrillic alphabet an obstacle to his progress (Clements, *Mao Zedong*, 2006, p. 36).

Mao and the emergence of the CPC

One reason Mao and other like-minded protestors were drawn to the Soviet Union was because it rejected imperialism – echoing decades of Chinese opposition to the influence of foreign powers. Furthermore, according to Hsu, the promise of rapid economic development was particularly appealing (*The Rise of Modern China*, 1995, p. 515). In this way, the ideology of communism came to represent a way to reject the West while also surpassing its achievements. A group devoted to the study of Marxism–Leninism, known as the New Tide Society, was set up in 1918 at Peking University, where Mao was a library assistant. Along with many other groups of similar political views, the New Tide Society was to lead to the establishment of the CPC. Prior to this, there had been two branches of the society: one in Shanghai (set up secretly at the Po-Wen Middle School for Girls, located in the French Concession) under the leadership of Chen Duxui, and one in Beijing under Li Dazhao. With the assistance of representatives from the Comintern, the two branches were united to form the CPC.

> **TOK**
>
> It is not always easy to find reliable sources on modern Chinese history as, even today, there is control over access to archival material. In the 1970s, Hong Kong became a base for many academics, journalists, and government officials, who became known as 'China watchers'. These people would look closely at any information coming out of China. For example, they would read *The People's Daily* (the official newspaper published also in English) and look for hints of news about the CPC to try to spot any changes in policy or personnel. How, do you think, did this very limited access to information about China affect what the West knew about it?

Activity 2   **Knowledge and research skills**

Study the source below and answer the questions that follow.

❝ *When the news of the Paris Peace Conference finally reached us we were greatly shocked. We at once awoke to the fact that foreign nations were still selfish and militaristic and that they were all great liars. I remember the night of May 2ⁿᵈ and very few of us slept. A group of my friends and I talked almost the whole night. We came to the conclusion that a greater world war would be coming sooner or later, and that this great war would be fought in the East. We had nothing to do with our Government, that we knew very well, and at the same time we could no longer depend upon the principles of any so-called great leader like Woodrow Wilson, for example. Looking at our people and at the pitiful ignorant masses, we couldn't help but feel that we must struggle.*

From Tse-Tsung Chow, *The May 4ᵗʰ Movement: Intellectual Revolution in Modern China*

1. The above extract is from an account of a student who had attended a meeting on 3 May 1919, held at Peking (Beijing) University. The students wanted to send telegrams to Paris begging the Chinese delegates not to sign the Treaty of Versailles. In what way does knowing the background to this extract help you to analyse the value and limitations of this source?

2. What was it about the treatment of China in Paris that had so incensed the students?

Towards the First United Front

The year 1919 was a tempestuous one for Chinese nationalists. There was considerable unease at the way in which China's interests appeared to have been overlooked at the meetings in Paris; the May Fourth Movement was a strident response to this disappointment. There still was no centralized government, with the warlords continuing to dominate much of the country. In the north, Feng Yuxiang, a warlord and supporter of the GMD, established a military government. In the south, there was another government under the leadership of Sun Yixian, who had growing ties with the Comintern and the Soviet Union, where Sun's Three Principles were seen as akin to socialism. Sun was looking for foreign assistance at this time as he was attempting to unite China, and the Soviet Union responded positively. In this way, according to Jonathan Fenby, these neighbouring states developed closer ties and the Comintern, already instrumental in the creation of the CPC, now instructed its members to join forces with the GMD (*The Penguin History of Modern China*, 2008, p. 159).

The CPC had to tone down their radical policies and, according to Fenby, the CPC had to accept they were now in a party that included their **class enemies**, such as businessmen and landlords. Stalin, apparently, was quite at ease with this, but Trotsky criticized what he viewed as a betrayal of the ideology of a 'permanent revolution' (for more on this, see page 63). Meanwhile, Sun sent his best general Jiang Jieshi to Moscow to ask for military aid for what was to become known as the Northern Expedition. Although military experts in Moscow advised Jiang against such a military adventure, another Comintern agent, Mikhail Borodin, was actively helping Sun, not only to apply Leninist principles to organizing the GMD, but also to help train the army. According to Fenby, Lenin was hopeful that China – with its vast population, high levels of poverty, and a growing labour movement in the cities – resembled pre-revolutionary Russia and was ripe for revolution (*The Penguin History of Modern China*, 2008, p. 161).

The United Front was established in 1923. In 1924, the Central Executive Committee (CEC) was set up. Out of 41 seats, the CPC was given ten. Among the CPC representatives on the CEC was Mao Zedong, who was put in charge of the Propaganda Department. In 1926, Mao was promoted and given the leadership of the Peasant Movement Committee (Fenby, p. 161).

As part of the United Front, the CPC grew significantly in popularity, its membership number increasing from a mere 57 in 1921 to 58,000 in 1927, with an additional 30,000 in the Communist Youth League. Sun knew that the United Front would not make progress against the warlords without a strong army, and this led to the establishment of the Whampoa Military Academy in 1924. The Commandant of the Academy was Jiang Jieshi and, under his leadership, it became the training ground for the army of the GMD, which later became the National Revolutionary Army (NRA).

When Sun died of liver cancer in 1925, Jiang became the next leader of the GMD even though he was not the most likely choice. Like Sun, Jiang was determined to unite China and bring the warlords under control, either through alliances or through force. Unlike Sun, however, Jiang was a military man leading a well-trained army. In 1926, he began the Northern Expedition. As it turned out, this would challenge the authority of the warlords and lead to a purge against the CPC.

Communication, thinking, research, and social skills (ATL)

During a visit to the United States, Sun Yixian once referred to Mikhail Borodin as 'China's Lafayette'. With a classmate, do some research on both Borodin and Marquis de Lafayette. Although they were from different centuries, both men were involved with nascent revolutionary movements. See if you can discover what they might have had in common in order to help you understand why Sun made this comment, and what the impact might have been on Sun's American audience.

CHALLENGE YOURSELF

(ATL) **Research and thinking skills**

When Sun Yixian died, Jiang Jieshi became his successor as the leader of the GMD. This was unexpected, but Jiang was ambitious, energetic, and had told his wife, 'If I control the army, I will have the power to control the country. It is my road to leadership.' (Quoted in Fenby, *The Penguin History of Modern China*, 2008, p. 167.) Can you think of any other successors to authoritarian leaders who had, at first, been overlooked? Compare and contrast their rise to power. What methods did they use? Were there certain conditions that helped them rise to power?

The Nanjing Decade, 1928–37

Historians refer to the period 1928–37 as the Nanjing Decade because, in 1928, Jiang Jieshi made Nanjing the capital of China. This city was on the Yangtze River and was located in the heart of GMD-controlled territory between Shanghai and Wuhan. For ten years, Nanjing remained under the control of the GMD and their army.

The end of the First United Front

The Northern Expedition got off to a very successful start as the United Front moved northwards from Guangdong province. At this early stage, Jiang still needed the support of the CPC, but it soon became clear that the NRA was strong enough. The expedition was successful enough for Jiang to achieve another aim – to purge the United Front of Communists. Jiang had long suspected that the Soviet Union had plans to use the CPC as a way to take over the GMD from the inside; in his words, the CPC were 'a disease of the heart'.

Known as the White Terror, the purge of the CPC began in Shanghai in 1927. Here, the workers had been organized by the CPC and, through trade unions, had taken part in strikes for better working conditions. They had been a formidable threat to the many different factions involved in the economy of Shanghai, such as drug lords, triad gangs, and the foreign diplomats who oversaw the different legations. All of these interested groups now helped the GMD establish control of the city. Once this was done, the NRA searched out and executed trade union members and those suspected of sympathizing with the Communists. In doing so, Jiang had the support of the wealthy middle classes, as well as the residents of the international settlements in the city, who feared the anti-imperialist sentiments of the Communists. According to Michael Lynch, over 5,000 Communists, as well as their sympathizers, were executed and similar purges took place in other cities (*China: From Empire to People's Republic*, 1996, p. 37).

The CPC was badly affected by this, although the instructions from Moscow were that the remnants of the CPC should continue to resist for as long as possible. In an attempt to carry out a workers' uprising, Mao was tasked with leading what became known

'A disease of the heart'

Jiang maintained that 'the Japanese are a disease of the skin, but the Communists are a disease of the heart'. By this he meant the Japanese threat was only skin-deep, but that the Communists threatened China in a far more dangerous way and should always to be seen as the real enemy of the GMD.

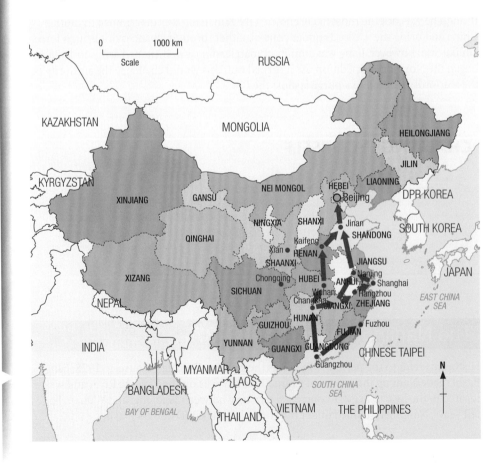

Map of China showing the progress of the GMD, 1926–28.

as the Autumn Harvest Uprising in 1927, but this, too, failed, even though it was to have a deep influence on Mao's interpretation of Marxism–Leninism. Regardless of instructions from Moscow, the surviving members of the CPC either went 'underground' (into hiding) in Shanghai or scattered to remote regions of China, such as Yan'an in Shaanxi province and Jiangxi.

In 1928, the GMD moved north towards Beijing, attempting to negotiate with Zhang Zuolin (also known as the Old Marshal), a warlord who held sway in this area of China and over Manchuria. The Japanese Kwangtung army, which had a powerful presence in Manchuria, was also concerned that Zhang was not sufficiently under its control. It plotted to remove Zhang and did so by assassinating him on 3 June 1928. Zhang's son, Zhang Xueliang (the Young Marshal), who was westernized in his habits, succeeded him. Zhang Xueliang enjoyed driving fast cars and played polo, but he was also a morphine addict. We will hear more of him later (see page 122).

The Northern Expedition was a success. Jiang set up the structure of a national government in Nanjing, while holding on to the reins of power. Although there was little in the way of democracy, the country experienced modest economic growth and there was some semblance of political structure. The CPC had not disappeared, however.

The emergence of Mao as leader of the CPC

As you read this part of the chapter, consider the methods that were used by Mao to rise to the leadership of the CPC. This, after all, was the first step to his becoming the leader of China. The difficult conditions in China certainly helped the CPC to make an impact, but Mao himself also possessed important qualities, such as the ability to make Marxism–Leninism relevant to the condition of the Chinese peasantry and to implement guerrilla warfare against the GMD. You will see that Mao was able to deal with opposition and to challenge, successfully, Communist officials who criticized his ideas and methods.

Mao and the Jiangxi Soviet

After the failure of the Autumn Harvest Uprising in 1927, Mao travelled to Jiangxi (see map on page 118) where he joined other Communists. In the following years, Mao was able to participate in setting up a soviet, where land was redistributed among the peasants to whom Mao tried to teach the principles of communism. In 1931, this area became the Chinese Soviet Republic, or the Jiangxi Soviet as it was more commonly known. According to Edwin Moïse, during this time Mao was closely allied to Zhu De, whose military experience as an officer in the GMD army was to prove invaluable (*Modern China*, 1994, p. 70).

Ideology

Mao now made an important departure from the traditional Marxist–Leninist party line. According to Moïse, Marxists believed it was the proletariat that would lead revolutions and that the peasantry were 'uneducated and technologically primitive'. Even though the 1917 Bolshevik Revolution in Russia recognized the contribution of the peasants, the leaders believed the 'real base remained in the cities'. Mao, however, understood that China lacked significant numbers of proletarians, and so any hope of revolution had to lie with the peasants. As Moïse points out, '[Mao's] actual policies placed the main theatre of the revolution entirely in the countryside, and reduced the role of the proletariat to a negligible level' (*Modern China*, 1994, p. 73). Moïse also claims that, unlike Lenin, Mao was able to do more than just promising change and a more egalitarian future: through a practical application of his ideology, Mao was able to convince supporters to join him.

This did not follow the party line from Moscow, however, and Mao's ideas were challenged in 1931 upon the arrival in Jiangxi of the 28 Bolsheviks, a group of CPC members who had gone to the Soviet Union to be trained for leadership. To the 28 Bolsheviks, a 'correct revolutionary attitude' was the key factor and they criticized Mao's pragmatic interpretations of communist ideology (Moïse, *Modern China*, 1994, p. 75). Furthermore, they disagreed with Mao's willingness to include richer peasants in the redistribution of land and his cautious approach to land reform. This was particularly difficult to reconcile with the Soviet Union policy of 1931, when collectivization was being introduced, and the **kulaks** (richer peasants) were exiled or executed. Another way in which Mao did not see eye to eye with the 28 Bolsheviks was over the use of guerrilla warfare.

CHALLENGE YOURSELF

Thinking and research skills

Sun Zi was a famous Chinese military strategist who lived during the 4th century BCE. His famous book, *The Art of War*, has now become very well known, but Mao was already well aware of Sun's theories and applied them when fighting the GMD. See what you can find out about these strategies.

Activity 3

ATL Research and thinking skills

Study the sources below and answer the questions that follow.

Source A

“ *All revolutionary parties and all revolutionary comrades will stand before them [the peasants] to be tested, to be accepted or rejected as they decide. To march at their head and lead them? To stand behind them, gesticulating and criticizing them? Or to stand opposite them and oppose them. Every Chinese is free to choose among the three, but by force of circumstances you are fated to make the choice quickly.*

From a report submitted to the CPC in February 1927 by Mao

1. What does Source A tell us about Mao's views on how peasants would be an important element in directing the revolution in China?
2. To what extent does Source A agree with the Marxist–Leninist theories of revolution?

Source B

“ *Confiscate all land, and turn ownership over to the soviet government, which should use the following three methods to redistribute it:*

a. Distribution to the peasants for them to cultivate individually

b. Distribution to the peasants for them to cultivate in common

c. Organization by the soviet government of model farms to cultivate the land.

Of the above three methods, the first is to be the primary one. Under special circumstances, or when the soviet government is strong, the second and third methods may also be employed.

From *The Jinggangshan to the Establishment of the Jiangxi Soviets, July 1927–December 1930*

3. How and why did Mao say different methods of land redistribution should be applied?

In 1937, Mao wrote his famous treatise on war called 'On the Art of Guerrilla Warfare'. Mao used guerrilla tactics very effectively against the GMD who were, once more, hunting the Communists. Jiang had launched his five Extermination Campaigns against the Jiangxi Soviet but, with limited resources and far fewer men, Mao and Zhu De organized a successful defence, using strategies such as sudden attacks rather than pitched battles. The 28 Bolsheviks disagreed with Mao's guerrilla methods, calling them 'cowardly'; they demanded the guerrilla tactics be replaced with methods that were more conventional. Although these conventional tactics made the defence of the Soviet less effective, credit for the near defeat of the Communists must also be given to changes in GMD tactics. By 1933, the GMD had a number of excellent German advisors, including General von Seeckt, and their tactics included encircling the Soviet and steadily tightening their control of the region surrounding the Communists. This proved effective and, once again, the survival of the CPC was at risk. For the Communists, the solution was to try to escape Jiangxi and to make their way to Yan'an, a distant, northern region of China to join another group of Communists. This epic journey of some 6,000 miles lasted a year and was called the Long March. According to Moïse, of the 100,000 people (including women and children) who left Jiangxi, only 10,000 survived (*Modern China*, 1994, p. 78).

The Long March – Mao consolidates his leadership of the CPC

When the Long March began, Mao no longer had a prominent role in the leadership of the CPC. He had been rebuked by the 28 Bolsheviks, and had lost his authority over the ideology and military strategy of the Jiangxi Soviet. The route to the north was long and arduous, made more difficult because of constant harassment by the GMD that followed in the wake of the Long Marchers.

Three months into the journey, in January 1935, events came to head at Zunyi, where a meeting of the CPC leadership was held. Mao criticized the 28 Bolsheviks for their insistence on adopting disastrous military tactics. He also argued that it was wrong to abandon guerrilla tactics and for the under-manned and under-equipped Communists to have to apply conventional battle tactics. Furthermore, Mao disputed the wisdom of following a predictable route to Yan'an and argued for a more circuitous route that would make it more difficult for the GMD to follow them. By the end of the meeting, Mao gained enough support to establish authority over the party. He had shown strong conviction and, whatever the opinion of the 'experts' – as the 28 Bolsheviks were also known – Mao's ideas worked. Pragmatism had won the day. The Long March continued and eventually reached Yan'an, where another soviet was established.

This episode in the life of Mao Zedong was mythologized in the history of the CPC; to have been a 'Long Marcher' added to the credentials of party members. The Long March offered endless material for plays, operas, and ballets in the People's Republic of China, adding an element of highly romanticized narrative to the rise of the Communist state.

Zunyi Conference

A meeting of the leaders of the CPC took place here to try and halt its defeat by the GMD. It was an important conference because this was where Mao established his prominence among the leadership.

Exam questions will sometimes ask you to analyse the rise to power of an authoritarian leader. If you are discussing Mao, it may be relevant to mention the Chinese Civil War. This may be divided into two parts as the First Chinese Civil War, which was fought from 1927 (the White Terror) until the truce that occurred with the establishment of the Second United Front in 1936. The Second Chinese Civil War began in 1946 and ended in 1949. Both would be relevant to the rise to power of Mao.

Activity 4 ATL Thinking skills

Study the sources below and answer the question that follows.

Source A

Source B

◀ Mao Zedong, seen here as a young man.

◀ Jiang Jieshi

1. These photographs of Mao and Jiang were taken around the same time. If you didn't know anything about their backgrounds or their occupations, what could you say about them based only on these sources?

Map of China and its provinces.

Puyi (1906–67)

Puyi was the last Emperor of the Qing dynasty. Born in 1906, he became Emperor in 1908 when he was just two years old. He was deposed in 1911, but became the puppet-emperor of Manchukuo in 1934. Much later, under the Communist regime, he was given the job of assistant gardener at the Beijing Botanical Gardens. He died in 1967 at the age of 61.

Manchurian Incident/ The Invasion of Manchuria

The events of 1931 can be called the Manchurian Incident or The Invasion of Manchuria. Strictly speaking, as the Kwangtung Army was already based in the region, some historians would argue it was not an 'invasion'.

Japan and China

In 1931, Japan invaded Manchuria (the northeast region of China), renaming it Manchukuo. Japan also installed Puyi, the boy emperor of 1911, as the puppet-emperor. Although he held the title of Emperor, Puyi was no freer to rule Manchukuo than he had been, as a five-year-old, to rule China. The invasion was viewed by the League of Nations as an act of aggression against China, but its rather limp response (by sending a Commission of Enquiry) had little impact. In many ways, this was less of an invasion than a takeover of territory governed by Zhang Xueliang, the Young Marshal, and threatened by the advancing New Revolutionary Army of the GMD. The Japanese Kwangtung army was already in Manchuria, where it had the duty of protecting Japanese trading interests. What became clear was that, to a great extent, it was the military, not the civilian government in Tokyo, that had planned and carried out the invasion/ occupation in Manchuria. It was successful, and when the League of Nations criticized Japan (which had been one of its founding members), it left the League.

China had been viewed for some time as 'living space' for Japan's expanding population as well as as a source of natural resources (for more on this concept, see *Lebensraum*, page 96), and now Japan needed territory in China to help with its economic recovery from the Great Depression. The encroaching Northern Expedition also affected the timing of the Japanese takeover of Manchuria, especially as the Young Marshal had thrown in his lot with Jiang and the GMD (unsurprising perhaps, as the Japanese had assassinated his father, the Old Marshal). All these events formed the backdrop to Jiang's campaign against the CPC in Jiangxi. As we know, however, the Japanese threat did not stop Jiang's campaign against 'the disease of the heart' (the Communists). Despite cries of outrage from the 50,000 strong anti-Japanese demonstrations in Shanghai and the 6,000 in Nanjing who asked to be sent to fight in Manchuria, Jiang knew he did not have the capacity or perhaps the will to go north (Fenby, *The Penguin History of Modern China*, 2008, p. 235). Even so, there was some limited response, as Japanese goods were boycotted and, when the Japanese attacked Shanghai in 1932, the GMD did respond and a settlement was finally reached whereby the city was demilitarized.

If you have studied the causes of World War II, you will be familiar with the concept of appeasement. It is worth asking whether or not appeasement began here.

Activity 5 (ATL) Research and thinking skills

Study the sources below and answer the questions that follow.

Source A

This cartoon is from the 1930s. It satirizes the way in which Japan ignored international treaties.

Source B

> The Long March is a manifesto. It has proclaimed to the world that the Red Army is an army of heroes, while the imperialists and their running dogs, Chiang Kai-shek and his like, are impotent. It has proclaimed their utter failure to encircle, pursue, obstruct and intercept us. The Long March is also a propaganda force. It has announced to some 200 million people in eleven provinces that the road of the Red Army is their only road to liberation.

From Mao's speech 'On Tactics against Japanese Imperialism', 27 December 1935

1. In Source A, the names of the two treaties are shown: the Kellogg–Briand Pact and the Nine Power Treaty. What did the signatories of these treaties promise to do and, according to the message of the cartoon, why did Japan break them?

2. In Source B, there are several terms Mao used to denigrate the GMD. What did Mao mean to imply by referring to them as 'imperialists', 'running dogs', and being 'impotent'?

The Second United Front, 1936–45

Jiang's policy of prioritizing the fight against the Communists over the struggle with Japan did not meet with the approval of all his officers. In particular, Jiang met opposition from two generals who had been in command of the campaign against the

Zhou Enlai (1898–1976)

Zhou Enlai was an important member of the CPC from the time he led worker uprisings in Shanghai. He remained an important supporter of Mao, becoming premier in 1949. He was one of the 'survivors' of the CPC as, despite his moderate views, he was not purged during the Cultural Revolution (1966–76) and remained close to Mao.

The Second Sino-Japanese War, 1937–45

The Marco Polo Bridge Incident of July 1937 led to all-out war between Japan and China, the destruction of Nanjing, and the occupation by Japan of much of the densely populated, coastal regions of China. Despite their ruthless policy of the 'Three Alls' (see page 117), the Japanese army could not possibly occupy all of China and were never able to secure the surrender of Jiang's forces. The GMD government moved inland to Chongqing, a city that was out of reach of the Japanese army but was, nevertheless, heavily bombed by the Japanese Air Force.

Communists in Yan'an: 'Young Marshal' Zhang Xueliang, who was apparently now cured of his morphine addiction, and Yang Hucheng, a former warlord (Fenby, *The Penguin History of Modern China*, 2008, p. 269).

In 1935, however, the Comintern ruled that Communist parties should ally with anti-fascists wherever possible to form Popular Fronts against the spread of fascism. This was a departure from its previous policy (which forbade such alliances) and allowed Mao to suggest an alliance against the Japanese. Through his close friend and comrade, Zhou Enlai, Mao contacted Jiang, who agreed that the 'real enemy' was Japan and that the forces of the GMD and the CPC needed to unite. A plot was hatched by Zhang and Yang to lure Jiang to Xian, kidnap him, and hold him hostage until he agreed to end the campaign against the Communists and to revive the United Front to fight the Japanese. In December 1936, the plan was put into operation. Jiang, reluctantly, agreed to end the struggle against the Communists and to give them some autonomy in the north. The Red Army in Yan'an was renamed the Eighth Route Army and a much smaller – but equally tenacious – group of Communists in the south were named the New Fourth Army.

It is also likely that Zhang Xueliang and Yang Hucheng were afraid that they were about to be removed from their command and so wanted to pre-empt this by kidnapping Jiang and to remove him as leader of the GMD.

It is worth noting, however, that in 1936, Mao had made clear his aims in initiating the Second United Front, saying 'our fixed policy should be 70 per-cent expansion, 20 per-cent dealing with the Kuomintang and 10 per-cent resisting Japan' (Mao quoted in Hsu, *The Rise of Modern China*, 1995, p. 589).

As events unfolded, the Second United Front turned out to greatly benefit the CPC. Meanwhile, the threat of Japan did not end with the seizure of Manchukuo but resumed in 1937 with the Second Sino-Japanese War. This was very important in Mao's rise to power. It brought a temporary end to the civil war, but it allowed the Eighth Route Army to develop its fighting skills in skirmishes against the Japanese army and, as we shall see, gave the CPC the opportunity to expand their control over the north of China.

Today, there is much controversy over the role of the Communist forces in the Sino-Japanese War, with official Communist Party sources emphasizing the immeasurable contribution of the Eighth Route Army to the war in Manchuria and the failure of the GMD forces to do more than wait for the United States to come to their rescue. Not all historians agree with this view, however. Jonathan Fenby refers to how both American and Soviet observers noted that the Communists did 'far less fighting than they claimed and certainly less than the Nationalists'. Even so, 'the myth that it was the CPC which constituted the prime source of armed resistance persists as one of the key claims to legitimacy of the regime since 1949' (*The Penguin History of Modern China*, 2008, p. 309).

Although Japan (as a member of the Anti-Comintern Pact of 1936 and the Tripartite Pact of 1940) was vehemently anti-communist ideologically, it realized that defeating the Eighth Route Army and the New Fourth Army was not its main objective; Japan's main enemy in China was the army of the GMD.

 ATL Knowledge, research, and self-management skills

World War II was fought with great savagery in many countries, especially where armies were told that the people they were fighting were subhuman. See what you can find out about the ideology that lay behind the Nazi attacks on the Slav populations in the Soviet Union. Can these be compared to the Japanese attacks on the Chinese? Why, do you think, did racist beliefs gain such credence at this time?

CHALLENGE YOURSELF

 **Thinking skills**

Study the following sources and answer the question that follows.

Source A

Having defeated the GMD forces in the north and driven them south, the CPC moved into the areas that were now lightly defended by the Japanese. Edwin Moïse refers to the period as:

> ❝ *a power vacuum in which large areas were almost empty of armed forces. By 1940, without even having to do a great deal of fighting, the CPC made itself ruler of perhaps 100 million people scattered across the North China Plain.*
>
> **From Edwin Moïse, *Modern China*, Routledge, 2008, p. 89**

Source B

Jonathan Fenby, meanwhile, argues that:

> ❝ *while nurturing the propaganda line that it alone was fighting the invaders, the CPC restricted itself to scattered guerrilla operations and was, in fact, considerably less active than the Nationalists, as Mao concentrated on building up a power base from which he would be able to challenge for supreme power in China once somebody else had defeated Japan.*
>
> **From Jonathan Fenby, *The Penguin History of Modern China: The Fall and Rise of a Great Power, 1850 to the Present*, 2nd ed., Penguin, 2008, p.309**

Once you have read the two sources, consider what they tell us about the aims and methods of the CPC during the Second Sino-Japanese War. How far do the two sources agree with each other? Are there points on which they disagree?

Mao in Yan'an – ideology, propaganda, and the use of force

Mao's decade in Yan'an was very important for the development of both CPC ideology as well as control over the party structure. Mao continued to develop his interpretations of Marxism–Leninism. In particular, he was very critical of Communists who were able to quote Marx and Lenin but did not understand how to apply these ideas in real-life situations. In this way, Mao was able to criticize the remnants of the 28 Bolsheviks, as well as to carry out what was called a 'rectification campaign' against 'subjectivism, sectarianism, and party formalism'. Mao used these terms to target party members who knew the theory of Marxism but not its application (subjectivism), those who challenged the authority of the party (sectarianism), and those who did not speak plainly in a way that could be easily understood by everyone (party formalism). One important aspect of this purge was that it provided a way to screen new arrivals at Yan'an.

Since the start of the war and the weakening of GMD rule, many young urbanites (often middle-class and well educated) who had made their way to Yan'an to join Mao now risked being identified as spies. Fenby states that, by 1943, 1,000 'enemy agents' had been arrested; a 'witch hunt' was carried out, leading to the expulsion of 40,000 party members and 'a wave of suicides'. This purge, known as the 'rescue movement', ended when it succeeded in consolidating Mao as the undisputed leader of the party. Afterwards, Mao made a formal apology for any 'excesses' caused during this period (*The Penguin History of Modern China*, 2008, p. 310). In this way, Mao's approach to the **mass line** – with a strong focus on the needs of the peasants, land reform, and the

---

The Rape of Nanjing

In December 1937, Nanjing was devastated by the Japanese army during the Second Sino-Japanese War (1937–45); the episode is known as the 'Rape of Nanjing'. Instructed to apply the rule known as the 'Three Alls' ('Kill All, Burn All, Destroy All'), Japanese soldiers behaved with extreme impunity against the Chinese population, who were thought to be an inferior race. Hundreds of thousands of civilians were slaughtered; tens of thousands of women and girls were raped. After the massacre, the GMD moved their capital to Chongqing, a city in the interior of China.

According to Jonathan Fenby, who refers to the work of historian Cheng Yung-fa, trade in opium was a main source of income for the Communists in Yan'an. In their financial accounting, opium was referred to as 'soap', 'foreign trade', and 'special product'. The use of drugs was banned within the party, but by 1943, the Communists were 'producing nearly a million boxes of opium p.a. and in 1944, profits from the sale of drugs amounted to 40 per cent of the total revenue of the Yan'an Soviet'. Two sources mentioning the drug trade are Soviet advisor to Yan'an, Petr Parfenovich Vladimirov, who wrote about it in 1974, and Chen Yung-fa, who wrote about it in 1995 (*The Penguin History of Modern China*, 2008, pp. 308–9).

Thinking and research skills

Read about the time Mao spent in Yan'an and what he achieved there. Then, read about the time that Fidel Castro spent in the Sierra Maestra Mountains in Cuba (see Chapter 1). Compare and contrast how these two leaders used propaganda and also the ways they used ideology to gain support.

inclusion of peasants into the political and economic life of the Yan'an Soviet – was established (Hsu, *The Rise of Modern China*, 1995, p. 591).

During this time, Mao's cult of personality also flourished in Yan'an. Songs such as 'The East is Red' called him 'the Great Saviour', with children at the school being taught to write slogans such as 'we are all Chairman Mao's good little children' (Fenby, *The Penguin History of Modern China*, 2008, p. 310).

Mao also wrote many pamphlets whilst in Yan'an, including 'On New Democracy', which he wrote and published in 1940. Michael Lynch points out that this emphasized that Mao's revolution was not 'a class movement, but a national one' and that the aim was one of 'co-operation among all classes, groups and individuals willing to fight Japan to the end' (*China: From Empire to People's Republic 1900–49*, 1996, p. 50).

By this time, Mao's fame spread through not just China but also abroad, through visits by foreign journalists who were able to make their way to Yan'an and see for themselves that conditions seemed to compare favourably with those in Chongqing. For many of these foreign reporters, life in the Yan'an Soviet seemed more democratic, less corrupt, and better organized than in the GMD-ruled China. Not surprisingly, Jiang dismissed these reports as biased. Meanwhile, an American Military Observers Mission (also known as the Dixie Mission) visited Yan'an in July and August 1944. In their report, they referred positively to Yan'an as 'a different country' and 'the most modern place in China'. Although the Mission were aware that the United States could not abandon Jiang, they concluded that the Communists were 'in China to stay'. Immanuel Hsu argues that such visits gave a quasi-international recognition to Mao and recognized that he had 'created another China, in competition with the Nationalist government for the supreme power of the Chinese state' (*The Rise of Modern China*, 1995, p. 598).

Reflecting on this period, you can see how the period in Yan'an against the backdrop of the Sino-Japanese War and, indeed, World War II in the Pacific and Asia, gave Mao an important opportunity to consolidate his undisputed leadership of the Party and prepared him for the next step to be the leader of China.

The GMD at the end of World War II

It is worth reflecting here on how the GMD fared during what became known as the Pacific War, when the Japanese attacked Pearl Harbor on 7 December 1941. This had catapulted the United States into a war against Japan and, consequently, into an alliance with China. According to Fenby, this was a huge relief for Jiang: On hearing of the attack on Pearl Harbor, 'to celebrate the news, Jiang put on a recording of Ave Maria'. Two days later, China declared war on Germany, Italy, and Japan (Fenby, *The Penguin History of Modern China*, 2008, p. 302).

The United States provided Jiang with aid and sent General Joseph Stilwell to help train the GMD army. Stilwell and Jiang did not get along, however, and according to an interview given by Stilwell to Theodore White of *Time* magazine, Stilwell had condemned Jiang by saying that 'the trouble in China is simple. We are allied to an ignorant, illiterate, superstitious peasant'. Stilwell also contemptuously referred to Jiang as 'Peanut', and 'that rattlesnake'; Jiang's wife, the socialite Soong Meiling, meanwhile was referred to as 'Madame Empress' (Fenby, *The Penguin History of Modern China*, 2008, p. 305). A Wellesley graduate, Soong was far more sophisticated than her husband. In 1943, she was invited to address a joint session of the US Congress, where she pleaded for aid to China. Soong made a very positive impression, and both she and Jiang were lauded in the US press as staunch allies of the United States.

Soong Meiling,
Madame Jiang Jieshi

There was rampant corruption in the administration of the GMD government as well as very high inflation in Chongqing. Although Mao had fewer soldiers and fewer arms, inside China he was winning the propaganda war. He gained a reputation primarily as a nationalist, ready to sacrifice all to save China and this gained him supporters. Clearly, the Dixie Mission also showed that the United States was interested in supporting the Communists and ready to provide them with the arms necessary to help drive the Japanese out of Manchuria. However, despite what may have been more realistic reports coming from US representatives on the ground in China, Jiang retained the image of a strong leader among the Americans and, indeed, many of his detractors would find themselves castigated as pro-communist during the McCarthy era.

The war against Japan came to an end in August 1945, when atom bombs were dropped on the Japanese cities of Hiroshima and Nagasaki. The Soviet Union, as agreed at the Yalta Conference, entered the war against Japan almost exactly three months after the end of the war in Europe. The Soviet Red Army of 1.5 million soldiers crossed the border into Manchuria and Operation August Storm led to the defeat of the Japanese army. Along with the use of the atom bombs, this is considered as one of the main reasons Japan finally surrendered without much resistance. On 14 August 1945, Stalin signed a Treaty of Alliance and Friendship with Jiang and promised that, in return for some territorial gains, he would support Jiang and no one else. Stalin agreed to withdraw from Manchuria by December 1945 but, at Jiang's request, delayed this departure until the GMD were ready to take over. Edwin Moïse points out that this was remarkably prescient of Jiang who was clearly aware that sharing an ideology did not necessarily mean that the Soviet Union and the CPC were close allies (*Modern China*, 1994, p. 102). Even so, Jiang was a little overoptimistic. As it withdrew, the Red Army allowed the Eighth Route Army, now renamed the People's Liberation Army (PLA), to occupy the territory it vacated, as well as to receive the weapons confiscated from the Japanese army.

Soong Meiling was one of three sisters known collectively as the Soong sisters. While Meiling married Jiang Jieshi, sister Ailing had been courted by Sun Yixian but did not return his advances. Sun ended up marrying third sister Qingling instead. Their brother, TV Soong, became Jiang's minister of finance.

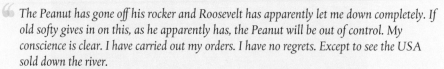

Activity 6

ATL **Thinking and research skills**

Study the following sources and answer the questions that follow.

Source A

❝ *Other Americans, including General Stilwell himself, were equally horrified at the campaigns of enforced conscription carried out by the Guomindang armies, and at the sight of ragged, barefooted men being led to the front roped together, already weakened almost to death by beriberi or malnutrition. Random executions of recruiting officers, occasionally ordered by Chiang Kai-shek, did nothing to end the abuses. It was estimated that of 1.67 million Chinese men drafted for active service in 1943, 44 per cent deserted or died on the way to join their units. Those draftees who died before seeing combat between 1937 and 1945 numbered 1.4 million, approximately 1 in 10 of all men drafted.*

From Jonathan Spence, *The Search for Modern China*, W.W. Norton & Company, 2001

Source B

❝ *The Peanut has gone off his rocker and Roosevelt has apparently let me down completely. If old softy gives in on this, as he apparently has, the Peanut will be out of control. My conscience is clear. I have carried out my orders. I have no regrets. Except to see the USA sold down the river.*

Stilwell's letter to his wife just before his recall, 1944. From Joseph W. Stilwell and Theodore H. White (ed.), *The Stilwell Papers*, Da Capo Press, 1991

Source C

General Stilwell with Jiang Jieshi and Madame Jiang Jieshi. This photo was taken when they met in Burma in July 1942.

1. According to Source A, Jiang appears not to have considered the wellbeing of his soldiers. Why, do you think, did he treat them so badly?

2. In Source B, General Stilwell called Jiang 'the Peanut'. He was also known to have referred to Madame Jiang as 'Madame Empress' (behind her back). What does this tell you about how Stilwell viewed the President and First Lady of China? Compare the tone of the letter with the photo in Source C. Does this give a different impression of their relationship? Give reasons for your answer.

The Second Chinese Civil War, 1946–49

In December 1945, President Harry S. Truman of the United States sent General George Marshall (later to be US Secretary of State) to meet with Jiang, in order to ensure a peaceful resolution of the conflict that threatened to accompany the disintegration of the Second United Front. It was a difficult task, made more difficult for Marshall, who had to appear neutral at a time when the United States continued to consider Jiang as its ally and to supply him with aid and weapons. This continued more or less even after a US embargo was placed on sales of weapons to the GMD. A negotiated truce was signed in January 1946 that required both sides (the GMD and the CPC) to reduce the size of their armies, but neither had any intention of keeping to its terms. Edwin Moïse notes that US Marines were present in northern China and that the embargo on sales of weapons 'did not stop the marines giving the GMD large quantities of surplus ammunition when they did withdraw in 1947' (*Modern China*, 1994, p. 105). In addition, Jiang had been greatly assisted by the United States in the airlifting of GMD forces to Manchuria in 1946.

By this time, the civil war was well underway. During his time in China, General Stilwell had been horrified by the treatment of conscript soldiers by their GMD officers and this was to be a factor in the civil war. Although the GMD forces outnumbered the PLA by a ratio of four to one, the loyalty of GMD soldiers was often limited, as demonstrated by high rates of desertion as well as the numbers that quickly surrendered and joined the PLA.

Inflation was still spiralling out of control. Michael Lynch, as quoted by Jonathan Fenby, states that 'in 1940, 100 yuan bought a pig; in 1943, a chicken; in 1945, a fish; in 1946, an egg; and in 1947, one-third of a box of matches'. Furthermore, corruption was endemic and US aid was often sold for profit, including blood plasma that 'was on sale in shops in Shanghai for $25 a pint'. According to Fenby, unemployment soared as factories closed, because resources were scarce. There were many strikes, including 4,200 in Shanghai alone between 1946 and 1947 (*The Penguin History of Modern China*, 2008, p. 335).

You can see that Jiang was not successful in providing good governance to the Chinese and this had a negative impact on support for the GMD. President Truman also lost patience with the Chinese government, claiming that it had stolen 'a billion dollars in US loans'. In Truman's opinion, they were 'all thieves, every damn one of them' and according to Fenby, it is therefore not surprising that the Truman administration refused to continue aid to the GMD after 1948 (*The Penguin History of Modern China*, 2008, p. 336).

The CPC, meanwhile, used guerrilla tactics very successfully as it gained more territory in northern China, gradually isolating the GMD forces in towns or 'islets' surrounded by PLA-held countryside, where 'the peasants were the sea and the PLA were the fish', to use a phrase made famous by Mao. This was a fundamental tactic of guerrilla warfare, as the revolutionaries were dependent on the goodwill of the people who could be persuaded to provide cover, food, and shelter. In practice, of course, guerrillas could also threaten peasants into helping them.

Guerrilla warfare had previously been used successfully by the CPC in Jiangxi (until the 28 Bolsheviks had halted it) and on the Long March to Yan'an and against the Japanese. Now, it would be used very effectively once again as Mao's soldiers had been trained well in the art of fighting a seemingly stronger enemy.

CHALLENGE YOURSELF

ATL Thinking and research skills

Source A

Nationalist army bandsmen captured by the PLA on 1 October 1949, during the Second Chinese Civil War.

Source B

❝ The key to a successful guerrilla campaign was summed up as follows:

When the enemy advances, we retreat;
When the enemy escapes, we harass;
When they retreat, we pursue;
When they tire, we attack.

From Michael Lynch, *China: From Empire to People's Republic 1900–49*, Hodder, 1996, p. 55

Source C

❝ There were basic principles of conduct that Mao conveyed to his soldiers. These included:

1. *Replace all doors when you leave the house*
2. *Roll up and return the straw matting on which you sleep*
3. *Be courteous and help out when you can*
4. *Return all borrowed articles*
5. *Replace all damaged goods*
6. *Be honest in all transactions with the peasants*
7. *Pay for all articles purchased*
8. *Be sanitary and especially establish latrines at a distance from people's houses*
9. *Don't take liberties with women*
10. *Don't kill prisoners of war*

From Michael Lynch, *China: From Empire to People's Republic 1900–49*, Hodder, 1996, pp. 49–50

1. Study the photograph in Source A. How could an image like this be used for propaganda purposes? What message would it convey?

2. How, do you think, did the instructions in Source B help a poorly equipped army to defeat a stronger enemy? The outcome of most wars is determined by the side that holds the largest territory. How would these rules help guerrillas to conquer and hold territory?

3. What does Source C tell you about how Mao wanted the PLA soldiers to behave? Do these rules tell us anything about how armies usually behaved towards Chinese peasants? Do you think the GMD forces also behaved like this? Be sure to support your answers with evidence.

 **ATL** Thinking skills

Below are two examples of introductions written by students responding to the question:

For what reasons did the Guomindang fail to win the Chinese Civil War?

Read both and give your reasons as to which you think is the better answer.

Student answer A – Susan

The Chinese Civil War was a conflict between the nationalist Guomindang under Jiang Jieshi and the Communist Party of China ruled by Mao Zedong. The war broke out in 1927 after the Shanghai Massacre. The civil war was interrupted by two United Fronts, where nationalists and communists fought together to defeat the warlords as well as the invading Japanese. With the support of the Americans, and ultimately the dropping of the atomic bombs, China's external issues were resolved and old conflicts between nationalists and communists resurfaced. This led to the outbreak of a full-scale war in 1946. The communists referred to the war as their revolution or the War of Liberation. The civil war ended in 1949 with a communist victory: Mao founded the People's Republic of China and the nationalist leaders fled to Taiwan.

Student answer B – Paul

The Chinese Civil War 1946 to 1949 was the continuation of the conflict between the Nationalists and Communists that had started after the Qing dynasty was overthrown in 1911 and the Guomindang, the Nationalist party, took control of China under Jiang Jieshi. That the GMD lost the Civil War, even though the Chinese Communist Party under Mao Zedong remained relatively small until long after the proclamation of the People's Republic of China in 1949, is the result of the devastated economic situation of China, and the Guomindang's general policies, especially concerning foreign affairs.

Examiner's comments

Susan's answer begins with some focus on defining the Chinese Civil War and she goes on to identify which groups were involved. Unfortunately, she then loses focus as she brings in less relevant information. She is broadening her scope when she actually needs to keep a tight focus on the question. She needs to show the examiner that she is going to discuss the reasons the GMD lost; there is little indication of that in her introduction.

Paul also begins quite well but he then goes on to identify two reasons for the defeat of the GMD and this gives the impression that this will be the main argument. If this is indeed Paul's intention, his essay will be quite narrow in scope and many important factors will be left out. A better approach would have been for Paul to write in more general terms in his introduction.

Don't forget, there is no need to make a thesis statement (to state your argument) in the introduction. This is possible, of course, but it is not compulsory and it may be better to keep your introduction focused on the actual question but less specific on what your answer will be.

A possible question on the Civil War may read something like this:

Examine the factors that led to a Communist victory in the Chinese Civil War.

Alternatively, a question may ask about the defeat of the Guomindang. In both cases, you would need to select quite similar evidence to support your arguments, even though the approaches to the questions would be different. Just make sure you answer the question that is being asked.

Remember, the introduction to an essay is where you indicate that you have understood the question. A good way to do this is to include words from the actual question. Think of it this way: If you read through your introduction and it is not immediately clear what question it is you are answering, then an examiner is probably not going to know either!

As the war continued, the PLA gained strength, while the GMD weakened due to a lack of popular support and a loss of control of large swathes of countryside to the PLA. Michael Lynch notes that the GMD were unable to achieve any victories between 1947 and 1949. In fact, as Edwin Moïse points out, the GMD forces still heavily outnumbered the PLA in 1948, yet they were isolated from each other and this left them exposed to PLA encirclement and attack. By the autumn of 1948, the GMD had been driven out of Manchuria.

In January 1949, Jiang Jieshi resigned as president of China, knowing that his forces were heading towards defeat. Although Vice-President Li Zongren took over as president, military control remained with Jiang, who prepared his withdrawal to Taiwan. The PLA crossed the Yangtze River and headed south to Guangdong, bringing almost all of China under its control. There were huge problems to overcome in a country that had been disunited and at war for almost 40 years. The civil war, however, was over and in Beijing, on 1 October 1949, Mao announced the establishment of the People's Republic of China.

> **Activity 8**   (ATL)   **Research, thinking, and communication skills**
>
> **1.** Use a table like the one below to organize your ideas about what factors influenced the outcome of the civil war.
>
> | GMD weaknesses | CPC strengths |
> | --- | --- |
> | | |

> Mao took a long time to rise to power. If you use him as an example in a question that asks about his rise to power, you could begin in 1921 with the establishment of the CPC. You would need to think about what factors helped him to rise to power and how important they were. For example, consider the importance of the following events:
>
> - The White Terror and the Autumn Harvest Uprising
> - The Jiangxi Soviet
> - The Long March
> - The Second United Front
> - The Yan'an Soviet
> - The Second Sino-Japanese War
> - The Second Chinese Civil War
>
> Explain how each one of the events above was used effectively by Mao to a) to establish his control over the CPC and b) increase the popularity of the CPC.

3.2   Consolidation and maintenance of power

This section deals with Mao's time in power. When authoritarian leaders come to power, they usually have to consolidate their control over the state and they can do this in a number of ways. These may include:

- legal changes to the political structure and/or the constitution so that the leaders can govern without having to consult with a governing body such as a parliament
- the use of force to arrest opponents, purging the ruling party of rivals, persuading the population that opposition will be punished
- the use of propaganda and populist policies to gain the support of the people
- a successful foreign policy that can increase feelings of nationalism and support for the regime (sometimes both internally and externally).

Consider these points as you read through this section to see how they apply to Mao's rule in China.

Domestic policies and their impact, 1949–76

The country that Mao took over in 1949 was in a poor state. Inflation was among the first problems to be tackled and this was done effectively as inflation dropped from 1,000 per cent in 1949 to only 15 per cent in 1951. A new system of taxation was also introduced and the CPC made every effort to maintain or to restore public services.

At first, Mao's aims can be summed up as follows:

• To maintain public services
• To establish law and order
• To keep the administration of China running.

Edwin Moïse believes that without this initial pragmatic approach, the goal of a socialist revolution could not be reached (*Modern China*, 1994, p. 115).

The initial changes that took place are outlined below.

The structure of the state

The Organic Law of 1949 determined that the PRC was a 'democratic dictatorship' led by the Communist Party. It was 'democratic' because it included the four classes: the workers, peasants, petty bourgeois, and national bourgeois. It was a 'dictatorship' because of its 'unyielding attitude towards the revolutionaries'. As in the Soviet Union, the principle of democratic centralism applied. This meant that party representatives at various levels were elected democratically, but they had to show obedience towards the decisions made by the top officials of the party.

Mao became the chairman of the Central People's Government Council. The Council met twice a month, but when not in session, affairs of state were handled by the State Administrative Council headed by Premier Zhou Enlai.

The Organic Law remained in place until a constitution was introduced in 1955 that established the National People's Congress. Alongside this state structure was that of the CPC, with the National Party Congress, from which representatives were elected to sit on the Central Committee that met twice a year and when not in session delegated authority to the Politburo. Above that was the Standing Committee, which included Mao (as chairman), five vice-chairmen, and a general secretary. As in the Soviet Union, the state and the party were closely aligned with the same personnel present at the highest level of both structures (Hsu, *The Rise of Modern China*, 1995, pp. 647–49).

Democratic centralism

In 1921, at the 10th Party Congress of the Soviet Union, Lenin proposed the Resolution on Party Unity (also known as 'the ban on factions'). It enshrined the principle of democratic centralism, as it recognized the democratic election of party representatives (from a party-approved list, of course), but also stipulated that once decisions had been made by the party leaders there could be no further disagreement. The party line had to be accepted and applied. This became the model for all 20th-century communist parties.

Activity 9  ATL Thinking skills

Below is an extract from the Organic Law. It was an important indicator of how Mao planned to run China, at least at first.

Study the extract and answer the questions that follow.

> *CHAPTER I. GENERAL PROVISIONS ARTICLE 1. The Chinese People's Political Consultative Conference … is the organization of the democratic united front of the entire Chinese people. Its aim is to unite all democratic classes and all nationalities throughout China by establishing the unity of all democratic parties and groups and people's organizations. This will enable them to put forward their combined efforts in carrying out New Democracy, opposing imperialism, feudalism and bureaucratic capitalism, overthrowing the reactionary rule of the Guomindang, eliminating open and secret remnant counter-revolutionary forces. It will also enable them to heal the wounds of war,*

rehabilitate and develop the people's economic, cultural and educational work, consolidate national defence, and unite with all the nations and countries which treat us on a footing of equality. All this is for the purpose of establishing and consolidating an independent, democratic, peaceful, unified, prosperous and strong People's Republic of China of the People's Democratic Dictatorship, led by the working class and based on the alliance of workers and peasants.

From 'The Organic Law of the Chinese People's Political Consultative Conference', Beijing, 29 September 1949

1. What reasons are given in this extract for keeping the Chinese population united? How was this to be achieved?

2. Is there an indication in the source that all classes would not be equal?

Economic policies

Agriculture – the Agrarian Land Reform Law of 1950

In the countryside, Mao had already gained a wealth of experience by introducing land reform in Jiangxi and Yan'an. He had encountered considerable difficulties in breaking the ancient bond between landlord and peasant, and determined that the only way to do this was by destroying the landlord class. In order to do so, he sent party officials (work teams) to villages to establish peasant associations, with the most enthusiastic members encouraged to become village leaders. It was by no means guaranteed that the peasants would want to get rid of their landlords or, indeed, that this was considered even remotely possible. There was also the fear that expelled landlords might return to exact their revenge on the peasants and it was very difficult to convince the peasants that there could be any long-term shift in power. Work teams were tasked to carry out 're-education' programmes and peasants would be encouraged to take part in 'Speak Bitterness' campaigns. These would involve gathering the peasants of a village for 'struggle meetings' where the peasants were encouraged to express their sorrow and anger against harsh landlords who were then put on trial and punished. According to Michael Lynch, it is estimated that as many as 1 million people were executed at these meetings (*The People's Republic of China, 1949–1976*, 2008, p. 22).

The Agrarian Land Reform Law was brought into force in June 1950. It called for an end to 'the land ownership system of feudal exploitation' and a redistribution of land and implements to landless peasants. Immanuel Hsu states that the 'agrarian revolution' had been completed by December 1952, with some 300 million peasants benefiting – mostly those classified either as 'poor peasants', who had not had sufficient land to eke out a living and so had to rent additional land, or 'hired hands', who had owned no land at all. This was rapidly followed by the next phase of the revolution, which was to encourage peasants to collectivize (*The Rise of Modern China*, 1995, pp. 652–53).

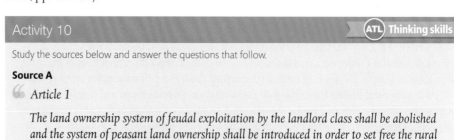

Activity 10
ATL Thinking skills

Study the sources below and answer the questions that follow.

Source A

❝ *Article 1*

The land ownership system of feudal exploitation by the landlord class shall be abolished and the system of peasant land ownership shall be introduced in order to set free the rural productive forces, develop agricultural production and thus pave the way for New China's industrialization.

Article 2

The land, draught animals, farm implements and surplus grain of the landlords, and their surplus houses in the countryside shall be confiscated, but their other properties shall not be confiscated.

From the Agrarian Land Reform Law 1950

Source B

At a struggle meeting, targeted individuals are humiliated with dunces' caps.

1. According to Article 1 in Source A, how do you think agriculture production was supposed to contribute to China's industrialization?
2. According to Article 2 in Source A, what did landlords get to keep? Why, do you think, was this exception included?
3. Find out what were 'dunces' caps', as shown in Source B. What do you think is the message that would have been conveyed to people who saw this photograph?

Industry

At first, the CPC had no choice but to depend on people with the appropriate skills rather than with the correct ideological background. For example, party officials realized that in the cities businessmen were considered 'bourgeois' but also had the kind of expertise that was vital to keeping the economy running – this meant they needed to be included and not excluded from the revolution. They were referred to as 'national capitalists' and were allowed, initially, to retain ownership of their factories and then to share ownership by entering into 'joint ownership' of businesses with the state. Edwin Moïse points out that heavy industry and transportation (what Lenin had called the 'commanding heights' of the economy) quickly came under state control but there was still, at first, a measure of private ownership (*Modern China*, 1994, p. 121).

Once party members acquired management skills and businesses were taken over by the state, campaigns were started to target the bourgeois businessmen. By 1952, it was thought that there was enough expertise among the party members for the Five Antis and Three Antis Campaigns to be introduced, to target bribery, fraud, and tax evasion. Employees were encouraged to denounce their employers in much the same way as peasants had been encouraged to speak out against landlords. This was part of a new rectification campaign, which was introduced between 1950 and 1951 to target class enemies and counter-revolutionaries; an estimated 22,000 people were killed in Guangdong province alone. As well as the Five and the Three Antis, there was a 'thought reform' campaign, which was meant to expose those who did not support the revolution. Street committees were set up to keep files on everyone and to encourage neighbours to spy on each other. Increasingly, the CPC tightened its grip on people's lives and it became more difficult to remain anonymous or to passively oppose the Party by not actively supporting it or helping to carry out its policies.

Stamping out the opposition

Campaigns like those mentioned earlier brought everyone within the sphere of the CPC and encouraged 'self-criticism' by those who were not sufficiently zealous. Moreover, a pamphlet was produced entitled 'How to Hold an Accusation Meeting', giving instructions on how to 'try' those accused of crimes against the party. In Shanghai, for example, an estimated 99 per cent of businessmen were found guilty of at least one of the Antis, more than 3,000 were arrested and an estimated 500 executions took place. Propaganda was spread through political meetings that city employees had to attend and in 1951, all urban residents had to register with the Public Security Bureau, which kept track of where people lived and prevented their free movement. In 1952, peasant migration from the countryside to the city was restricted. In this way, the party also extended its control over the movement of the population.

> ### Activity 11   **ATL** Thinking skills
>
> Below are the results of the Five Antis movement in Shanghai, 1952. Study the information and answer the question that follows.
>
> | | Small firms | | Medium firms | |
> |---|---|---|---|---|
> | **Law-abiding** | 59,471 | (76.6%) | 7,782 | (42.5%) |
> | **Basically law-abiding** | 17,407 | (22.4%) | 9,005 | (49.1%) |
> | **Semi law-abiding** | 736 | (0.9%) | 1,529 | (8.3%) |
> | **Serious lawbreakers** | 2 | | 9 | |
> | **Total** | 77,616 | | 18,325 | |
>
> **Source: Jonathan Spence, *The Search for Modern China*, W.W. Norton & Company, 2001**
>
> 1. What is the message conveyed in the source above? Is the government targeting 'small firms' or 'medium firms'? Explain your answer.

Social policies – the role of women

'Women hold up half the sky' was one of Mao's famous expressions and reflected his belief (in theory) in gender equality. China was a very patriarchal society, with obedience being required of daughters to fathers and wives to husbands. In traditional culture, especially of the countryside, arranged marriages were still common and, although now dying out, foot binding was still practised. Mao declared that women were equal to men; polygamy was outlawed and the Marriage Law Reform of 1950 banned arranged marriages. For women, these changes were significant, even though in practice, especially in rural areas, arranged marriages still happened, as did female infanticide. A law was unlikely to change deeply ingrained social practices in a short period of time. Nevertheless, a change had been introduced and through 're-education' and propaganda, it eventually took effect.

After 1949, Hong Kong benefited enormously from the number of entrepreneurs who fled there to escape, especially from Shanghai. These businessmen set up textile industries in the then-British colony and contributed enormously to its economic growth. In the 1980s, these entrepreneurs would contribute to the success of the Special Economic Zones that were part of Deng Xiaoping's economic reform.

Activity 12 **ATL** **Thinking and communication skills**

Study the two propaganda posters (both from 1953) below and answer the question that follows.

Source A

▲ The slogan reads 'Freedom of marriage, happiness, and good luck'.

Source B

▲ The slogan reads 'A free and independent marriage is good; there is great happiness in unified production'.

1. How, would you say, do these posters convey a message of gender equality? How effective are they at doing so?

You can see that Mao did not attempt to introduce rapid change immediately in 1949, even though the CPC needed to demonstrate to their supporters that changes were afoot; this was because they wanted to avoid rousing opposition from non-party members (who were the vast majority of the population). Even so, as Jonathan Fenby notes, from 1951 onwards, class enemies became a target, and the rest of the population were now included in the process of identifying and punishing these so-called 'dirty rich people' (*The Penguin History of Modern China*, 2008, p. 372).

The First Five-Year Plan, 1953–57

In 1953, Mao launched China's First Five-Year Plan that was intended to follow the Soviet model of developing heavy industry as rapidly as possible. The government centrally planned the economy, allocating resource, labour, and production targets as necessary. In theory, the First Five-Year Plan began in 1953, but in practice it was not written until 1955.

In the countryside, the peasants who had received plots of land in 1950 were now encouraged to join mutual-aid teams. This was meant to be the first stage of bringing peasants together to work collectively. They were told to share land, tools, and animals; those who had nothing to share could 'borrow' them in exchange for their labour. This did not always work well however, and the wealthier peasants, who didn't want to share their resources, often resisted joining these teams. The result of this first stage was low yields and poor harvests, so that by 1954 the party decided to move on

 Foot binding

It had been customary in China for women to bind their feet. This was done by folding both feet of a young girl back under the heels (the process would often start when she was around three years old) and binding them tightly with cloth so that they ceased to grow. Over time, the feet would resemble stumps of flesh, small enough to fit into tiny silk slippers. This fetish was considered to be erotic, as women with bound feet had difficulty walking; when they did so, they would have to swing their hips to keep their balance. Obviously, girls born into poor families were spared this practice, as they had to work, so foot binding was the preserve of better-off families to prepare their daughters for marriage. By the early 20th century, this practice had died out in the cities, partly as a result of many wealthy young women adopting Western styles of dress and behaviour.

to a second stage that was intended to push Chinese agriculture towards a production process similar to the Soviet collectivization of agriculture. Farming needed to become more efficient and one way to do this was to make plots bigger by forming agricultural producers' cooperatives. Liu Shaoqi suggested that machinery should be provided to the cooperatives to encourage farmers to adopt this policy, but Mao insisted that no such incentive was required and that, above all else, China's abundance of labour would be the solution to all its economic problems.

Indeed, Mao was determined to push ahead with these changes in the countryside. He always maintained that it was the peasants who were leading the way forward and that the CPC was becoming too reactionary. In a speech given in July 1955 entitled 'The Question of Agricultural Cooperatives' Mao claimed that many members were 'tottering along like a woman with bound feet, always complaining that others were going too fast'.

Party officials such as Liu Shaoqi were concerned that moving too quickly towards collectivization would arouse a similar resistance among Chinese peasants to that of the kulaks (rich peasants) in the Soviet Union. It seems that these fears were unfounded as by 1956, 92 per cent of households had been collectivized (an increase of 78 per cent in one year); by 1957, according to Hsu, 800,000 cooperatives had been established, each made up of around 160 families (*The Rise of Modern China*, 1995, p. 653). Mao's aim was to make farming more productive by following an **economies of scale** model. In theory, bigger farms meant increased productivity, but farmers were now being paid only for their labour and no longer received compensation for the use of the animals or implements that they may have contributed to the collective.

Despite there being little organized resistance, the changes mentioned above, coupled with the application of collectivization, prompted many peasants to leave the countryside to find work in the cities. This led to a doubling of the urban population by 1957, which made it increasingly difficult for the countryside to produce enough food to feed the cities. It is also worth noting that although by far the greatest percentage of people still lived in the countryside, government investment in agriculture was no more than 7.6 per cent as opposed to the 58.2 per cent that went into industry.

Mao Zedong and Liu Shaoqi

In 1956, Mao resigned as chairman of the Central Secretariat (one step below the Central Committee) and as chairman of the People's Republic (effectively, head of state) in 1959. He was succeeded by Vice-Chairman Liu Shaoqi (1898–1969). Liu was one of the victims of the Cultural Revolution and died in prison in 1969 after being denied medical care.

It is always useful to memorize a few statistics so that you can use them to support an argument in an exam essay.

Activity 13
ATL **Thinking and research skills**

Source analysis

We often judge the success of an authoritarian leader on how far they achieved their aims. Study Sources A to F. Start this exercise by thinking about what Mao aimed to achieve for the economy of China when he began the Five-Year Plan and then use these sources to estimate how far he was successful. Use a table, like the one below, to help you to organize your ideas.

First Five-Year Plan, 1953–57

Successes	Failures

Source A

Percentage of peasant households that became part of mutual aid teams/co-operatives, 1950–57

	Mutual aid teams (%)	Agricultural producer cooperatives (%)	
Year		Lower stage	Higher stage
1950	10.7	negl.	negl.
1951	19.2	negl.	negl.
1952	39.9	0.1	negl.
1953	39.3	0.2	negl.
1954	58.3	1.9	negl.
1955			
End of autumn	50.7	14.2	0.03
Year end	32.7	63.3	4.00
1956			
End of January	19.7	49.6	30.70
End of July	7.6	29.0	63.40
Year end	3.7	8.5	87.80
1957	None	negl.	93.50

Source: Jonathan Spence, *The Search for Modern China*, W.W. Norton & Company, 2001

Source B

The First Five-Year Plan, 1953–57

Indicator (unit)	1952 Data	1957 Plan	1957 Actual	1957 Actual as a percentage of plan
Gross output value (in million 1952 yuan)				
Industry (excluding handicrafts)	27,010	53,560	65,020	121.4
Producer sector	10,730	24,303	34,330	141.0
Machinery	1,404	3,470	6,177	178.0
Chemicals	864	2,271	4,291	188.9
Producer sector less machinery and chemicals	8,462	18,562	23,862	128.5
Physical output				
Coal (mmt)	68.50	113.00	130.00	115.0
Crude oil (tmt)	436	2,012	1,458	72.5
Steel ingot (mmt)	1.35	4.12	5.35	129.8
Cement (mmt)	2.86	6.00	6.86	114.3
Electric power (billion kWh)	7.26	15.90	19.34	121.6

Indicator (unit)	1952 Data	1957 Plan	1957 Actual	1957 Actual as a percentage of plan
Internal combustion engines (thousand hp)	27.6	260.2	609.0	234.2
Hydroelectric turbines (kW)	6,664	79,500	74,900	94.2
Generators (thousand kW)	29.7	227.0	312.2	137.5
Electric motors (thousand kW)	639	1,048	1,455	138.8
Transformers (thousand kva)	1,167	2,610	3,500	134.1
Machine tools (units)	13,734	12,720	28,000	220.1
Locomotives (units)	20	200	167	83.5
Railway freight cars (units)	5,792	8,500	7,300	85.9
Merchant ships (thousand dwt tons)	21.5	179.1	54.0	30.2
Trucks (units)	0	4,000	7,500	187.5
Bicycles (thousand units)	80	555	1,174	211.5
Caustic soda (tmt)	79	154	198	128.6
Soda ash (tmt)	192	476	506	106.3
Ammonium sulphate (tmt)	181	504	631	125.2
Ammonium nitrate (tmt)	7	44	120	272.7
Automobile tires (thousand sets)	417	760	873	114.9
Sulphuric acid (tmt)	149	402	632	157.2
'666' insecticide (tons)	600	70,000	61,000	87.1

Note: mmt = million metric tons; tmt = thousand metric tons; kva = kilovolts-amperes; dwt = deadweight tonnage; kWh = kilowatt hour; kW = kilowatt

Source: Jonathan Spence, *The Search for Modern China*, W.W. Norton & Company, 2001

Source C

" *Despite the speed of compliance with the call for higher-level cooperatives, agricultural production figures for 1957 were disappointing. Grain production increased only 1 percent over the year, in the face of a 2 percent population rise. Cotton-cloth rations had to be cut because of shortages. Indeed although the First Five-Year Plan had met its quotas well enough, it had also revealed disturbing imbalances in the Chinese economic system. While industrial output rose at about 18.7 percent per year during the plan period, agricultural production rose only about 3.8 percent. Per capita grain consumption grew even less, at just under 3 percent per year. With rural markets booming, local purchasers bought up most of the grains, edible oils, and cotton that was for sale, decreasing the amount available for state procurement or for urban consumers.*

From Jonathan Spence, *The Search for Modern China*, W.W. Norton & Company, 2001

Source D

Distribution of government budget expenditures, 1950–57

Expenditure category (per cent)	1950	1952	1957
Economic construction	25.5	45.4	51.4
Social, cultural, and educational outlays	11.1	13.6	16.0
National defence	41.5	26.0	19.0
Government administration	19.3	10.3	7.8
Other	2.6	4.7	5.8
Total in per cent	100.0	100.0	100.0
Total in millions of yuan	6,810.0	16,790.0	29,020.0

Source: Jonathan Spence, *The Search for Modern China*, W.W. Norton & Company, 2001

Source E

Per capita annual consumption, Shanghai, 1929–30 and 1956 (in catties, except as noted)

Commodity	1929–30	1956	% increase
Rice	240.17	270.74	12.5
Wheat flour	15.17	15.68	3.4
Pork	9.78	16.21	65.7
Beef, mutton	1.89	2.29	21.2
Chicken, duck	0.76	2.70	255.3
Fish, shellfish	10.17	27.39	169.3
Eggs	1.85	7.02	379.5
Vegetables	159.57	193.50	21.2
Vegetable oil	612.58	10.20	-18.9
Animal oil	0.47	0.71	73.2
Sugar	2.40	4.17	73.8
Cigarettes (20)	24.21	32.36	33.7
Alcoholic beverages	13.43	6.46	-51.9
Tea	0.55	0.15	-72.3
Cotton fabrics (m²)	6.43	14.00	117.7
Kerosene	19.17	0.40	-91.9
Coal and charcoal	43.14	228.17	428.9
Combustible gasses	242.77	78.24	-67.8
Leather shoes (pair)	0.17	0.27	58.8
Rubber shoes (pair)	0.10	0.51	410.0
Stockings (pair)	1.26	2.08	65.0
Living space (m²)	3.22	4.78	48.5
Units: 1 catty = 0.5 grams			

Source: Jonathan Spence, *The Search for Modern China*, W.W. Norton & Company, 2001

'History – among many other and more important things – is the record of the crimes and follies of mankind.' (Eric Hobsbawm, *Age of Extremes*, 1994)

To what extent would you agree with Hobsbawm's judgement?

TOK

Source F

> *National income grew at an average annual rate of 8.9 percent (measured in constant prices), with agriculture and industrial output expanding annually by about 3.8 and 18.7 percent respectively. On top of the large increase recorded from 1949 to 1953, this was a stunning rise. Since population growth was 2.4 percent and output grew at 6.5 percent per person, the growth rate, if sustained, would double national income every eleven years.*

From Lee Feigon, *Mao: A Reinterpretation*, Ivan R Dee, Inc., 2002

How did Mao deal with opposition?

Throughout this chapter you will come across instances when, in order to maintain or to recover power, Mao would introduce campaigns to target enemies, real or imagined. For example, the Five- and Three-Anti Campaigns targeted remnants of the bourgeois class. Historians are less clear about the Hundred Flowers Campaign however, in terms of whether it was meant to allow greater freedom or, more cynically, to encourage (and so to uncover) dissent.

The Hundred Flowers Campaign and the Anti-Rightist Movement, 1956–57

In April 1956, the slogan 'let a hundred flowers bloom; let a hundred schools of thought contend' heralded the beginning of what may have been a sincere attempt by Mao to allow a little more freedom of speech. Edwin Moïse argues that Mao had hoped the Hundred Flowers Campaign would encourage intellectuals to criticize arrogant party bureaucrats, and be an effective and positive step moving the revolution forward (*Modern China*, 1994, p. 128). It may be that Mao was disturbed by Khrushchev's secret speech of 1956 (see the section on foreign policy, page 147) and the impact it had upon events in Hungary and Poland, where there were calls for greater independence from Moscow and more freedom for the communist parties to run their own affairs. Just as the secret speech and its apparent promise of greater freedom appeared to have encouraged the expression of discontent in the Eastern Bloc, Mao was concerned that there might be a similar level of discontent simmering beneath the surface in China.

Whatever the motive, Mao was surprised by the extent of criticism that poured forth and how negative much of it was with regard to the party. In 1957, a crackdown on dissent took the form of the Anti-Rightist Movement organized by Deng Xiaoping. According to Edwin Moïse, every organization that employed intellectuals (schools, universities, and the media) was expected to find at least 5 per cent of 'rightists' on their staff and, regardless of whether there were so many, the quota had to be filled (*Modern China*, 1994, p. 129). Many were sent to *laogai* (labour camps) for thought reform. The campaign undermined trust in intellectuals, a prejudice that was to resurface with vehemence during the Cultural Revolution, when they were categorized in the hierarchy of classes as the 'Stinking Ninth'.

The Second Five-Year Plan – the Great Leap Forward, 1958–63

Energized by belief in the enormous resource available to China with its vast population and being a firm believer in the economies of scale, Mao began the Great Leap Forward in 1958. Edwin Moïse notes that, at the heart of this project lay the People's Communes, which totalled 26,000 and contained 5,000 households

Deng Xiaoping (1904–97)

Deng Xiaoping was a member of the CPC during the 1920s. He had taken part in the Long March and became General Secretary of the CPC. He was a protégé of Zhou Enlai, who protected him from more severe punishment during the Cultural Revolution. By 1979, Deng had become the paramount leader of China and put in place the economic reforms of the 1980s. He also determined that Mao had been '70 per cent right but 30 per cent wrong'. He died in 1997.

(*Modern China*, 1994, p. 138). There would be communal dining halls, nurseries, hospitals, and boarding schools. The aim was, as far as possible, to make daily life more efficient, so that workers could spend more time in the factories or in the fields. Communes incorporated both agriculture and light industry, and Mao emphasized the policy of 'walking on two legs', which would allow the development of both areas of the economy in tandem. Agricultural production was set to double in 1958 and double again in 1959.

One of the most memorable aspects of the Great Leap Forward was the building of backyard furnaces that would allow everyone to be part of the industrialization of China. These furnaces were built out of mud and straw, or whatever material was at hand, and, in a frenzy of enthusiasm, all manner of metal objects were collected for smelting. Despite the tremendous energy that was put into this, the end product was, as might be expected, of very poor quality. In their spare time, people were also expected to take part in Anti-Pest campaigns, where rats, insects, and birds were exterminated because they ate the grain before it was harvested; the illogicality of killing sparrows, a natural predator of insects, was immediately obvious. Of paramount importance, however, was that everyone felt they could, and should, contribute to the unstoppable advance of Chinese socialism.

The Great Leap Forward mobilized the country in an unprecedented manner and it could be argued that it cemented the unity of the country and firmly established party control. In economic terms, however, it was a disaster.

Communes set themselves unrealistic targets that were clearly impossible to achieve. Levels of agricultural production, though good, could not possibly be good enough to reach what the communes had promised. According to Jonathan Fenby, a commune in Wuchang claimed that its grain output for 1958 was 450 million tonnes. Not even Mao thought that this was possible and he accepted a revised estimate of 370 million tonnes, but in reality the output was only 200 million tonnes. Did it matter that these targets were untrue? As a matter of fact, it did, as the government was basing the distribution of food, as well as its grain exports, on false statistics (*The Penguin History of Modern China*, 2008, p. 407).

In the new communal dining halls, people were encouraged to eat more than they needed – even more than was realistically available! Propaganda constantly emphasized the bounty of the PRC and calls to 'fill your bellies' meant that those who did not eat a lot risked being targeted as unpatriotic. Farmers also had to neglect their fields to tend backyard furnaces and were encouraged to give up metal farming tools for smelting. Trees were cut to fuel the furnaces so when there was a drought followed by floods, the topsoil was washed away, leaving the land less fertile. An additional problem was that Mao accepted the pseudo-scientific claims of Trofim Lysenko, a Soviet scientist (see page 104), and so China tried to produce 'super crops' with extremely high production yields by deep ploughing and close planting. Sometimes these methods worked, but, for the most part, they exhausted the soil and produced lower crop yields.

How Mao handled criticism

In 1958, during a visit to Hunan, minister of defence Peng Dehuai noticed that the Great Leap Forward was off course. He hesitated before voicing his doubt in front of the party leadership, as he knew that Mao might take this criticism personally and the consequences could be severe. In fact, it is likely that Mao had known the Great Leap Forward was not working, as he stood down as state chairman in 1959 and was replaced by Liu Shaoqi. According to Jonathan Fenby, the Party Plenum (a meeting to discuss policy issues) was held that year in Lushan, and it was there that Peng spoke up, asking if 'the call for the whole people to make steel was correct or not' (*The Penguin History of Modern China*, 2008, p. 409).

Peng then wrote Mao a letter outlining the dangers of depending on false statistics. At a meeting that followed, several of the officials present also expressed muted but clear criticism of the impact of the Great Leap Forward. Mao responded with indignation, making it clear that no hint of criticism would be tolerated. He turned on the CPC and threatened to 'go to the countryside to lead the peasants to overthrow the government. If those of you in the Liberation Army won't follow me, then I will go and find a Red Army, and organize another Liberation Army' (quoted in Zhisui Li, *The Private Life of Chairman Mao*, 1994). Peng resigned and was replaced by Lin Biao, who would take Mao's cult of personality to new heights with his compilation of Mao's sayings in the *Little Red Book of the Thoughts of Chairman Mao*.

Meanwhile, the impact of the Great Leap Forward was devastating, as a terrible famine killed an estimated 30 to 50 million people during the Three Bitter Years of 1959–61. Peasants resorted to eating tree bark and grass just to stay alive and, in some extreme cases, killed and ate their children.

Activity 14
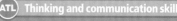 **ATL** **Thinking and communication skills**

Study the source below and answer the question that follows.

> *Towards the people … it uses the method of democracy and not of compulsion, that is, it must necessarily let them take part in political activity and does not compel them to do this or that but uses the method of democracy to educate and persuade. Such education is self-education for the people, and its basic method is criticism and self-criticism… Literally the two slogans – let a hundred flowers blossom and let a hundred schools of thought contend – have no class character; the proletariat can turn them to account, and so can the bourgeoisie or others. Different classes, strata and social groups each have their own views on what are fragrant flowers and what are poisonous weeds. Then, from the point of view of the masses, what should be the criteria today for distinguishing fragrant flowers from poisonous weeds? In their political activities, how should our people judge whether a person's words and deeds are right or wrong? On the basis of the principles of our Constitution, the will of the overwhelming majority of our people and the common political positions, which have been proclaimed on various occasions by our political parties.*

From Mao's speech 'On the correct handling of contradictions amongst the people', 27 February 1957

1. What does the above source tell us about how Mao wanted the Hundred Flowers Campaign to work?

Activity 15
ATL **Thinking and communication skills**

There are several different points of view about why Mao initiated the Hundred Flowers Campaign. Here are two interpretations.

Source A

> *The Party, he [Mao] said he needed to be accountable and 'under supervision'. He sounded reasonable, criticizing Stalin for his 'excessive purges', and giving the impression there were going to be no more of these in China.*
>
> *Few guessed that Mao was setting a trap, and that he was inviting people to speak out so that he could use what they said as an excuse to victimize them. Mao's targets were intellectuals and the educated, the people most likely to speak out.*

From Jung Chang and Jon Halliday, *Mao: The Unknown Story*, Vintage, 2007

Source B

> The Hundred Flowers campaign was not a simple plot by Mao to reveal the hidden rightists in his country, as some critics later charged and as he himself seemed to claim in the published version of his speech. It was, rather, a muddled and inconclusive movement, that grew out of conflicting attitudes within the CPC leadership. At its centre was an argument about the pace and type of development that was best for China.

From Jonathan Spence, *The Search for Modern China*, W.W. Norton & Company, 2001

1. Which of these two views do you find more compelling? Give reasons for your answer.

Activity 16

Study the sources below and answer the questions that follow.

Source A

> The party has become more united, the morale of the people further heightened, and the party–masses relationship greatly improved. We are now witnessing greater activity and creativity of the popular masses on the production front than we have ever witnessed before. A new high tide of production has risen, and is still rising, as the people of the whole country are inspired by the slogan – 'Overtake Britain in Iron and Steel and Other Major Industrial Production in Fifteen or More Years'. To meet this new situation certain methods of work of the party Centre and local committees have to be modified.

From Mao Zedong, 'Sixty Points on Working Methods', 1958

Source B

The backyard furnaces, like this one here, were often very rudimentary constructions. They were built in response to Mao's call for the whole population to be involved in the production of steel.

Source C

> The Communist Party is really wonderful.
> In three days more than a thousand furnaces were built.
> The masses' strength is really tremendous.
> The American imperialists will run off, tails between legs.
> The Chinese people will now surpass Britain.
> The East wind will always prevail over the West wind.

Song composed by workers in Hsinhua County in 1958

Source D

❝ Millet is scattered all over the ground,
The leaves of the sweet potatoes are withered.
The young and the strong have gone to smelt iron,
To harvest the grain there are children and old women.
How shall we get through next year?
I shall agitate and speak out on behalf of the people.

Poem written by Peng Dehuai, 1959, from R. MacFarquhar, *The Origins of the Cultural Revolution*, **Volume 1, Columbia University Press, 1959**

1. 'The backyard furnaces were a failure.' How could you use Source B to support this assertion?
2. What, do you think, was the purpose of songs like the one in Source C? How reliable are songs like this as evidence of how the Chinese population felt about the Great Leap Forward?
3. Compare and contrast the origin and the purpose of Source C with those of Source D.

Activity 17

ATL Thinking skills

Statistical analysis of China, 1957–61

Study the statistics below on China's outputs and answer the questions that follow.

Grain output (million metric tons)

	Total grain	Rice	Wheat
1957	185	86.8	23.6
1958	200	80.8	22.6
1959	170	69.3	22.2
1960	143.3	59.7	22.2
1961	147.5	53.6	14.25

Other crop output (million metric tons)

	1958	1961
Sugar cane	12.50	4.27
Beets	3.00	0.80
Oil-bearing plants	4.77	1.80
Cotton	1.97	0.80

Livestock numbers (millions)

Pigs	138.29	75.50
Draught animals	53.60	38.10

Industrial output (billions yuan)

1958	1959	1960	1961	1962
121	163	183	113	94

Steel, coal, and cement output (million metric tons)

	1958	1959	1960	1961	1962
Steel	8.8	13.87	18.66	8.70	6.67
Coal	270.0	369.00	397.00	278.00	220.00
Cement	9.3	12.27	15.65	6.21	6.0

Source: Jonathan Fenby, *The Penguin History of Modern China: The Fall and Rise of a Great Power, 1850 to the Present*, 2nd Revised ed., Penguin, 2013

1. How would you use the above statistics to support an argument that the Great Leap Forward was a disaster for China?

2. Why did livestock numbers fall so drastically?

Mao's foreign policy

Authoritarian leaders often used foreign policy as a way to consolidate or to maintain power. They might have used fear of an external enemy to justify increased security and a reduction of individual freedom, or the conquest of new territory to heighten nationalism and help build a cult of personality. For Mao, his main concern was to build up China's economy and to consolidate the rule of the CPC over this vast country. An additional factor was the Cold War and how, by the late 1940s, this was dividing the world into spheres of influence. In terms of ideology, Mao stood with the Soviet Union, but, as we shall see, this could not be taken for granted.

The Sino-Soviet Treaty of Friendship, Alliance, and Mutual Assistance, 1950

Mao announced in 1949 that China would lean towards the Soviet Union and away from the United States. This was not so surprising given that China and the Soviet Union shared a common ideology, and that the Cold War was now a major factor in international diplomacy. Although Mao did not intend China to become a 'satellite' of the Soviet Union, he knew that aid was essential for developing the Chinese economy and that the Soviet Union was the likeliest source of funds and technology for China, just as it was for the countries of the Eastern Bloc.

In December 1949, Mao was invited to the festivities that celebrated Stalin's 70th birthday; this would be his first visit to the Soviet Union. One of Mao's key aims was to get Stalin to **abrogate** the treaty that had been signed with Jiang Jieshi in 1945, which had given key territorial concessions to the Soviet Union. Mao found, however, that it was very difficult to have a meeting with Stalin; only by threatening to leave immediately did Mao finally get an invitation to the Kremlin in January 1950. It then took several weeks to complete the negotiations, but by 14 February 1950, the treaty had been signed. It stipulated that the Soviet Union would aid China if it went to war. It also said that 50 industrial projects would be set up with Soviet assistance and that China would receive a loan of $300 million over a period of five years. Jonathan Fenby concludes that Mao was 'reasonably satisfied' as, after all, China desperately needed aid and it was unlikely to get it elsewhere (*The Penguin History of Modern China*, 2008, p. 364).

The Korean War, 1950–53

Almost as soon as the PRC was established, China became embroiled in a war that was taking place in Korea. This had broken out in June 1950, when North Korea, a communist state led by Kim Il Sung, invaded South Korea, a capitalist state led by Syngman Rhee. Stalin had given Kim tacit support to attempt the reunification of Korea under communist rule. Kim had informed Mao that an invasion was planned although it was unlikely that Mao thought China would get involved. Indeed, Mao's main preoccupation at this time was with Taiwan, also known as the Republic of China (ROC), where Jiang and the GMD had taken refuge. Mao's priority was to stage an invasion of the island.

In Korea, the initial campaign waged by Kim was a success with the North Korean Army, which included veterans who had fought alongside the PLA in the Chinese Civil War, moving swiftly to Pusan, in the very southern tip of South Korea. The invasion provoked the United States, however, and President Truman took this violation of South Korean sovereignty to the United Nations (UN) Security Council. A resolution was passed to support a 'peace-making' force to be sent to aid South Korea. The Soviet Union had been unable to veto this resolution, as it was boycotting the Council in protest of the occupation of China's seat in the UN by the Nationalist government of ROC, instead of the PRC. The UN Army was, in practice, made up mostly of US troops led by General Douglas MacArthur. He carried out a daring plan to cut North Korean supply lines by landing troops behind enemy lines at Inchon. This was a resounding success: the UN forces crossed the 38th parallel that divided Korea, and by October 1950, they were advancing towards the Yalu River, the border with China.

Stalin urged China to intervene, so Zhou Enlai visited Moscow for consultations, receiving assurances that the Soviet Union would provide air support. This, for Mao, was the deciding factor and 300,000 'volunteer' soldiers (there would be 3 million in all) crossed the Yalu to fight on behalf of North Korea. According to Jonathan Fenby, they fought in difficult conditions, with temperatures in winter falling to minus 20 degrees Celsius (*The Penguin History of Modern China*, 2008). In China, the war was known as the 'the War to resist US aggression and to aid Korea'.

The UN forces were swept back towards the 38th parallel, as the Chinese and North Koreans took Seoul, the South Korean capital that now changed hands for the third time. The Chinese supply lines were too long, however, and they suffered enormous casualties. MacArthur urged Truman to use the atom bomb and to attack China. Famously, the US Chief of Staff, General Omar Bradley, strongly advised against this, stating that this would be 'the wrong war in the wrong place at the wrong time and against the wrong enemy' (Fenby, *The Penguin History of Modern China*, 2008, p. 368).

The Korean War was a long drawn-out war of attrition. It did not end until 1953, when an armistice, still in place today, was finally signed. An estimated 400,000 Chinese soldiers were killed, including Mao's eldest son Anying.

For Mao the outcome of the Korean War was important in many ways:

- It showed that China could stand up to the United States and not be defeated.
- It demonstrated that the United States was reluctant to use the A bomb (Mao called the bomb a 'paper tiger').
- China was able to receive the latest arms from the Soviet Union, including 3,000 planes.

Kim Il Sung (1912–94)

Still known today as the Universal Leader, Kim returned with the Red Army in 1945 to become the communist leader of North Korea. His son Kim Jong Il succeeded him; his grandson, Kim Jong Un, is the current leader.

One of the main obstacles to signing the armistice was the fate of the prisoners of war (POWs). There were thousands of Chinese and North Korean POWs held in camps and many of them did not want to return to their homeland, preferring to stay in South Korea. This was totally unacceptable to both China and North Korea so, in retaliation, they refused to release UN POWs. The matter was finally resolved in 1953 when, after the death of Stalin (probably the main block to peace, as he preferred the United States to be held down in a long war), an armistice was signed. Guards were taken off POW camps and the gates left open.

- It raised China's status as a revolutionary and anti-imperialist power.
- It confirmed an alliance between the United States and the ROC and its hostility towards the PRC.
- On the domestic front, it may also be argued that the Korean War assisted with the implementation of the Five- and Three-Anti Campaigns, as the threat of an external enemy appeared very real and could justify the tightening up of security and the strengthening of the revolution at home.

Mao saw China as a champion of anti-imperialism; he identified closely with the independence struggles of former colonial powers. In 1955, Zhou Enlai attended the Bandung Conference in Indonesia. This was a gathering of representatives from 29 countries, such as India, Ceylon (Sri Lanka), Yugoslavia, Egypt, and Burma, to discuss Asian–African affairs, focusing on the need for post-colonial states to assist each other in their economic progress and to adopt a neutral stance on the Cold War. To some extent, it was also a reaction to the creation of the Southeast Asia Treaty Organization (SEATO) that had been put together under US auspices in the aftermath of the Korean War.

For the most part, post-colonial states were unlikely, at this stage, to gain much support from the United States as it was reluctant to alienate its allies, among whom were the colonial powers of Britain and France. There was a tendency therefore for the representatives who came to Bandung to lean towards communism, although at the Belgrade Conference of 1961, the formal name of 'Non-Aligned Movement' was adopted. China's aim was to become the beacon for development among developing countries, but it did not achieve this during Mao's rule, as it was always overshadowed by the Soviet Union.

Taiwan and the Chinese Off-Shore Islands Crisis, 1958

Taiwan (the ROC) remained a thorn in the side of China. In 1958, a conflict broke out over the strategic islands of Quemoy and Matsu, which lay in the Taiwan Straits, a narrow stretch of water between China and Taiwan. After the outbreak of the Korean War, the United States had pledged support to Taiwan, sent the Seventh Fleet to patrol the Straits, and sent arms to Jiang Jieshi. This dissuaded Mao from attempting an invasion of the island, but the PLA did shell the islands from time to time, and in 1958, this, along with the build-up of Chinese troops, suggested that an invasion might take place. The US response was quick and strong; there was even a discussion of a rapid escalation to nuclear war if an invasion was attempted. The crisis passed, however, and a tense peace was restored. Relations between Taiwan and China continued to be hostile but, as we shall see, improved Sino-American relations led to the UN accepting the PRC as a member in 1971 with Taiwan's status as 'China' being rescinded.

Sino-Soviet relations, 1953–76

Stalin died in March 1953 and, after an internal power struggle, was succeeded by Nikita Khrushchev. With the passing of Stalin, Mao considered himself to be the leader of world revolution, although Khrushchev did not agree! In 1956, during the 20th Party Congress in Moscow, Khrushchev delivered his 'secret speech' that denounced Stalin's purges and began a process of de-Stalinization. Mao was infuriated by this speech, in part because Khrushchev had criticized Stalin's cult of personality; Mao, who had developed his own personality cult, wondered if this had been a slight against him. Mao also disagreed with Khrushchev's proposal of 'peaceful coexistence' with the West. Relations deteriorated, with Khrushchev criticizing Mao's behaviour over the Off-Shore Islands Crisis in 1958. Khrushchev had a growing suspicion that

China could not be trusted with the nuclear bomb that it wanted Russian help to build. Although aid and technological assistance were withdrawn, China did go on to build its own atomic bomb, which was tested in 1964. Meanwhile, antipathy between the Soviet Union and China deepened, and matters came to a head in 1961 over the 'Albanian Question'.

The socialist leader of Albania, Enver Hoxha, had also been deeply offended by Krushchev's 1956 secret speech, and Soviet aid to Albania had been withdrawn. China stepped in 'with money and technical assistance', mostly to annoy Khrushchev, who, as blunt as ever, later called Mao an 'Asian Hitler' and 'a living corpse', according to Michael Lynch (*The People's Republic of China since 1949*, 1998, p. 120). The Sino-Soviet dispute resembled a religious conflict, with one side charging the other with heresy. Antipathy deepened and troop numbers were increased significantly along the border. Despite China and the Soviet Union both supporting North Vietnam during the Vietnam War, they were barely on speaking terms. In fact, during the Cultural Revolution, the 'Soviet running dogs' were considered among the chief ideological enemies of China. Border conflicts did break out along the Ussuri River in 1969 and, although these were limited in scope and duration, they reflected how serious the Sino-Soviet split had become. Relations did not improve until long after the death of Mao.

Tibet and Xinjiang

Although not strictly 'foreign', the PRC's attitude towards Tibet and Xinjiang, China's border regions, was imperial in nature, given that the local populations there differed in ethnicity (and religion) from China's majority population, the Han Chinese.

On the basis that it belonged, historically, to China, Tibet was invaded in 1950–51, leading to the Agreement on the Peaceful Liberation of Tibet or Xizang, as it was now renamed. Although the agreement promised to preserve the culture, religion, and tradition of Tibetan society, in practice a military committee was put in place to run the country. Many new projects, for example to improve infrastructure, were completed, but there was little regard for the traditional structures of society, which were described by the CPC as 'feudal'. Han Chinese were settled in large numbers as workers and as party representatives, not only to implement projects but also to dilute the ethnicity of the local population. In 1959, the suppression of Tibetan unrest became more serious; the Dalai Lama, fearing the consequences if he stayed, escaped to India. Another impact of the Chinese policy towards Tibet was to worsen China's relations with India, leading to the outbreak of the Sino-Indian War of 1962, fought along the border that lay in the Himalayas. The Chinese forces were victorious, but relations remained tense.

Another autonomous region was Xinjiang, where although the majority Muslim Uyghur population were given representation on the People's Council, real control lay with the army. Jonathan Fenby states that Wang Zeng, the head of the Xinjiang Production and Construction Corps, was described as 'the closest any CPC military man came to being a warlord' and that he 'presided over a vast conglomerate that ran businesses, farms and prisons, while offering Beijing border security and keeping the Uyghurs down' (*The Penguin History of Modern China*, 2008, p. 370).

There will be more on foreign policy when we come to discuss the changing nature of China's relations with America in the early 1970s. At this point, however, it is worth considering whether Mao did have a 'foreign policy' or whether, as mentioned earlier, he merely responded to external events. He certainly had expansionist policies, but these lay inside rather than outside of China.

Towards the Cultural Revolution

After the failure of the Great Leap Forward, Mao allowed Deng Xiaoping and Liu Shaoqi to take the necessary measures to achieve economic recovery. They responded by reducing the size of the communes and allowing a revival of private markets so that farmers would be encouraged to sell their surplus stocks and to increase grain production. Mao did not approve, as he felt that China was moving away from socialism, but he was also aware that these policies were working and could not yet be halted. He was increasingly concerned that he was losing authority and popularity. In particular, as Frank Dikotter states, Mao grew suspicious of Liu, especially when he expressed concerns about how the party would be judged when the calamities of the Great Leap Forward became widely known. In a meeting with Mao, Liu had said that 'history will judge you and me, and even cannibalism will go into the books'. Dikotter also mentions that Mao had suspected Liu would become 'his Khrushchev, the servant who had denounced his master, Stalin'. Indeed, Liu would be one of the victims of the Cultural Revolution when Mao felt able to strike at his enemies (*Mao's Great Famine*, 2010, p. 337).

Meanwhile, under the supervision of Liu and Deng, grain output rose, industrial production grew by 17 to 27 per cent between 1963 and 1965, and the production of trucks, cement, steel, and electricity had doubled since 1957 (Fenby, *The Penguin History of Modern China*, 2008, p. 426). With Mao's support, Liu started the Socialist Education Movement that aimed to increase collectivism, socialism, and patriotism. This was to be achieved through the 'Four Clean-ups' of politics, the economy, the organization of the CPC, and ideology. The mass line was reintroduced and party members were encouraged to go and learn from the peasants. There were warning signs however, as, according to Mao, the ideology of the CPC now clashed with socialism, and the party was under threat from 'capitalist roaders', a phrase that was to gain wide currency during a period later to be called the Great Proletarian Cultural Revolution.

With Lin Biao as minister of defence, Mao was sure of control over the PLA. His *Little Red Book* was distributed to all the soldiers; its size conveniently formatted to fit in the top pocket of their uniforms. In this way, the army became a propaganda mouthpiece for Mao. Soldiers wore identical green uniforms, devoid of all insignia, and military ranks were abolished, emphasizing the egalitarian nature of the armed forces and their allegiance to Mao. The role of the army was also glorified in *The Diary of Lei Feng*, a book that told the story of an ordinary army driver whose every moment was given over to reading and learning the Thoughts of Chairman Mao. His untimely death (crushed under the wheels of a truck) made him a martyr for the revolution. As Michael Lynch points out, the story was fictional, but it had a clear propaganda message: ordinary soldiers were honest and devoted and, by implication, self-important party officials were not (*The People's Republic of China since 1949*, 1998, p. 36).

In 1965, the split between Mao and the party deepened when Yao Wenyuan, a writer, criticized a play called *The Dismissal of Hai Rui from Office*, written by Wu Han, Deputy Mayor of Beijing. Although it was set in the Soong dynasty (960–1279 CE), the play was interpreted as a veiled attack on Mao. Yao's article accused Wu Han of having written an allegory of Peng Dehuai's dismissal by Mao, and Wu stood accused of betraying Marxism–Leninism. This was a serious accusation and it emphasized the growing division in the CPC between those who wanted to slow down and those who wanted to speed up the revolution.

Mao's wife, Jiang Qing, played a very important role in the Cultural Revolution. She was a leftist and stood firmly on the side of radicalizing the revolution. Along with Lin

Jiang Qing (1914–91)

Jiang Qing was Mao's third wife. A former actress, she had married Mao during their time in Yan'an. She was to become a strong supporter and initiator of the most radical policies of the Cultural Revolution and, together with three colleagues, was to form what was disparagingly known as the Gang of Four. After Mao's death, they were arrested and imprisoned, though not put on trial until 1980. When accused of the excesses of the Cultural Revolution, Jiang blamed Mao, claiming, 'I was Chairman Mao's dog. Whomever he told me to bite, I bit.'

Biao, she called for a move against the rightists, especially Liu and Deng, and so began the Cultural Revolution. In May 1966, students at Peking University criticized the educational system and called for educational reform. Liu and Deng sent work teams to control the students, but Mao supported the rebels. The students were to become known as Red Guards.

Mao returned to the public eye in May 1966 when he swam in the Yangtze River. This event was intended to show that he was still alive and energetic (in other words, still fit to lead) and that the Great Helmsman was back in charge. He promoted Lin Biao to vice-chairman, and encouraged revolution in August 1966 when he called upon the Red Guards to 'bombard the headquarters'. In this way, Mao was encouraging an attack not only on schools and universities but also on the CPC. In the same month, encouraging the youth of China to support him, Mao called on them to denounce the 'Four Olds': old thoughts, old habits, old culture, and old customs. In doing so, he was calling on the younger generation to follow his edicts and to overthrow the system put in place by the older generation of party officials. He told his Red Guards 'to rebel is justified', and they heeded his command by abandoning their work and studies to become the vanguard of the revolution and the reformers of the CPC.

Because they had the support of Chairman Mao, these young revolutionaries knew that they could attack, with impunity, all those accused of being rightists. Names were changed, for example: the road outside the Soviet Embassy in Beijing was now called Anti-Revisionism Road; Hong Kong was referred to as 'Expel the Imperialists' City. Red Guards, many of them elementary school students, poured into Beijing to attend rallies, where they marched through Tiananmen Square and, if they were lucky, achieved their dream of seeing Mao Zedong. From Beijing, millions of Red Guards travelled to distant parts of the country to carry the message of the Cultural Revolution. For many, it was a salutary lesson in how impoverished much of China was at this time, only a few years after the famine.

The criticism of Western influence, now branded as bourgeois, extended to 'a ban on magic and wrestling, use of poker cards, private shoe repairing and the purchase of snacks'. The brutality of the Red Guards was notorious, with pupils attacking teachers (some of whom were made to sit on a box of explosives and then to set it alight); others were beaten to death. Intellectuals were especially targeted. Jiang Qing set herself up as the censor of all artistic works, condemning authors, artists, composers, and opera singers. According to Jonathan Fenby, some of these artists committed suicide as a way to avoid punishment for being counter-revolutionaries (*The Penguin History of Modern China*, 2008, pp. 448–9).

Mao's cult of personality was hugely influential during the Cultural Revolution. He was the Great Teacher and the Great Helmsman, achieving the status of a deity. He had succeeded in purging the party of rivals as Liu Shoqui was sent to prison, where he fell sick and died. Meanwhile, Deng Xiaoping was sent to work in a factory and his son, caught up in a Red Guard attack, was thrown out of a high window, suffering serious injuries that led to his being paralysed. Not only had Mao reasserted his authority, he had placed himself in a position of power and influence that few authoritarian leaders have rivalled.

By 1967, Mao had achieved his aims for the Cultural Revolution and, ready to scale back the excesses of the Red Guards, sent in the PLA to restore order. The Red Guards had split into different factions, with the worker-led Scarlet Guards in Shanghai overthrowing the city government. As many as 12 million eager young enthusiasts were now 'sent down to the countryside to learn from the peasants'.

For many of them this was the beginning of a long exile, as many were forbidden from returning to the cities until after Mao's death in 1976. They had helped Mao to maintain power, at a terrible cost to the country and to themselves, as many of them now lost the opportunity to complete their education.

Employees at the Government Printing House in 1971 packing up boxes of Mao's *Little Red Book* for distribution. It was expected that everyone should have a copy of this book, carrying it with them. There were reports that it had 'cured illnesses and raised a man from the dead' (Fenby, *The Penguin History of Modern China*, 2008, p. 457).

Activity 18

ATL   Thinking

Study the sources below and answer the questions that follow.

Source A

A propaganda poster used during the Cultural Revolution.

The poster, from the Great Proletarian Cultural Revolution, reads: 'Advance victoriously while following Chairman Mao's revolutionary line in literature and the arts' (1968).

Source B

沿着毛主席的革命文艺路线胜利前进

1. What is the message conveyed by Source A?
2. Look carefully at the poster in Source B, what does it tell you about how the Cultural Revolution intended to influence the arts in China?

Towards the end of the Cultural Revolution

Although the Red Guards were brought under control, the Cultural Revolution was not yet over. The PLA, led by Jiang Qing and Lin Biao, now continued a campaign of terror against the rightists. Indeed, the Cultural Revolution did not end until Mao died in 1976. It was ever-present as a threat to be used against counter-revolutionaries, should Mao, once again, sense that he was losing power. According to Immanuel Hsu, the Cultural Revolution was 'anti-cultural, anti-intellectual and anti-scientific' (*The Rise of Modern China*, 1995, p. 703). Once again, Mao had chosen revolution over economic progress, with the result that China's economy was almost destroyed.

Lin Biao survived until 1971, but his ambition was clear to all, including Mao, who suspected that, having built up the strength of the PLA during the Cultural Revolution, Lin was planning a military coup. Lin's subsequent fall from grace reflected the growing factionalism that was now dividing those who had supported and implemented the Cultural Revolution. It still isn't clear if Lin really had planned a coup, but he was killed in a plane crash when he was allegedly escaping to the Soviet Union. Conspiracy theories abound, including a claim that Lin had been killed earlier and it was his dead body that was placed on the plane that subsequently crashed.

One of the great survivors of the Cultural Revolution was Zhou Enlai, who managed to convince Mao of his loyalty. When the economy needed reviving in the early 1970s, it was Zhou who quietly called Deng Xiaoping back from the countryside; together, they worked on what would later become known as the Four Modernizations. Zhou, suffering from throat cancer, died in January 1976, just months before Mao.

The purpose of the Cultural Revolution

The Cultural Revolution was a momentous event, especially in urban areas, and it had a huge impact upon people's lives. Propaganda and terror were used in equal measure to tighten Mao's grip on power and to renew the revolution in China. In 1976, when Mao was near the end of his life, he maintained that one of the great victories of his life had been the Cultural Revolution, although it was a process that he believed was still unfinished.

Below is a summary of some main reasons for the Cultural Revolution:

- After the failure of the Great Leap Forward, Mao stepped back to allow Zhou Enlai and Deng Xiaoping to revive the economy but, in doing so, he felt he had lost power and that China was heading along a capitalist road. Mao wanted to put a halt to this and to restore socialism.

- One of Mao's great concerns was that the impact of the Communist Revolution would be short-lived and that the bourgeois class would reassert itself. In particular, he feared that education was still the preserve of the elite (in this case, the children of party cadres), and that the children who proceeded on to further education would not be the children of the peasants in the countryside. By challenging the authorities in schools and universities, the Red Guards were breaking down a system that Mao believed perpetuated privilege among the few.

- Mao also felt that the younger generation, who had not experienced the civil war, did not appreciate how bad circumstances had been in China before 1949; the Cultural Revolution would therefore give them some idea of the struggle required to make a revolution and to keep it alive.

- Mao felt that he had enemies within the party hierarchy intending to wrest power from him. By calling on the Red Guards to 'bombard the headquarters', he was encouraging them to challenge and remove even the most senior party officials, such as Liu Shaoqi and Deng Xiaoping.

- Mao had around him people who also saw the revolution as an opportunity to gain power. These included Lin Biao, who wanted Mao to revive the presidency (Mao refused, and Lin was killed soon after), and Jiang Qing (who led a political faction known as the **Gang of Four**). Jiang, a former actress, had insisted that all the arts had to be revolutionary in content and purpose, thus banning Western classical music and ballet. When Mao died, Jiang wanted to become his successor, but she was not popular, and the Gang of Four was pushed aside.

What did the Cultural Revolution achieve?

- Mao's cult of personality reached new heights of adulation: he was the sole (and unquestioned) authoritarian ruler of China.

- He removed his perceived enemies from the leadership of the CPC, although Deng was allowed to return to Beijing in 1973 under the protection of Zhou Enlai and, to some extent, to replace Lin Biao.

- The Red Guards, after a frenzied period of attacking all symbols of bourgeois sentiment and counter-revolutionary behaviour, became a 'lost generation' whose education had been interrupted and whose lives were blighted by long periods of exile in the countryside. In 1971, the Communist Youth League was reinstated to restore control over the generation that had been instrumental in blindly carrying out the wishes of Chairman Mao.

- Outside of China, the Cultural Revolution inspired students in the 1968 student uprisings. The Communism of the Soviet Union had lost its appeal, especially after the suppression of the Prague Spring in 1968, and many young communists turned instead to China and would brandish copies of the *Little Red Book*.

In July 1981, the CPC gave its own assessment of the Cultural Revolution: 'The Great Cultural Revolution from May 1966 to October 1976 caused the most devastating setback and heavy losses to the party, the state, and the people in the history of the People's Republic, and this Great Cultural Revolution was initiated and led by Comrade Mao Zedong' ('Resolution on Certain Questions in the History of our Party Since the Founding of the People's Republic', *Beijing Review*, no. 27, 6 July 1981).

Women enact a political drama for a large crowd during the Cultural Revolution.

CHALLENGE YOURSELF

ATL Thinking, research, social, and communication skills

Working with a classmate, see what you can find out about the impact of the Cultural Revolution on Hong Kong, as well as on Albania where its leader Enver Hoxha was a close ally of Beijing. Then make a slide show presentation for the class.

ATL Research and thinking skills

Compare Mao's foreign policy with that of another authoritarian leader who shared the same ideology but from a different region. How far, do you think, did both leaders' commitment to Marxism–Leninism influence their decision-making when it came to international diplomacy?

An unexpected shift in China's foreign policy

In 1972, as the Cultural Revolution abated, China's foreign policy took an unexpected turn when President Nixon of the United States visited Beijing and met with Mao. Despite its claim to be the leading country of world revolution and a beacon for anti-imperialists everywhere, China was still a second-tier power compared to the Soviet Union. As the Sino-Soviet split deepened, there was an opportunity for China to improve its relations with the United States.

The 1970s became known as the decade of *détente*, as relations between the United States and the Soviet Union improved with arms treaties being signed, a joint-space mission was planned, and the Organization for Security and Cooperation in Europe was established. There are many reasons that motivated the policy of *détente*, but ending the war in Vietnam was one of the most important. Richard Nixon won the US presidential election in November 1968, against a background of civil unrest and the war in Vietnam. He wanted to find a way to leave the war and to secure 'peace with honour'; to accomplish this, he needed to secure the support of both the Soviet Union and China. The two countries, although not on friendly terms, were both supporting North Vietnam. Nixon knew that he needed the agreement of not just one but both allies of North Vietnam, and so was open to improving relations with China.

The initial communication was kept highly secret and the first public inkling of a change in relations came with what became known as 'ping-pong diplomacy'. This was literally about ping-pong (table tennis) to begin with, as the US team visiting Japan at that time was invited to play in China. Highly secret diplomatic meetings followed and, finally, Nixon made his famous visit to China in February 1972. For Mao, this was a significant coup, as closer relations with the United States alarmed the Soviet Union and provided China with an important ally. Meanwhile, in October 1971, the UN General Assembly had voted in favour of the PRC taking over the seat on the Security Council held until now by nationalist Taiwan (the ROC). For Mao, this was significant, because it gave China a right of veto, bolstering China's growing status as a world power. The shift in relations with the United States came as a shock to the Chinese people who, for decades, had been compelled to consider the country as an arch enemy, but it was also very welcome and signalled a return of China to world affairs.

The death of Mao

By the early 1970s, Mao was in poor health. He had been suffering from Parkinson's disease, a degenerative illness that worsened over time. In January 1976, Zhou Enlai died; he was deeply and sincerely mourned, especially by those who saw him as a moderating influence at a time when the excesses of the Cultural Revolution might return. Deng Xiaoping gave the oration at Zhou's funeral, but Mao, being too sick, was unable to attend. A month later, during the Ching Ming Festival (a traditional holiday when respect is paid to dead ancestors), thousands came to Tiananmen Square to lay wreaths in memory of Zhou. Jiang Qing, an arch-rival of Zhou, called this a 'counter-revolutionary' act and blamed it on Deng who, on the advice of powerful friends he had in the military, once again left Beijing to bide his time until he could safely return.

Mao's health continued to deteriorate and by June 1976, he was no longer able to receive foreign visitors. It was clear that he did not have long to live. In July, the Tangshan earthquake – the worst earthquake of the 20th century – hit China. It reached 7.8 on the Richter scale with aftershocks of 7.1; a city of 1.6 million people was destroyed, with the estimated number of deaths ranging from 260,000 to 600,000. According to traditional Chinese belief, such a major disaster was an omen that a dynasty was coming to an end. Indeed, a 'dynasty' did end when Mao died on 9 September 1976. In his last months, he designated Hua Guofeng, the party secretary from Hunan, as his successor, although Jiang Qing still plotted to take power. According to Immanuel Hsu, she was thwarted, however, by failing to gain the support of senior military commanders, most of whom, along with other senior party cadres, loathed her and the other members of the Gang of Four (*The Rise of Modern China*, 1995, p. 779).

Activity 19   Thinking, research, and communication skills

Consider this question:

Analyse the successes and failures of the domestic policies of one authoritarian leader.

Below are the introductions of two essay answers to the question, using Mao's policies between 1949 and 1976. What do you think are the strengths of these answers? Are there areas for improvement?

Student answer A – Kevin

On the 1 October 1949, after Mao proclaimed the People's Republic of China (PRC), he became its unquestionable leader, destined to change its future forever in an attempt to industrialize and transform China into a modern superpower. The following years from 1949 to 1976, which became known as the 'Mao years', are characterized by huge economic programmes as well as very controversial social policies. However, the assessments of Mao as well as those of his policies vary greatly.

Examiner's comments

This is a good introduction and it begins well. It manages to include references to Mao's leadership and his aims. These would be the strengths. The last sentence could be improved upon, however, as it drifts away from the question and mention 'assessments', which would fit better in a conclusion rather than in an introduction.

Some questions may ask you to discuss specific types of policies, such as social or economic policies. You may also be asked to compare the policies of two leaders from different regions, so be prepared for this.

Student answer B – Anna

Throughout history many great leaders have walked this planet with leadership qualities such as a deep understanding of business, charisma, willingness to admit mistakes etc. The communist leader of China, Mao Zedong, who ruled from 1949 to 1976 is arguably both a successful and unsuccessful leader. He managed to save the previously corrupt China, but also created great poverty and more violence in his country. His successes and failures are what defined him as a person and as a leader of China.

Examiner's comments

The opening sentence could be improved, as it is rather whimsical with its reference about leaders who have 'walked this planet'. It does improve with the second sentence pointing out the different points of view and ends with a nicely phrased sentence that link back to the question.

Activity 20   **Research, communication, social, and thinking skills**

Study the sources below and answer the questions that follow.

Source A

A meeting between Mao Zedong and Richard Nixon, 1972.

Source B

Cartoon by Pat Oliphant in the *Denver Post*, 1971.

1. The meeting between Nixon and Mao was very important. Source A is one of the famous images taken at this time. Even though it is quite simple and shows just the two men shaking hands, what can you infer from this photograph about Nixon and Mao's relationship at this time?

2. In a small group, discuss Source B and try to determine what its message is meant to be. Be sure to look at all the different symbolism and, in particular, pay attention to the comment in the bottom left-hand corner. Do you think this could be added to a cartoon nowadays? Give reasons for your answer.

3.3 Assessing Mao as an authoritarian leader

Mao turned China into a unified, tightly controlled state that became a world power. He did this by providing an ideology that offered hope of change to a nation that endured poverty, famine, invasion, and civil war. He also introduced campaigns to provide basic healthcare and education. Strenuous efforts were made to turn China into an industrialized country and to provide it with a strong army and nuclear capability. This was surely a transformation that can be attributed largely to Mao's leadership.

What did Mao achieve?

In terms of social policies, Mao addressed women's rights with the Marriage Reform Law, although it took time for this to be accepted, especially in the deeply traditional rural areas. He also gave land to the peasants in accordance with the Agrarian Land Reform Law, although this land was then taken away, with the peasants being herded into the vast communes of the Great Leap Forward and suffering greatly during the Three Bitter Years. Overall, it is difficult to estimate how far the lives of peasants changed for the better, but millions moved to the cities, where they found work in factories and where the 'iron rice bowl' ensured some economic security. Literacy levels increased from 20 per cent in 1949 to over 70 per cent in 1976 and, although the Cultural Revolution had a damaging impact on education, overall there was progress. In terms of healthcare, there was immunization against diseases such as polio. The '**barefoot doctors**' were sent out to provide basic healthcare in the countryside and, although these were peasants who received only a few months of training, they were able to offer some rudimentary care. Certainly, according to Edwin Moïse, they were much cheaper to train than professional doctors and more willing to spend their time in the countryside, rather than in the city hospitals (*Modern China*, 1994, p. 175). Life expectancy can also be a guide to living conditions, and this went up from an average of 35 years in 1949 to 68 years in 1976. We can take this as an indication of improved life opportunities and general living standards in Mao's China.

Neither religion nor traditional Chinese beliefs were encouraged. Also, when we look back at Mao's rule, it is easy to see periodic bursts of revolutionary zeal that would denounce counter-revolutionaries and put innocent people at risk. In this way, Mao's control could be enforced, as it was never clear when someone might become a target and be sent off for punishment, which made everyone all the more mindful of their own (and each other's) behaviour.

Historians' assessments of Mao

Immanuel Hsu, an American-Chinese historian who wrote several books on Chinese history states that 'historians will agree that Mao was supremely successful as a revolutionary but extremely erratic as a nation builder. His great achievements before 1957 may serve as an inspiration to others, but his major mistakes thereafter must serve as a lesson to all' (*China without Mao*, 1982). In particular, Hsu considers Mao's fixation with population growth to have been a mistake. Unlike Stalin and Hitler, Mao did not give out medals to mothers who had eight or 10 children, but he did make it extremely difficult for women to access birth control or to have abortions. As a result, the population almost doubled from 500 million in 1949 to 925 million by 1976, an enormous increase that China could barely afford. Hsu also criticizes Mao's ill-planned and erratic economic policies that were driven by ideological zeal and a drive for industrialization, rather than taking into account China's predominantly agrarian economy. Finally, Mao ruled China like the feudal emperors that he despised. His cult of personality reached into every corner of China, with propaganda posters and the *Little Red Book*. Hsu comments that, 'like the emperors of the past, Mao was a patriarch, Helmsman, and even god-hero, who could do no wrong' (*China without Mao*, 1982, p. 154).

Jung Chang and Jon Halliday, writing in 2005, made the following claim: 'While feeling deeply discontented at having failed to achieve his world ambition, Mao spared no thought for the mammoth human and material losses that his destructive quest had cost his people. Well over 70 million people had perished – in peacetime – as a result of his misrule, yet Mao felt sorry only for himself' (*Mao: The Unknown Story*, 2005).

There are yet other assessments of Mao. Maurice Meisner, for example, refers to the statistics of an Australian economist who considers China's economic development to have been remarkable: 'This sharp rise [of almost 30 per cent] in industry's share in China's national income is a rare historical phenomenon. For example, during the first four or five decades of their drive to modern industrialization, the industrial share rose by only 11 per cent in Britain (1801–41) and 22 per cent in Japan (1878/82–1923/27)' (From Kueh, 'The Maoist Legacy and China's New Industrialization Strategy', *The China Quarterly*, September 1989). As Meisner indicates, China received very little external assistance once the Sino-Soviet split had taken place, and so, in light of this, the impact of modernization on China's economy was quite impressive.

Study the following historians' views of Mao' rule, and answer the questions that follow.

Source A

" *Impatient for change, he wanted to transform the state, the society and human nature in one stroke: "Ten thousand years are too long; seize the day, seize the hour". A purist at heart, he kept up the revolution by creating incessant upheaval, exhausting both country and people. His twenty-seven year rule brought little improvement.*

From Immanuel Hsu, *The Rise of Modern China*, Oxford University Press, 1995, p. 780

Source B

" *Mao had cast his followers adrift again in 1966. He demanded that they abandon the patterns of thought and behaviour that had become standard since the Revolution of 1949. Once again, they were left frantically trying to learn how to apply a new worldview to the complexities of the world. The results were the same as they had been a generation before: confusion, bad decisions, and a tendency to mask one's own inner uncertainties by acting self-righteously and attacking one's opponents with exceptional fanaticism and ferocity.*

From Edwin Moïse, *Modern China*, 3rd ed., Routledge, 2008, p. 184

Source C

" *Backed by the immense cult of his personality, the charismatic, narcissistic Son of Heaven, who thought himself capable of changing human nature through his mass campaigns, could demand complete loyalty to the cause of revolution as he chose to define it. Nobody and nothing could be excused from utter dedication and readiness to contribute whatever was demanded. Private life meant nothing. People were a blank sheet of paper, mere numbers to be used as the leader saw fit. Maoist autocracy reached heights of totalitarianism unparalleled by Hitler or Stalin, accompanied by massive hypocrisy as the leader who preached simplicity, morality and proletarian values.*

A potent terror organization ensured obedience, a huge gulag swallowed up real or imagined opponents, and a massive propaganda machine fed the myths. Yet it is hard to argue that Mao did not inspire adulation. He was a monster, but a monster whom people revered as the symbol of a new China that would wipe away all the suffering and weakness of the hundred years before 1949 and who offered at least a promise of an 'iron rice bowl' of food and welfare however much it was contradicted by his actions.

From Jonathan Fenby, *The Penguin History of Modern China: The Fall and Rise of a Great Power, 1850 to the Present*, 2nd Revised ed., Penguin, 2013

1. How far do these historians share the same view of Mao? In what ways do they a) agree and b) disagree on Mao's legacy?

2. What evidence would you use to support the argument made in Sources A and B?

3. Compare Mao's authoritarian rule with that of another leader you have studied. How would you support the argument made in Source C that Mao's authoritarianism was 'unparalleled'?

Consider this question:

Analyse the successes and failures of Mao's domestic policies between 1949 and 1976.

Below are the conclusions of two essay answers. What do you think are the strengths of these answers? Which, do you think, is the better conclusion?

Student answer A – Denise

A leader of a country can never be perfect and fulfil all the people's expectations. Mao is a memorable leader who helped China, but he also made several mistakes that harmed the people and the country. It can be concluded that he had the people's best interest at heart and fought for what he believed in. Up until 1957 Mao managed to save China from corruption and gain the support and admiration of his people. This was his greatest success. However from 1958 onwards, the economy declined and millions of deaths were caused due to the Second Five Year Plan and his Cultural Revolution. Whether he was an unsuccessful or successful leader is still debated, but what he will be remembered by is his love for his people and the people's love for him.

Examiner's comments

Denise has written quite a good conclusion but it could do with being a bit more factual. It has rather too many vague assertions about Mao's character and depicts him in a rather saintly manner, which could be quite difficult to support!

Student answer B – Risa

Chairman Mao achieved a great deal during his rule of the People's Republic of China. Though he celebrated many successes, failures followed often too. Some of his greatest achievements include the rapid increase in production during the first Five-Year Plan and the unification of his country during the agrarian land reforms. However, many of his foreign affairs were not successful, and campaigns such as the Proletarian Revolution and the Great Leap Forward caused great losses.

Examiner's comments

Risa has written quite a straightforward conclusion. It is a good summing-up.

Study the source below and answer the question that follows.

 20 September 1954

ARTICLE 40 The Chairman of the People's Republic of China, in pursuance of decisions of the National People's Congress or the Standing Committee of the National People's Congress, promulgates laws and decrees; appoints or removes the Premier, Vice Premiers, Ministers, Heads of Commissions and the Secretary-General of the State Council; appoints or removes the Vice-Chairmen and other members of the Council of National Defence; confers state orders, medals and titles of honour; proclaims general amnesties and grants pardons; proclaims martial law; proclaims a state of war; and orders mobilization.

From the Constitution of the People's Republic of China

1. How far does this source help you to assess Mao as an authoritarian leader?
2. To help you assess how far Mao was able to achieve his aims, complete a table like the one below.

	Aim	Policy	Success	Failure
Economic				
Political				
Cultural				
Social				

Activity 24

 **ATL Thinking skills**

Revision activity

Look back at the chapter breakdown on page 111. Do you feel confident that you could answer an examination question on all of these topics? Pick your weakest topic and spend some time revising it, then try out one of the practice questions contained in this chapter. Go to the chapter titled 'Comparing and contrasting authoritarian states' and compare Mao or China with another leader or region. There are lots of ideas in that chapter to help you draw out relevant points for comparison.

To access websites relevant to this chapter, go to www.pearsonhotlinks. com, search for the book title or ISBN, and click on 'Chapter 3'.

04

Benito Mussolini and Italy

This chapter examines the rise to power and rule of Benito Mussolini in Italy between 1919 and 1945. It focuses on:

- the conditions that led to Mussolini's rise to power
- the methods he used to consolidate power
- the nature, implementation, and effects of his social, political, economic, and foreign policies
- Fascist culture, propaganda, and education
- the role of minorities and women
- the nature and extent of opposition during Mussolini's time in power.

The photograph opposite shows Mussolini speaking to a crowd in Rome after the annexation of Abyssinia, 1936. These rallies were common at the time; the fact they were filmed and photographed illustrates the importance of propaganda in Fascist Italy.

> **Key concepts:**
>
> As you work through this chapter, bear in mind the key concepts that we use when studying history:
>
> - **Change**: Think about the ways in which the lives of Italian citizens changed as a result of Mussolini's rise and rule. For example, how far did the lives of peasants in the south or industrial workers in the north improve as a result of Mussolini's policies? How far was the role of women different under Fascism?
>
> - **Continuity**: Reflect on the extent to which the Fascist state was a new state. Which political institutions existing before 1922 remained in place? Which ones either changed their nature or disappeared? Which new institutions were created?
>
> - **Causation**: Which do you consider to be the most important reasons to explain Mussolini's rise to power? Consider factors such as his opportunism and the weakness of the Italian political system. Can you suggest other reasons for his rise?
>
> - **Consequence**: What were the consequences, for both Mussolini and for the Italians, of Italy's entry into World War II?
>
> - **Significance**: As you read through the chapter, reflect on how significant Mussolini's successes and failures in foreign policy were to his maintenance of power. For example: To what extent did foreign policy make him more popular both at home and internationally? When and why did this change?
>
> - **Perspective**: When assessing Mussolini's domestic policies, historians are not always in agreement as to whether he implemented them to boost his own image or whether he was serving the interests of particular social classes. As you work though the chapter, try to come up with your own explanation as to what motivated Mussolini's policies.

Under Benito Mussolini, Italy became the first country in the world to experience a fascist government. As you work your way through this chapter, think about how much continuity and change Italy experienced under Mussolini. To what extent did he transform Italy between 1922 and 1943?

Timeline of events – 1870–1945	
1870	The unification of Italy is completed.
1883	Benito Mussolini is born on 29 July in the town of Predappio.
1915	Italy enters World War I as an ally of France and Britain.
1919	Versailles Settlement; Mussolini establishes the first Italian Combat Group (*Fasci di Combattimento*) in Milan.
1919–21	Red Two Years (*Biennio Rosso*).
1921	Mussolini is elected Deputy; the National Fascist Party is created.
1922	March on Rome; Mussolini is appointed prime minister.
1923	Creation of the Fascist Grand Council; the Acerbo Law is passed; Italian occupation of Corfu.

1924	Mussolini seizes Fiume; the murder of Socialist deputy Giacomo Matteotti.
1925	Aventine Secession; Battle for Grain; the Locarno Pact is signed with Italy as one of its guarantors.
1926	Creation of OVRA; Battle for the Lira.
1927	Battle for Births.
1929	Mussolini and Pope Pius XI sign the Lateran Treaty.
1933	Adolf Hitler is appointed chancellor of Germany.
1934	Mussolini mobilizes the army to Austria after the assassination of the Austrian Chancellor Dolfuss.
1935	Italy, Britain, and France sign the Stresa Front; Italy invades Abyssinia and the League of Nations imposes sanctions.
1936	Mussolini and Hitler sign the Rome–Berlin Axis.
1936–39	Italy takes part of the Spanish Civil War.
1937	Italy becomes a member of the Anti-Comintern Pact.
1938	The Manifesto on Race, which revokes citizenship to Italian Jews, is passed.
1939	Mussolini occupies Albania; Italy and Germany sign the Pact of Steel; World War II starts on 1 September.
1940	Italy enters the World War II on 10 June.
1941	Italian troops are defeated in the Balkans and North Africa.
1943	The Allies land on Italy; the king dismisses and arrests Mussolini, appointing Pietro Badoglio as prime minister; Italy signs an armistice and declares war on Germany; Mussolini is rescued from imprisonment by the Germans and is put as the head of the Salò Republic in the north of Italy.
1945	The Salò Republic collapses; Mussolini is assassinated on 27 April.

4.1 The emergence of an authoritarian state

Historical background of Italy, 1861–1914

Modern Italy was established in 1861 when Victor Emanuel II, king of Piedmont, was proclaimed king of Italy under a constitutional monarchy. The acquisition of Venetia in 1866 and of Rome in 1870 completed the political unification of the country. However, Italy remained a divided nation, as claimed by former Piedmontese prime minister Massimo d'Azeglio: 'We have made Italy; now we must make Italians.' The new nation was far from consolidated; it faced economic, social, and political challenges.

Economically, there were underdeveloped regions throughout Italy, particularly in the south where malnutrition, malaria, and cholera were widespread. The north, with prosperous cities like Turin, Genoa, and Milan, enjoyed higher living standards. After unification, peasants in the south had hoped for policies of land redistribution and agricultural modernization that would improve their living conditions, but these did not come about. By the turn of the 20th century, illiteracy in the north was only 11 per cent but soared to 90 per cent in some areas of the south. This social divide between north and south became known as the 'Southern Question'.

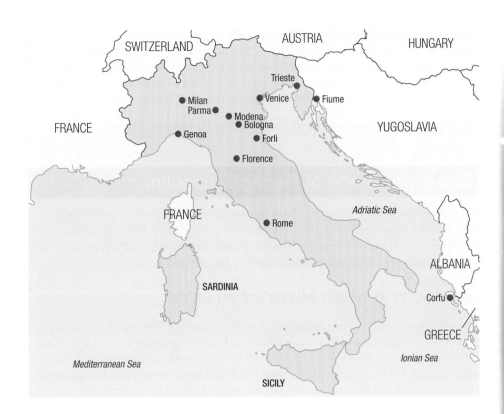

Map of Italy and surrounding countries in 1919.

The Italian unification had also bred conflict between the Catholic Church and the national government. As a result of the annexation of the Papal States, the Pope lost territories and political power in Italy. Considering themselves prisoners in Rome, successive popes refused to recognize the legitimacy of the Italian state and, until 1904, demanded Catholics to boycott elections. Italian Catholics, a vast majority of the population, saw themselves torn between political citizenship and their religious beliefs. This dispute became known as the 'Roman Question' and was to remain unresolved until 1929.

Peasant revolts in demand for land, combined with the increasing claims for the improvement of working conditions in cities, contributed to the expansion of socialist and anarchist parties. The protests and the resulting government repression increased in violence towards the end of the 19th century.

Another source of tension was the rise of nationalist groups demanding territorial expansion towards the end of the 19th century. At the time, other European countries (like Britain, France, and Germany) were expanding their influence in Africa and Asia. Italian nationalists demanded that Italy did the same and claimed that economic prosperity could only be achieved if Italy became an empire. Overseas territories would provide raw materials for industrial development and become markets for Italian products. Also, foreign expansion would unite Italians as a nation behind the war efforts. Somaliland became a colonial territory in 1888, followed by Eritrea in 1890. However, these territories did not provide the rich raw materials that Italy had expected to obtain. To increase its gains, Italy invaded Abyssinia (known as Ethiopia today) in 1895. However, the defeat in Abyssinia at the Battle of Adowa (1896) was a humiliation for the country. By the time of the outbreak of World War I (1914–18), it was clear that Italy was not the rich colonial empire it had aspired to be.

By the turn of the 20th century, Italian industrialization was making progress. Agricultural production continued to be the main source of income for Italy, although the steel and automobile industries, together with the railways, had developed significantly by 1914. Even if the Southern Question had by no means been solved, southern Italy also experienced some level of improvement. Nevertheless, rising urbanization, coupled with poor working conditions, led to continued strikes and protests, which reached a peak of violence during the **Red Week** of June 1914.

This was the background against which World War I broke out in Europe.

The emergence of Benito Mussolini

The following section explains how and why Mussolini rose to power in 1922. It addresses the influence of long-term conditions, represented by Italy's structural problems, as well as that of more immediate events, like World War I and its aftermath. It also examines the methods used by Mussolini to come to power.

Conditions in which Mussolini emerged

Mussolini was named after Benito Juárez, the charismatic leader who was president of Mexico in the 19th century. Juárez had fought against the French occupation of Mexico.

Benito Mussolini was born in Predappio (near Forli) in 1883. The son of a socialist republican blacksmith and a Catholic schoolteacher, young Benito was influenced by his father's ideology. Mussolini's gifted oratorical skills made an impression on those who met him. He became involved in socialist politics and was arrested for agitation several times both in Italy and in Switzerland, where he lived for a short while. Upon his return, Mussolini became secretary of the local socialist party in the town of Forli and editor of the socialist newspaper, *La Lotta di Classe* (Class Struggle). In 1912, he became editor of one of the most important socialist newspapers, *Avanti* (Forward), and was working there when World War I broke out.

Why did Mussolini come to power?

Several conditions in Italy contributed to Mussolini's rise. It is important that you understand how these long- and short-term factors relate to one another, and how, together, they contributed to Mussolini in his rise to power.

World War I (1914–18)

Exam questions on authoritarian states may ask about the conditions in which a leader came to power. To analyse these conditions, you should focus on the reasons that enabled a leader to emerge. In other words, think of the question as one asking you to *explain why* a leader rose to power.

Consistent with his socialist ideology, Mussolini wrote extensively against Italian intervention when World War I broke out in 1914. However, soon after, he changed his views and wrote in support of intervention. Among the arguments in favour of Italian participation in the war, Mussolini claimed Italy would have the opportunity to reclaim the land Italians considered they should receive from the Austro-Hungarian Empire. As result of his support for the war, he was expelled from the **Italian Socialist Party (*Partito Socialista Italiano*, PSI).** He resigned from *Avanti* and founded *Il Popolo d'Italia* (The People of Italy), where he continued to write in support of intervention. At the same time, Mussolini fought in the Italian army from 1915 until 1917, when he was dismissed as a result of war injuries.

| Activity 1 | **ATL** Research, communication, self-management, and social skills |

Study the source below and answer the questions that follow.

Source A

    With the Austrian ultimatum to Serbia known among the public, and with the war drums beating, Mussolini declared on 26 July that the Italian working class would give 'not a man, not a penny!' and that it would spill 'not one drop of blood' for a cause 'that has nothing to do with it'. He demanded a declaration of absolute neutrality from the Italian government and warned that if this were not forthcoming the proletariat would 'impose it by all means necessary'. He subsequently issued slogans such as 'Down with the war!', 'Long live the international solidarity of the proletariat! Long live socialism!'

From Paul O'Brien, *Mussolini in the First World War: The Journalist, the Soldier, the Fascist*, Bloomsbury, 2005, pp. 31–32

1. Explain the meaning of 'the Austrian ultimatum to Serbia' in Source A.
2. With reference to its origin, purpose, and content, analyse the value and limitations of Source A for a historian studying the response to World War I in Italy.
3. Divide the class into two groups. One group needs to argue the case for the interventionists and another group will argue against Italy's entry into World War I. Put forward well supported arguments that consider what Italy hoped to gain as well as the war efforts required.

The aftermath of war

World War I was not the war that many Italians, like Mussolini, had expected. In 1917, Italian troops faced a dramatic defeat at the Battle of Caporetto. Although they defeated the Austrians at the Battle of Vittorio Veneto the following year, the war demonstrated that Italy was unprepared for it. The army was underequipped, soldiers died from cold and starvation, and morale was low. The economy was unable to sustain the war effort, military leaders were incompetent, and politicians were seriously undermined by the war and its results. In short, World War I did not unite the nation, nor did it provide the territories that Italians had expected in exchange for their participation.

At an international level, Italy was dissatisfied both with the territorial settlement as well as with the treatment received by the Italian delegation during the Peace Conference in 1919. The **Treaty of London** (1915) had promised Italy South Tyrol, Istria, Trentino, Trieste, part of Dalmatia, Adalia, some Aegean islands, and a protectorate over Albania. Although Italy did receive a large part of what had been agreed upon in 1915, the **Treaty of St Germain** (1919) did not grant Italy Dalmatia, which was integrated into the Kingdom of Yugoslavia. The city of Fiume, which had not been explicitly promised by the Treaty of London, was placed under Yugoslavia even though 50 per cent of Fiume's population was Italian speaking. Coupled with the fact that Italy did not receive any of the former German colonies, Italians became increasingly resentful of the treaty.

When the war ended, Italy was left in great debt and experienced high levels of inflation. Demobilized soldiers joined the unemployed, which had reached 2 million by 1920. These economic problems affected the savings of the middle class as well as the wages of the workers. Consequently, discontent and political radicalization became widespread.

Italy was a parliamentary constitutional monarchy that, as a relatively young country in Europe, had limited democratic experience. The largest parties were the PSI and the Italian People's Party (*Partito Populare Italiano*, PPI) of Christian Democrats. Other political groups included socialist, communist, liberal, and nationalist parties. This multi-party democracy made it very difficult for any single party to obtain 50 per cent of the votes and form a government without having to resort to coalitions with others.

CHALLENGE YOURSELF

 Thinking skills

You may have already studied the Russian Revolution of 1917, which established the first Marxist government. Bolshevism promoted a form of communism that believed in violent revolution as a way to overthrow capitalism. Can you explain why it became a source of inspiration to workers and peasants across many European countries in the interwar period? If you have not come across this revolution in class before, find out about its aims and about the events that took place in Russia in 1917.

Giovanni Giolitti (1842–1928) became prime minister of Italy five times between 1892 and 1921, leading liberal coalition governments. He opposed Italy's entry into World War I. He played an important part in Mussolini's rise to power.

If asked how a leader came to power, you should focus on the methods used by the leader. In other words, if you argue that social unrest was a condition that contributed to Mussolini's rise, you should analyse how he responded to such a condition and how his response contributed to his political achievements. Did he use legal methods? Did his methods include the use of force? You could also refer to events that may have either weakened the opposition or strengthened Mussolini's position.

CHALLENGE YOURSELF

 **Research skills**

Find out additional information on the nature of coalition parties. What are their strengths and limitations? Why do you think it was difficult for coalition governments to rule in post-war Italy?

Coalitions were difficult to maintain and caused political instability, which in turn promoted social and political agitation. The 1919 elections were an example of this, where the PSI had obtained over 32 per cent of the votes and yet the result did not enable them to form a government of their own. A period of great instability followed.

The Red Two Years, 1919–21

The years between 1919 and 1921 are known as the Red Two Years (*Biennio Rosso*). In protest against the post-war social and economic conditions, and inspired by the events of the Russian Revolution, industrial workers and peasants across Italy occupied factories and land.

Food riots, looting, and street violence spread throughout the country. The government was unable to control the situation, partly because of internal dissent as to how to respond to it, but also because Prime Minister Giolitti refused to use force against the protestors as he feared it could trigger a revolution. In fact, because the government (under Giolitti's policy) did not offer effective protection to their properties, industrialists and landowners turned to **paramilitary organizations** to defend them.

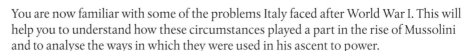

Activity 2   **Thinking and self-management skills**

1. Write a summary of the social, political, and economic problems of Italy between 1919 and 1921.
2. To what extent do you consider the Italian government to be responsible for the Red Two Years?

Methods used by Mussolini to rise to power

You are now familiar with some of the problems Italy faced after World War I. This will help you to understand how these circumstances played a part in the rise of Mussolini and to analyse the ways in which they were used in his ascent to power.

Unlike some other authoritarian leaders you may have studied, Mussolini's rise to power took place within a relatively short period of time, between 1919 and 1922, when he was appointed prime minister of Italy.

The Italian Combat Group, March 1919

In March 1919, Mussolini organized a meeting in Milan at which he announced the foundation of the Italian Combat Group (*Fasci Italiani di Combattimento*). The meeting was attended by ex-soldiers, discontented socialists, and anarchists, among others. The name of the party, which was inspired by ancient Roman history, evoked *fasces* – a bundle of rods tied about a **lictor**'s axe – a symbol of Roman authority, as well as a symbol of strength through unity: the rods are much stronger when bundled together. As you will discover later in the chapter, Mussolini very much looked to the image of the Roman Empire, which evoked ideas of prosperity and glory.

Study the symbol below.

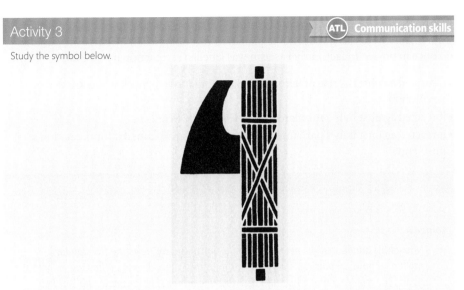

This image became the symbol of the Italian Fascist Party (Partito Nazionale Fascista, PNF) in 1921.

1. Explain what you think each of the elements of the Fascist symbol represents. In what ways did this symbol appeal to the Italians?

Mussolini was not the first one to use the term 'fascist' in contemporary Italy. Other *fasci* had already been organized in support of Italy's intervention in World War I in 1915. In 1919, fascist unions formed by ex-soldiers – outraged at the diplomatic defeat of the peace settlement and claiming to defend Italy against Bolshevism – were already acting in northern and central Italy. Each regional fascist group had its own leadership. However, Mussolini, a gifted orator and a perceptive journalist, was well known among most fascist groups. Regional leaders agreed that Mussolini could contribute with his charisma and political skills to the movement, at a national level.

The role of Mussolini's fascist ideology

As you will see in this section, Italian Fascism was not a new ideology but rather one that borrowed concepts from existing organizations and other ideologies. It represented different things at different times. For example, Mussolini opposed democracy and blamed it for the chaos prevailing in Italy, and yet he formed a political party and was elected as Deputy democratically. In 1922, he moved from republicanism to being a supporter of the monarchy. Similarly, Mussolini moved from a strong anti-clericalist stance and signed the Lateran Pact with the Pope in 1929 to end the Roman Question. In order to justify these changes, Mussolini often said that Fascism was not a doctrine but a movement and, therefore, had to change according to the circumstances.

There are, nevertheless, some elements of the Italian Fascist ideology you will read about in the following section, such as an extreme nationalism, which contributed to Mussolini's rise and prevailed throughout his entire rule.

What did Mussolini's Fascism stand for in 1919?

Earlier in this chapter, you read that Fascism was not a national party under a single leadership. Over 70 fascist groups existed rather independently across Italy, Mussolini's being one of them. In order to impose himself above the rest, Mussolini knew it was important to show he could offer solutions to the problems in Italy. So, in June 1919, Mussolini published a Fascist **Manifesto** to explain his party's ideology. Essentially,

Have you studied other *charismatic* authoritarian leaders? The word *charismatic* is often used to describe a leader who is set apart from other people because of his or her exceptional personal qualities or exemplary actions, both of which inspire loyalty among his or her followers. Think about why Mussolini could be considered as a charismatic leader. You will be able to find examples of this throughout the chapter (for example, see Source B from Activity 1). As you work through the chapter, analyse the role charisma played in Mussolini's rise and rule, and consider how this information can help you demonstrate your understanding of him as a leader.

it opposed socialism as well as the institutions like the monarchy and the Catholic Church, but there was not a lot of explanation regarding what the party proposed to do once in power. In fact, early Fascism was labelled as 'reactionary' in that:

- it reacted against the rise of leftist ideologies and movements like the Russian Revolution
- it reacted against Italy's mutilated victory in World War I
- it reacted against Italy's parliamentary democracy and blamed it for the nation's problems.

Thinking and communication skills

To what extent did ideological factors play a major role in the rise of other authoritarian rulers you have studied? Compare and contrast their ideologies to that of Mussolini.

Activity 4 **Thinking and communication skills**

Study the sources below and answer the questions that follow.

Source A

[Mussolini] announced the new movement as an 'antiparty', rejecting the standard structure of political parties... The goal was to attract a broad young following on both the left and the center, so that Mussolini described the minimal programme published on March 30 in Il Popolo d'Italia as not new 'and not even revolutionary' but designed to achieve democracy and renovate the nation... Mussolini did not, apparently believed that he was actually founding a new movement in March 1919 as much as creating some sort of front to rally left interventionism in the immediate post-war era.

From Stanley G. Payne, A *History of Fascism 1914–1945*, University of Wisconsin Press, 1995, p. 91

Source B

In 1919 the Fascist movement had been born as an 'anti-party' that looked to recruit those who had no place in traditional political parties. Fascism was presented as a pragmatic, anti-dogmatic, anticlerical, and republican political movement that advocated radical institutional, economic, and social reform. The Fascists were contemptuous of parliamentary government and liberalism; they supported the activist politics of minority groups and were prepared to use violence and the politics of the street both in support of Italy's territorial demands at the Peace Conference and to combat the socialists.

From 'Fascism in Power: The Totalitarian Experiment' in Adrian Lyttelton (ed.), *Liberal and Fascist Italy: 1900–1945 (Short Oxford History of Italy)*, Oxford University Press, 2002

1. What do you understand by the view expressed in both sources that Mussolini's movement in 1919 was an 'anti-party'?
2. Compare and contrast the views expressed by Sources A and B on the nature of the Fascist Party.
3. Evaluate the relationship between the conditions of Italy in the early 1920s and Mussolini's reactions against democracy, the left, and the post-war treaties.
4. Why do you think Mussolini considered it more important for Fascism to be a flexible movement rather than a political party at this time?

Mussolini's strategy, at this time, did not bring about positive results in terms of electoral support. In the elections held in November 1919, Mussolini's movement did not gain a single seat in parliament. As in many past elections, no single party obtained the necessary votes to form a government to rule over Italy on its own, with one coalition government succeeding another. Despite his complete defeat in the 1919 elections, Mussolini was able to exploit the instability during the Red Two Years (1919–21) to strengthen his position.

How and why did Fascism change between 1919 and 1922?

Between the defeat in the November 1919 elections and his appointment as prime minister in October 1922, Mussolini used a successful combination of legal methods and force to rise to power. As he had anticipated, he changed the ideology of the party accordingly to attract support.

The use of violence

As violence intensified during the Red Two Years, Fascist squads successfully rallied support across Italy from those who feared a Bolshevik revolution. Those who feared Bolshevism included not just large landowners and businessmen but also middle class shopkeepers and peasant leaseholders – and they were all ready to fund the movement.

Activity 5 **Thinking skills**

Study the sources below and answer the questions that follow.

Source A

 ... the unrest of the biennio rosso boosted Mussolini's group. He offered to send in squadre d'azione (action squads) to end the factory and land occupations that had been organized by the trade unions and peasant leagues. Industrialists in the north and landowners in the Po valley and Tuscany, frustrated and angered by the Liberal government's stance of concessions and inaction, were only too pleased to give money to Mussolini's group in return for the squadristi's violent attacks against the left's strikes and occupations. As well as attacking strikers, the squadristi also burned down offices and newspapers printing works of the Socialists and trade unions in many parts of the north and central Italy and tried to destroy the influence of the peasant leagues.

From Alan Todd, *The European Dictatorships: Hitler, Stalin, Mussolini*, Cambridge University Press, 2002, pp. 103–104

Source B

In 1921 and 1922, Mussolini exploited the anxieties of landlords, industrialists, and the middle class in the hope that they would turn to Fascism out of fear of a Bolshevik revolution. In his drive for political power, he had to maintain the support of rabid nationalists, syndicalists, veterans, futurists, and followers of D'Annunzio—the extremist elements of the early movement— while courting the newly won conservative forces that could both diversify his constituency and bankroll his movement. All the while, he had to reconcile internal tensions between urban and rural Fascists and between the dominant lower-middle-class rank-and-file and the newly recruited elites.

From: Charles L. Killinger, *The History of Italy*, Greenwood Press, 2002, p. 142

1. According to Sources A and B, who supported Mussolini and why?
2. To what extent do these sources support the view analysed earlier in this chapter that Fascism was 'reactionary'?

Whether Italy was ripe for a Bolshevik revolution or whether the Fascists skilfully exploited the idea to gain support continues to be a matter of contention among historians. The fact of the matter is that authorities often turned a blind eye to Fascist violence; the police repeatedly ignored orders to suppress Fascist attacks on opponents and, at times, even contributed by providing Fascists with weapons. Clearly, the idea of a Fascist intervention as a solution to the threat posed by Bolshevism was widely popular during the Red Two Years.

The adoption of legal methods

Although many fascists groups in Italy recognized Mussolini's authority by 1920, he had not yet become their undisputed leader. Loyalties towards the regional leaders, the **ras**, were often stronger. The ras enjoyed relative financial autonomy and had prestige in their regions.

Mussolini didn't necessarily agree with the rising levels of violence of the local squads, and was worried that it was alienating support for the Fascists. He believed that the Fascists needed greater acceptance to succeed in their bid for power and that violence would not contribute to it. However, he was not always able to restrain the other leaders who were anxious to seize political control by any means.

In order to increase the base of support, Mussolini decided to run in the May 1921 elections and to introduce changes to the ideas proposed by Fascism. With a focus on the restoration of order, the improvement of Italians' living and working conditions, a strong foreign policy, and the respect for private property and private enterprise, the support for Fascism expanded dramatically.

Activity 6 Thinking and communication skills

Study the source below and answer the questions that follow.

> Recruiting landowners, industrialists, and the middle class, the Fascist adopted a new, more conservative program that emphasized a pro-business, nationalist agenda, cutting taxes and diminishing the role of the government while boosting military spending and supporting the monarchy and the Catholic Church. However, at the very time Mussolini's new platform made him more appealing to moderates, black-shirted squadristi continued their punitive attacks, descending by the truckload on Socialist offices to dispense violence, virtually immune from justice despite mounting casualties.

From Charles L. Killinger, *The History of Italy*, Greenwood Press, 2002

1. According to the source, in what ways was the Fascist Party becoming more conservative? To what extent was that change challenged within the Fascists?
2. Which of the problems faced by Italy were being addressed by the new programme?
3. Which sectors of society was Mussolini trying to attract? What policies were proposed to that end?

May 1921 elections and the creation of the National Fascist Party

In May 1921, the Fascists obtained 38 seats in parliament. Although this was less than 7 per cent of the total number of seats and didn't make the Fascists influential in themselves, Mussolini had become a deputy using democratic means. Nevertheless, the more radical members of the movement continued to believe in the use of force, rather than parliamentary democracy, as the only way for Fascism to seize power.

However, Mussolini was more conciliatory and offered to sign a Pact of Pacification with the Socialists in August 1921 to end violence. He claimed it was 'ridiculous to talk as though the Italian working class were heading for Bolshevism'. Unsurprisingly, this was met with open opposition from many of the ras, supported by businessmen and industrialists who had been financing the Fascists to resist socialism. Consequently, Mussolini was forced to abandon the idea of a pact, and the failed strategy weakened his position within the movement.

Nonetheless, Mussolini's failure to achieve the Pact of Pacification is important to our understanding of the methods he used in his rise to power. First of all, the attempt to sign the pact with the Socialists demonstrated that Mussolini was prepared to become even more flexible in his views and aims. Secondly, it showed that Mussolini did not have total control of the ras and that many of them were prepared to challenge him in the open. Furthermore, it is clear that the ras did recognize the importance of Mussolini's political skills in making Fascism popular at a national level, and were fully aware of how necessary he was in the road to power.

Activity 7 — **Thinking and communication skills**

1. You may be familiar with other authoritarian states that have declared their opposition to socialism and liberalism. How do their ideologies compare to that of Mussolini?

2. To what extent do you agree with the view that Mussolini's strength lay in the fact that he did not have what some call 'an ideological straightjacket'?

Although support for Fascism had increased considerably, its popularity in the south of Italy continued to be more limited. By November 1921, the Fascist movement had become a national party called the National Fascist Party (*Partito Nazionale Fascista*, PNF). Under the principles of 'order, discipline, hierarchy', the PNF aimed at coordinating the *fasci* and spreading their influence at a national level. Mussolini became the head of the Executive Committee of the PNF and started to be referred to as Il Duce ('The Leader').

Activity 8 — **Thinking and self-management skills**

'The rise to power of authoritarian leaders is attributed more to promises of improved social and economic conditions than to ideology.'

With reference to one authoritarian leader, discuss the validity of this claim.

Now read the following introduction from a student's essay.

Introduction

It is often said that crises lead to the rise of authoritarian states. These situations include the negative outcome of wars, economic problems and civil unrest. This seems to be the case of Italy at the end of World War I. The war had not given Italians what they had expected, there was unemployment, political chaos and fear of a Bolshevik revolution. Mussolini came to power by offering to address these issues: he promised to revert international peace treaties, to improve the economy and to bring order. To what extent did Mussolini's promises play a more important role than the ideological considerations in gaining support for his movement?

Examiner's comments

Here is an interesting opening that shows a comprehensive understanding of the rise of authoritarian states. The student also shows some understanding of the conditions against which Mussolini came to power. It would have been useful to include information on the groups to whom Mussolini's promises appealed the most, and more detail as to the reasons why this was so. Also, although there is mention of 'ideological considerations', there is no specific detail of which, if any, Mussolini made.

Sidebar:

ⓘ Some of the most powerful *ras* leaders in the 1920s were Italo Balbo (Ferrara), Dino Grandi (Bologna), Roberto Farinacci (Cremona), and Filippo Turati (Brescia).

❗ To assess the validity of a claim in relation to specific examples, you need to show an understanding of the claim itself. In this case, you need to show what those promises were and explain Mussolini's ideology during his rise to power. It will not be enough to simply say that you agree, in Mussolini's case, his promises of better conditions gained him more support than his ideology. You need to give specific examples of both these aspects and analyse why one was more effective than the other. Or, you may consider them both to have been equally important, but again, you must explain why and how.

❗ Use your introduction to show the examiner you have understood the question. In this sense, the introduction above would have benefited from a clearer treatment of the ideological factors.

Use of coercion and the March on Rome, October 1922

Throughout 1922, clashes between Fascist and anti-Fascist forces spread across north and central Italy. One coalition government succeeded another, none of them able to pacify the country or to obtain support to rule, and placing Italy on the verge of civil war.

Having broken up a Socialist strike in July that year, the Fascists were now increasing their influence in many cities in the north and centre of the country. Rather than achieving anything for the Socialists, the strike played in favour of Mussolini, who was now seen as the only one capable of restoring order. Frustrated by the limited response from the government, coupled with the breaking up of the strike, some of the most prominent ras announced a march on Rome to seize power, with or without Mussolini. They planned to take control of railways and access points to the capital as well as strategic buildings, to drive the government out of office.

Mussolini was uncertain about the success of the march. Also, he was eager to avoid a clash between the Fascist forces and the national army, whose support he valued. Therefore, in an attempt to appease the ras, Mussolini announced the Fascist March on Rome on 28 October. As for himself, Mussolini remained in Milan and followed the course of the events from there.

TOK

'There is no such thing as innocent language.' To what extent do you agree with this view? Analyse the use of language in Mussolini's article in Activity 9. To what extent does his choice of words reflect his Fascist ideology?

Blackshirts

Members of the Italian Fascist Party were also known as the Blackshirts (or *camicie nere* in Italian) because of their uniform: the black shirts they wore were inspired by the uniform of the *arditi*, an Italian elite force in World War I. Many of the Blackshirts were ex-soldiers themselves.

Activity 9 **ATL Communication skills**

Study the source below and answer the questions that follow.

> *Fascism, furthermore, does not march against the police but against a political class both cowardly and imbecile, which in four long years has not been able to give a Government to the Nation. Those who form the productive class must know that Fascism wants to impose nothing more than order and discipline upon the Nation and to help to raise the strength which will renew progress and prosperity. The people who work in the fields and the factories, those who work in the railroads or in offices, have nothing to fear from the Fascist Government. Their just rights will be protected.*

From an article by Benito Mussolini published in *Il Popolo d'Italia* on October 27 1929, taken from Benito Mussolini, *My Autobiography*, Dover Publications Inc., 2006, p. 130

1. To what extent do you consider Mussolini's article to be both a threat and a promise to Italians?
2. Discuss how different social and economic groups might have reacted to the article?
3. What do you think the reaction of the members of the government in Rome might have been?

Liberals in Rome, such as former prime minister Giolitti, believed that the only way to stop the Fascists from attempting to seize control was to offer Mussolini and the Fascists positions in a coalition government. As the Fascists began to march towards the capital, Mussolini remained in Milan to wait for such an offer. When the Fascists took control of communication lines in the north of the country, Prime Minister Facta began preparations to defend the city. However, King Victor Emanuel III refused to sign the decree of **martial law**, leading to Facta's resignation and to greater political crisis. Finally, Mussolini received the offer to join a coalition government; he accepted it on the condition that he would be appointed prime minister of the new government. The king invited Mussolini to Rome and

This photograph shows Mussolini arriving in Rome on 29 October, 1929. A Blackshirt walks in front of him. What do you think this image tries to communicate?

formally offered him the opportunity to head a coalition government of 14 members, including three Fascists.

There are several theories as to why the king decided to negotiate with Mussolini on his terms and appoint him prime minister. For instance, the king may have been influenced by the opinion of some liberal politicians at the time, which was that it would be easier to control the Fascists if they were part of the government rather than in the opposition. Or, he may have feared that the army would join the Fascists – or worse still, a civil war that could bring about the end of the monarchy. He may even have been sympathetic to some Fascist ideas. Whatever the reasons behind the king's decisions, he played a major role in making Mussolini prime minister in 1922.

Activity 10 Thinking, communication, and self-management skills

Read the following interpretations of how Mussolini came to power before answering the questions.

Historian Denis Mack Smith claims that the March on Rome was 'a comfortable train ride, followed by a petty demonstration, and all in response to an express invitation from the monarch' (*Italy: A Modern History*, 1959, p. 372).

Historian Adrian Lyttelton considers the March on Rome as psychological warfare in which the threat of force frightened both the king and many Italian politicians, and brought Mussolini to power.

Historian William Ebenstein supports the idea that it was the weakness of the opposition, rather than the Fascist strengths, that explains Mussolini's rise in 1922. The opposition, be it socialist or liberal, had been unable to guarantee peace and, consequently, democracy had lost its value in Italy.

1. What supporting evidence can you provide for each of these views? Do you consider ay one of them a better explanation for Mussolini's rise? Explain your answer fully.

2. How important do you consider the March on Rome to have been in Mussolini's rise to power?

Now, take a look at the following questions. Then read the conclusion taken from a student's essay answering the second question.

Question 1

'Authoritarian leaders largely rose to power as a consequences of war.' With reference to one authoritarian leader, discuss the validity of this claim.

Question 2

With reference to the rise to power of one authoritarian leader, assess the extent to which ideology played a larger role than organization.

Conclusion

During his rise, Mussolini did not have a clear, consistent ideology. In fact, he started off a socialist only to become an enemy of socialism over Italian intervention in World War I. He did not explain clearly and explicitly how he meant to attain any of the objectives he mentioned: territorial expansion, improvement of working conditions, the protection of property. On the other hand, he made intensive use of the local ras, the blackshirts and rallies like the March on Rome of October 1922. In Mussolini's case, organization played a greater role than ideology.

Examiner's comments

This conclusion focuses on the question by identifying the ideological elements and organizational aspects that played a role in the rise of Mussolini. The candidate comes to a conclusion that organization played a greater role. Although she says that organization was more important than ideology in the rise of Mussolini, she does not clearly explain why this was the case, for example, what was so significant about the roles of the ras, Blackshirts, and the mass rallies, or why ideological considerations seemed less important at this stage.

Paper 2 questions often ask about the methods used by the leaders in their rise to power. They may have used force, legal methods, or a combination of both. The period in which Mussolini rose to power was relatively short, ending in his appointment as prime minister after the March on Rome. How would you explain the methods used by Mussolini to achieve his aim? How do these methods compare to those used by other leaders you have studied?

4.2 Aims and results of Mussolini's domestic policies

You are now familiar with how and why Mussolini came to power. This next section will analyse the political, economic, and social policies of his regime. It will explain his economic aims and plans, the impact of domestic policies on culture and education, the status of women, the role of the opposition, and the treatment of minorities. By the end of the section, you will be able to assess the extent to which you consider Mussolini as having achieved his domestic aims. While working on this chapter, consider whether it could be argued that Mussolini created a 'new order'.

Political policies

The March on Rome gave Mussolini access to political power but, in 1922, his power was not yet consolidated. In the words of James B. Whisker, Mussolini was 'in charge of the state but without a guiding and inspirational system of thought'; he still had to devise the structure of the Fascist state. Mussolini's power was also limited; the king had the power to dismiss and replace him. Furthermore, Mussolini had to prevent those who opposed Fascism from forming an alternative coalition of enough strength to challenge him. Finally, Mussolini did not have undisputed control within the Fascist Party itself.

Under these conditions, Mussolini implemented several policies to consolidate his power – policies that, gradually, moved the country away from a democracy towards an authoritarian state. While you work through this section, think about how far you consider Mussolini's position was made secure by 1939.

What methods did Mussolini use to consolidate his power?

In the previous section, you have analysed how Mussolini rose to power by successfully combining the use of force with legal methods. His consolidation of power bears similar features.

Activity 11 Thinking skills

During his first speech to parliament after having been appointed prime minister, Mussolini stated:

> *I could have abused my victory, but I refused to do so. I imposed limits on myself. I told myself that the better wisdom is that which does not lose control of itself after victory. With 300,000 youths armed to the teeth, fully determined and almost mystically ready to act on any command of mine, I could have punished all those who defamed and tried to sully Fascism. […] I could have barred the doors of Parliament and formed a government exclusively of Fascists. I could have done so; but I chose not to, at least not for the present.*

From Mussolini's first speech as Prime Minister to the Chamber of Deputies, 16 November 1922

Study the speech above before answering the following questions.

1. What is the significance of Mussolini's first speech to parliament?
2. With reference to its origins, purpose, and content, assess the value and limitations of the extract above to a historian studying Mussolini's political aims.

Coercion and intimidation

Mussolini soon persuaded the king to give him extraordinary powers for one year. These powers granted him relative freedom to introduce significant changes and enabled him to consolidate his position. They also bought him time to obtain from parliament a new electoral law that would secure him the majority he then lacked.

In the months following Mussolini's appointment as prime minister, thousands of political opponents were arrested by the government. The local ras also exercised much violence against the opposition, with the government turning a blind eye. However instrumental this may have been to Mussolini, he was concerned that excessive violence could lead him to lose social support.

In order to appease the Blackshirts, as well as to create a loyal armed force to protect his government, Mussolini created a Fascist militia, the Voluntary Militia for National Security (MVSN), to work alongside the police and the army 'to defend the Fascist revolution'. This paramilitary organization responded directly to him and was paid for by state funds; its members swore an oath of loyalty to Italy, not the king. Although there was some initial resistance from other political parties, the MVSN was seen as a way of keeping the Blackshirts under the control of the state and also to limit the power of the ras. Mussolini defended the MVSN on the grounds that 'Fascism cannot renounce the armed force of the Blackshirts… until the state has become integrally Fascist.'

However, the Italian army became rather suspicious of the MVSN as a paramilitary force over which they had no jurisdiction. In the years that followed, Mussolini played the rivalries between the police (*Carabinieri*), the MVSN, and the Italian armed forces to his advantage. At the same time, Mussolini used various tactics to limit the power of the ras and put them under his control. These ranged from transferring them away from their own regions so they would lose local support, to offering them positions within the government.

Reforming the state

Although Mussolini held the positions of prime minister, foreign and interior minister, in 1922 the Fascists remained a very small party in parliament. Even after the Nationalist Party merged with the Fascists, they only had 47 of 535 seats. This prompted Mussolini to find a way to change the electoral law to gain majority in parliament.

The Acerbo Law, 1923

The task of drafting a new electoral law to enable the PNF to gain a majority in parliament was handed to Giacomo Acerbo.

The Acerbo Law proposed that the party gaining the largest number of votes in an election – providing it had reached a minimum of 25 per cent – automatically obtained two-thirds of the seats in parliament, while the remaining third were to be proportionally distributed among other parties. In effect, the law ensured that the Fascists obtained majority in parliament whilst weakening the opposition at the same time.

Mussolini claimed that the Acerbo Law would bring political stability in Italy by ending the problems caused by the collapse of coalitions. The Socialist Party opposed it openly, having seen it for what it was: a manoeuvre to obtain Fascist supremacy in the chamber. Although other parties, like the Liberals and the Catholics, were not supportive of the law, they feared the consequences of not supporting it since the

Giacomo Acerbo (1888–1969)

Giacomo Acerbo was a decorated World War I captain from an Italian noble family. He was elected Deputy in 1921, and had participated in the political negotiations during the events of the March on Rome as well as in Mussolini's government. Acerbo voted for Mussolini's removal during the crisis that led to the fall of Mussolini.

Fascists threatened to use force to have it passed. It was in this atmosphere of threat that the Acerbo Law was voted.

Study the source below and answer the questions that follow.

❝ *The Acerbo Bill, however, involved such a radical modification in the system of representative government that, even if honestly applied, it was hardly compatible with parliamentary government as it had previously been understood. … The battle over the law therefore had high symbolic value as a measure of the determination of the defenders of parliamentary liberty. It was the first decisive test of strength that Mussolini had had to undergo and its outcome was critical for the consolidation of the regime. … Rejection of the bill would have weakened Mussolini's position in relation to the Crown, and harmed his prestige. It would have multiplied discontent among his supporters. Approval, on the contrary, would dishearten the Opposition and would allow Mussolini to use parliamentary and legal methods as a cover for the transformation of the State, which, once the majority was safe, could be carried through without any formal break in constitutional continuity.*

From Adrian Lyttelton, *The Seizure of Power: Fascism in Italy, 1919–1929*, Routledge, 2009

1. According to the source, why did the battle over Acerbo Law have a 'high symbolic value'? Explain with reference to both Mussolini and the opposition.

2. Why do you think it was important for Mussolini's consolidation of power to have the Acerbo Law passed?

During the 1924 elections, the PNF gained over 65 per cent of the votes, obtaining the largest electoral victory for a political party since unification. The significance of the 1924 elections was the fact that Mussolini, who did not come to power by popular vote, was now being endorsed by it.

Giacomo Matteotti, whose murder in 1924 led to one of the greatest political crises faced by Mussolini.

The murder of Giacomo Matteotti and the Aventine Secession

One of the spokesmen against the Acerbo Law was a Socialist deputy from Rovigo called Giacomo Matteotti. He was a highly respected politician who had been critical of Fascism. According to Richard G. Massock, chief of the Rome Bureau of the Associated Press (1938–41):

❝ *Matteotti had denounced Fascism as 'an association of criminals' on the floor of the Chamber in 1921. He contested the April election of 1924. He denounced Fascist rule, he charged it with frauds and outrages. He declared the Fascist militia had rolled up 4,500,000 votes against the 3,000,000 of the opposition parties by beating up anti-Fascist candidates and forcibly detaining them at their homes. He demanded annulment of the election.*

From *Italy from Within*, The Macmillan Company, 1943

In 1924, Matteotti was kidnapped by Fascist thugs and beaten to death, his body thrown into the river. His murder constituted a political crisis for Mussolini for a number of reasons. The men who abducted Matteotti were associated with the Fascists. Although there was no evidence of his direct involvement, Mussolini bore the moral responsibility for Matteotti's murder. It was also questioned whether Mussolini could control the most radical and violent people in his party.

For some time, it seemed that Mussolini could lose his position. Over 100 deputies withdrew from parliament in protest, hoping their 'Aventine Secession' would persuade the king to dismiss Mussolini and call for a new government. However, Mussolini survived the crisis, largely due to the weaknesses of both the opposition and the king: Without the presence of the deputies who had walked out in protest, the Fascists were in control of parliament and gave Mussolini a vote of confidence; in view of this vote, the king, who had the power to remove Mussolini, remained silent.

> The Aventine Secession was named after an event in ancient Roman history (493 BCE), when the Roman population withdrew to the Aventine Hill in protest against a ruling class known as the Patricians.

Activity 13 ATL Communication and thinking skills

Study the source below and answer the questions that follow.

> 'I declare here in front of this assembly,' [Mussolini] said, 'and in front of the Italian people that I and I alone assume the political, moral and historic responsibility for everything that has happened. If misquoted words are enough to hang a man, then out with the noose and the gallows! If Fascism has been castor oil and club and not a proud passion of the best Italian youth, the blame is on me. If Fascism has been a criminal plot, if violence has resulted from a certain historic, political and moral atmosphere, the responsibility is mine, because I have deliberately created this atmosphere. [...] Italy wants peace and quiet, work and calm. I will give these things with love if possible and with force if necessary.'

From Christopher Hibbert, *Il Duce: The Life of Benito Mussolini*, Palgrave Macmillan, 1962, p. 50

1. For what reasons did Mussolini assume political responsibility for the murder of Matteotti?
2. With reference to its origins, purpose and content, assess the value and limitations of the above source to a historian studying Mussolini's consolidation of power.

As revealed by the crisis following Matteotti's murder, Mussolini's consolidation of power had not yet been fully secured – though it seemed to speed up his pace towards dictatorship: Mussolini's opponents (those who had played an important part in the Matteotti crisis) were either killed or had to leave Italy; censorship was strengthened and anti-Fascist newspapers were brought into line or closed down; to strengthen control in all of Italy, local elections were abolished and local officials (*podestá*) became appointed directly by Rome. By 1926, all opposition parties were banned. Italy had become an authoritarian state.

In 1927, a secret police force called the Organization for Vigilance and Repression of Anti-Fascism (*Organizzazione per la Vigilanza e la Repressione dell'Antifascismo*, OVRA), was founded. At the time it was argued that the OVRA was created after a number of attempts were made on Mussolini's life. It exercised surveillance of Italian citizens, including important politicians. However, given the existence of MVSN and the state police, frictions among these organizations on matters of jurisdiction and hierarchy were frequent. Rather than seeing this as a miscalculation on the part of Mussolini, it illustrates another method he used to consolidate power: by dividing (thus weakening) those who could threaten his position. Similar to what he had done with the ras before, Mussolini was now playing the different institutions that formed the bureaucratic Fascist state against one another.

By 1926, Mussolini was ruling by decree, which meant he no longer responded to parliament. Although parliament continued to meet, it did not play any active role in Italian politics. Opposition to Mussolini had failed to prevent his consolidation of power, partly because of Mussolini's use of coercion and force. However, there were other reasons why the role of opposition became limited in this period.

According to Professor Christopher Duggan:

> 66 *... the idea that the liberal regime had been synonymous with chaos and could never safely be returned to became an important factor in limiting opposition in the years ahead. Fascism might have its faults, but what was the alternative? (...) The consideration that fascism was responsible for much of the turmoil, that a socialist revolution had never been a serious possibility and that much of the recovery after 1922 might have occurred anyway as the economy picked up, was not given currency.*
>
> **From *Fascist Voices: An Intimate History of Mussolini's Italy*, Vintage, 2012, p. 72**

The Fascist Grand Council

This institution, created by Mussolini to consolidate his power, served two distinct purposes. Firstly, it was a parallel cabinet formed by Fascists that, in time, had more influence than the official cabinet. Secondly, it aimed at coordinating the party and all other Fascist organizations that were being created with the government. A further change to the electoral law, this time in 1928, meant that the Fascist Grand Council was to produce a single list of PFN candidates for the upcoming elections. The candidates were to be selected from professional and industrial organizations. All one could do at the time of voting was to accept or reject the whole list.

The Fascist Grand Council was in theory a check on Mussolini's power as its faculties included that of recommending to the king the removal of the prime minister from office. However, the institution was under the tight control of Mussolini, who always had the final say on its membership and on the topics that were to be put forward before it.

The Corporate State

Mussolini was determined to end social conflicts by offering a 'third way' between capitalism and communism – corporativism – which aimed at ending the strikes and protests that had been negatively affecting productivity, as well as to improve the Italian economy. Economic success was important to Mussolini, in terms of maintaining power and achieving his expansionist aims. Under the Corporate State, Mussolini abolished the traditional trade unions and replaced them with corporations. Each corporation included representatives of workers, employers, and those from government. They were created to supervise negotiations related to wages and working conditions. Strikes and protests were banned; all conflicts were to be solved within the corporations. In 1927, a new Charter of Labour introduced workers' rights such as paid holidays and social security, but there was no freedom to protest or negotiate outside the corporation. The Corporate State also aimed at gaining some level of state control over production, while maintaining private enterprise. To that end, a Ministry of Corporations was created, headed by Mussolini himself. However, as you will see later in the chapter, centralization didn't necessarily make the economy more efficient. Eventually, the Chamber of Fasces and Corporations of 1939 came to replace the Italian parliament, the latter of which had by now become obsolete. Rather than representing regions, members of this chamber represented different branches of economic activity.

The Corporate State was an extremely bureaucratic creation: it contributed a lot of confusion; what it achieved was to guarantee that the government authority could not be successfully challenged. However, having made social protests illegal thus ending them, the creation of the Corporate State could be viewed as a concession Mussolini made to his landowning and industrialist supporters – as a way of preventing anyone with sufficient economic power from challenging him.

Study the source below and answer the questions that follow.

> Most of the decisions that were made were not made by the corporations but by the government and the employers, including the decision to cut wages. [...] Employers had undue influence within the corporations, especially as the workers' representatives were usually selected by the Fascist Party rather than being chosen directly by the workers... In addition employers were nearly always supported by the three government representatives, who were Fascist members, even though they were supposed to be neutral.

From Alan Todd, *The European Dictatorships: Hitler, Stalin, Mussolini*, Cambridge University Press, 2002, p. 119

1. According to the source above, what were the structural problems of the Corporate State?
2. Using the source and your own knowledge, discuss why Mussolini created the Corporate State.

Relations with the Catholic Church – the Lateran Pact

Relations between the Church and Mussolini experienced moments of tension, especially over education and the indoctrination of young people. However, in 1929, Mussolini and Pope Pius XI ended a long-lasting dispute between the Italian state and the Vatican, which had resulted from the Italian annexation of the Papal States during Italian unification. The Lateran Pact created an independent Vatican State with the Pope at its head, thus restoring an element of temporal authority to the papacy. The pact made Catholicism the official Italian religion, outlawed divorce, and extended religious education to secondary schools. The Pope was also economically compensated for the loss of territories in 1870. In return, he recognized the 1870 territorial settlement as definitive.

According to Laura Fermi:

> Gaetano Salvemini, in his book Mussolini Diplomatico, says that the reconciliation was Mussolini's greatest publicity stunt and points out that, rather than a moulder of events, Mussolini was an opportunist taking advantage of very favorable circumstances. Despite the popes' firm and intransigent stand, things were not as bad as they seemed; the passage of time had shown that the dissension between church and state was more formal than real; the Holy See was much better off without the burden of a territory that the popes had administered poorly.

From *Mussolini*, Chicago University Press, 1966, p. 256

The Pope and Mussolini signing the Lateran Pact. What is the message of this image?

Although at first you could think Mussolini gained little from the pact, the agreement provided him with enormous political prestige. He received the credit for solving a conflict that had troubled the conscience of Roman Catholic Italians since 1870. His popularity increased, not only at home where Catholics were a significant majority but, also, among the Catholics worldwide, who considered Mussolini as having done a great justice to their spiritual leader.

With time, conflicts between the state and the Church resurfaced over different issues, such as the extent of the Church's authority over education. In 1931, Pope Pius XI published the encyclical *Non abbiamo bisogno* ('We do not need'), a document condemning aspects of Mussolini's Fascist regime. Although relations between the two sides remained cordial, tensions were renewed following Mussolini's shift to anti-Semitism, especially from 1938 onwards.

Research and thinking skills (ATL)

Relations with the Church seemed to have provided Mussolini with an opportunity to reinforce himself as leader. What role did religion play in the consolidation and maintenance of power for other authoritarian leaders you have studied? Where religion didn't play a significant role, can you suggest reasons why this was the case?

The question asks you to assess the contributing factors to an authoritarian leader's consolidation of power. In Mussolini's case, it could be argued that this period begins with the March on Rome (1922) and extends to the Lateran Pact (1929). In order to answer the question effectively, you should look at both the use of terror (for example, the murder of Matteotti, the intimidation used to pass the Acerbo Law, the roles of the Blackshirts and the ras), as well as other contributing factors (for instance, the Lateran Pact, the use of propaganda, the support of some sectors of society such as the industrialists, and the weaknesses of the opposition) in order to determine whether or not the use of terror played a greater part in Mussolini's consolidation of power.

Remember, there is no set answer, so if it up to you to conclude whether or not the use of terror did play a more significant role in Mussolini's case. However, you do need to provide detailed arguments supported by evidence that show you have examined both sides of the question before you arrive to your conclusion.

Activity 15

 Self-management and thinking skills

1. To what extent is an authoritarian leader's consolidation of power a result of the use of terror?

Economic policies

In the previous sections of this chapter, you have looked at the economic problems in Italy that were caused by World War I. It is now your opportunity to assess whether or not Mussolini was able to solve these problems.

The Italian economy was relatively small in comparison to those of other European nations; it depended on imports. After World War I, unemployment levels were high; the gap between the industrial regions of the north and the countryside in the south – where methods of production needed modernization – continued to exist. Mussolini's aim was to make Italy rich and powerful by expanding its territories. To achieve this, he implemented different economic policies. As you work through this section, consider how far Mussolini was able to make Italy economically stronger.

The liberal years, 1922–25

When Mussolini came to power in 1922, he did not implement radical economic policies. Still trying to consolidate his power at this stage, Mussolini focused his attention more on political issues, leaving the liberal economist Alberto De Stefani to run the Ministry of Finance. De Stefani reduced government spending and allowed a liberal economy in which prices were settled by the market rather than by state intervention. Combined with the European post-war recovery, these policies led to an increase in economic activity. During this period, the unemployment figure dropped from 500,000 to 122,000, and living standards in general improved.

State interventionism, 1926–29

However, once he felt his political position was more secure, Mussolini's policies turned more interventionist and he became directly involved in their design and implementation. Many of his economic policies in this period were referred to as 'battles'. Why do you think Mussolini chose to call his policies so?

The Battle over the Southern Problem, 1924

To address the ongoing problems of the Southern Question, Mussolini had promised rapid urbanization of southern Italy together with some extent of land redistribution. However, the Battle did little to solve the poverty and backwardness in the region. Plans to redistribute large estates and make land available to small farmers were never put into practice. By the end of the 1920s, 87 per cent of peasants owned 13 per cent of the land, and little progress had been made on urbanization projects. This is an indication that social inequality had not been solved.

The Battle for Grain, 1925

The purpose of this policy was for Italy to become more self-sufficient in agriculture – by increasing productivity in the country and reducing the import of cereals, particularly wheat. More land was dedicated to grain production and an emphasis was put on the mechanization of farming.

In order to achieve higher levels of grain production, land previously used for traditional products – such as olives and citrus – was now used for wheat. As a result, the exports of traditional Italian products dropped. Although some level of mechanization was achieved, especially in the north where the most affluent farmers lived, the south did not see significant mechanization. Nonetheless, by 1931, Italy became self-sufficient in wheat production.

Activity 16   (ATL) Communication skills

Study the source below and answer the questions that follow.

Benito Mussolini and Victor Emmanuel III inspecting a field of wheat in the year the Battle for Grain was launched.

1. What is the message of this source?
2. With reference to the origins, purpose, and content of this source, assess its value and limitations to a historian studying the Battle for Grain.

The Battle for Land, 1926

In an attempt to increase the availability of arable land, Mussolini ordered the draining of marshes and swamps. The most famous of these projects was the draining of the Pontine Marshes near Rome. Under government financing, these newly created farms were then given to unemployed farmers.

Activity 17   (ATL) Thinking skills

Study the source and answer the question that follows.

> [New villages] were colonized by war veterans while journalists and foreign observers looked on. 'This is where we have waged a veritable war', Mussolini declared in Littoria in 1932. 'This is the war that we prefer.' Propaganda was to pour out panegyrics on an undertaking that was only partly completed at a cost of six hundred million dollars to the state and often to the greater enrichment of landowners the value of whose properties was increased by the investment of public funds in them. Meanwhile, covered with wreaths, Mussolini dedicated the colonists' little houses, on the walls of which were inscribed one of the aphorisms of Il Duce: 'It is the plow that makes the furrow, but it is the sword that defends it.'

From Max Gallo, *Mussolini's Italy*, Macmillan Publishing, 1973, pp. 233–34

1. According to the source above, how successful was Mussolini's Battle for Land?

The Battle for the Lira, 1926

In order to show the lira – the Italian national currency at the time – as a strong currency, Mussolini had the lira revalued to make it stronger against other currencies. Behind the Battle for the Lira was essentially a desire by Mussolini to increase national prestige and his own image at home: 'I will defend the lira to my last breath, to the last drop of my blood.' As a result of the lira's increased value, Italian imports benefited from the new exchange rates, but exports suffered. This was because a stronger lira made Italian-made products more expensive to other countries. The car industry, for example, was badly affected and this took a toll on the employment levels of the sector. Tourism, which had been a main source of income, also declined.

The Battle for Births, 1927

One of Mussolini's ambitions was to create a large army of people to enable Italy to build an extensive empire that would provide the homeland with raw materials from around the world and develop a market for Italian industrialized products. To achieve that aim, he announced the Battle for Births, with the objective of increasing the Italian population from 40 million at the time to 60 million by 1950. Legislation and a new taxation system were introduced to reward large families and penalize bachelors. Propaganda was directed at promoting women's roles as housewives and mothers.

Although Italy experienced a growth in population, the Battle for Births did not reach the expected levels. In fact it is very difficult to determine whether the achieved population growth resulted from the battle, or whether there were other contributing factors, for example, the influence of Catholicism. Furthermore, despite Mussolini's efforts to keep women in their homes, female employment levels remained the same. You will find out more about this in the section on women's policies later on.

Economic policies after 1929

The year 1929 brought about an international economic crisis known as the **Great Depression**. Like many countries, Italy suffered the effects of the Depression. Mussolini's response to this was to become more interventionist in matters relating to the Italian economy, in order for the country to achieve **autarky** in all areas. This required a further increase in production levels. You have read earlier in this chapter how the Battle for Grain achieved some level of self-sufficiency; Mussolini now wanted more and, to achieve it, he had to increase employment levels.

Unemployment caused by the Depression had led to a decline in wages. In the countryside, these dropped by as much as 30 per cent, thus forcing rural workers to migrate to the cities or leave Italy for the Americas in search of better opportunities. To prevent a shortage of hand labour in the countryside, Mussolini restricted the movements of peasants within Italy by introducing travel permission documents that had to be obtained from the Fascist authorities. While this provided landowners with a surplus of labour, it also contributed to a further reduction in peasants' wages.

Mussolini also sought to create employment opportunities in other areas. In the area of construction, Mussolini promoted the building of highways, railways, bridges, aqueducts, and other public works. The Italian state absorbed banks and private companies that went bankrupt as a result of the Depression, in order to save jobs. The armament industry, partly funded by the state, absorbed unemployed workers. Price controls were established to protect the purchasing value of salaries. Furthermore, greater state intervention after 1929 called for new institutions and legislation. New commercial and civil codes were drafted, all of which continued to be in use in Italy after 1945.

Although Mussolini's economic policies lacked coordination, it is true that, by 1940, Italian industrial output surpassed agricultural production for the first time in history. However, autarky was never fully achieved; the Italian economy suffered as a result of Italy's aggressive foreign policy after 1935, as well as from the participation in World

War II. You will find out more about this when analysing Mussolini's foreign policy later on in the chapter.

Activity 18   (ATL) Social, communication, and self-management skills

1. Consider the following question:

> *To what extent did an authoritarian state you have studied bring about significant economic change?*

How would you answer this question with reference to Mussolini?

Paper 2 questions may ask you to assess the policies of authoritarian states. In this case, if you were to answer the question with reference to Mussolini's economic policies, you need to explain what you understand by 'economic change' in this context. Does it refer to whether Mussolini was able to improve the existing economic conditions? Does it ask whether the economy became different, for example, more centralized? The introduction to the essay is your opportunity to explain how you understood the question.

Before you take your exam, you will be revising different authoritarian leaders you have studied. It may therefore be useful to create a chart for each leader, like the one below, to help you with your revision. Charts like this will help you get a sense of how you can compare and contrast different leaders, as well as work out which pairings of leaders are the most effective.

Complete the missing elements in the following chart and discuss with your classmates how you would answer the question in Activity 18.

Problem	Policy	Aim	Result
Southern Question			
		Self-sufficiency	
			Limited land reclaimed; mostly used for propaganda
	Battle for Births		

Propaganda

The use of propaganda for the consolidation and maintenance of his regime was as important to Mussolini as it had been during his rise to power. Previous sections of the chapter have discussed how Mussolini used his journalistic talent and oratorical skills in his rise to power. This section will analyse the use of propaganda in the Fascist state. As you work through it, think about whether you agree with Denis Mack Smith's view that 'Fascism was essentially rhetoric and blather.'

What were the aims of Fascist propaganda?

Propaganda in Mussolini's regime aimed at inspiring in Italians a pride for their nation and persuading them that Mussolini was an extraordinary leader. This involved the development of a cult of Mussolini by praising his actions and, often, overstating the achievements of his policies.

TOK Consider the claim that 'propaganda is the art and science of controlling the mind by overwhelming insistence upon a point of view'. How would you define propaganda? To what extent do you consider it to be 'an art and a science'?

This photograph from 1938 shows Mussolini giving a speech to inaugurate the wheat harvest. Can you think of some reasons why he chose to be photographed stripped to the waist?

What were the methods of propaganda?

Fascist propaganda made use of a wide range of methods to spread its ideas. It insisted on key concepts, such as 'Mussolini is always right' or 'Believe, obey, fight'. Catchphrases like these reflected the role of submission Mussolini wanted the population to adopt towards him. Mass rallies, such as the one shown in the opening photograph of this chapter, were an effective way to reach vast numbers of people as well as to demonstrate the extent of Mussolini's popularity. His speeches focused on key ideas relating to nationalism, such as the importance of the state above individuals ('Everything in the state, nothing outside the state, nothing against the state.') or Italian territorial expansion.

Mussolini also made use of the mass media. He published articles in newspapers as he had done before coming to power. Later, he incorporated the use of radio as an effective way to reach the population nationwide. The use of posters and photographs was also extensive: these were very carefully designed and created in order to enhance the idea of Mussolini as a strong leader.

The restoration of Roman ruins, the draining of marshes, and the inauguration of ambitious works of infrastructure were also methods used to demonstrate the achievements of Mussolini and to show him as a contemporary Caesar.

This poster illustrates an Italian factory in Mussolini's Italy. What message is being conveyed by the poster?

The poster above was designed in 1937 to commemorate the first anniversary of the invasion of Abyssinia. The caption calls Mussolini 'the victorious Duce'. How is this message supported by the image?

Education or indoctrination?

Mussolini's aim was to raise a generation of Fascists by promoting patriotism and obedience in boys, and the concepts of family and motherhood in girls. The figure of Mussolini was honoured as the protector of the nation and the leader who was returning Italy to an age of splendour.

In order to achieve this aim, public schools introduced standardized texts in 1928; every subject in the curriculum was used for propaganda. Political indoctrination in the lower forms at school was given particular importance. Portraits of Mussolini were placed in all classrooms; every day, students recited the Fascist creed 'I believe in the genius of Mussolini and in our Holy Father Fascism'.

These pages are from a second-grade reading book, 1941. On the left, we see a beautiful colour image of Il Duce embracing and kissing a little *Balilla*. The child offers Il Duce some beautiful flowers. The text reads: 'Duce, Duce, you are so good to children and children love you with all our heart. You are a like a father to us; you make us strong and robust you make us happy. Viva Il Duce D'Italia!' (Translation by D. Senés)
On the opposite page you can see the uniform of the Blackshirts.

The administration of education was centralized and a purge of non-Fascist teachers was carried out. From 1931 onwards, teachers were required to swear of an oath of loyalty to Mussolini.

Youth organizations – the ONB

Different youth organizations such as the Sons of the She-Wolf, the *Avanguardisti*, and the Young Fascists were created and, in 1926, became united under the coordination of the *Opera Nazionale Balilla* (ONB).

The aim of ONB was to become the training grounds of the future military. To that end, its members wore uniforms, paraded like troops, and engaged in highly organized activities often involving physical action. The ONB activities provided ample opportunities to develop the cult of Il Duce further as well as for political indoctrination. Additionally, all other organizations, except for some under the jurisdiction of the Church, were dissolved in 1928.

Here is a photograph of Young Fascists acclaiming Benito Mussolini as 'Founder of the Empire', on a train in Italy in 1930. To what extent does it show the aims of the youth organizations being achieved? How useful would this photograph be for a historian studying education and indoctrination under Mussolini?

Study the two sources below and answer the questions that follow.

Source A

 The principal function of the ONB was to prepare the young for their future role in society: boys to be soldiers and girls to be the mothers of warriors... Boys dressed in uniforms, paraded, sang marching songs and engaged in competitive sports. Girls practised first aid, danced around poles, went to concerts and attended courses on such topics as flower arranging, embroidery, knitting and typing. Part of the training of future maternity consisted of a military-style drill, in which girls were passed in review carrying dolls in the correct manner of a mother holding a baby.

From Christopher Duggan, *Fascist Voices. An Intimate History of Mussolini's Italy*, Vintage, 2012, p. 192

Source B

Although it is certainly true that many activities undertaken by the ONB gave numerous Italian children opportunities that would otherwise have not have been available, the introduction of compulsory membership in 1935 catalysed the development of a climate of resentment and disillusionment surrounding Fascist youth organisations. Furthermore the ideological impact of such groups is difficult to assess given the prevalence of opposition youth movements, such as the Catholic Boy Scouts. The rapidity at which support for Fascism disappeared following the overthrow of Mussolini in 1943 is clearly relevant here.

From Thomas Meakin, 'Mussolini's Fascism: St Hugh's College, Oxford, in Association with History Review: Julia Wood Prize Thomas Meakin Asks to What Extent Italian Fascism Represented a Triumph of Style over Substance', *History Review*, no. 59, 2007

1. According to the sources, to what extent were the youth organizations successful in promoting Fascist aims?

2. In pairs, find out if any non-Fascist youth organizations existed between the 1920s and 1930s, and what they represented. Using your own knowledge, why were the Catholic Boy Scouts allowed to continue after 1935?

After-work organizations

The *Opera Nazionale Dopolavoro* (OND) was set up in 1925 with the aim of increasing support for Fascism by offering recreational activities and becoming a socialization network within the PNF. It promoted cultural activities by opening theatres, cinemas, libraries, and orchestras. It also offered subsidized holidays to Italian workers. By 1939, 40 per cent of urban workers and 25 per cent of peasants had joined the OND. However, it is questionable whether it was an effective instrument of indoctrination as opposed to being only a recreational organization.

According to Adrian Lyttelton:

 Organized recreation served several purposes; first, the real advantages of cheap excursions, youth camps and subsidized seaside holidays were good material for the propaganda of the regime abroad: second, these initiatives aimed to imprint upon the popular mind (and especially on youth) an impression of the beneficence and ubiquity of the regime: third, they could be used as channels and instruments for direct political propaganda and for reinforcing social discipline.

From *The Seizure of Power: Fascism in Italy, 1919–1929*, Routledge, 2009, p. 402

Sport

Sport became important under Mussolini. As part of education, it was used to develop the virtues of manliness and obedience. But it also become a significant tool for Fascist propaganda and provided the opportunity to put Italy on the international stage: Italy hosted the FIFA World Cup in 1934, winning it in 1934 and again in 1938; the Italian football team also won gold in the 1936 Summer Olympics in Berlin.

As written in an Italian newspaper at the time:

> *The Olympics, European championships, World Cup and International Student Games have been the sieve and the evidence of our rise. The blue shirt has become, in all fields, a symbol of ability ... of ardour, of assertion.*
>
> *The number of individual successes blend into the bright dazzling size of the collective success, and abroad our superiority is recognized, admired and envied.*
>
> **Extract from *La Gazzetta*, 31 May 1938, quoted in Simon Martin, *Football and Fascism: The National Game under Mussolini*, Berg, 2004, p. 211**

Activity 20 Social and communication skills

Below is a colour card to promote the 1934 FIFA World Cup.

1. Discuss how you think this card promoted ideas of success. Do you think it contains an element of nationalism? Explain your answer.

2. In groups, discuss how sport has been used by authoritarian leaders to maintain power. Can you think of other authoritarian states where sport has been politically manipulated by leaders? In those cases, how successful was this policy?

Arts and culture

Mussolini, unlike other authoritarian leaders you may have studied, was relatively open as regards the artistic expressions that could exist under his regime. As such, no specific 'Fascist Art' developed, nor did Mussolini instigate a specific purge of Italian artists and writers.

One of the most important Italian artistic movements of the time was Futurism. Born in 1909, it transmitted a passion for movement and fearlessness as well as an admiration for industrial progress, together with a cult of military force. The most popular representative of Italian Futurism was Filippo T. Marinetti. Like Mussolini, Marinetti supported Italy's intervention in World War I as an opportunity to rebuild Italy. Coincidences between the Futurists and Mussolini continued after the war, and Marinetti became an early member of the PNF. Marinetti wanted Futurism to become the visual representation of Fascism. Although Mussolini used Futurist art and techniques for propaganda, he was not interested in committing to one single artistic movement.

Although Mussolini did not personally appreciate art very much, he recognized its usefulness as a tool to communicate Fascist aims and achievements. The government encouraged literary and artistic exhibitions and competitions on Fascist topics such as ancient Roman history and nationalism. One of the clearest examples of this policy was the Exhibition of the Fascist Revolution of 1932, held in Milan to mark the 10th anniversary of Mussolini's rise to power. The purpose of the exhibition was to show the achievements of Fascism as well as to project the image of Mussolini leading Italians into a promising future. To encourage people from all across Italy to attend the exhibition, Mussolini reduced train fares. For many citizens, this was the first time they travelled outside their region. The exhibition was a huge success.

Activity 21   (ATL)   Communication and thinking skills

Study the images below and answer the questions that follow.

Source A

Source B

▲ *Myths of the Action* (1939) by Futurist artist Enrico Prampolini.

Poster of the Exhibition of the Fascist Revolution, 1933. ▶

1. Source A is a painting showing Mussolini on horseback. What feelings do you think the artist wanted to evoke? In what ways does the painting help to communicate the aims and policies of Fascism?

2. Source B was designed to advertise the Exhibition of the Fascist Revolution using the aesthetics of Futurism. In what ways does it help to communicate Fascist ideals?

As part of propaganda, policies to support Italian cinema were also implemented. In 1932, the Venice International Film Festival was created – it remains one of the most prestigious festivals worldwide to this day. Under the slogan 'Cinema is the strongest weapon', Mussolini inaugurated Cinecitta – Italy's own version of Hollywood – in 1937. The studios produced as many as 100 films a year. Although some films were used to promote themes in the Fascist agenda, such as the role of women as exemplar mothers and wives or stories that praised militarism, most films were for general entertainment rather than propaganda. Indoctrination came with the newsreels that, as of 1926, were compulsorily projected at every film session.

1. Examine the role of education and the arts in the maintenance of power of one authoritarian state.

Before you can examine the role of education and the arts, you need to consider what this role was from the outset: In the case of Mussolini, what role did the government want education and the arts to play in Italy during that period? Once you have done that, you can think about whether or not they did in fact play such a role, or, alternatively, whether they became areas that reflected weaknesses of the regimes. For example, if the role of education was to indoctrinate people, you can evaluate the extent to which this was achieved and the challenges Mussolini faced in this area. Or, if the arts were meant to help portray a new model of **nationhood**, consider how far it reflected this; think about whether or not the arts were also used to express dissent.

The impact of policies on minorities and women

The following section focuses on Mussolini's policies on minorities in Italy, in particular its Jewish population, as well as his policies on women.

Treatment of minorities

At the turn of the 20th century, the Jewish population in Italy was relatively small; according to the 1911 census, its size was estimated to be 2 per cent of the entire population. The Jewish community concentrated mostly around cities like Rome, Milan, and Trieste. Although Fascist Italy was not anti-Semitic at first, the Jews suffered discrimination and, later, persecution under Mussolini.

Mussolini's rise did not constitute an immediate danger to the Jewish community in Italy. His nationalist political speeches did not contain anti-Semitic elements. In fact, a significant number of Italian Jews supported Mussolini's anti-communism and his defence of law and order; many became PNF members in the early days. After 1922, a number of Italian Jews held important positions, including Edoardo Polacco (general secretary of the Fascist Party in the province of Brindisi), Giorgio del Vecchio (first Fascist rector of the University of Rome), and Guido Jung (minister of finance between 1932 and 1935).

However, Fascist policy changed radically in the mid-1930s as Mussolini moved into a diplomatic, and later a military, alliance with Hitler's anti-Semitic Third Reich. In July 1938, the Ministry of Popular Culture issued the Manifesto of Italian Race. The document tried to provide a scientific basis for anti-Semitism and declared that Jews did not belong to the Italian (defined as Aryan) race. It made anti-Semitism an official Italian policy by severely reducing the civil rights of the Italian Jews. The Manifesto removed Jewish teachers and students from the school system, placing them in separate schools; Jews were expelled from the PNF and all other major institutions; they could no longer own large businesses or estates; restrictions were also placed on their ownership and inheritance rights. Soon after, mixed marriages were outlawed by a Law for the Defence of the Race.

Initially, these anti-Semitic policies had limited effect; they were badly received by many sectors of the Italian population as well as by many PNF members. Anti-Semitism troubled Catholic Italians, who often chose to ignore it. The Italian Jews were fully integrated into Italian society, and people were reluctant to denounce them to the authorities. The authorities in turn were not fully supportive of the anti-Semitic legislation either, according to Nicola Caracciolo:

> " *Then, this other thing happened, when I was running around downtown Genoa, and someone comes near me and says, 'Look, I'm a police agent, and I have an order to pick you up. Grosser, do me a favor, don't go around the city like this, go home and stay there.' When I'm some ten or twelve steps away from that agent, another plainclothes agent comes and says, 'Listen, Grosser, I'm with the police, don't run around town so much, because I've got orders to bring you in. Go home, hide there, and this way we forget about it.' And this was a most lovely action on the part of the police.*
>
> **From Nicola Caracciolo, *Uncertain Refuge: Italy and the Jews during the Holocaust*, trans. Florette Rechnitz Koffler and Richard Koffler, University of Illinois Press, 1995**

However, when World War II broke out, a vast number of Jews from Nazi Germany and beyond were interned in concentration camps. Although Italian officers sometimes refused to hand over Italian Jews to Nazi authorities, thousands of Italian Jews were deported to Nazi camps.

Although anti-Semitism in Italy was largely perceived as a result of Hitler's influence on Mussolini, it is also true to say that race had already been a public issue in Italy during the period of Italian expansion in Africa, when the idea of the Italians being superior to the African races began to spread (for more, see page 199).

Treatment of women

In order to understand Mussolini's policies towards women, you should consider the historical context in which they were conceived. During World War I, women helped the war effort socially and economically: By replacing men in factories and the countryside, they showed they could contribute positively to the economy. The great challenge came, however, when the men had returned from the front and peace had been restored: Should women continue to work, or should they return to the more traditional roles of being housewives and mothers? This question was of particular relevance in Italy, as the Catholic Church played a large part in shaping social traditions, and the role of women before the war had been mostly limited to their home environment.

Along these lines, Mussolini declared that 'women's place, in the present as in the past, is in the home'. Earlier, you studied how the Battle for Births aimed at increasing the Italian population from 40 to 60 million by 1950. Thus, Mussolini encouraged women to stay home and become mothers. By 1932, contraception, sterilization, and abortion were banned. The state granted marriage and birth loans to couples, and gave medals to mothers who had a large number of children. A married status and the number of children one had became criteria for the selection of civil servants.

Apart from increasing the Italian population, Mussolini's policies towards women at work also partly aimed at solving the high levels of male unemployment. By forcing women out of the labour market, he created job opportunities for unemployed men. Legislation was passed in 1933 and again in 1938, restricting the number of women in the workforce in all Italian companies. It could be argued that life became more demanding for women under Mussolini. Due to the low wages paid to the men, many women had to work in the informal market anyway to support their families, even though they would be underpaid and would remain unprotected by work legislation. In addition, women had to play an active role in the 'Fascistization' of the family.

Fascist women could not expect to hold important positions within the structure of the PNF. Instead, they formed the *Fasci Femminili*, which were female branches of the

PNF that carried out welfare activities. The *Massaie Rurali*, for example, was a branch that provided assistance to rural women by instructing them on farming techniques, childcare, and craft manufacturing. Under Mussolini, women were briefly granted the right to vote in local elections in 1925, but these elections were abolished the following year. Italian women did not vote again until after World War II. Existing feminist organizations were only allowed to continue if they dedicated themselves to welfare activities and not to political life. However, with the outbreak of World War II and the rise of opposition to Mussolini, many women became involved in political life by joining the resistance movements across Italy. They helped spread anti-Fascist propaganda, organized strikes and sabotages, carried secret information across enemy lines, and engaged in actual fighting.

Activity 23 Thinking and communication skills

Study the sources below and answer the questions that follow.

Source A

A chart showing the percentage female participation in the total labour force, 1921–36

	Agriculture	Industry	Other
1921	44.7	39	38.5
1931	40.5	34.4	40
1936	41.3	33.1	42.8

Data adapted from Rosa Anna Pernicone (1972), in Victoria de Grazia, *How Fascism Ruled Women. Italy 1922–1945*, University of California Press, 1992, pp. 35–36

Source B

 In an effort to manage these trends, the regime intervene to make public sector employment a male preserve with special privileges and good pay. It tolerated women working while young, then induced them to leave the official labor market when they married and had children. Finally the Fascist state promoted the formation of a largely female submerged economy of unprotected, underemployed and ill paid home workers. As a result, the several million Italian women who toiled outside the home during the interwar years experienced significant changes in occupational opportunities, work routines, and career patterns under especially disabling conditions.

From Victoria de Grazia, *How Fascism Ruled Women. Italy 1922–1945*, University of California Press, 1992

Source C

 The woman-mother was responsive to the state's interest in the following very concrete way: she had her children as fascist citizens, engage herself and them in the fascist youth organisations such as the ONMI, direct her household according to the national interests, make her children – against her will – good soldiers who would in all likelihood sacrifice their lives for the good of the nation, be a good wife and back up fascist ideology. In other words, the state's expectation was 'to fascistize the family as the smallest unit of the authoritarian regime, whose motto was to 'Believe, Obey, Fight'.

From Efharis Mascha, *Contradiction and the Role of the 'Floating Signifier': Identity and the 'New Woman' in Italian Cartoons During Fascism*, University of Essex, 2010

Source D

This war propaganda poster shows women replacing male workers in a munition factory.

Fronte del lavoro. - Negli stabilimenti per la produzione di guerra le donne italiane lavorano attente, assidue, sostituendo con cosciente dedizione la maestranza maschile.
(Disegno di A. Beltrame)

1. What is the message conveyed by Source A?
2. What is the poster in Source D trying to promote?
3. Using the sources and your own knowledge, discuss the extent of change in the lives of women in Fascist Italy.
4. With reference to one authoritarian state, discuss the view that authoritarian states allowed women to play a fuller role in society.

A good starting point for question 4 would be to define what you understand by 'a fuller role in society'. Did improvements in women's political rights reflect a wider participation in society? If women entered their workforce in great numbers as a result of government policies, did it necessarily mean their role in society was 'fuller'? Some regimes may offer you the possibility of focusing on specific cases of individual women who played a significant part – but to what extent are these cases representative of the role of women in general?

Questions on Paper 2 Topic 10 will only ask about the foreign policy of leaders in relation to their domestic policies. In other words, you may be asked to assess how events in Mussolini's foreign policy were a response to his needs to attain objectives in his domestic policies. You may also be asked about the impact his foreign policies had on events at a national level.

4.3 The use of foreign policy in Mussolini's consolidation and maintenance of power

This section aims at analysing the impact of Mussolini's foreign policy on his domestic policies. It explores Italy's role in some of the most significant events in both the interwar period and in World War II, as well as how they affected both the nation as well as Mussolini himself. As you work through this section, ask yourself the following questions: What was the impact of the different events of Mussolini's foreign policy on his rule as well as on Italy as a nation? To what extent did Mussolini's foreign policy contribute to his fall from power in 1943?

To what extent did Mussolini use Italy's foreign policy to consolidate his power?

One of Mussolini's most well-known phrases is 'I want to make Italy great, feared, and respected'. This phrase echoed the feeling of many Italians who wanted a revision of the 'the mutilated victory' after World War I and to put Italy back on the map. Mussolini's aim was to re-establish the glory of the ancient Roman Empire by territorially expanding Italy. His main strategic objectives were the control of the Mediterranean Sea, and the acquisition of territory in Africa and the Balkans region.

Even before his rise to power, Mussolini had demanded that Italy took opportunities for aggrandizement. In previous sections of this chapter you have studied how he changed his view about World War I: seeing an opportunity to promote nationalism and to achieve territorial expansion, he quickly went from being a non-interventionist to a full supporter of Italy's entry in the war. Once in power, Mussolini showed full awareness of how both domestic and foreign policies were interrelated. He considered war as a necessary stage in the development of history: 'only blood can turn the blood-stained wheels of history'; consequently, Fascism promoted the importance of physical strength in all aspects of society.

You have also studied how Mussolini aimed at making Italy an autarkic nation, for which he put into practice an expansionist foreign policy. His education and indoctrination policies focused on the preparation of future soldiers. The Battle for Births is another example of an economic policy designed to serve Italian foreign policy, as a growing population could strengthen the army. At times, Mussolini used foreign policy to enhance his image politically, and as a distraction from other internal problems in Italy. At an international level, Mussolini's aim was to be considered as a great leader, as he thought it would also serve to increase his popularity in Italy. This led him to play an active diplomatic role in the interwar period. As time progressed, however, he shifted from the role of a negotiator to that of an aggressive leader who refused to cooperate with international organizations.

However, rather than being interpreted as calculated, Mussolini's foreign policy has also been understood as one in which he seized international opportunities as they arose in order to serve his own interests.

Activity 24

 Social and communication skills

1. In groups, chose one aspect of Mussolini's domestic policies that you have studied (for example, economic, political, social, culture) and explain how the aims and implementation of such policies can be related to the aims in his foreign policy.

Foreign policy between 1922 and 1934

This section assesses the ambitions and achievements of Mussolini's foreign policy from his rise to power up to the invasion of Abyssinia. After his rise, Mussolini tried to keep in good diplomatic relations with both France and Britain, the most powerful European countries at the end of World War I. However, he did not miss the opportunity to reclaim territory in Corfu (1923) and Fiume (1924).

The Corfu Incident, 1923

In 1923, Mussolini blamed Greece for the murder of Italian diplomats working on the Greek–Albanian border and demanded economic compensation. He successfully defied the League of Nations by invading the Greek island of Corfu and making Greece pay.

Activity 25

Study the source below and answer the question that follows.

> ❝ It should not be forgotten that if Mussolini fell he would not merely be succeeded by some other premier such as Giolitti but that period of anarchy might possibly ensue which would be followed by either military dictatorship or some other worse form of government.

From a telegram from Howard Kennard, a counsellor of the British Embassy in Rome, to British Foreign Secretary Lord Curzon, 6 September 1923

1. What does this source reveal about the ways in which the international context aided Mussolini's foreign policy in Corfu?

In many ways, the invasion of Corfu could be seen as a failure for Mussolini. He was forced to withdraw from the island and received only an economic compensation for the loss of Italian citizens instead. Relations, particularly with Britain, became strained. However, in Italy, Mussolini made certain the Corfu incident was perceived as a victory. The attack on Corfu was to be interpreted as a shift in foreign policy. Mussolini claimed he would not tolerate any attack against the honour of the nation.

Fiume, 1924

Fiume was set up as a free city between Yugoslavia and Italy after the war; its population was largely Italian-speaking. In 1919, Gabriele D'Annunzio, together with some nationalist supporters, occupied Fiume in the name of Italy and held it for 15 months. In 1920, Prime Minister Giovanni Giolitti removed D'Annunzio and his men from Fiume.

In 1924, Mussolini invaded Fiume under the pretext that its Italian population was in danger. Even when Fiume had not been a territory promised to Italy by the Treaty of London, it was nevertheless associated with the *Italia irredenta*, the territories Italians believed should be incorporated into their kingdom. Because of this, and because the events had evoked the romanticism and nationalism of D'Annunzio, when the king of Yugoslavia signed a pact of friendship with Mussolini and handed over Fiume to Italy, he helped Mussolini obtain a great propaganda victory.

The Locarno Pact, 1925

The Locarno Pact was a series of treaties signed by France, Germany, Britain, Belgium, and Italy in 1925 to guarantee Germany's frontiers with France and Belgium. By the Treaty of Mutual Guarantee included in the pact, Italy and Britain agreed to defend any signatory victim of a violation of the terms of the pact.

With this pact, Mussolini sought to improve relations with Britain after Corfu and Fiume. However, the pact did not guarantee Germany's eastern frontiers, and Mussolini was concerned that a potential expansion of Germany into Austria would affect Italian security. The failure to address this issue at Locarno deprived Mussolini of a more categorical diplomatic triumph. This would have been of utmost significance to Mussolini as the conference was contemporary to the events surrounding the murder of Giacomo Matteotti, which had seriously hampered his reputation both at home and abroad (see page 180).

The impact of the rise of Adolf Hitler in Germany

In 1933, Adolf Hitler came to power in Germany. Although German Nazism shared many ideological principles with Italian Fascism, they initially clashed in 1934 over

Gabriele D'Annunzio (1863–1938) Gabriele D'Annunzio was an important Italian poet and journalist who lost an eye whilst fighting in World War I. He was associated with the *arditi*. Disappointed that Italy had not been given the land promised at the Secret Treaty of London, D'Annunzio coined the term 'mutilated victory' to refer to the humiliating outcome of negotiations at the Paris Peace Conference.

Austria. Hitler had territorial ambitions in Austria, but post-war treaties prohibited the union of these two countries. Mussolini feared the effects of the **anschluss** on the South Tyrol region of northern Italy, which had German-speaking minorities.

When Austrian Nazis murdered Chancellor Dollfuss in 1934, Mussolini mobilized troops to the Brenner Pass, the border between Italy and Austria, in protection of Austrian integrity. This had a positive impact on Mussolini's reputation and, also, paved the way for the **Stresa Pact** in 1935. Although shortlived, this agreement between Britain, France, and Italy was a propaganda opportunity for Mussolini to show he had become a statesman of international importance.

Activity 26  Thinking skills

1. To what extent was Mussolini's foreign policy in this period consistent with his aims? Is there evidence to suggest he was only taking advantage of international events?

2. To what extent did Mussolini's foreign policy between 1922 and 1933 contribute to his domestic policies?

Foreign policy, 1935–39

After 1935, Mussolini aimed to strengthen his power in Italy through his foreign policy, but it proved to be a major contributor to his downfall. The following section focuses on some of the most important international events after 1935 and Italy's role in them. When working through this section, consider the ways in which Mussolini aimed at strengthening his domestic policies through foreign policy, and the extent to which this was achieved.

The Italian Invasion of Abyssinia, 1935

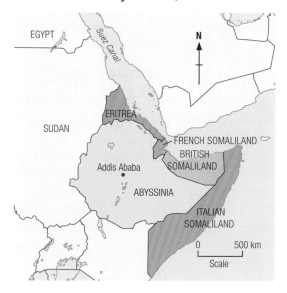

Map of Abyssinia and surrounding regions, 1934.

Abyssinia (Ethiopia) was an independent monarchy between the less-rewarding Italian colonies of Eritrea and Somaliland. In the introduction to this chapter, you briefly read about Italy's defeat at the Battle of Adowa in 1896. The Italian invasion of Abyssinia was of both historical and contemporary significance to Mussolini. Because Adowa had previously been a humiliation for Italy, the 1935 victory was experienced as a moment of great historical significance.

At the time, the success of the invasion played a large part in enhancing Mussolini's prestige. He became the hero who transformed Italy into an empire by proclaiming the king of Italy the new Emperor of Abyssinia. However, the expansion over Abyssinia ultimately aimed at addressing domestic problems.

Activity 27

 Thinking and communication skills

Study the source below and answer the questions that follow.

> *Motivations are always difficult for historians to decipher, and the Ethiopian War is no exception. It appears, however, that the Fascist revolution was growing stale by the mid-1930s. There was little else that Mussolini could do domestically without alienating one of the major conservative groups supporting him. Italy was also significantly slower to recover from the Great Depression than either Germany or Britain. A war against Ethiopia would solve several problems at once. It would divert attention from the economy, avenge Italian defeats at the hands of the Ethiopians in 1889 and 1896, and bring glory to Italy (and especially to Mussolini). All this would be accomplished by establishing an empire in Africa.*

From Bruce F. Pauley, *Hitler, Stalin, and Mussolini: Totalitarianism in the Twentieth Century*, 4th ed., John Wiley & Sons, 2014, p. 196

1. According to the source above, what problems did Mussolini hope to address with the war in Abyssinia?
2. Using your own knowledge of Italian domestic policies, to what extent do you agree with the view that 'the Fascist revolution was growing stale by the mid-1930s'?
3. Which were the 'major conservative groups' that were being alienated by Mussolini in 1935?

However, Mussolini's invasion of Abyssinia damaged his reputation at an international level; he was no longer perceived by Britain and France as a leader that could be trusted.

Activity 28

 Communication and thinking skills

Study the sources below and answer the questions that follow.

Source A

This is the front page of the British newspaper *Daily Sketch* on 4 October 1935.

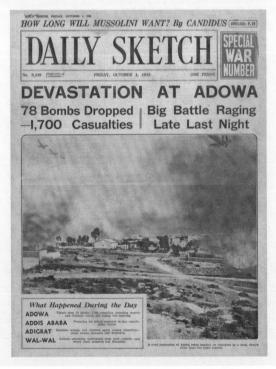

Source B

This photograph shows Italians donating gold to contribute to the war cause on 18 December 1935. Among other donations, thousands of women donated their wedding rings; in exchange, they received an iron ring with this date engraved on it.

TOK

18 December 1935 was known as *Giornata della Fede*. The Italian word *fede* stands for both the name given to a wedding ring as well as for 'faith'. Therefore, the name *Giornata della fede* could be interpreted in more than one way. How does understanding this influence the significance of this photograph?

1. How does Source A help you understand the international reaction towards the invasion of Abyssinia?

2. Source B is a propaganda photograph showing Italians donating gold, including their wedding rings, towards the war effort. How effective do you think this photograph is as an example of Fascist propaganda? In what ways do you think this campaign strengthened the image of Mussolini, both in Italy and abroad?

Mussolini justified the invasion of Abyssinia on the grounds that the Italian population needed more territory and that it was 'an African country universally branded as a country without the slightest shadow of civilization'. This was a warning that Italy's racial policies were to take a turn for the worse, as the 1938 Manifesto on Race later demonstrated.

If Mussolini had been looking for raw materials and resources to justify his mission in Abyssinia, he was to be disappointed: Abyssinia didn't have oil, nor did its farming conditions ensure high levels of production of coffee or sugar. Not only did Abyssinia fail to provide much in terms of additional sources of income, it also continued to cost the Italian government a significant amount of money. For three years, Italian troops remained engaged in local clashes with the guerrillas; moreover, the intended resettlement of Italians in Abyssinia was unsuccessful and many Italians returned home, disappointed by what they had (or had not) found.

Activity 29 **Thinking and communication skills**

1. With reference to the sources in this chapter and your own knowledge, discuss the extent to which you consider the Abyssinian crisis of 1935 a contribution to Mussolini's rule in Italy.

The Spanish Civil War, 1936–39

The Spanish Civil War broke out in 1936 as a result of the political, social, and economic conflicts that had been affecting Spain for many years. A group of generals from the Spanish army, including General Francisco Franco, led the Nationalist forces against the Second Spanish Republic.

1. Divide the class into groups. Each group should make a brief presentation on one of the causes leading to the outbreak of the Spanish Civil War: a) weakness of the Republic, b) the role of the Spanish army, c) the role of the Church, d) economic causes, e) regionalism.
2. Discuss why you think Mussolini was interested in events in Spain in 1936.

Why did Mussolini enter the Spanish Civil War?

Mussolini's Italy became committed to the Nationalist cause from the beginning. Here are several reasons explaining Italy's involvement:

• Mussolini wanted to show himself as a leader in the fight against communism, and to gain support from both the Pope and the Catholics in Italy.
• A new successful war would provide him an opportunity to promote nationalism and rally the nation behind him.
• A war would keep employment levels high, especially in the armament industry, thus contributing to the Italian economy.
• Particularly after Abyssinia, Mussolini's interest in the control of the Mediterranean Sea could be safer with Franco in power, since France also had interests in North Africa.

By early 1937, almost 50,000 Italian troops, formed by infantry and artillery men alongside the Blackshirts, had landed in Spain. Mussolini continued to supply troops, airplanes, tanks, and even submarines to aid the Nationalists. The Italian naval and air support were a significant contribution to the Nationalists.

What was the impact of the Spanish Civil War on Italy?

Although Mussolini received support from the Vatican and many Italian Catholics, the civil war was a strain on the Italian economy. Also, the Italians were defeated at the Battle of Guadalajara, where the lives of 2,000 soldiers were lost and 4,000 were wounded. Even more embarrassing was the fact that the Italian army was defeated by Italians fighting on the side of the Republicans.

Participation in the civil war left Italy exhausted. By the time World War II broke out in 1939, the strain on Italy's economy and its armament industry led Mussolini to declare himself non-belligerent. He only entered the conflict in 1940, when he thought the war would soon be over.

Some historians disagree with the idea that intervention in the Spanish Civil War had weakened the Italian military. John Coverdale, for example, argues that because Italy had been sending obsolete weaponry to Spain, it made little impact on Italy's preparedness for war when World War II broke out. Instead, Coverdale claims that Italy's problem at the time of World War II was that it had not learned the valuable military and strategic lessons from the Spanish Civil War.

German–Italian relations, 1936–39

Mussolini and Hitler signed several international agreements before they became war allies. The Rome–Berlin Axis was an understanding of friendship between Italy and Germany, signed in 1936. It was followed, in 1937, by Italy joining Germany and Japan in the Anti-Comintern Pact against Bolshevism. In 1939, Mussolini signed the Pact of Steel, a full military alliance, with Hitler, thus bringing Italy into the war in June 1940.

This photograph shows German Chancellor Adolf Hitler and Prime Minister Benito Mussolini shaking hands in 1938. By then, the two leaders had become diplomatic allies. Later, they were to fight on the same side in World War II.

The impact of World War II on Italy

Italy entered World War II in June 1940. At that time, France was about to surrender to Germany, and Mussolini interpreted this as a sign that war would soon be over. He thought of the war as an opportunity to renew his popularity and prestige. Many Italians, persuaded that war would be short and victorious, also supported it due to the prospect of glory for Italy. A growing number of anti-Fascists who, considering the war as an opportunity to end Mussolini's rule over Italy, also welcomed it to some extent.

However, Italian participation in the war led to disastrous consequences for both Mussolini and Italy. The war was neither short nor successful. In fact, it was humiliating for Italy, as Mussolini's forces had to be repeatedly aided by the Germans. Italian citizens suffered the destruction of their homes, the industries, and the transportation networks. Agricultural output fell dramatically during the war, causing famine; rationing had to be introduced in 1941. In spite of censorship, news of defeat and of the high casualty numbers reached the Italian citizens. Strikes and riots broke out.

Mussolini was personally responsible for much of this, since he was the one who centralized many of the economic decisions in the years before the war. His economic policies never achieved autarky, and Italy lacked raw materials to sustain the war effort. Supplies of oil were short; the armament industry depended on German steel and iron to sustain war production. Also, Mussolini's earlier foreign adventures, such as Abyssinia and the Spanish Civil War, had used up much of the resources now needed by the country.

▲ Ruins of Recco town centre after the heavy aerial bombing by Allied Forces 1944.

In 1943, after the Axis lost control of North Africa, the Allies invaded Sicily. This time, many Fascists turned against Mussolini and the Fascist Grand Council demanded his dismissal. Consequently, in July 1943, the king dismissed Mussolini and placed him under arrest. Italy surrendered and, under Mussolini's successor Marshal Pietro Badoglio, signed an armistice with the Allies. Shortly after that, the country started fighting on the Allies' side. However, the war was to continue on Italian territory until April 1945.

Activity 31   ⏵ (ATL) Thinking skills

Study the source below and answer the question that follows.

> 66 The armistice and the botched changing of sides prolonged the war still further; opened up the country to invasion, occupation, and division by Nazi Germany and the Allied powers; led to the destruction by death, disbandment, and internment of Italy's armies; and discredited the monarchy and the military as national institutions, nearly but not quite to the point of extinction. Thereafter, Italians, increasingly confused about where they were and would be, and where they felt they belonged, participated in a struggle for survival in worsening wartime conditions. It was a struggle for personal and family survival, but also one to determine not so much the survival of the nation, as the kind of nation it would be after the war.

From Philip Morgan, *The Fall of Mussolini: Italy, the Italians, and the Second World War*, Oxford University Press, 2008, p. 228

1. According to the source above, what were the effects of World War II on Italy?

Having occupied northen Italy, the Nazis now established the Italian Social Republic, also known as **Salò Republic**. They rescued Mussolini from imprisonment and made him its leader.

A map of Italy in 1943, showing the Italian Social Republic as well as territories occupied by the Allies.

Key
- Italian Social Republic
- Allied gains between 1943–1944
- Allied occupation

However, the Italian Social Republic did not live long. Why did it collapse?

- It lacked legitimacy – the fact that it was a republic antagonized the traditional sectors of society, who were still loyal to the king. Because it was separate from Italy, it was difficult to promote nationalism there.

- Nazi control of the territory was based on violence and repression, so it was difficult to gain support from the Italian citizens in the republic. It also increased the presence of resistance groups that wanted an end to foreign occupation.

- Mussolini had lost his popular appeal: defeated and ill, he was a shadow of his former figure as Il Duce; also, in the present conditions, he could no longer rely on the support generated by the propaganda apparatus. Consequently, he was left with a limited base of support from the radical sectors of the Blackshirts.

In April 1945, Mussolini attempted to escape Italy but was discovered by Italian partisans. On 28 April 1945, along with his mistress and a number of associates, Mussolini was shot and hanged for public display in Milan.

CHALLENGE YOURSELF

 Research skills

Find out more about the partisans who were involved in the death of Mussolini. What roles did these people play in the event?

This question asks that you make explicit links between the domestic and foreign policies of the leader of your choice. You need to provide specific examples of foreign policies and discuss in detail whether you think they were conditioned by domestic policies.

Activity 32

 Thinking and self-management skills

Consider the following question:

> *To what extent were the domestic policies of one authoritarian leader subordinated to his foreign policy?*

Now read the following extract from a student essay.

Student answer

From the beginning of his political career, Mussolini had made no secret of his ambition to restore Italy to greatness. This included, but was not limited to, having the 1919 Peace Treaties revised. He also wanted Italy to have a large empire that would bring glory to the nation and to himself. In order to achieve this, he set out organizing the Italian economy so that it developed to sustain the war effort. He also promoted the Battle for Births to increase the Italian population so that the country could have a large army. He tried to make Italy a self-sufficient nation by encouraging the production of wheat. Self-sufficiency was important to Mussolini's foreign policy because it allowed the country to have an aggressive foreign policy without having to think of supplies.

Examiner's comments

This paragraph attempts to link Mussolini's economic and foreign policies, and identifies some of the aims in each of them. It also tries to argue that the foreign policy drove the economy (using the Battle for Births as an example), which indicates an understanding of the demands of the question. However, it lacks detail, especially in relation to Mussolini's foreign policy. It would have been helpful to specify which territories Mussolini wanted for Italy and why obtaining them required support from his domestic policies. For example, did the Italian armament industry expand more in the 1930s as a response to Mussolini's decision to pursue a more aggressive foreign policy? Or could it be argued that it developed in order to cope with the effects of the Great Depression and that, as a result of the increase in the production of armaments, Mussolini pursued a more aggressive policy? Do not be afraid to challenge the assumptions of the question; make sure you include sufficient analysis and detail.

4.4 Assessing Benito Mussolini as an authoritarian leader

In *The Origins of the Second World War* (1991), A. J. P. Taylor said of Mussolini: 'The social peril from which it saved Italy was a fraud; the revolution by which it seized power was a fraud; the ability and policy of Mussolini were fraudulent. Fascist rule was corrupt, incompetent, empty: Mussolini himself a vain, blundering, boaster without either ideas or aims.'

To what extent do you agree with this claim?

Mussolini's regime experienced some domestic and foreign successes. He encouraged a stronger sense of nationalism than Italy had ever experienced. The Lateran Pact ended the dispute that had divided the loyalties of Italian citizens between the Church and the state since unification. The modernization of legislation, with the adoption of new codes, far outlived the Fascist regime. In the international field, much was undone by his aggressive policies, but there were circumstances when Mussolini was a positive influence in international relations, such as during the events in Austria in 1934.

However, these achievements were overstated by propaganda and the cult of Il Duce. Mussolini himself fell victim to his own propaganda and refused to listen to critics. In the words of Thomas Meakin, Mussolini's Italy was 'a triumph of style over substance'. When put to the test during World War II, neither Mussolini nor the Fascist state survived the challenge. Propaganda aside, this can be attributed to policies that had not been coordinated appropriately and, consequently, failed to deliver under pressure, as with the case of the Fascist economy.

In your revision of Mussolini, return to some of the questions we have analysed in this chapter, such as:

- To what extent did he transform Italy between 1922 and 1945?
- Did he come to power because of his strengths or because of the weaknesses of his opponents?
- Did Mussolini have a programme or was his regime all 'rhetoric and blather'?
- To what extent could it be argued that he was an opportunist in his rise and rule?
- How far did his domestic policies help or hinder his foreign policy?

CHALLENGE YOURSELF

Research skills

Carry out research on the influence of Mussolini's regime outside Italy. Did either he or the ideas he stood for serve as a source of inspiration to other authoritarian regimes? In what ways were these regimes similar to or different from Mussolini's Italy?

Activity 33 Thinking skills

Revision activity

Look back at the chapter breakdown on page 165. Do you feel confident that you could answer an examination question on all of these topics? Pick your weakest topic and spend some time revising it, then try out one of the practice questions contained in this chapter. Go to the chapter titled 'Comparing and contrasting authoritarian states' and compare Mussolini or Italy with another leader or region. There are lots of ideas in that chapter to help you draw out relevant points for comparison.

 To access websites relevant to this chapter, go to www.pearsonhotlinks. com, search for the book title or ISBN, and click on 'Chapter 4'.

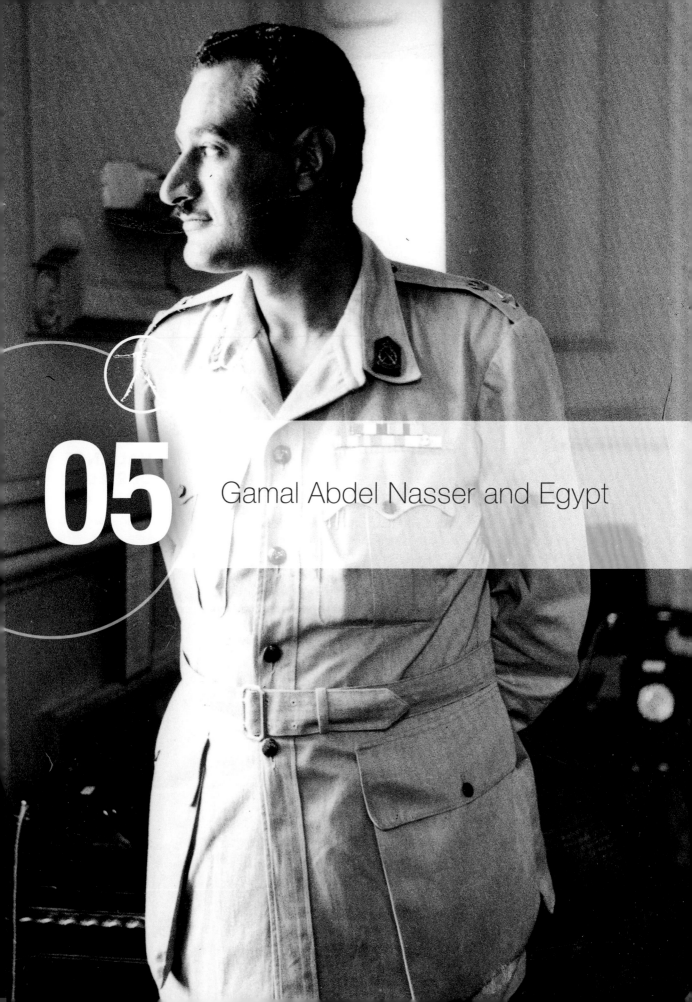

05 Gamal Abdel Nasser and Egypt

This chapter covers the rise to power and the rule of Nasser as the leader of Egypt. In particular, it focuses on:

- how Nasser, along with the Free Officers' Movement, came to organize and carry out the coup against King Farouk, and to establish a new government
- the social, economic, and political reforms that were carried out by the Revolutionary Command Council
- the emergence of Nasser as the president and authoritarian leader of Egypt
- the period from the Suez Crisis to the United Arab Republic, and how these events had an impact upon Nasser's popularity and policies
- the implementation of pan-Arabism and Arab nationalism
- the methods used by Nasser to remain in power; what he aimed to achieve; and an assessment of his successes and failures as an authoritarian leader.

August 1953, Lt, Col, Gamal Abdel Nasser, when he was president of Egypt.

> ### Key concepts:
>
> As you work through this chapter, bear in mind the key concepts we use when studying history.
>
> - **Causation**: What events caused the emergence of the Free Officers' Movement?
> - **Continuity**: Which aspects of Egyptian society remained the same, despite the abdication of the king and the establishment of an authoritarian state? For example, was religion affected?
> - **Change**: How did Egypt's position in world affairs change under Nasser? Did it play a more important role in world politics?
> - **Consequence** and **Significance**: The Suez Crisis had important consequences both in Egypt and elsewhere. Which were the most significant?
> - **Perspective**: When Nasser died in 1970, he was mourned as a hero. Has his reputation changed at all since then?

This chapter will focus on the rise to power and the rule of Gamal Abdel Nasser, the president of Egypt from 1955 until his death in 1970. A very charismatic leader, Nasser was an avowed anti-imperialist and a strong supporter of Egyptian and Arab nationalism. This chapter will give background information on the following topics: Egypt prior to the coup that brought Nasser and the Free Officers to power in 1952; the emergence of Nasser as the authoritarian leader of Egypt; and the introduction of his own brand of 'Arab socialism' that included land reform and some state ownership of industry. Extracts from both primary and secondary sources will be included, as well as maps, cartoons, and photographs along with samples of student work and hints on how to use Nasser as an example of an authoritarian leader for IB exam questions.

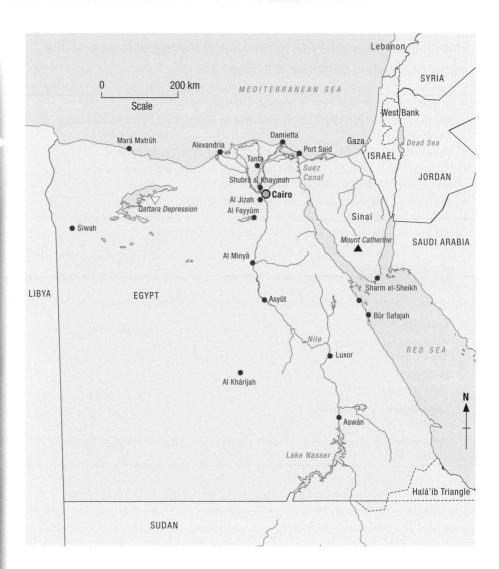

Map of Egypt and the Middle East.

Timeline of events – 1918–1970

1918	Gamal Abdel Nasser is born on 15 January in Alexandria.
1926	Fahima Mahad, Nasser's mother, dies while Nasser is away at school.
1936	Nasser is involved in an anti-British demonstration in Cairo; the Anglo-Egyptian Treaty is signed with Britain.
1937	Nasser completes his schooling at Nahda School in Cairo; Nasser is admitted to the Military College in Cairo.
1939	World War II breaks out in Europe.
1948	The first Arab–Israeli conflict breaks out.
1949	The Free Officers' Movement is set up by Nasser and like-minded army officers.
1952	The Free Officers carry out a military coup; King Farouk leaves for exile in Europe; in July a government is set up with General Mohammad Naguib as president.
1953	The monarchy is abolished; Egypt becomes a republic.

1954	An assassination attempt on Nasser fails; President Naguib is removed from office, and then reinstated; Nasser becomes prime minister; a new treaty is signed with Britain regarding the Suez Canal.
1955	Nasser becomes chairman of the Revolutionary Command Council.
1956	Nasser writes the new constitution and is elected president in the June elections with 98% of the votes; in July, he nationalizes the Suez Canal, resulting in an international crisis.
1958	The United Arab Republic (UAR) is established with Syria.
1961	The UAR comes to an end with the separation of Egypt and Syria.
1962	Nasser introduces the National Charter.
1967	The Six-Day War ends with the defeat of Egypt and the loss of Sinai and Gaza to Israel.
1969	The War of Attrition leads to continual low-level conflict in Sinai.
1970	Nasser dies of a heart attack on 28 September.

5.1 The emergence of an authoritarian state

A brief overview of Egypt up to 1945

Nasser was the first Egyptian leader of Egypt since the time of the pharaohs. As Anthony Nutting, one of Nasser's best known biographers, states, 'After two and a half thousand years of taking orders successively from Persian, Greek, Roman, Byzantine, Arab, Kurdish, Turkish, French and British pro-consuls, the people of Egypt were at long last to regain their national statehood' (*Nasser*, 1972).

Although this chapter will examine the rise to power of Nasser and analyse the methods by which he consolidated his control over Egypt, it will begin with an overview of the political events that shaped the development of Nasser's political philosophy.

Egypt before and after World War I

Nominally a part of the Ottoman Empire, Egypt was a British protectorate. The British governor-general was hugely influential in Egyptian politics alongside a ruling class whose origins were Turkish rather than Egyptian. In 1914, the outbreak of World War I led to a crisis in which Turkey allied itself with Germany and declared war on Britain. To secure its position, Britain declared Egypt a British protectorate, although in practice the same dynasty of Turkish rulers continued to occupy the throne. By the end of the war, as in so many other colonies, Egyptian nationalism was given a boost by the ideology outlined in President Wilson's Fourteen Points embraced at the Paris Peace Conference of 1919.

Fourteen Points

In January 1918, President Woodrow Wilson of the United States made a speech in which he described Fourteen Points outlining the landscape of post-war Europe.

Egypt as a British protectorate

Egypt became a protectorate of the British government in 1882. This action was prompted by a nationalist uprising that threatened the rule of the Sultan (Khedive) Taufiq Pasha. The British government did not want direct rule over Egypt or to make it into a British colony, but wanted to ensure its stability, as this was crucial for British control over the strategically important Suez Canal. The method of government chosen was that of a 'protectorate', which ensured influence but without removing the ruling family.

Among them was the right of **self-determination**. Although this was not to be applied to the colonial states of the European powers, Egyptian nationalists were nevertheless keen to try to gain independence from Britain.

A group of nationalists, led by Saad Zaghlul, planned to go to Paris to plead the case for Egyptian independence. This, in 1919, was the beginning of the Wafd Party, a name derived from *al-wafd al-misry* meaning 'Egyptian delegation'. At first, Zaghlul was forbidden from leaving Egypt, but this decision was revoked after a series of strikes and demonstrations by his supporters. In Paris, rather predictably, Britain proved unsympathetic to calls for early Egyptian independence.

Egyptian independence

In February 1922, Egypt was given recognition by Britain as a sovereign state with a constitutional monarchy. The nephew of Khedive Abbas was crowned as King Fuad and a new constitution, drawn up in 1923, allowed the king to appoint the prime minister, dismiss his ministers and, if he so wished, to dissolve parliament. Full independence was limited, however, by four provisions:

- Britain retained control of 'imperial communications' (Stephens, *Nasser*, 1971), which effectively meant the Suez Canal.
- Britain had the right to defend Egypt in the event of an invasion, which meant it could continue to have its army stationed there.
- Britain had the right to defend the rights of foreigners and minorities.
- Britain had the right to determine the status of Sudan.

The Wafd Party grew in popularity, but was limited in its influence not only by the British High Commissioner (the highest-ranking British official now that Egypt was officially independent) but also the king, who suspended the constitution and ruled by decree. Robert Stephens comments on how the political landscape in Egypt revolved around the three power blocs of the king, the British and the Wafdists. In addition, the 'Young Egypt' (*Misr el Fatat*) movement – or 'Green Shirts', as they became known – conducted paramilitary parades in support of the king.

A new party, the **Muslim Brotherhood**, was established in 1928. Founded by Hassan el-Banna, the Sheikh (leader) of the al-Azhar University in Cairo, it was both a nationalist and an Islamic party. Its manifesto demanded the restoration of the **Islamic Caliphate**, to be based in Cairo, and for a 'holy war' to be declared against the British.

Activity 1

1. Having read the first part of this chapter, what, do you think, had the Egyptian nationalists achieved by the end of the 1920s and what obstacles did they continue to face?

The Anglo-Egyptian Treaty of 1936

Following the death of King Fuad in 1936, there were increasingly strident calls for the restoration of the 1923 constitution. King Fuad was succeeded by his young nephew, Farouk, who was studying at a boarding school in England at the time. Concerns about growing threats to peace in Europe and the Italian invasion of Abyssinia contributed to British readiness to negotiate a treaty with the Wafd Party, which had won the election in 1936. This 'treaty of alliance', as it came to be known, guaranteed the right to station up to 10,000 British troops in the Canal Zone for at least another 20 years; allowed Egyptian troops to be stationed in the Sudan; and permitted Egypt to become a member of the **League of Nations**.

The Suez Canal

Opened to shipping in 1869, the Suez Canal was built by the French but the commercial Suez Canal Company ended up being owned mostly by the British and French governments, who were the majority shareholders. British control over the canal was secured in 1888 and affirmed by the Anglo-Egyptian treaty of 1936.

Sudan

In 1899, a 'condominium' was established that enabled Britain and Egypt to have joint control over Sudan. The 'unity of the Nile valley' was important to Egypt, as the waters of the River Nile flowed down from Sudan and control over the river was considered vital to the Egyptian economy. While Britain became more sympathetic to the cause of Sudanese self-determination, Egypt remained bitterly opposed to this proposal and so the question of Sudan became a sticking point in Anglo-Egyptian relations.

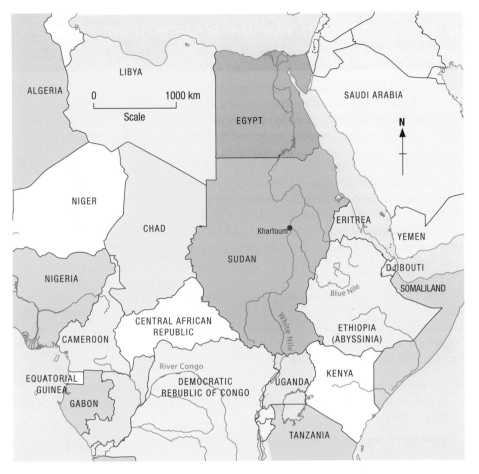

Map of north-east Africa in 2000.

King Farouk, Queen Narriman, and Crown Prince Ahmed Fuad II. King Farouk's divorce from his first wife, the popular Queen Farida, was an event that added to his unpopularity by the time of his abdication.

Most sources refer to this treaty as a false dawn for Egyptian independence, as Britain continued to occupy the country. Certainly, many nationalists were disappointed by the negotiations that had been led by the Wafd Party and, as we shall see, a schoolboy by the name of Gamal Abdel Nasser was among those who demonstrated their opposition. The Wafd Party's negotiations with the British made them less popular, but boosted the public approval of the young King Farouk, who succeeded to the throne shortly before the treaty was signed and was widely believed to be a nationalist. The Muslim Brotherhood, who took a strongly anti-British stance, also gained popular support.

The Italian invasion of Abyssinia

Under the leadership of Mussolini, Italy invaded Abyssinia (now Ethiopia) in 1935. This ancient Christian kingdom was the only independent nation in Africa, although Italy had attempted to occupy it in 1896 from its neighbouring colonies in Eritrea and Somaliland. The League of Nations applied sanctions in response to Italy's invasion, but the Italians fought a cruel and bitter campaign, and defeated Abyssinia in 1936. The British did not oppose Mussolini with any real determination because they were concerned about the emergence of Nazi Germany and feared driving Italy into the arms of Hitler. For more information, see page 199.

Egypt and World War II – a state of limited independence

World War II began in 1939, and the European conflict spread to North Africa in 1940 when Italian forces launched an attack on the British in Egypt. German reinforcements drove the British back to El Alamein but were defeated here after a five-day battle in 1943. Many Egyptian nationalists supported the Germans in the hope that they would finally get rid of the British. A political crisis in 1942, however, led to the British High Commissioner, Sir Miles Lampson, insisting that King Farouk appoint the Wafdist, pro-British Mustafa el-Nahhas Pasha as prime minister. Although there was tacit agreement to the appointment, the government protested that this act challenged the independence of Egypt. British tanks surrounded the palace and the king was told either to agree or to abdicate. This episode, known as the Abdin Palace coup, not only humiliated the king but also gave the impression that the Wafdists were no more than puppets of the British. Was Egypt a sovereign state or was it a British colony? There were further stirrings of rebellion in the army when General Mohammad Naguib wrote to King Farouk stating, 'I am ashamed to wear my uniform … and request permission to resign.' The king refused Naguib's resignation but army officers, including Nasser, were incensed. Upon hearing the details of the Abdin Palace coup, Nasser wrote to a friend, regretting that the Egyptian army had failed to retaliate when British tanks surrounded the palace:

> '… as for the army, this event has been a deep shock; hitherto the officers talked only enjoyment and pleasure. Now, they talk of sacrifice and of defending dignity at the cost of their lives … but the future is ours.'

From Robert Stephens, *Nasser*, Simon & Schuster, 1971, p. 56

Nasser called it a 'severe lesson'. As we shall see, it was such events that highlighted the apparent failure of the army to take action that were to ferment the officers' rebellion in 1952.

It was not until 1945 that Egypt officially declared war on Germany and Japan, partially in order to gain a seat in the United Nations. So Egypt ended the war 'neither victor nor vanquished nor neutral' (Stephens, *Nasser*, 1971). The declaration of war was unpopular and resulted in the assassination of Prime Minister Aly Maher by a young nationalist lawyer. (Prime Minister Mustafa el-Nahhas Pasha had been dismissed in 1944.) There was considerable frustration among Egyptians at being theoretically independent but, in practice, still subject to a domineering Britain.

Now that you have an overview of Egypt in the first half of the 20th century, you can read about how Nasser fits into this background. If you were to consider the conditions that helped Nasser in his rise to power, remember that you would need to think about background events. You could assess the importance of World War II, for instance, and consider whether or not this is why Britain chose to, or felt it had to, reassert its authority over Egypt. You could examine the impact this had upon idealistic young nationalists like Nasser. The Abdin Palace coup could certainly be mentioned and how this provoked a reaction from politicians and army officers. The next section begins with a narrative of Nasser's early years. You would not necessarily include such details in an essay, but they may help you to get a better understanding of the political experiences that influenced Nasser. A discussion follows on his rise to power set against the backdrop of political events.

CHALLENGE YOURSELF

 Research, thinking, social, and self-management skills

What does the Abdin Palace coup tell you about the nature of the British presence in Egypt at this time?

Can you think of other examples where opposition to interference by external powers influenced the growth of nationalism that fuelled the rise of authoritarian leaders? Work in groups to come up with examples and present your research to the class.

Nasser's early years

Gamal Abdel Nasser was born on 15 January 1918, in Alexandria. His father came from the south of Egypt (or Upper Egypt) and was a low- to middle-level civil servant. His mother came from a better-off family, and she had been born and brought up in Alexandria. Nasser, therefore, had family connections in both **Upper and Lower Egypt**, although he is often described as having the physique and the temperament of his father's people.

A photograph of Captain Gamal Abdel Nasser in the Egyptian army.

In 1924, at the age of six, Nasser went to live with his uncle so that he could attend primary school. Two years later, his mother passed away and, according to his biographers, the loss of a deeply loved parent had a lasting impact upon the young boy. When his father remarried in 1928, Nasser went to stay with his grandparents in Cairo before returning to live with his father in Alexandria a year later. His ambition was to join the army, a career that had become possible for a young man from a humble background only after the treaty of 1936, when the British government agreed to an expanded Egyptian army being placed under the command of its own officers. At first, Nasser's application to enter the Military Academy was unsuccessful. This rejection was possibly because he lacked the social connections still required of the less well-off, or perhaps because he had a police record from when he was arrested in 1936 for participating in an anti-British demonstration. Before he made another application to the academy, Nasser approached the Secretary of State, Ibrahim Kheiry Pasha, who gave him his support. This tale, along with other anecdotes, is mentioned by many of Nasser's biographers, who also relate how he devoured books on military strategy and the lives of great warriors from Alexander the Great to Napoleon. Interestingly, in his biography of Nasser, Robert Stephens emphasizes that Nasser was 'not so much a soldier who went into politics as a politician who went into the army', arguing that he would have been political in his interests and ambitions, regardless of his profession (*Nasser*, 1971).

The Free Officers' Movement

Nasser rose quickly within the army and had been promoted to captain by 1942, when he became involved in what would become the Free Officers' Movement. This organization, if it can be referred to as such in 1942, arose out of frustration with the failure of the king and the government of Egypt to stand up to the British. Although its members, who were army officers, wanted King Farouk to be more assertive towards the British, they were also careful to remain loyal. This, they hoped, would widen their support base in the army and among a population that was mostly pro-monarchist.

The Muslim Brotherhood was also vocal in its opposition to the British, although its members supported the king. Said Aburish describes the group as 'right wing' and says that its members '... did not object to the ways of the king and the landlords, provided

Note on sources

There are rather limited sources available on the life of Nasser, and many depend upon each other, so the same stories are often repeated by several biographers. Given that the anecdotes tend to be rather flattering, it is best to be rather cautious in their use and to be aware of the limitations as well as the value of these sources.

TOK

It is said that Nasser, like two other authoritarian leaders, Stalin and Hitler, was deeply attached to his mother. Do you think that studying the psychology of authoritarian leaders helps us to understand them better? How important is it to historians that these three leaders were said to have adored their mothers but had cool, even unfriendly relations with their fathers? How far, do you think, is this kind of information useful to a historical assessment of the careers of these leaders?

Feudalism in Egypt

In European history, the system of feudalism refers to a system of government whereby the king would parcel out land to his knights, who swore loyalty to him. They would be given ownership of both the land and the peasants who farmed it. Feudalism is also used to describe the system in Egypt where, during the 1930s, 6 per cent of the population owned 65 per cent of the land. These landowners did not 'own' the farmers who rented the land (tenant farmers), but the farmers had to pay part of what they produced to the landowner and, in practice, had very few rights.

they toed an Islamic line' (*Nasser: The Last Arab*, 2004). Another political faction with communist leanings that came to the fore at this time was the **Democratic Movement for National Liberation (DMNL)**.

The ideology of the Free Officers was fairly moderate or, as Aburish suggests, both 'diluted' and 'naïve'. The aims of their Six-Point Plan, as it was known, can be summed up as follows:

- The liquidation of colonialism and the Egyptian traitors who supported it
- The end of domination of power by wealth
- The liquidation of feudalism
- The establishment of social equality
- The building up of a powerful army
- The establishment of free elections and a healthy democratic atmosphere.

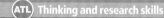

Activity 2

ATL Thinking and research skills

Study the source below and answer the questions that follow. The author of this source was a British politician who knew Nasser and who resigned from his position in the British Foreign Office (over the Suez Crisis).

> But at the outset, Nasser's aims and ambitions were strictly limited to the eviction of the British. Far from being directed against the throne, his initial object was, so he subsequently told me, to try to put some stuffing (courage) into the King and, by creating a militant opposition to British imperialism within the army, to strengthen Farouk's resistance to further encroachments on Egypt's sovereignty. Neither Nasser nor any of his fellow conspirators had any love for the King as a man, still less for the corrupt palace clique…

From Anthony Nutting, *Nasser*, Constable, 1972

1. In the source, Nutting writes 'so he subsequently told me', indicating that his information came directly from Nasser. How does this affect the reliability of this source?
2. So far, this chapter has mentioned three different 'nationalist' groups in Egyptian politics: the Wafd Party, the Muslim Brotherhood, and the Free Officers' Movement. How would you explain their similarities and also their differences?

Post-war Egypt

Social and economic conditions

Egypt had suffered badly in the economic depression during the 1930s and most of its population lived at just above the poverty level. In his book, *Nasser*, Robert Stephens notes that the average per capita income was £42 p.a. or one-tenth of what it was in Britain at this time. Farmers earned an average income of £22 p.a. and landless labourers, whose income was also dependent on seasonal work, earned an average of £7 p.a. (All amounts are given in Egyptian pounds.) Fewer than 6 per cent of landowners owned 65 per cent of all cultivable land and the remaining 94 per cent owned just 35 per cent. More than 77 per cent of the population over five years old was illiterate and life expectancy was just 36 years, compared with 69 years for American males at this time. In an attempt to escape the poverty of the countryside, peasants would go to the cities, where they lived in sprawling slums. Living conditions were poor and lack of housing led to overcrowding, especially as the urban population started to increase. Workers' rights were almost non-existent and trade unions were either controlled by the state or banned. The gap between the lives of the rich and the poor was enormous; Stephens even compares conditions in Egypt with those of pre-revolutionary France.

In addition to the tension that arose from economic hardship, there was always the shadow of an ever-present imperialism. Economically, World War II brought some prosperity to Egypt, but after it was over, the economy faltered, unemployment increased and there was growing discontent with the government. The balance of payments deficit in 1952 was £38 million and there was a budget deficit of £81 million.

Political conditions

Inevitably, demands for complete independence were voiced again once the war was over. Mahmoud Fahmi al-Nuqrashi, the prime minister, called for a renegotiation of the treaty of 1936 and the complete withdrawal of British troops. In addition to this, there was a call for the unification of Sudan with Egypt, a subject very dear to the hearts of the nationalists and the king, who included 'King of Sudan' among his titles. According to Robert Stephens, the British did not respond enthusiastically to these proposals and believed that the invasion of Egypt by the Axis Powers in 1940 had more than justified the cautious terms of the 1936 treaty. Popular demonstrations broke out and in 1946, at the Abbas Bridge in Cairo, 170 casualties resulted from a clash with police. Amid this tense atmosphere, Anglo-Egyptian talks began under the leadership of Ismail Sidky Pasha, the new prime minister.

Post-war Palestine and the 1948 Arab–Israeli War

The British **mandate** over Palestine was returned to the United Nations (UN) in 1947, but events were unfolding that would have an impact throughout the Middle East and would culminate in the first Arab–Israeli conflict. Discussions at the UN in November 1947 led to the partition of Palestine into an Arab and a Jewish state, but with direct UN control over Jerusalem. The establishment of the State of Israel in May 1948 led, almost immediately, to conflict with the **Arab League**. Said Aburish claims that King Farouk seized this opportunity to pose as king of all the Arabs, partially to divert attention away from economic problems in Egypt.

For Nasser, this first taste of war was a formative experience. The king, it seemed, cared little for the lives of his soldiers, who were ill-equipped and badly led by high-ranking officers often promoted not for their military skill but because of family connections. In 1949, Egypt retreated from a humiliating war that, contrary to the aims of the Arab League, had established the statehood of Israel but not of Palestine. In the opinion of the anti-imperialist Nasser, the outcome of the war had been decided not on the field of battle but in the corridors of Washington, Paris, and London where, he suspected, decisions had been made to support Israel (Stephens, *Nasser*, 1971).

Nasser's biographers agree that the 1948 war was an important step in the radicalization of the Free Officers' Movement with its aim to '... uphold the honour of the army and to liberate Egypt'. Political tension worsened in December 1948, when a member of the Muslim Brotherhood assassinated Prime Minister al-Nuqrashi, who had returned to power. His successor, Ibrahim Abdel Hadi, called for the suppression of the Brotherhood. When elections were held in 1950, it was the Wafd Party that won and, once again, Mustafa el-Nahhas Pasha became prime minister. Calm was not restored however and, although, on the surface, the Free Officers shared many of the aims of both the Wafdists and the Muslim Brotherhood, the army's frustration remained.

The **Tripartite Agreement of 1950** – signed by the United States, Britain, and France – intended to restore stability by enforcing boundary lines and imposing

TOK

There are many comparisons made here between the living conditions of the poor in Egypt and lives of people elsewhere. How useful, do you think, are these comparisons? Do they help us to 'empathize' with a) people who lived in the past, and b) people who currently live in very different circumstances from our own?

Research skills ATL

See what you can find out about the 'bigger picture' during the period of the Arab–Israeli War of 1948. In theory, Britain still had a large empire, but what was it like in practice? For example, find out when Britain withdrew from India and gave up the mandate over Palestine.

Also, see if you can link Britain's 'retreat from empire' to the decision by President Truman of the United States to announce the Truman Doctrine in 1947.

restrictions on the sale of arms to countries in the Middle East. This was to become very controversial and led to speculation about the way in which some countries were able to purchase arms while others were not. For Egypt, there was a feeling that it was not able to access arms, which created tension.

The coup of 1952

A failure to reach an agreement with the British government over the continued presence of British troops in Egypt led to the abrogation of the 1936 treaty by Prime Minister Mustafa el-Nahhas Pasha in October 1951. The British government responded with a proposal to replace the treaty with a Middle East Defence Organization, of which Egypt would be a founding member. This was intended to be the equivalent of the **North Atlantic Treaty Organization (NATO)**, but specifically for the Middle East. It was rejected by the Egyptian government, who saw it as a proposal for the occupation of the Canal Zone not by one power (Britain) but by four (United States, Britain, France, and Turkey).

A policy of non-cooperation with the British followed, with a boycott imposed on the use of Egyptian labour in the Canal Zone and a refusal to allow the movement of supplies. Conflict with the British troops in the Canal Zone erupted in Ismailia when General Erskine, the British army commander in the region, ordered tanks to fire on the headquarters of auxiliary police suspected of supporting guerrilla fighters known as 'liberation commandos'. As well as three British soldiers, 41 auxiliary policemen were killed and 71 wounded. This excessive use of force caused public outrage, and demonstrations in Cairo led to widespread unrest. 25 January 1952 became known as 'Black Saturday', as more than 700 buildings were attacked or looted, and an estimated 17 Europeans and 50 Egyptians were killed. Afraid of 'turning the clock back seventy years' (Stephens, *Nasser*, 1971), the British ambassador held off calling in British troops. The King, unsure of the loyalty of his officers, also hesitated before finally calling in the army to restore order. 'The King, the Wafd and the British who between them had ruled Egypt for the previous thirty years had now between them made Egypt ungovernable' (Stephens, *Nasser*, 1971).

Robert Stephens maintains that the Egyptian army was about to become the most powerful element in Egyptian politics, as the Free Officers met to plan a coup to overthrow the monarchy. The Free Officers had been encouraged by elections on 6 January 1952 for the president and Committee of the Army Officers' Club in Cairo. Largely ceremonial, these elections were significant because, although the King had put forward his own candidate for the presidency, it was General Mohammad Naguib, the candidate of the Free Officers, who won a resounding victory. This demonstrated a measure of defiance among army officers and, according to Anthony Nutting, showed that there was more support in the army for the Free Officers than for the king.

After the debacle of Black Saturday, Prime Minister Mustafa el-Nahhas Pasha was dismissed, but his three successors lacked the confidence of either the government or the king. The last of these, Hussein Sirri Pasha, appointed General Naguib as the minister of war, but the king insisted on the appointment of General Hussein Sirri Amer and dismissed Hussein Sirri Pasha. The number of royal appointments and dismissals was a clear indication of a rapidly weakening monarchy and, in one last effort to retain power, measures were put in place to get rid of the Free Officers, whom the king dismissed as 'that bunch of pimps'. All of these events brought matters to a head and the Free Officers conducted a coup on the evening of 22 July 1952.

When asked to abdicate in favour of his baby son, King Farouk agreed and prepared to leave for exile in Europe. At the port of Alexandria, the king embarked on the royal

In an essay, it is always useful to place events in a wider context. This demonstrates that you understand how events, especially in the post-war world, have an impact upon each other. For example, if you are discussing the policies of an authoritarian leader, it helps to consider what is happening in other countries. Political leaders always consider how their actions will impact, or be impacted by, external events so if we want to analyse their actions, it is important to consider these influences.

yacht along with his young wife, baby son, three daughters, and large quantities of luggage. It had been agreed that he could make this journey on the royal yacht but, as this vessel was the property of the Egyptian people, it would have to sail back as soon as its royal passengers disembarked at Naples. King Farouk also took with him gold from the Bank of Egypt, although this was not discovered until after he had left. To replace the king, a Regency Council was appointed to govern until the Crown Prince was old enough to succeed to the throne. This Council was composed of Brigadier Rashad Muhana, sympathetic to the Muslim Brotherhood; Bahieddine Barakat Pasha, a judge and member of an aristocratic family; and Prince Mohammad Abdel Munim. In reality, however, the Revolutionary Command Council (RCC), composed of members of the Free Officers' Movement, was now in charge.

Why was the coup successful?

Black Saturday had shown that there was considerable discontent amongst the Egyptian people, and that the king and his government were not confident about using the army to suppress popular demonstrations. The coup was considered a success for a number of reasons. Firstly, the Muslim Brotherhood and the Wafdists agreed not to oppose the coup, nor did the British and the United States, who agreed to the removal of King Farouk. The king, widely seen as a corrupt and decadent monarch, did not have the support needed to oppose the coup. The population in general welcomed a government that they hoped would finally end the British occupation of the Canal Zone, improve social and economic conditions, and restore national pride. Furthermore, the Free Officers had the support of General Mohammad Naguib, who was well known and had widespread support among the population. To a large extent, Naguib was to be a figurehead as his name was recognizable to the Egyptian people and his reputation was that of a moderate.

It must be noted, however, that the Free Officers' Movement did not take power by legal methods. Nasser and the Free Officers were part of a political/military faction that used the threat of force to persuade a monarch to abdicate. Nasser was adamant that the role of the RCC was that of a 'commando vanguard' to rule as a '… guardian for a definite period of time.'

Activity 3

ATL Research and thinking skills

1. Using two (or more) examples of authoritarian leaders, make a list of the similarities and differences in the conditions that helped them rise to power. To do this, ask yourself the following questions:

   - Did most people work on the land or in industry?
   - What was the level of literacy?
   - How was the economy performing?
   - What kind of political system was in place?
   - How democratic was the political system?
   - What was the level of opposition to the government?
   - Was the army loyal to the government?

Exam questions on Paper 2 Topic 10 may ask for comparisons and contrasts. If, for instance, you consider the rise to power of an authoritarian leader, are there comparisons to be made with similar events elsewhere? In Egypt in 1952, it could be said that the following factors were important:

- Defeat in a war
- Rejection of colonialism
- An unpopular monarch
- Complaints about corruption
- The need for radical land reform
- The lack of organization of the government
- Failure to introduce social and economic reform.

Do some or all of these conditions also apply in the cases of other authoritarian leaders you have studied?

To what extent was the use of force the main reason for the rise to power of Nasser?

(In the exam, you would not be asked specifically about Nasser but, in this case, we will use him as an example.)

The following are extracts from the main body of two sample answers:

Student answer A – Jenny

(Jenny has written her introduction and now she is beginning to state her arguments, so this is her second paragraph.)

The use of force was not very important for Nasser to be able to rise to power because the Free Officers' Movement took power by threatening to use force against the King and the government. In fact, the main reason for their (and Nasser's) rise to power was the poverty of the people. Most of the land was owned by a few people and the peasants were barely able to make a living. There wasn't much industry and most people were illiterate. It was because of this that the FOM were able to get so much support and although they did use force by threatening the King, they could not have come to power without there being so much economic discontent.

Examiner's comments

Jenny moved on rather briskly to discuss factors other than the use of force. If you are asked in a 'to what extent' question to discuss the importance of a particular factor, you have to address it. You cannot dismiss it by saying, '… this was not important' as this may give the impression that perhaps you don't know very much about the topic and are trying to change the question topic to what you want to write about.

Student answer B – Iris

(This is also the second paragraph of Iris's essay.)

Among the conditions that Nasser and the Free Officers were able to use to come to power in 1952 was the use of force. Although Nasser did not yet become the leader of Egypt, he has been referred to as 'the power behind the throne' and the one who really held power even though General Naguib was the nominal head of the Revolutionary Committee and President. In 1952 the focus of their seizure of power was the army. It had been disappointed by how the King had not helped them in 1948 when the Egyptian army had not done so well against Israel and when they felt that the leadership of the army was also inadequate for winning the war. Nasser, especially, was disappointed by the lack of concern about the safety of the soldiers or their lack of supplies. The presence of Britain as a very powerful influence in Egypt was also a reason for the coup of 1952 as it followed on from the events of Black Saturday. It seemed that the King and the government were unable to govern Egypt. It could be argued that, for the most part, force was used to threaten the King and so was not used to threaten the population, although a proclamation was read out that warned people not to be violent or they would be arrested. The way in which sources of opposition such as the Communists and the Muslim Brotherhood were treated does, however, show that the new rulers were quite prepared to use violence. In this way, force was very important in 1952 but it was, perhaps, even more important in events that led up to Nasser becoming President in 1956.

Examiner's comments

Iris has written a better paragraph that starts well by addressing the use of force. She has also explained why she begins in 1952 by describing Nasser's importance in these events. In this way, she makes sure that the examiner sees that she has understood the demands of the question and why she has chosen to address it in this way. She does not mention other factors yet but, instead, is focused on the factor that is mentioned specifically in the question.

If you use Nasser as an example in a question that asks about how an authoritarian leader was able to rise to power, you would need to bear in mind that although Nasser was a leading member of the Free Officers' Movement and played a crucial role in their collective rise to power in 1952, it wasn't until later that he succeeded Naguib. It would certainly be relevant to begin with the coup of 1952, even though it was not Nasser, strictly speaking, who came to power at this time. You could argue that Nasser's role was very important, however, and that some biographers consider him to have been the 'power behind the throne'.

In answering a question on Nasser's rise to power, you could list possible relevant factors like this:

Up to 1952:

• The unpopularity of King Farouk

• Black Saturday

• The 1948 Arab–Israeli War

• The elections at the Officers' Club

• The Six Points

• The failure of the Wafdists to renegotiate the 1936 treaty

• The reluctance of the British government to withdraw its troops from Egypt

• Economic problems in post-war Egypt.

After 1952:

• The charismatic personality of Nasser who had a stronger popular following than Naguib

• The ideology of the Free Officers' Movement

• The attempted assassination of Nasser in 1954.

As with most revolutions, there will always be people who feel that the level of change has been insufficient or incomplete. In August 1952, groups of Communists who had hoped for changes similar to those of October 1917 in Russia led riots in the port city of Alexandria. In some cases, soviets were set up in factories and, after these were suppressed, the leaders were arrested and two were condemned to death. The application of the death penalty was a serious matter and Nasser, along with a few of his colleagues, protested that this punishment was too harsh, but they were in a minority on the RCC. After two leaders were hanged, the Communist Party withdrew its support from the RCC.

Despite having earlier described the Free Officers' Movement as 'the blessed movement', the Muslim Brotherhood had also withdrawn their support from the RCC by October 1952. Their hope for an Islamic constitution had not been fulfilled and their request for four ministerial positions in the government had been rejected.

The military coup that took place in 1952 was not a legal method of taking power. The threat of violence was used to intimidate the king into leaving and to impose the authority of the Free Officers on the government.

Activity 5 **Thinking and research skills**

Eric Hobsbawm, the British historian, wrote about the nature of military involvement in revolutions in his book *Revolutionaries*. He noted that in Egypt in 1952, the military takeover was, quite exceptionally, a 'genuinely innovating military regime'. In his opinion, such regimes appeared where:

> ... the necessity of social revolution is evident, where several of the objective conditions of it are present, but also where the social bases or institutions of civilian life are too feeble to carry it out. The armed forces, being in some cases the only available force with the capacity to take and carry out decisions, may have to take the place of the absent civilian forces, even to the point of turning their officers into administrators.

From Eric Hobsbawm, *Revolutionaries*, Abacus, 2007

Once you have read the source above, answer the questions that follow.

1. Can you think of other occasions when military coups led to the rise of an authoritarian state?
2. How far would you agree with Hobsbawm that military coups usually take place where civilian institutions are 'too feeble' to carry out necessary social change?
3. Hobsbawm was a Marxist historian: in what way(s) does knowing this influence how you would evaluate the source above?

Domestic policies up to 1955

Economic change – land reform

One of the main aims of the Free Officers was to carry out measures for land reform. They considered this to be essential in order to improve Egypt's impoverished agrarian economy. Out of a population of around 22 million, 16 million Egyptians were dependent upon farming and land shortage was a significant problem, especially as the population was growing rapidly. There were calls to end what the Free Officers' Six Points had termed 'feudalism', but was Egypt really a 'feudal' country?

Activity 6 **Thinking skills**

In the source below, Anne Alexander argues that Egypt was not a feudal country.

> At an economic level, Egyptian agriculture was anything but feudal. It was highly capitalized, mechanized and well-integrated into the world economy. At a social and political level, the officers' campaign against 'feudalism' struck a chord with millions of Egyptians. As a contemporary observer noted: 'when an Egyptian economist was asked what he meant by a feudal estate, he replied, "It means that the landowner keeps a private army to defend his house and his person; and that armed men stand guard over the crops."'

From Anne Alexander, *Nasser (Life and Times)*, Haus Publishing, 2005

Read the source above and answer the questions that follow.

1. What does this source tell you about the way 'feudalism' was perceived in Egypt?
2. Why, do you think, did the Free Officers use the term 'feudalism'?

The Free Officers were not the first group to attempt land reform in Egypt, as attempts had been made to pass bills through parliament in the 1940s. These were intended to limit the size of farms, but the king, as the owner of large estates, had not wanted land reform and neither had the Wafdists, who represented the middle class. The extent of the reforms was rather modest, however, although both prominent Marxists and the US government had been consulted on how the reforms should be carried out. Ultimately, only 10 per cent of cultivable land was set aside for redistribution and large landowners could keep up to 300 *feddans* (acres) as well as being compensated for any land that was expropriated. Anne Alexander notes that only between 15 and 20 families had land taken away from them and royal estates alone accounted for one-third of all expropriations. Nevertheless, this was a highly symbolic reform and was a very important method to show that the Free Officers meant to push through social and economic change.

Political change – the road to a republic and an authoritarian state

The Liberation Rally

The Wafd Party, the Muslim Brotherhood, and the Communist Party were still popular political parties in Egypt and, initially, the RCC had intended to include what they called 'purged' parties to be part of the government. By January 1953, however, all political parties with the exception of the Muslim Brotherhood (whose religious affiliation made it too sensitive to be treated too harshly) were abolished, along with independent trade unions and student political groups. In their place, the Liberation Rally was set up to become a mass movement of the people. Nasser became its secretary-general and he promised that the Rally would deliver 'unity, discipline and work' (Alexander, *Nasser*, 2005). This was to give Nasser a strong position from which to launch his own bid for power.

Ideology – *The Philosophy of Revolution*

By 1953, Nasser was the leading member of the Free Officers' Movement, if not yet its public figurehead. He had to grapple with the challenge of how to achieve social and economic change in Egypt. He saw the risks of a military government evolving into a dictatorship, and expressed his determination that the military officers should only lead the way and not become a long-term government. Robert Stephens notes, however, that Nasser 'had been dismayed to find that the masses did not follow the army's desperate charge but hung back as onlookers' (*Nasser*, 1971). In his manifesto *The Philosophy of Revolution*, which was written in 1953 and published in 1954, Nasser spoke of his concern that creating a truly democratic system was proving difficult in a land where a class system was so entrenched. Over the next 17 years, he would struggle to turn Egypt into a state where his vision of political freedom and economic progress could be realized. Nasser also wrote about his belief that Egypt was central to the Arab, African, and Islamic worlds. These three, he argued, were linked together and Egypt played a role that went beyond its national borders. According to Said Aburish, this was a hint of the role Nasser would aspire to a few years later as that of a pan-Arab leader suggesting that, in this case, ideology preceded action.

The abolition of the monarchy and the entry of Nasser into the government

In the summer of 1953, the monarchy was abolished and Egypt officially became a republic. General Naguib became president and prime minister, and Nasser entered the government as deputy prime minister along with his close friend, Abdel Hakim Amer, who was appointed commander-in-chief of the armed forces. Despite Nasser's assurances that the Free Officers were a temporary solution and that parliamentary democracy would soon return to Egypt, this now seemed increasingly unlikely.

Who authored *The Philosophy of Revolution*?

Said Aburish claims that it was Nasser's close friend, the journalist Mohammad Heikal, who actually wrote *The Philosophy of Revolution* and that he was 'an ardent Arab nationalist' (*Nasser*, 2004), which is why this booklet signalled a shift away from Egyptian to pan-Arab nationalism.

Activity 7   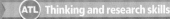 **ATL** **Thinking and research skills**

In 1954, in an interview with Jean Lacouture, Nasser explained:

> *In a year and a half we have been able to wipe out corruption. If the right to vote were now restored, the same landowners would be elected – the feudal interests. We don't want the capitalists and the wealthy back in power. If we open the government to them now, the revolution might just as well be forgotten.*
>
> **Nasser quoted in Anne Alexander, *Nasser (Life and Times)*, Haus Publishing, 2005**

1. In this source, Nasser seems to be saying that the Free Officers have to stay in control because to give up power now would endanger the revolution. Can you think of other authoritarian leaders who may have used a similar excuse to justify their refusal to relinquish power?

Methods used by Nasser to become the leader of Egypt

Step one: Naguib is undermined

By 1954, Nasser was growing in confidence and was less prepared to wait patiently for reforms that seemed too radical for President Naguib. There were growing divisions that Anne Alexander in *Nasser* summarizes as follows:

- Naguib wanted a return to parliamentary democracy but Nasser did not.
- Naguib wanted better relations with the Muslim Brotherhood but Nasser did not.
- Naguib wanted an end to military rule in Egypt but Nasser wanted to continue to use the army to achieve his goals.
- Naguib called the events of July 1952 a 'coup' but Nasser called them a 'revolution'.

In February 1954, Naguib offered his resignation, having lost the struggle for support within the RCC. His resignation was accepted because, it was claimed, he had wanted to establish a dictatorship.

Activity 8   **ATL** **Thinking skills**

Read the source below and answer the question that follows.

> *We had to break with Naguib who aimed at dictatorship, criticised in public and to foreigners decisions that had been made by a majority, and with no thought but his own popularity, played a double game by coming to an understanding with the opposition.*
>
> **By Salah Salem, a member of the RCC, quoted in Anne Alexander, *Nasser (Life and Times)*, Haus Publishing, 2005**

1. How reliable is this source? What evidence can you find to refute the allegations made here?

It was not so easy to remove a popular president, however, and crucially there was a pro-Naguib faction within the army. Aware of the dangers posed by this group, the reinstatement of Naguib was agreed to by Nasser, but with himself as prime minister.

Step two: popular unrest is used to call for change

Nasser had suffered a temporary setback by reinstating Naguib, but he did not give up. On 25 March, Nasser gave a speech in which he pledged the following:

- To restore parliamentary government by July 1954
- To lift the ban on political parties

- To end censorship
- To facilitate the gradual release of political prisoners
- 'The Council of the Revolution will surrender its powers to a constituent assembly on 24 July 1954, at which time it will declare the end of the Egyptian revolution.'

As anticipated by Nasser, however, the promise to restore democracy was not popular among all sections of the Egyptian population, including those who supported the Liberation Rally and feared that a democracy would lead to the return of pre-revolutionary social and political elites. Nasser now used his position as secretary-general of the Liberation Rally to organize strikes and demonstrations that called for the continuation of the revolution. He was supported not only by workers in the cities, but also by peasants who feared the end of land reform, and by members of the middle class who wanted the continuation of strong government.

Step three: Nasser's response to attempted assassination

A crucial event was the attempted assassination of Nasser in October 1954 by Mahmud Abdul Latif of the Muslim Brotherhood. A swift crackdown followed, with – according to Said Aburish – as many as 700 members of the Brotherhood rounded up, although Robert Stephens quotes the official figure as having been 1,800. After being tried in a hastily established 'People's Court', eight of the conspirators were sentenced to death. Of these, six were executed and two had their sentences commuted to life imprisonment. Prison camps were built to contain those who were suspected of plotting against the government, and the Muslim Brotherhood was dissolved. Naguib now stood accused of conspiring with the Muslim Brotherhood and the Communists and was finally removed from office.

Step four: the presidency

The removal of Naguib in 1954 made Nasser the de facto leader of Egypt. In 1955, he was appointed the chairman of the Revolutionary Command Council and began to write a new constitution. The position of president, meanwhile, remained vacant until elections were held in 1956. Nasser was the only candidate and was elected with 99.9 per cent of the vote. He was to be re-elected in 1958 and again in 1965.

Activity 9　　　　　　　　　　**ATL** **Research and thinking skills**

The attempted assassination of Nasser may be seen as one of those events that can prove useful when leaders want a crackdown on dissent and to increase state security. Such an incident that can often lead to panic, and fears for the security of the state may be followed by a 'necessary' suppression of all perceived 'threats'. For example, political parties may be disbanded, freedoms curtailed, and opponents imprisoned or even executed.

If you have studied the rise and/or consolidation of power of Mussolini or Stalin, can you think of similar moments when an event was used as a turning point towards the establishment of a stronger, more authoritarian government?

Below is a list of factors that may contribute to the rise to power of an authoritarian leader, with a specific example of how they can be applied to Nasser. You could use the same template for other leaders you have studied to help you examine how they got into power.

- The creation of a revolutionary organization: the Free Officers' Movement
- The deposition of head of state: the abdication of King Farouk
- The appointment of a public figurehead: General Mohammad Naguib
- The introduction of popular reform: land reform
- The propagation of a revolutionary ideology: *The Philosophy of Revolution*
- The exploitation of a seminal moment: the attempted assassination of Nasser

---

Dividing the period from 1952 to 1955 into different stages will give you a structure to help you remember how Nasser came to power. Using these six points as headings, see if you can add a paragraph briefly under each one to explain what happened. You would not include a narrative of events in an exam essay, but it helps to place events in a chronological order so that you can consider causation, in other words, how and why each event follows on from the last.

An overview of Nasser's rise to power

Points to remember:

- The establishment of the Free Officers' Movement: its programme and its choice of leader
- The political, social, and economic conditions that led to the coup of 1952
- The setting up of the Revolutionary Command Council and preliminary reforms
- The establishment of the Republic, after which Nasser joins the government
- The attempted assassination of Nasser and the removal of President Naguib
- Nasser's election as president.

5.2 Consolidation and maintenance of power

The impact of foreign policy on the maintenance of power

As with most authoritarian leaders, it is quite difficult to separate foreign policy from domestic policy. With Nasser, especially, his role as a regional Arab leader was very important and his policies at home were also popular in neighbouring countries. In turn, popularity abroad reflected well on Egypt and increased his popularity at home. When you read about the Suez Crisis, for example, you will see how this made him a hero not only in Egypt but throughout the Middle East and Africa. However, such popularity also led to increased expectations from supporters who looked to Nasser for leadership. The United Arab Republic (UAR) can be interpreted as a consequence of Suez, and it is debatable whether or not Nasser wanted a union with Syria. Similarly, as the leader of Egypt, he was expected to play a leading role in Middle Eastern affairs and this was not always successful. As you read through this section on Nasser's foreign policy, think about what his aims appeared to be and how far he achieved them. It may also be interesting to consider whether his policies were a result of his own will or of obligations to help neighbouring countries. You might even ask: Was he too charismatic for his own good?

> **!** Don't forget that Nasser saw himself as a pan-Arab as well as an Egyptian leader, and his policy decisions were influenced by relations with neighbouring countries and with the superpowers of the Cold War.

Nasser and the Non-Aligned Movement

In 1955, Nasser attended the African–Asian Bandung Conference in Indonesia where, according to Said Aburish, 29 countries represented half of mankind. Among the world leaders present were Prime Minister Nehru of India, President Sukarno of Indonesia, President Nkrumah of Ghana, Premier Zhou Enlai of China, and Marshal Tito of Yugoslavia. For Nasser, the concept of **non-alignment** fitted easily with his anti-imperialist policies, and he wholeheartedly embraced the concept of **positive neutralism**. This meeting was also important because Nasser had already asked the United States for arms and been refused (remember the Tripartite Agreement, see page 215). At Bandung, it was suggested that he approach the Soviet Union instead for arms; when he returned to Egypt, Nasser made a fateful decision to do so by contacting the Soviet embassy in Cairo. This set in motion a series of events that led to the nationalization of the Suez Crisis – a huge gamble that, nevertheless, as we shall see, paid off. In 1961, Nasser attended the Non-Aligned Conference in Belgrade and strengthened his friendship with Marshal Tito. Like many members of this movement, Nasser embraced socialism. He was also staunchly anti-imperialist: he wanted to make Egypt truly independent of external control – something that was not easy to achieve in a bi-polar world, where less powerful countries usually fell into the sphere of influence of either the United States or the Soviet Union.

This photo shows Nasser, Prime Minister U Nu of Burma, Prime Minister Nehru of India, and Nasser's adjutant Major Salah Salem dressed in traditional Burmese costume to celebrate the Burmese New Year.

Nasser and the United States

When the Free Officers staged their coup in 1952, as long as they were clearly anti-communist, they were accepted by the United States. Scott Lucas in *Divided We Stand* (1996) suggests that the Central Intelligence Agency (CIA) was keeping a close watch on events in Egypt well before the coup. Nasser gradually formed a friendship with Kermit Roosevelt, one of the CIA's Middle Eastern specialists, who was also the grandson of the former US president, Theodore Roosevelt. Nasser was repeatedly disappointed, however, by the refusal of the United States to sell arms to Egypt. Nasser was frustrated by what he saw as the problem of Israeli cross-border raids in response to attacks by Palestinian *fedayeen*. Despite the Tripartite Agreement, France was selling Mystère jets to Israel but refused to sell them to Egypt as long as Nasser supported the Front de Libération Nationale (FLN) in Algeria.

Although the United States, especially the Secretary of State John Foster Dulles, tried to persuade Nasser to bring Egypt into the **Baghdad Pact** in 1955, Nasser refused to consider it, as he thought the pact was too 'colonial' given that it would be led by Britain on behalf of the United States. Nasser strongly believed that if there were to be a mutual defence pact in the Middle East, it should be organized independently by the Arab states, a view that, again, reflected Nasser's anti-imperialism.

The role played by Egypt in the Algerian War of Independence remains controversial, with historians divided over whether Nasser contributed in a meaningful way to the victory of the FLN or whether he did little other than offer verbal support. There is further discussion of this topic in the section on the Suez Crisis.

TOK

How important, do you think, is the naming of organizations like the Non-Aligned Movement, or the wording of the phrase 'positive neutralism'? Can you think of other examples of names given to political movements or policies that were meant to convey a positive image? How important, do you think, is 'naming' in gathering popular support?

CHALLENGE YOURSELF

Social, self-management, and research skills

Working in small groups, find out which countries joined the Non-Aligned Movement and choose two from different regions. Compare and contrast the similarities and differences in their history after 1945. For example, you could investigate the following: colonial past, changes in GNP/economic condition, levels of literacy, membership of (other) international organizations, type of government, affiliation to either the United States or the Soviet Union during the Cold War.

Nasser and the Soviet Union

After attending the Bandung Conference in 1955, Nasser was encouraged to assert his independence of the West by approaching the Soviet Union for arms. Nikita Khrushchev had more or less assumed the leadership of the Soviet Union by this time. He was General Secretary of the Communist Party but also became prime minister in 1958 (although he had been leader of the Soviet Union in all but name since 1955). Khrushchev agreed to provide Egypt with arms from Czechoslovakia. This was the beginning of a relationship that, although close, was not as close as the Soviet Union would have liked. Nasser was never a communist, and had imprisoned and executed Egyptian Communists. Inevitably, there were tensions in the relationship between the Soviet Union and those of its client states that did not embrace communism. This did not prevent generous aid being given to Egypt, however, and inside the Soviet Union, Egypt was referred to as a 'state of socialist orientation', in order to make it seem as though it shared a similar ideology.

The Suez Crisis, 1956

Egypt took over Gaza after the 1948 war and had Palestinian refugees living under its administration. Border raids staged by *fedayeen* into Israel were commonplace and often met with reprisals. In 1955, 39 Egyptians and Palestinians were killed in an incident that worsened relations between Israel and Egypt. As we have seen, Nasser turned to the Soviet Union for arms in an act described by John Foster Dulles, the American Secretary of State, as 'the most dangerous development since Korea'. This growing concern led to the withdrawal of Western funding for the construction of Nasser's most important project, the building of the Aswan Dam. Nasser now made the most controversial, but also the most popular, decision of his career by announcing on 26 July 1956 that the Suez Canal would be nationalized. More an act of bravado than of economic necessity, as the income from the canal was insufficient to build the dam, it won Nasser huge acclaim at home, in neighbouring Arab states, and elsewhere in Africa. If Egypt was indeed at the heart of the intersecting circles of Islam, Arabia, and Africa, then Nasser now came close to demonstrating this.

When it was announced that the Suez Canal would be nationalized, the reaction in London and Paris was one of outrage. Anthony Eden, the British prime minister, compared Nasser to a fascist dictator, referring to him as 'Mussolini on the Nile'. Having resigned as British foreign secretary in 1938 as a protest against the policy of appeasement and now predicting that history was about to repeat itself, Eden was determined to remove Nasser. French prime minister Guy Mollet was also eager to take this opportunity to remove Nasser who had supported the FLN in Algeria. Meanwhile, Israel was interested in striking against Nasser because he aided the *fedayeen* in Gaza. These three powers now came together to challenge Nasser: in September 1956, Israel, Britain, and France met secretly in Paris to discuss how to remove Nasser and to recover control of the canal. Given that *fedayeen* raids happened regularly across the border into Israel, it would be possible to use one of these as a motive for Israel to cross the border into Egypt, and to move towards the canal. It was assumed that Egypt would respond by also moving its army towards the canal, prompting Britain and France to send their troops to 'protect' it on the pretext that it was an important international waterway. The plan went ahead in October but Britain, especially, underestimated the vehemence of US condemnation of what it viewed as its ally's behaviour reminiscent of pre-war imperialism. The crisis was referred to the UN and the United States supported a resolution condemning the actions of Britain and France.

Although it is usually said that Nasser nationalized the Suez Canal, strictly speaking, he nationalized The Suez Canal Company. As long as he compensated the shareholders, this action was, in fact, perfectly legal.

Aswan Dam

More correctly known as the Aswan High Dam (the Low Dam was an earlier construction), this structure was built on the River Nile near the town of Aswan. The intention was to increase the amount of cultivable land by 30 per cent, to store water, and to make flooding and drought less likely. It was also a hydroelectric project to provide power to thousands of small villages. Some 60,000 people were moved from areas that were submerged in the building of the dam. UNESCO financed the removal and rebuilding of the Temple of Abu Simbel, one of the great historical sites of ancient Egypt. The building of the dam began in 1960 and was completed in 1970.

The Suez Crisis erupted at the same time as the Hungarian Revolution, and the actions of Britain and France were blamed by some for US reluctance to act against the Soviet Union's suppression of this uprising. After all, its own allies were involved in the invasion of Egypt. In turn, the behaviour of Britain and France was noted in Moscow and may have influenced the decision to send Soviet troops into Budapest as, although this would surely be criticized by the western powers, criticism was likely to be less vehement if they no longer felt they held the moral high ground (Archie Brown, *The Rise and Fall of Communism*, HarperCollins, 2009, p. 284).

The UN Security Council passed a resolution on 5 November condemning the invasion of Egypt but of course, Britain and France had a veto, and so discussion of the crisis was transferred to a special meeting of the General Assembly where a decision was made to send a UN peacekeeping force to the Middle East.

Lester Pearson, later to be prime minister of Canada, brokered a peace and UN peacekeeping forces were sent to patrol the border with Israel. According to his memoirs, Khrushchev, the leader of the Soviet Union at this time, told the British, French, and Israeli governments:

 You have attacked Egypt, knowing that it is considerably weaker than you are, that it does not have much of an army, and that it does not have many weapons. There are other countries which are entirely capable of coming to Egypt's defence… I have been told that when Guy Mollet received our note, he ran to the telephone in his pyjamas and called Eden. I don't know if this story is true, but whether or not he had his trousers on doesn't change the fact that twenty-two hours after the delivery of our note the aggression was halted.

From Nikita Sergeevich Khrushchev, *Khrushchev Remembers*, transl by Strobe Talbott, Little Brown, 1970

Activity 10 — **ATL Thinking and research skills**

Source analysis

1. The extract above is taken from '*Khrushchev Remembers*', an autobiography written by Nikita Khrushchev after his retirement as the prime minister of the Soviet Union. It is well known that Khrushchev had not retired so much as been sent into exile to his dacha (house) in the countryside outside Moscow. In what way does knowing the background to this autobiography help you to analyse the value and limitations of this source?

2. What impression was Khrushchev trying to give of the role of the Soviet Union in the outcome of the Suez Crisis?

Nasser was the first Arab statesman to grasp fully the geo-political potential of a united Arab world with a unified or coordinated control over the world's main oil reserves and the means of moving them through the Suez Canal and the pipelines. (Anthony Eden also understood this possibility and that was the main reason for his going to war over Suez. When Eden and Mollet denounced Nasser as another Hitler, Nasser retorted 'What they are frightened of really is the impact of the Afro-Asian revolution on their economic interests'.)

Nasser emerged as the hero who had faced down this last gasp of imperialism, and his reputation reached new heights. Buoyed by this level of support, both at home and abroad, he was ready to take the revolution a stage further.

How the canal was nationalized

The takeover of the offices of the Suez Canal Company was carried out by Colonel Mahmoud Younes, who was told to listen to the broadcast of Nasser's speech on the evening of 26 July and to go ahead with the plan if Nasser mentioned the name Ferdinand de Lesseps (the French architect who had built the canal). Nasser had decided to go ahead with the nationalization and was so anxious that, according to Nasser's friend, Mohammad Heikal, de Lesseps' name was repeated about ten times and people began to wonder why he was making such a fuss about de Lesseps.

The Eisenhower Doctrine

In 1957, president Eisenhower of the United States expressed concern that the end of British and French influence in the Middle East might encourage the Soviet Union to 'fill the vacuum' left behind by the departure of these colonial powers. In a policy named the 'Eisenhower Doctrine' and in a speech delivered to Congress in January 1957, Eisenhower stated that the United States would offer aid to Middle Eastern countries that requested it, and that $200 million p.a. should be set aside for this. He also stated that the United States would give military assistance to countries that requested it to combat armed aggression from 'any nation controlled by International Communism'. This was approved by the Congress (Stephens, *Nasser*, 1971, p. 255).

Map showing the movement of troops during the Suez Crisis of 1956.

The results of the Suez Crisis

The results of the Suez Crisis can be summarized as follows:

- Nasser's popularity in Egypt was well and truly established.
- Nasser's fame spread beyond Egypt to neighbouring states in the Middle East and Africa.
- The United States criticized British intervention but became increasingly suspicious of Nasser.
- In 1957, the Eisenhower Doctrine expressed US interest in the Middle East as a sphere of influence.
- Relations between Egypt and the Soviet Union grew warmer.
- UN peacekeepers moved in to patrol the border between Egypt and Israel.
- Relations with Israel deteriorated.
- Nasser's increased popularity contributed to the establishment of the UAR.

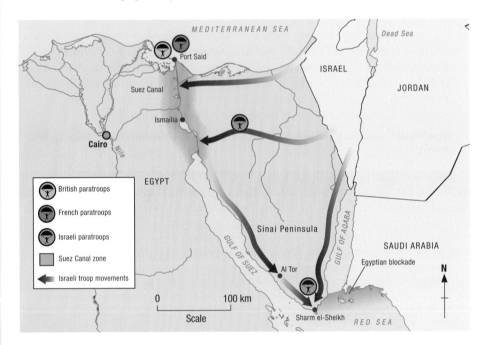

5.3 Aims and results of Nasser's policies

Domestic policies – Nasser after Suez

Political change

In June 1956, Nasser introduced a new constitution for the Egyptian republic. This stated that Islam was the state religion and that Egypt was part of the 'Arab nation'. Meanwhile, the structure of the government was changed: it consisted of a president (who would hold office for a six-year term), a council of ministers, and a National Assembly to be elected by **universal suffrage**. The Liberation Rally was replaced in

1957 by the National Union, which would take the place of all political parties. Nasser was reluctant to grant political freedom because he still feared that voters would be drawn to the Muslim Brotherhood and the Communists. He was also still convinced that a more democratic system would only result in the restoration of a political system that acted in the interests of the bourgeoisie.

The National Assembly became the 'national representative body' (Aburish, *Nasser*, 2004), and when elections were held in July 1957, women voted for the first time. Although it was intended that this body would have a majority of representatives from the lower classes, including workers and poor peasants, in fact it was full of middle-class professionals. There were very few peasants in the assembly, possibly because an equivalent of £50 was charged as a deposit to all candidates standing for election. Robert Stephens argues that, for all its restrictions, the National Assembly was a dynamic and often critical institution where different political opinions were aired.

The assembly was closed down in March 1958 after the declaration of the UAR. During its lifespan, however, significant changes did come about, including the following:

• A ban on the employment of children under the age of 12
• Increased measures taken to improve working conditions
• The provision of healthcare
• The distribution of free food to the needy.

Nasser wanted to take Egypt into a new future and embraced what can be described as 'Islamic modernism'. He began by secularizing the religious courts and advancing women's rights, although both of these measures were criticized by the Muslim Brotherhood. Undeterred, Nasser pressed on with measures to make primary education compulsory, as he considered this to be fundamental to the process of modernization.

Activity 11　　　　　　　　　　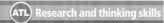 **ATL** **Research and thinking skills**

Study the source below and answer the questions that follow.

❝ *The National Union is one means for us to enforce our internal conditions and the necessities of our foreign policy. It is the cadre through which we will realize our revolution, for the security of the homeland and to safeguard its independence. It is a form of peaceful co-existence between the social classes.*

From an article by Nasser published in *al-Ahram* in 1959

1. What did Nasser mean by 'peaceful co-existence between the social classes'?
2. What does this tell us about his political ideology?

Economic change

The success of the nationalization of the Suez Canal led to further confiscation of foreign-owned businesses. In 1957, Nasser had already spoken of the 'Egyptianization' of all foreign banks, insurance companies, and import–export agencies in order to reduce the dependence of Egypt on foreign investment. To organize this change, a National Planning Committee was set up as well as an institution known as the Economic Organization, which would deal with the nationalized property. A Five-Year Plan was started in 1958 to increase the growth of industrial output from around 6 per cent p.a. to 16 per cent p.a. It was intended that although the bulk of investment would come from the government, private investment would also be encouraged.

Nasser was disappointed at the limited success of this mixed public–private investment plan and we shall see that this pushed him towards further nationalization after 1960. Meanwhile, he recognized that corruption was becoming endemic, as government officials directed grants and contracts towards friends and family, or in exchange for bribes.

In agriculture, Nasser was disappointed that the land reform had achieved so little. Production levels had risen, but it was estimated that only 5 per cent of the peasantry had actually benefited from the redistribution of land.

> ❝ *The laws controlling rent and fixing minimum agricultural wages were being widely evaded, often with the connivance of the tenants and farm workers themselves, owing to the acute shortage of land and jobs. There was criticism in the press of the amount that farmers had to pay the government in interest and annual repayments for the land they acquired under the agrarian reform… There was also evasion of the law limiting the amount of land that could be owned by one person or his family. By exploiting the allowance made for relatives and the use of 'straw men' (a fictitious person who could be the nominal owner of land but who didn't really exist), it was possible for a former big landowner whose personal holding should not have exceeded 200 feddans to control effectively as much as two or three thousand feddans. Thus, he was able to maintain in his district the kind of power and influence over the peasantry that the revolution had branded as 'feudalism' and had tried to eradicate.*

From Robert Stephens, *Nasser*, Simon & Schuster, 1971

Activity 12   (ATL) Research and thinking skills

1. Based on what you have read so far, how successful, would you say, were Nasser's economic reforms?

The nationalization of major companies also took place, although two-thirds of businesses continued to be privately owned. Said Aburish says that Nasser wanted total government control of the economy, but this was not achieved. Agricultural production gradually increased, and there was higher investment in industry with the expansion, in particular, of the Helwan steelworks, but progress was disappointing.

The UAR, 1958–61 – 'three-and-a-half years of troubles'

You can consider the United Arab Republic (UAR) as both domestic and foreign policies as it involved union with neighbouring Syria. It did not last long but affected other countries such as Iraq and Jordan.

If we consider anti-imperialism to be at the core of Nasser's political ideology, then the Suez Crisis was his defining moment. He had acted audaciously to challenge the former great powers of Britain and France, and they had been humiliated at the hands of a former colony. Such moments fed into the development of a cult of personality that made Nasser well known not only throughout Egypt, but also beyond its borders. This led to the establishment of a pan-Arab experiment in 1958, when Nasser was asked if Egypt would unite with Syria to establish the UAR.

On 1 February 1958, Nasser and the Syrian president, Shukri el Kuwatly, signed a union treaty. Syria and Egypt were united and became the UAR. The union lasted until 1961, when a military coup in Damascus precipitated Syria's withdrawal from the UAR. It is unlikely that union with Syria was one of Nasser's aims but the events of 1957 in Syria, when a US-backed coup was rumoured, probably pushed Nasser into saving the Ba'athists and so avoiding the emergence of a pro-US government in line with those of Turkey, Iraq, and Jordan.

There were strong similarities between the Free Officers' Movement and the **Ba'athist Party** in Syria. Both used the slogan 'unity, freedom and socialism', and the Syrian Ba'athists had looked to Egypt for support against the growing influence of Syria's Communist Party. In January 1958, a group of Syrian army officers asked Nasser if he would agree to a union of the two countries. Robert Stephens mentions how Nasser did not want to be rushed into a union and that he thought such a policy would need at least five years to prepare (*Nasser*, 1971, p. 273). Even so, Nasser could see the benefit of increased security for Egypt, plus an improved economy with the provision within the UAR of new markets for Egyptian goods and jobs for Egyptian workers. After the UAR was set up, it was further approved by a **plebiscite** held three weeks later on 22 February 1958. Although the UAR could have been interpreted as a step towards closer unity among the Arab states, Aburish suggests that Nasser may not have fully considered the many significant differences between Syria and Egypt. With a population of only 5 million, Syria was far smaller than Egypt and was also more heavily influenced by the Muslim Brotherhood and the Communist Party, two groups that Nasser had placed under strict control in Egypt.

Nasser's appointment of his commander-in-chief, Abdel Hakim Amer, as governor-general of Syria possibly made it seem that this was less a union than an annexation, as suggested by this British cartoon from 1961.

Cartoon by Michael Cummings, published in the *Daily Express*, 29 September 1961.
▼

Tension in the Middle East was heightened by the assassination of King Faisal of Iraq and his prime minister, Nur al-Said, in July 1958. This was followed by an attempted coup in Lebanon, which led to US intervention, or expansion, into the Middle East, as there was no doubt that the United States viewed Nasser as a profoundly destabilizing force. Nasser's next step was to visit Moscow to consult with Khrushchev who, eager to prevent any further rise in Cold War tension, suggested a summit. Robert Stephens emphasizes that Nasser, too, wanted tempers to cool and did not want the Middle East to be embroiled in a superpower conflict that could result, in the extreme case, in nuclear war. Nasser was, nevertheless, gratified that the coup in Iraq had broken its links with the Baghdad Pact, and that it was now allied with Syria and Egypt. By the

In an exam question where you are asked to discuss the ideology of an authoritarian leader, it is often not straightforward to decide what to make of Nasser. He was not a communist but he was anti-capitalist, and he described his policies as socialism. So, on the one hand, Nasser could be compared to leaders such as Stalin, Mao, and Castro. His ideology, however, as you can see, was not fixed by any allegiance to a predetermined political manifesto. He was very pragmatic and driven, it would seem, by a desire to rid Egypt of all the trappings of imperialism and to improve the lives of the poorest people. His biggest problem lay in knowing how best to achieve these goals.

end of the year, US troops had been withdrawn from Lebanon and the crisis was over. According to Nasser, 1958 had been a 'year of victory' for Arab nationalism, but differences among the Arab states remained a serious obstacle to unity. Nasser clashed with General Abdel Karim Kassim, the leader of Iraq, amid concerns that communism would infiltrate the Middle East through Syria and Iraq. In 1959, Nasser carried out a purge of suspected communists in Syria and Egypt; 280 leaders were arrested. Stephens states that many were sent to the 'notoriously brutal desert concentration camp of Abu Zaabal and to military prisons, where several were reported to have died as a result of torture' (*Nasser*, 1971). It is remarkable to consider that while Nasser imprisoned communists, he continued to promote socialist policies and maintain a close relationship with the Soviet Union. Khrushchev said, 'Abdel Nasser is a young man, passionate and hot-headed', but he still chose to lend him a helping hand and Soviet aid flowed into Egypt to help finance the building of the Aswan Dam.

Eventually, the UAR foundered on Nasser's socialist and political policies. He wanted a tightly controlled state with increased levels of nationalization and socialism, and when the UAR ended in 1961 Nasser reflected that it had been 'three and a half years of troubles'.

Post-UAR – from the National Union to the Arab Socialist Union

The failure of the UAR resulted in a period of radical reform in Egypt. According to Anthony Nutting, Nasser blamed the collapse of the UAR on the Egyptian 'business community' or bourgeoisie. Egyptian businessmen had done very well out of the expulsion of foreign interests in 1956, and had been very much in favour of the UAR as they felt it might open up access to trade with France, which had close ties with Syria since the days when Syria was put under a French mandate. Nasser suspected that, once these business interests realized the UAR meant both the Egyptian and Syrian economies would become more socialist, they worked to undermine it.

When the UAR collapsed, Nasser was determined to show that the implementation of socialism had not come to a halt, and in October 1961 he confiscated the property of 167 'reactionary capitalists'. This step was followed in December by further confiscations, and the seizure of more than 80 banks and corporations that were now put under 'emergency administration'. Said Aburish comments on how difficult it was for Nasser to move the economy along in the direction he wanted, as he was against 'extreme socialist measures such as collective ownership', but was opposed by the influential 'old bourgeois and industrial bloc' who advised foreign investors to stay away (*Nasser: The Last Arab*, 2004). Meanwhile, Anthony Nutting maintains that 'Nasser's evolution to socialism was thus an essentially pragmatic process, based largely on reaction to the collapse of the union with Syria and with little, if any, ideological motivation' (*Nasser*, 1972). He cites Nasser's nationalization of the press in 1960 as an example of this, when he feared that the capitalists had succeeded in dominating the 'political and social media'. Furthermore, Nasser feared that Egypt was on the brink of a counter-revolution, and so he pushed onwards to socialism as the only way to proceed with his revolution.

Ideology – Arab socialism

After the collapse of the UAR, Nasser seized upon Arab socialism as the key to change. In October 1961, he stated in a radio broadcast that 'socialism is our only road to justice … the national income must be shared among citizens, to each according to the efforts he makes to produce it. But there also had to be equal opportunities' (Stephens,

Nasser, 1971). In the new structure, Nasser claimed, room had to be made for peasants and workers, but not for 'reactionary forces'. Individual ownership was acceptable, but not what Nasser described as 'exploitative ownership'.

The National Charter, introduced in May 1962, is considered by Robert Stephens to be 'the key document' in understanding Nasser's political ideology post-UAR. Once again, Nasser saw political reform in Egypt as the catalyst for change elsewhere.

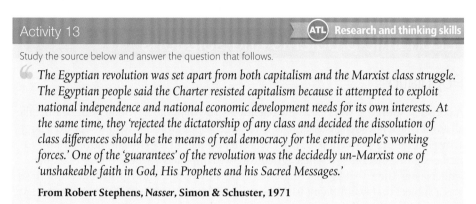

Activity 13 — (ATL) **Research and thinking skills**

Study the source below and answer the question that follows.

> The Egyptian revolution was set apart from both capitalism and the Marxist class struggle. The Egyptian people said the Charter resisted capitalism because it attempted to exploit national independence and national economic development needs for its own interests. At the same time, they 'rejected the dictatorship of any class and decided the dissolution of class differences should be the means of real democracy for the entire people's working forces.' One of the 'guarantees' of the revolution was the decidedly un-Marxist one of 'unshakeable faith in God, His Prophets and his Sacred Messages.'

From Robert Stephens, *Nasser*, Simon & Schuster, 1971

1. Explain briefly how the source above would help you to argue that Nasser was not a communist.

Economic change

In 1958, Nasser announced the First Five-Year Plan which embraced more radical land reform. Once again, there would be a limit on the amount of land owned by an individual farmer and there would also be a system of cooperatives to boost production by providing better access to irrigation projects financed by the state. There would also be access to credit and cheap technology to help the *fellahin*. Again, however, vested interests made it difficult for him to push through the practical application of land redistribution, as only 17 per cent of cultivable land was redistributed and only 8 per cent of the *fellahin* benefited.

Ali A. Mazrui and Michael Tidy maintain, however, that despite the limited success of the land reform programme, the cooperative system did bring considerable benefit to the Egyptian countryside (*Nationalism and New States in Africa*, 1984). For Nasser, capitalism was not the answer for Egypt because, for him, it was inextricably linked to imperialism. He did draw a line, however, at total nationalization of the means of production and the state ownership of land. These, he argued, were not necessary for socialism, Egyptian-style. Nasser argued for the nationalization of infrastructure and financial institutions, along with heavy industry and mining, although there could be private ownership of light industry. Some progress was made, with economic growth averaging between 6.4 and 6.6 per cent p.a. in the years 1960 to 1965. This compared with a lower rate of 4.7 per cent p.a. in 1945–52. Manufacturing output grew by 15.5 per cent in 1960–61 and by 10 per cent in 1963–64.

Political change

Following the collapse of the UAR, the government was restructured in 1963 based on the National Charter, the Arab Socialist Union, and the National Assembly. The National Assembly had 350 elected and 10 appointed members, half of whom had to come from the peasant and worker class. It met for the first time in March 1964 and although martial law was lifted the day before, new emergency measures were introduced the day after, so the internal security system barely changed. Nasser was nominated for re-election as president by the National Assembly and this was later confirmed by a 99.9-per-cent vote in a plebiscite. Nasser reorganized the army, stating that half the officers would continue as professional soldiers and the remainder would transfer into civilian posts either in the government or in private business. Biographers of Nasser comment on this system of government as a military-bureaucracy. Said Aburish calls it a 'military-bureaucratic society' made up of the old clique of the Free Officers who were promoted or demoted according to Nasser's wishes (*Nasser: The Last Arab*, 2004).

Economic problems and solutions

Population

A constant source of worry was the relentless growth in the Egyptian population. Like all authoritarian leaders, Nasser relished a large population that would support a large army, but the 2.5-per-cent p.a. growth rate in population also meant more mouths to feed, a significant concern when agriculture was impeded by the shortage of arable land. Nasser knew that Egypt could not support this population growth rate, but this was a subject that was difficult to address in an Islamic country that did not, in theory, support birth control.

Divisions between the rich and the poor

Plans to bring more of Egyptian industry under the control of the state were overly ambitious and, in practice, production fell short of the intended goals of a 16-per-cent growth p.a. In reality, much of the planned expansion of industry did not take place and expensive imported machinery lay idle. As there was a shortage of basic goods, Egypt came to depend increasingly on imported goods. This led to grumblings about the economy and a sharp criticism of the 'elite' who seemed to live very well indeed. These included the former Free Officers and those who had secured well-paid jobs in the government bureaucracy. A social class had appeared, similar to the ***nomenklatura*** of the Soviet Union, leaving those who led privileged lives immune to the economic problems that accompanied a startling 10-per-cent inflation rate. The high inflation rate was partially due to higher indirect taxes, which were levied instead of a rise in income tax, something that Nasser did not feel able to impose on an already heavily taxed population.

Gamal Abdel Nasser and Nikita Khrushchev at the opening of the first stage of the Aswan Dam in 1964.

The Aswan Dam

In 1964, the first stage of the Aswan Dam – Nasser's most important project – was completed (it would be finished in 1970) and Premier Khrushchev of the Soviet Union attended the opening ceremony. More than £500 million worth of Soviet aid had been granted to Egypt and Khrushchev now pledged another £100 million to help with the industrialization programme of the Second Five-Year Plan. Nasser was also awarded the Order of Lenin and the Hero of the Soviet Union and relations were amicable, made better by his having arranged parole for all who had been imprisoned for communist activities.

Oddly enough, among the many allegations of misbehaviour levelled against Khrushchev in 1964 when he was removed from office, was the fact that he had made Gamal Abdel Nasser a Hero of the Soviet Union! (Archie Brown, *The Rise and Fall of Communism*, 2009)

Grain

Egypt was dependent on the United States for 50 per cent of its wheat imports under a deal negotiated with President Kennedy, but this deal was in danger of not being renewed in 1965. Nasser also obtained grain from the Soviet Union and China, but there was still a shortfall. Egypt needed US wheat, and a new agreement was reached with the Johnson administration. In 1966, however, there were serious grain shortages, and when the United States sent its surplus to India instead of Egypt, Nasser, in a fit of anger, decided that his relationship with the United States would never improve as long as Lyndon Johnson was president.

Foreign policy – Entanglement and defeat

It is difficult to separate Nasser's foreign policy from his domestic policy, given that he saw himself (and was seen by others) at one time or another as the leader of Egypt, the leader of the Arab people, and representative of Pan-Arab and Pan-African anti-colonialism. Nasser felt that, under his leadership, Egypt had a duty to fulfil to its neighbours, although his enemies tended to see such policies as ambitious and expansionist. In what became known as 'Egypt's Vietnam', Nasser became involved in a civil war in Yemen that cost the Egyptian people dearly in money and troops. Its involvement not only made Egypt an enemy of Saudi Arabia, but it also tied up soldiers at the time of the Six-Day War in 1967. According to Jesse Ferris in *Nasser's Gamble* (2012), this may have been one reason for Egypt's defeat in the war.

The Yemeni Civil War

By 1960, Yemen was divided into two regions: a **theocracy** ruled by Imam Ahmad based in Sanaa and the British protectorate of Aden that bordered the Red Sea. Although the Imamate was not opposed to closer unity amongst the Arab states, as had been proposed by Nasser, Egypt's socialist policies were denounced by the deeply conservative Imam as 'ungodly'. When the Imam died in 1962, there was hope among the growing Yemeni middle-class for change. A revolt broke out, and the Imam's son and heir, Mohammad al-Badr, was presumed killed. The Yemen Arab Republic was then officially declared, under the leadership of Abdallah al-Sallal, an army chief of staff. It was recognized by both the Soviet Union and the United States. Mohammad al-Badr was alive, however, and with help from Saudi Arabia he raised enough support to hold on to around one-third of the country.

Nasser, in an attempt to shore up the Yemen Arab Republic, sent a total of 60,000 Egyptian troops to Yemen. It is unclear why Nasser decided to commit Egypt to this conflict but it is possible he was worried that, by remaining neutral, he would have enabled Saudi Arabia to increase its influence in Yemen. Rashid Khalidi describes this period as an Arab Cold War, when Nasser led the 'revolutionary and radical' regimes and Saudi Arabia led the 'monarchical and conservative' regimes. The civil war in Yemen, which lasted until 1967 when Yemen was divided into two states, has been described as 'Egypt's Vietnam' because it turned into a long drawn-out conflict that proved expensive and difficult to win. It also left Egypt weakened in 1967 when the Six-Day War broke out.

Research and thinking skills

Historians have compared Egyptian involvement in Yemen to the United States' involvement in the Vietnam War. How would you support such an assertion? Can you think of other civil wars that have been compared to the Vietnam War?

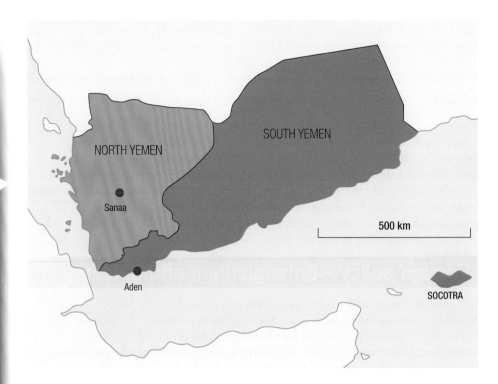

A map showing the division of Yemen in 1967 into two states by the end of the Yemeni Civil War.

How defeat was handled

At the beginning of the Six-Day War, the devastating air attacks by the Israeli Air Force were kept from the public and Eugene Rogan mentions how one Egyptian intelligence officer, hearing news of the war on the radio, recalled, 'The whole world thought that our forces were at the outskirts of Tel Aviv'. When the time came for the people to be told about the defeat of their army, Nasser, along with King Hussein of Jordan, blamed US and British planes 'for taking part against us from aircraft carriers'. Finally, on 9 June, Nasser told the people of *al-Naksa* ('the reversal') and offered his resignation.

The Six-Day War

In June 1967, after a build-up of tension that took place over many months, Israel launched a pre-emptive air strike against its neighbours Egypt, Jordan, and Syria. In just a few days, Israel managed to secure victory. A disaster for Egypt and for Nasser, the Arab–Israeli War of 1967 was the low point of his political career. Said Aburish suggests that Nasser had not planned to attack Israel, but more orthodox interpretations indicate that an escalating war of words and actions aroused Israeli fears. In May 1967, Syrian attacks on Israeli farmers ploughing land that was officially 'demilitarized' resulted in a quick Egyptian response, including the closing of the Straits of Tiran and the dismissal of the UN forces from the Egyptian border. Meanwhile, the United States refused to promise Israel that an attack on Israel's borders would be considered as an attack on the United States itself. Furthermore, the United States warned Israel not to take any kind of pre-emptive action.

General Moshe Dayan joined the Israeli cabinet as minister of war in June 1967. He planned a surprise attack that he considered essential if Israel, a country small enough to be overrun in a day, were to survive a war with its neighbours. So, on 5 June 1967, an air attack was launched on Egyptian, Syrian, and Jordanian air bases, giving Israel vital control of the skies. This caught the coalition of Egypt, Syria, and Jordan unprepared and a rout followed, leading to the Israeli occupation of Gaza, Sinai, the Golan Heights, East Jerusalem, and the West Bank. Following this deeply humiliating defeat, Nasser offered his resignation on 9 June, but withdrew it the following day when his supporters took to the streets shouting, 'No leader but Gamal!'

Nasser remained tied to the Soviet Union – an ally he needed now more than ever – as Egypt's armed forces needed to be rebuilt. President Podgorny of the Soviet Union visited Cairo just two weeks after the end of the war; Anthony Nutting describes how Nasser had to 'beg' for free arms, and also for instructors and technicians to be attached to the Egyptian army (*Nasser*, 1972). A cartoon in the *Evening Standard*, a British newspaper, commented wryly on President Podgorny's visit:

Cartoon by Raymond Jackson (Jak), *Evening Standard*, 23 June 1967. The caption to the cartoon has Podgorny saying, 'As far as Russia is concerned, we will fight – to the last Egyptian!'

The conflict with Israel did not end with the ceasefire, and a War of Attrition followed in 1969–70. This low-level but continuous conflict with Israel required arms, and these could only come from the Soviet Union.

TOK

This is a British cartoon of Nasser published during the Six-Day War in 1967. How is Nasser portrayed here? What kind of emotional response do you have to this? How important, do you think, are political cartoonists in influencing public opinion? See if you can compare this cartoon to cartoons published today about current political leaders.

The political and economic impact of the war

Blame for the disastrous outcome of the war in 1967 was placed on the army, and on 11 June Nasser sacked his Chief of Staff and close friend, Abdel Hakim Amer, along with 50 senior commanders. Amer was accused of 'gross dereliction of duty' but, according to Anthony Nutting, Nasser let him know that he could leave immediately and go into exile (*Nasser*, 1972, p. 429). Amer rejected this offer of clemency and committed suicide before his trial by taking poison; there were rumours that he had been 'allowed' to do so, although these were not substantiated. Nasser had arisen from a power base within the army and his fellow officers had played a central role in the

Abdel Hakim Amer (1919–67)

Nasser and Amer had been young officers together in the Egyptian army during the 1940s. One of the founding members of the Free Officers' Movement, Amer became commander-in-chief of the armed forces in 1953, a position he retained until the defeat of Egypt in the Six-Day War in 1967.

administration and ideology of the Arab Revolution. Now, because of their culpability for the defeat of Egypt, many of Nasser's former colleagues and supporters were put on trial and imprisoned; Nasser was increasingly isolated.

The Egyptian economy was not so badly affected by the war, despite the loss of the Sinai oilfields and the closure of the Suez Canal. By 1969, the discovery of new fields increased oil production to 14 million metric tons. An increase in world prices for cotton and a fall in the price of wheat also helped the trade balance between imports and exports, and by 1969 there was a trade surplus of £43 million, the first surplus since 1930 (Stephens, *Nasser*, 1971). At the same time, the Soviet Union provided support in the form of arms and aid vital for the completion of the Aswan Dam in 1970.

Nasser tried to keep inflation under control through the implementation of something called 'austerity measures', meaning cuts in government expenditure, including subsidized food prices, but this was met with limited success. In July 1969, Nasser pushed forward plans to place under state ownership the 283,000 hectares of cultivable land made available as a result of the construction of the Aswan Dam. New limits were placed on the maximum acreage that could be owned by an individual (20 hectares) or a family (40 hectares).

Though industry's share of national output rose by 50 per cent by around 1970, the price of Nasser's over-ambitious economic plans was inflation, shortages of basic essential commodities, debt, an inflated public-sector payroll, stifling controls, and urban overcrowding (Meredith, *The State of Africa*, 2006). Nasser was increasingly aware of criticism levelled against those who had done well out of the revolution. He was also aware that the limited purge of the military after the 1967 war had not satisfied workers and students, who took to the streets to protest in early 1968. The sentences given to the officers who had been put on trial were considered too lenient, while the students, in particular, were strident in their demands for greater freedom of the press. There was no liberalization, however, and it was foreign affairs that once again entangled Nasser through the summer of 1970.

The successful hijacking of three commercial airlines by members of the **Popular Front for the Liberation of Palestine (PFLP)** in September 1970 led to a major international crisis. Nasser was asked by the United States to broker negotiations between King Hussein of Jordan and Yasser Arafat of the **Palestine Liberation Organization (PLO)**. A ceasefire was agreed but Nasser, already suffering from heart problems aggravated by diabetes, died late in the evening of 28 September 1970. The news of his death brought crowds onto the streets of Cairo to lament the loss of a leader who had come to symbolize Egypt.

> *The years 1956 to 1959 marked the high tide of Nasserism as he seemed to sweep all before him. His appeal to the Arabs – and especially to the younger generation, who formed the majority – was overwhelming. They saw him as a modern Saladin who would unite them in order to drive out the Zionists – the crusaders of the twentieth century. The danger for Nasser was that he was raising expectations which neither he nor Egypt could fulfil.*

From Peter Mansfield, *A History of the Middle East*, Penguin, 2013

Nasser had played an important part in the establishment of the PLO in 1964. This had taken place at an Arab League meeting in Cairo and, although Fatah (led by Yassir Arafat) had not joined the PLO, this 'umbrella organisation of Palestinian groups' was, according to Said Aburish, a method used to control Palestinian actions and to avoid a war with Israel that Nasser knew Egypt could not win (*Nasser: The Last Arab*, 2004, p. 224).

The results of Nasser's social and cultural policies

Education

Nasser knew that the high level of illiteracy and inadequate access to education was a major stumbling block to political reform in Egypt. Of course, what he wanted was for the population to be educated in such a way that they would support and follow his political aspirations. He made primary schooling compulsory, and between 1952 and 1957 the number of students attending technical and vocational schools increased by 40 per cent. Literacy reached 50 per cent by 1970, an improvement on the 80-per-cent illiteracy rate measured in 1952. In his attempt to modernize Islam, he encouraged the teaching of science and technology, a change that had a significant impact upon the curriculum at the al-Azhar University in Cairo, the seat of Islamic learning not only in Egypt but throughout the Arabic-speaking world. Numbers receiving both primary and secondary education rose significantly, and out of 80,000 secondary school graduates in 1969, 34,000 went on to higher education.

University tuition was free and there were small grants for students who could not afford to support themselves.

The role of women

Nasser also tackled the role of women in Egypt. The **veil** was banned, which affected the towns more than the countryside where, traditionally, women had been unveiled. Girls had better access to education and professions were opened up to them. Nasser was a man of his times; he was accustomed to women being mothers and wives rather than having careers. According to Anthony Nutting, however, Madam Tito 'talked him round' to including in the National Charter a pledge to recognize the equality of women. He was persuaded that this was needed to push forward the economic growth of Egypt. Along with this came a realization that family planning was necessary. As we have seen, the population of Egypt, which stood at 26 million in 1960, was growing rapidly, and Nasser was concerned that the economy would not keep pace. Nasser appointed Hikmat Abu-Zayd to the post of minister of social affairs in 1962, the first time a female had held a cabinet post in Egypt. Generally, the role of women did not change so much. In Cairo and Alexandria, the two main cities, the role of women was not so dissimilar to that of their European or North American counterparts. In the countryside, however, especially in Upper Egypt, women still led traditional lives and young girls were often removed from school at an early age. Even so, the overall number of children receiving primary school education rose from 1,300,000 in 1952 to 3,400,000 in 1966 and more than 1,300,000 of these were girls (Stephens, *Nasser*, 1971). There were also 30,000 women in higher education in 1969 out of a total student population of 120,000.

Religion

Nasser was a devout Muslim, although he did not espouse the political Islam of the Muslim Brotherhood. Even so, his relations with this group were not entirely consistent. Before the coup, he had links with them as, indeed, did many army officers, but once in power he saw the Brotherhood as opponents and rivals for the support of the people. Said Aburish describes Nasser's attitude towards the Brotherhood in this way: 'Nasser was an observing Muslim and following the tenets of his religion came naturally to him. But his opposition to political Islam was rock solid, and from that he

TOK

How far, do you think, are values and beliefs something that we are born with or are they shaped by our social or political environment? Can authoritarian leaders change our values and beliefs? Discuss these issues in groups and see if you can come up with examples of leaders who have tried to impose new values or, perhaps, have attempted to suppress religious belief. Were they able to achieve this?

never deviated, nor did he consider compromise. He believed that you could not run a moderate state on the basis of the Koran'. Aburish mentions an incident at one of the prisons in 1957 when the police killed 21 members of the Muslim Brotherhood that were imprisoned there, but 'Nasser never expressed regret over the handling of this incident' (*Nasser: The Last Arab*, 2004).

Sayyed Qutub, the chief **ideologue** of the Muslim Brotherhood, repeatedly criticized Nasser for imposing a state of *Jahiliya* ('ignorance' or the state of a pre-Islamic movement) on Egypt. He was imprisoned several times by Nasser and, in 1966 having been linked to a Saudi plot, was sentenced to death and executed. In return, Aburish states that the brotherhood 'passed a death sentence on Nasser'. Nasser had always been a 'modernist', someone who believed that Muslim societies could embrace new technology and social change without ceasing to be Islamic. This brought him into conflict with the 'fundamentalists', who wanted to reject modernity.

Among the religious minorities in Egypt were the Coptic Christians who represented one of the earliest Christian communities and, during Nasser's rule, accounted for some 10 per cent of the population. Robert Stephens argues that although Egypt was now, officially, an Islamic state, Nasser, nevertheless, resisted attempts by Saudi Arabia to persuade him to bring Egypt into a Muslim alliance, just as he avoided too close a relationship with Pakistan, also an Islamic state, in part because he wanted to remain on good terms with India, a non-aligned partner. In this way, Nasser also allowed some religious freedom in Egypt. In particular, Nasser had a good relationship with Pope Kirollos VI of the Coptic Church and, in 1965, Nasser was invited to lay the cornerstone of the Cathedral of St Mark in Abbasiya.

The Jews were another religious minority in Egypt, although their numbers were significantly reduced after the Six-Day War in 1967 when many lost their property, were arrested, branded **Zionists**, and denied citizenship.

The media and culture

Egyptian newspapers came under state ownership in 1960, and there was strict censorship. Nasser was greeted enthusiastically at first by writers such as Nobel Prize winner Naguib Mahfouz, but encountered their opposition when there was so much suppression of the right to freedom of speech and expression. Nasser was not an avid reader, despite his fondness for military biographies when he was a schoolboy. He is said to have enjoyed films, however, but mostly of the sentimental kind that may have given him a release from the stresses of leadership.

One of the most important ways in which Nasser employed propaganda was through the broadcasts of the news programme, *Voice of the Arabs*. Nasser would give speeches that would be transmitted throughout the region; they were not only popular inside Egypt but also in Iraq and Syria. Nasser used this programme to denounce the Baghdad Pact and to gain support for the nationalization of the Suez Canal. It was a formidable and highly successful way to spread the message of Nasserism. Even so, Said Aburish states that the failure of the news broadcasts to give a true picture of events in the 1967 war meant that even army officers were turning to Israeli radio stations to get a more accurate account of what was really happening.

A recent photo of St Mark's Coptic Christian Cathedral in Abbasiya district of Cairo.

Mohammad Heikal, minister of national guidance and editor-in-chief of the national newspaper, *al-Ahram*, was said to be Nasser's closest friend. Having met in 1952, Heikal and Nasser remained in close contact and had a good mutual understanding. For foreign diplomats and journalists, reading Heikal's column in the daily edition of *al-Ahram* was considered to be the surest way to keep abreast of Egyptian politics.

An important source of entertainment was Egyptian cinema – not only within Egypt but throughout the Middle East. The film industry was nationalized in 1963 and class struggle became the theme of many popular films.

Voice of the Arabs (Radio Cairo)

The radio broadcasts of the *Voice of the Arabs* (or *Radio Cairo*) were an important propaganda tool for Nasser. Broadcast not only in Egypt but throughout the Middle East and Africa, programmes and speeches were, according to Robert Stephens, Nasser's 'most powerful political weapons' (*Nasser*, 1971). Nasser used them not only to criticize any vestiges of imperialism, but also to target any leaders with whom he disagreed, appealing directly to the people of countries such as Jordan and Iraq or Syria.

Activity 14

(ATL) Research and thinking skills

Study the sources below and answer the question that follows.

Source A

Al-Haram (*The Sin*), produced in 1965, is an example of a film with a theme of class struggle.

> [The film's] protagonist, a poor agricultural seasonal worker who had been raped, dies after having to deliver the resulting child in secret. Yet, contrary to the structure of a regular family melodrama in which the individual would have to bear their plight alone, the death of the woman incites the inhabitants of the village to develop solidarity with the seasonal workers to which the woman belonged.

Source B

An example of social realism in the cinema was *al-Mutamarridun* (*The Rebels*) produced in 1966.

> … the extraordinary al-Mutamarridun / The Rebels (1966), directed and written by Taufik Salih […] addressed the issue of class struggle most intensely. [It] focused on peasants versus feudal authorities and workers versus capitalists. In al-Mutamarridun the conflict was depicted in an entirely allegorical and pessimistic way by following the story of a rebellion. A group of infected people, who are kept in a desert camp in quarantine, take over the camp's direction but build up the same unjust and authoritarian structure as the former administration.

Both sources from Viola Shafik, *Companion Encyclopedia of Middle Eastern and North African Film*, Routledge, 2001

1. Read the plots of the two films discussed in Sources A and B, and consider how these may have reflected the themes of class struggle to an Egyptian audience. Which of the two films, do you think, would have been more 'politically correct'? Give reasons to support your answer.

Nasser and the treatment of opposition

Nasser was immensely charismatic, not only in Egypt but also in other Arab states, a quality that not all Arab leaders appreciated but that helped maintain his popularity both at home and abroad. Like all authoritarian leaders, however, Nasser was reluctant to allow freedoms that might imperil his control over the state, and opposition was dealt with harshly.

External opposition

Externally, the emergence of a charismatic *al-Rayyes* (the Captain), as Nasser was known, appealed to the people of neighbouring Arab states and led, inevitably perhaps, to a negative reaction from their own leaders. Nur al-Said, the prime minister of Iraq, saw Nasser as a dangerous rival, likely to incite Iraqis to demand union with Egypt. King Hussein of Jordan allowed the creation of a pro-Nasser government but was equally nervous about where this might lead. In Lebanon, President Camille

In an exam question, you may be asked to consider the 'nature, extent, and treatment of opposition in authoritarian states'. The best approach would be to consider what kind of opposition existed as well as how much of it there was (the extent). If you are asked to discuss how a leader dealt with opposition, don't forget that many leaders took measures to halt opposition by the imprisonment or even the execution of those they considered enemies. Don't forget, however, that as well as punishment, opposition to a ruler could be reduced or avoided by introducing popular policies, as well as by using propaganda to gain support.

CHALLENGE YOURSELF

 ATL Research and thinking skills

Nasser was involved in many of the political changes that took place in other Arab countries at this time. Do some research into how Nasser's policies a) influenced and b) were influenced by one of the following crises:

• Lebanon in 1958

• Iraq in 1958 and 1963

• Syria in 1963.

Chamoun reacted by leaning even further to the West in order to counter what he saw as a threat from Egypt. Indeed, in 1958, Chamoun invoked the Eisenhower Doctrine and US troops were sent, briefly, to Lebanon. In many ways, this was a reaction to the tide of Nasserism and its suspected links to the Soviet Union.

Internal opposition

Inside Egypt, opposition came from the Muslim Brotherhood, who considered Nasser un-Islamic, and from the Communists, who considered him un-socialist. Both groups were targeted and suppressed, and their members filled prisons and concentration camps.

Egyptian Communists

Even when Nasser was close to the Soviet Union, he maintained a ruthless policy of suppression towards the Communists. He was adamant that, although Egypt received aid from the Soviet Union, this would not lead to the introduction of communism in Egypt, and that it would not 'tie us to the wheel of dependency'. In January 1959, especially concerned about the activities of communist groups in both Syria and Iraq, Nasser carried out a purge of the Egyptian Communist Party; 280 of its leaders were arrested and imprisoned. For many of those arrested, this meant years of hardship at the desert 'concentration camp' of Abu Zaabal. Ultimately, because of events in Iraq, Nasser's harsh policy towards the communist opposition did not harm his relations with the Soviet Union. A more likely supporter of communism was Brigadier General Kassim, who, in 1958, had staged a coup in Iraq. In turn, he was overthrown in a CIA-backed coup in 1963. Nasser had outlasted a bitter rival and Khrushchev was ever-willing to ignore Nasser's vehement opposition to Egyptian Communists. Although already banned, the Egyptian Communist Party finally dissolved itself in 1965 and joined the National Committee, but the Muslim Brotherhood continued to be a source of concern for Nasser.

The Muslim Brotherhood

Nasser had cracked down on the Muslim Brotherhood after the attempt on his life in 1954. In 1965, there was a further spate of arrests when Nasser claimed that another plot to overthrow the government had been discovered. More than 400 suspects, including intellectuals, doctors, army officers, and lawyers, were rounded up. Amongst those arrested was Sayyed Qutub, the chief ideologue of the movement. He was tried, sentenced to death and executed, and, in response, the brotherhood passed a death sentence on Nasser. There is no doubt that, for Nasser, the brotherhood represented a threat to the success of the revolution. They opposed socialist policies, secularization, and women's rights; Nasser would not consider any compromise with a movement that promoted a form of political Islam.

Nasser's secret police, the *mukhabarat*, were relentless in chasing down conspiracies both real and imagined, and one of Nasser's ministers stated 'their main task – and source of livelihood – comprised in suggesting to their chief, Nasser, the existence of conspiracies against him, and that they were protecting him from them' (Meredith, *The State of Africa*, 2006).

Anthony Nutting claims that 'suspicion was Nasser's besetting sin and principal weakness' and claims that he would tap the telephone lines of his ministers to keep track of their misdemeanours. One minister was astonished when, asked for his resignation, he was played a recording of a telephone call to a mistress made many years before. Nasser himself was 'incorruptible', but seized upon faults that could be used, if necessary, to remove his 'enemies' from office (*Nasser*, 1972).

Aburish blames General Amer for keeping the details of his security activities hidden from Nasser, who he claims was unaware of the oppressive methods used to maintain the authoritarian state (*Nasser: The Last Arab*, 2004). This is a characteristic associated with many authoritarian leaders such as Stalin and Hitler, whose supporters also believed that their leaders were unaware of the acts of oppression carried out in their names. Aburish says that Nasser was never going to realize his dream of leading the Arab world because he was averse to blood and violence, which made him unfit to rule the Arab Middle East (*Nasser: The Last Arab*, 2004).

Activity 15
 **Thinking, research, and self-management skills**

1. Why is it, do you think, that the claim that the leader is unaware of what is being done in his name is common to many authoritarian states across regions and during different eras?

The personality cult of Nasser

Despite the disaster of 1967 and the economic crises, Nasser remained extremely popular both in Egypt and elsewhere in the Arab world. He was a very persuasive orator who spoke to the Egyptian people using a language that the ordinary 'man in the street' could understand. He knew how to express his ideas in different registers of language and this was a skill he perfected over time.

Said Aburish claims that Nasser was not guided by a strong ideology but that he listened to the people, following rather than leading popular opinion.

Activity 16
Research, thinking, and social skills

1. Successful foreign policies can often be an important method used by authoritarian leaders to stay in power. How far, do you think, is this true of the leaders you have studied?

2. Do you think Nasser's foreign policy decisions helped him to maintain power or did they undermine his hold on power? This is a difficult question and you will need to consider many factors before reaching a decision. In a group, first of all, discuss what Nasser aimed to achieve with his foreign policy and whether or not he was successful. Would you agree that some his actions were undertaken reluctantly?

Was Nasser authoritarian?

A man of the people, Nasser lived in a modest suburban villa rather than a presidential palace and would regularly go home for lunch, just as though he were a low-ranking civil servant. He would even invite visiting heads of state to eat dinner with him at his home, where his wife would prepare simple dishes.

Also, unlike many other authoritarian leaders, he did not create a 'dynasty' and had no plans for his children to follow him into political power. The CIA noted that Nasser was a very difficult target as 'he is too clean, he has no vices', and there was nothing they could find to use against him. Mohammad Heikal, editor of *al-Ahram*, called him the 'pious president'. Said Aburish does claim, however, that the British and the CIA planned to get rid of Nasser, and that there were at least 10 British and two French plots to assassinate him.

Nasser at home introducing his son to Prime Minister Nehru of India.

Nasser with his family outside his home.

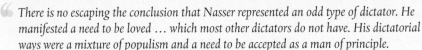

Activity 17 · ATL Thinking skills

Study the sources below and answer the question that follows.

Source A

❝ There is no escaping the conclusion that Nasser represented an odd type of dictator. He manifested a need to be loved … which most other dictators do not have. His dictatorial ways were a mixture of populism and a need to be accepted as a man of principle.

From Saïd Aburish, *Nasser: The Last Arab*, Duckworth, 2004

Source B

❝ He preferred plain Egyptian food and his friends with more sophisticated palates regarded it as a culinary penance to have to dine at the President's house; the menu seemed never to vary, nearly always the same dish of chicken, rice and vegetables – the Cairo middle-class equivalent of meat and two veg. ['Meat and two veg' refers to a British cliché that sums up very conservative British meals consisting of plainly cooked meat and two vegetables.]

From Robert Stephens, *Nasser*, Simon & Schuster, 1971

Source C

❝ Yet, whatever disasters befell Egypt, Nasser never lost his popularity with the masses. When, after the 1967 defeat, he announced his resignation, popular protests propelled him back into office. His reputation as the man who had stripped the old ruling class of their power, nationalised their wealth, booted out foreigners, restored to Egypt a sense of dignity and self-respect and led the country towards national regeneration – all of this counted for far more than the setbacks.

From Martin Meredith, *The State of Africa: A History of the Continent Since Independence*, The Free Press, 2006

1. How far do Sources A, B, and C convey a similar impression of Nasser as an authoritarian leader? How would you sum him up?

Nasserism

It is difficult to define Nasserism. It was often explained as a kind of Arab socialism, although Martin Meredith describes it as a 'system of personal rule', and one of Nasser's biographers, Professor P. J. Vatikiotis, says that Nasser 'managed to abolish the difference between state and government and between those two and himself'.

Nasserism was aimed at improving the lives of ordinary people while being anti-imperialist and firmly against external involvement in Egyptian policy-making. In some ways, Nasser's relations with Israel were always influenced by his belief that Zionism was a manifestation of Western imperialism.

Nasser's membership of the Non-Aligned Movement sums up his left-leaning but independent foreign policy.

Conclusion – Did Nasser achieve his aims?

Gamal Abdel Nasser, unlike many authoritarian leaders, was not inward-looking. He was strongly nationalist, but he also viewed Egypt within the context of the Middle East. Entranced by the concept of a pan-Arab union of states, Nasser tried many different ways to unite the disparate countries that had emerged from centuries of Ottoman rule only to become mandates of Britain and France. It was not until the 1950s that opportunities arose for true independence, and once Nasser and the Free Officers led the way, similar military coups took place in Syria and Iraq.

Whether or not an attempt was made to consolidate independence through membership of the Non-Aligned Movement, the reality of the Cold War meant that one side had to be chosen over the other. With the granting of aid and security, obligations to accede to the requests of the chosen superpower were unavoidable. Despite Nasser's avowed anti-imperialism, under his rule Egypt moved from the British sphere of influence briefly to that of the United States and, ultimately, to that of the Soviet Union.

At home, Nasser attempted to improve the lives of the impoverished masses, but came up against the obstacles of a weak economy and limited availability of education. He tried to remove the bourgeoisie from power, but in many ways the expulsion of foreign businessmen and investors opened new opportunities that benefited the very class that Nasser tried to undermine. In trying to nationalize and democratize Egypt, he created a vast bureaucracy and a new class of managers and administrators, many of whom had come up through the ranks of the army. Time and again, foreign policy intruded to impact on domestic policy, and from the Suez Crisis through the UAR to the Six-Day War, Nasser tried one method after another with mixed success. High inflation, along with an economy that never seemed to improve the lot of the poorest classes, left him frustrated and, increasingly, suffering from ill health. Despite all this, he remained overwhelmingly popular and his death in 1970 was mourned across not only Egypt but throughout the Arab world. The foreign dignitaries who attended the funeral were prevented from following the coffin, for fear they would be trampled by the estimated 5 million distraught mourners who filled the streets.

According to Said Aburish, Chinese Premier Zhou Enlai, who had met Nasser at Bandung in 1955, delivered the ultimate judgement: 'He died of sorrow; he died of a broken heart.'

Photograph of Nasser's funeral procession, from the *al-Ahram* newspaper.

You may be asked to compare and contrast the policies of two or more authoritarian leaders. This type of question requires careful planning, as it would work best if you used a 'comparative structure'. In other words, to compare the policies, in this case of Stalin and Nasser, and then to contrast them. Try not to simply describe first the policies of Nasser and then the policies of Stalin. Such an 'end-on' response, although it may be appropriate for some questions, would not be the best structure for this kind of answer. When you plan your answer, it is a good idea to list all the relevant policies and then jot down how they are similar or different. Perhaps the aims are the same but the methods are different, or some may succeed in one state but fail in the other?

Don't forget that 'social policies' refer to ways in which a leader tried to influence education, culture, the role of women, religion, and the media. Be careful not to confuse 'social' with 'political'.

Activity 18

ATL Thinking skills

Compare and contrast the economic and social policies of Nasser and Stalin.

Here is an extract from a student answer to this essay question:

Student answer – Wyn

Both Stalin and Nasser had a similar aim with regard to economic policy as both wanted their countries to develop and to prosper. Stalin wanted the Soviet Union to catch up with the West and to have industrial growth that would allow it to rearm effectively. In order to do this, Stalin introduced the collectivization of agriculture in 1929 so that food exports could finance industry that would grow by applying Five-Year Plans. Nasser also wanted Egypt to grow quickly and to develop its industry. Nasser also introduced central planning, but Nasser did not bring everything under state control and he did not introduce collectivization of farming. Unlike Stalin, Nasser was not a communist and although he did nationalize some industry and also foreign businesses, he also wanted private business and production to develop. Stalin was prepared to use slave labour to build canals and railways but Nasser, although he was often disappointed because economic growth and investment were difficult to achieve, never used methods like this.

Examiner comment

You can see that Wyn has used a comparative structure quite effectively. He begins the paragraph by comparing the economic aims of the two leaders and then goes on to show how they differ. He could go on to add some statistics to support his argument, but this extract shows a clear understanding of what the question requires.

Activity 19

 Thinking and research skills

1. Draw up a table like the one below to help you determine what Nasser aimed to achieve in Egypt and how successful he was.

Policy	Aims	Achievements	Failures

Activity 20

Revision activity

Look back at the chapter breakdown on page 207. Do you feel confident that you could answer an examination question on all of these topics? Pick your weakest topic and spend some time revising it, then try out one of the practice questions contained in this chapter. Go to the chapter titled 'Comparing and contrasting authoritarian states' and compare Nasser or Egypt with another leader or region. There are lots of ideas in that chapter to help you draw out relevant points for comparison.

To access websites relevant to this chapter, go to www.pearsonhotlinks. com, search for the book title or ISBN, and click on 'Chapter 5'.

Comparing and contrasting authoritarian states

◀ Nasser and Castro

Stalin and Mao ▼

◀ Mussolini and Hitler

Paper 2 Topic 10 only asks open questions, which means questions will not refer to specific leaders or countries in their wording. This means you will be able to select the leaders you would like to use as examples to answer any question on Topic 10.

Some of these questions will ask you to compare and/or contrast two leaders in relation to some of the prescribed content in a topic. They may ask you to choose authoritarian states from different regions, for example Mao (Asia) and Castro (Americas), or allow you to select any two leaders that you have studied.

How to select the appropriate leaders

When studying authoritarian leaders for Topic 10, you will come to realize that some leaders are more 'suitable' than others for specific questions. For example, if a question asks you to *compare and contrast the impact of the policies of two leaders on minorities*, you will probably conclude that Fidel Castro and Nasser may not be the most suitable leaders to write about as neither had particularly strong policies on minorities, which means you would quickly run out of things to say. The question could be addressed more effectively, however, if you choose to write about Mussolini and Hitler.

Likewise, if a question asks you to *discuss the establishment of an authoritarian state*, Stalin may not be the best example to use, because he succeeded Lenin and so an authoritarian state was already established when Stalin became leader. Nasser, however, would be a good example, as although he was not the first president of the Republic of Egypt, it was Nasser who influenced and introduced many of the methods that were used to turn Egypt into an authoritarian state. On the other hand, if the question asks about the rise to power of authoritarian leaders, you could certainly use Stalin.

So, as you work through the chapters in this book, it is important to consider how each of the authoritarian states you study compares with the others. You should also know which ones can be used more effectively for each prescribed content. Using charts like the ones below can help you do this.

Topic	Prescribed content	Leader 1	Leader 2	Leader 3
Emergence	Conditions in which they emerged			
	Methods used			

Topic	Prescribed content	Leader 1	Leader 2	Leader 3
Consolidation	Use of legal methods			
	Opposition			
	Foreign policy			

Topic	Prescribed content	Leader 1	Leader 2	Leader 3
Aims and results of policies	Political			
	Social			
	Economic			
	Cultural			
	Women			
	Minorities			

How to answer *compare and contrast* questions

It is very important that you offer running comparisons and contrasts. Suppose you were asked the following:

> **Compare and contrast the aims and effectiveness of the economic policies of two authoritarian states.**

A running comparison between Mussolini and Castro might read as follows:

Although both Mussolini and Castro aimed at making their economies less dependent of other countries, it could be argued that Mussolini was relatively more successful than Castro. Mussolini wanted to make Italy an autarkic country in order to be able to pursue an aggressive foreign policy. Among the policies he put into practice, we can mention the Battle for Wheat, which aimed at making Italy self-sufficient in grain. Although the battle achieved relatively good results in that the production of wheat increased as expected, it was at the expense of traditional Italian products such as wine and olives. In the case of Fidel Castro, his attempt to raise the production of sugar to 10 million tons to achieve economic independence failed dramatically. Unlike Italy, Cuba fell far from the target, and the impact of the policy on other areas of the economy was greater than in Mussolini's case, as Castro became even more dependent on Soviet aid.

What works in the comparison above?

Both the opening and closing remarks make explicit reference to the aims and the results of the economic policies discussed. This shows an understanding of the demands of the question.

There is sufficient level of detail. It would not be enough for you to say that both policies faced problems. It is always more effective to be able to provide examples of the type of problems faced (e.g. the cost, dependency) – this shows you have specific knowledge that you can effectively apply to address the question.

Planning your answer

You may be asked to compare and/or contrast the rise to power of authoritarian leaders from different regions. In this case, you would need to think quite carefully about what the question is asking. Consider the following question:

> **Compare and contrast how two leaders, each from a different region, used the following methods to establish an authoritarian state: a) ideology and b) use of force.**

Here, you could choose to write about Mao (Asia) and Nasser (Africa and the Middle East).

To help plan your answer, consider devising a two-step plan similar to the one shown on the next page. Start by noting down any points you can think of under each method (see step 1). Add as many relevant points under each method as you can. Using the notes you have gathered in step 1, you can then create a table to give you an overview of the similarities and differences between the leaders and their methods (see step 2).

Step 1: Ideas

Mao

- *Ideology:* Communism–Maoism; appealed to peasants who were the majority in China; united members of the Communist Party of China and gave them ideals to fight for; Mao was also seen as a nationalist and this ideology added to his appeal
- *Use of force:* Response to White Terror; civil war; purging of opponents in the CPC

Nasser

- *Ideology:* Nationalism was very important and linked with anti-colonialism; The Philosophy of Revolution; speeches; appeal of socialism and land reform as ways to improve the lives of the poor
- *Use of force:* the coup of 1952; the imprisonment of opponents such as the Muslim Brotherhood and the Communists

Step 2: Plan

Comparing and contrasting Mao and Nasser

	Comparison	Contrast
Ideology		
Use of force		

Now use the same steps to plan an answer to the following question:

> **Compare and contrast how two authoritarian leaders, each chosen from a different region, were able to use the following methods to rise to power: a) persuasion and coercion, and b) propaganda.**

Note that the question asks about *leaders*, not *states*, so you could choose Stalin as one of the leaders.

When preparing for the exam, do pay attention to the following:

- Avoid the 'one size fits all' approach – don't just revise two leaders and hope they will be good examples to use for all questions.
- Check a map of where the regions are, and make sure you have revised leaders from at least two.
- Make sure that you are familiar with the prescribed content from the IB History Guide and use this as a basis for your revision.
- It can be a good idea to revise leaders with different ideologies, for example, Mussolini and Stalin, as the contrasts as well as the comparisons may then be easier to find.
- Don't forget that the World history topics all have a global context, and that one aim of the course is to encourage you to look at examples from different regions to see how people respond in similar as well as different ways to events that may be local or global in their significance.

Theory of Knowledge

Introduction

The Theory of Knowledge (ToK) course is part of the core of the IB Diploma Programme and, along with the subject-specific courses, counts towards the Diploma. History is both one of the subject-specific courses in the IB Diploma and an area of knowledge in ToK. This chapter aims to discuss the key concepts of ToK, showing the interaction between the History course and its function as an area of knowledge within ToK.

There is a substantial overlap between history and ToK as both emphasize the importance of critical thinking. Both ask the question, 'How do we know?' Both want you to understand that your cultural identity is rooted in the past.

ToK uses knowledge frameworks as a concept to differentiate between areas of knowledge. This table helps you see how a knowledge framework could apply to IB History.

Scope/ applications	• It is the study of the recorded past. • It helps us to understand that our cultural identities are rooted in the past.
Concepts/ language	• It discusses change and continuity. • It explores causation and consequences. • It recognizes the power of language in influencing thoughts and actions.
Methodology	• It has a clear, strong, and demanding methodology. • It has recognized ways of collecting evidence, questioning sources, and constructing theories. • It tests significance. • It asks, 'How do we know?'
Historical development	• It recognizes that current values affect our views of the past. • It changes over time in subject matter and interpretations.

Links to personal knowledge	• It acknowledges the influence of individual historians on shared knowledge. • It allows for a range of perspectives. • It recognizes the importance of a shared history on a person's identity.

You will find that an understanding of ToK will help you to evaluate sources in your History course. It will also help you to complete the reflection section of the Internal Assessment component of the History course.

You may also find that an understanding of history is useful in your ToK course. It will help you to analyse the real-life issue in your ToK presentation and will provide a strong area of knowledge, with great examples, to refer to in your ToK essay.

Ways of knowing

Both ToK and history ask the question, 'How do we know?' ToK answers this question by identifying eight possible ways of knowing. Your knowledge must come from somewhere, and by analysing where it comes from, you are able to assess its reliability.

ToK identifies the eight ways of knowing as:

• Language
• Perception
• Reason
• Emotion
• Memory
• Intuition
• Imagination
• Faith.

You can use these concepts in ToK to assist in:

• checking the reliability of first-hand testimony
• analysing the way emotions influence the witness and the interviewer
• determining the possible bias in the language used
• assessing the fallibility of memory
• analysing the desire to see a rational explanation for events.

You can also use them in history to assist in establishing the origin, purpose, and content of sources, in order to assess their value and limitations.

Language is one of the key ways of knowing, so here is a case study exploring the use of language in the accumulation and communication of knowledge in history.

Case study: The role of language in Communist China

In Mao's China, language was very important in the communication of revolutionary rhetoric. For example, in 1956 the intellectuals were not exhorted to 'tell the Party what you think', but rather to 'let a hundred flowers bloom'.

In this way, the opportunity to express criticism was couched in benign, even romantic, terms.

Source A

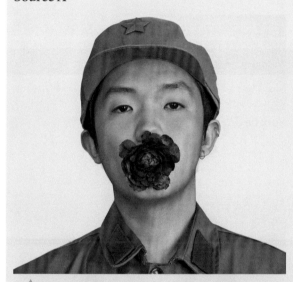

Mei Xian Qiu, 'Let a Thousand Flowers Bloom'.

This is an image created by a contemporary artist based in Los Angeles. Its title is 'Let a Thousand Flowers Bloom', a clear reference to the campaign of 1956. The subject of the image is wearing the traditional uniform of the People's Liberation Army during the Cultural Revolution and is holding a flower in his mouth. The artist described this work as 'a sweet conceit of romance and violence'.

Similarly, during the Cultural Revolution, language was condensed into slogans such as 'To Rebel Is Justified', 'Bombard the Headquarters', and 'The Four Olds'.

In *A Bitter Revolution*, historian Rana Mitter points out the following:

Source B

❝ *The combination of a dominant governing party, a leader with a particular political agenda and a culture hermetically sealed from the outside world meant that there was no tempering mechanism when that leader's project turned out to involve the assignation of violent meaning to words…*

From Rana Mitter, *A Bitter Revolution: China's Struggle with the Modern World*, Oxford University Press, 2005, p. 210

According to Mitter, there was also what he termed a 'verbal violence' of the big-character posters put up on walls to denounce enemies.

Iconoclasm is a term that is often used to describe how the Cultural Revolution (and the May 4th Movement of 1919) attempted to break down links with the past so that a new future could be created. *The Thoughts of Chairman Mao* enshrined the words of *The Great Helmsman*, and quotations were read out loud by study groups. These words were the weapons of the Cultural Revolution.

In *Modern China: A History*, Professor Edwin E. Moïse claims that,

Source C

 Neither Mao nor his followers (published) any clear, rational explanations of their goals during the Cultural Revolution. (They) … often referred to enemies as 'ghosts and monsters', 'freaks' or 'demons'. The intent of these phrases was to indicate that anyone so vile as to oppose the true revolutionary doctrines of Chairman Mao could hardly be considered human. With hindsight however, such language looks like a symptom of the fact that some of Mao's followers, not having been told exactly who or what they were struggling against, were having to conjure pictures of the enemy out of their imaginations. The result was chaos.

From Edwin E. Moïse, *Modern China: A History*, 3rd ed., Routledge, 2008

Activity 1

Study the sources in the case study above and answer the questions that follow.

1. What knowledge do you get from the photo in Source A? The artist described this image as 'a sweet conceit of romance and violence'. Why, do you think, did the artist use these words and how do they help us to understand the image? Why did the artist use 'a thousand' rather than 'a hundred' in the title?

2. To what extent do Sources B and C say the same thing about the use of language during the Cultural Revolution?

3. One of Mao's famous sayings was that 'a revolution is not a dinner party'. What image does this bring to mind? Do you think it is an accurate impression of what he meant to convey?

Areas of knowledge

History is one of the eight areas of knowledge identified by the ToK course. A full list of the areas of knowledge is:

• Mathematics
• Natural sciences
• Human sciences
• History
• The arts
• Ethics
• Religious knowledge systems
• Indigenous knowledge systems.

You can use these areas of knowledge to understand why we approach different types of knowledge in different ways. We recognize that a work of art is not the same as a chemical formula or a historical interpretation. We test them using subject-specific criteria, recognizing that a historical fact cannot be verified in the same way as a scientific fact. History uses a rigorous methodology to test its facts, but it is not the same method as used in the natural sciences. Here is a case study exploring the methodology of history.

Case study: Perceptions of Nasser

Historians writing in English about Nasser have a difficult time finding sources. One of the most well-known is a biography of Nasser written by Anthony Nutting, a politician rather than an academic historian. He knew and admired Nasser, and had resigned from the British government in 1956 over the Suez Crisis.

In the biography, Nutting concludes that:

Source A

❝ *Abdel Nasser was a remarkable man. His contribution to Egypt has guaranteed him a place in history. He gave a sense of national dignity and pride to a people who had known little but humiliation and oppression for two and a half thousand years.*

From Anthony Nutting, *Nasser*, Constable, 1972, p. 477

One of the most recent biographies of Nasser, *Nasser: The Last Arab*, by Said Aburish, was published in 2004. Aburish was a Palestinian-Egyptian journalist and in this biography, he describes his response to the news of Nasser's death in 1970:

Source B

❝ *In faraway California, I heard the news while driving a rented car. Momentarily I lost control of it. After I finally managed to stop it I put my head in my hands and sobbed uncontrollably.*

A state trooper stopped to ask the reason I had parked the car so awkwardly, but after he had a look at me, he asked, "What seems to be the matter, sir?"

"Officer, there has been a death in my family. I've just heard it on the radio."

From Saïd Aburish, *Nasser: The Last Arab*, Duckworth, 2004, p. 311

Finally, here is a photograph of Nasser, who is considered to have been immensely charismatic.

Source C

▲
Photograph taken in 1960.

Activity 2

Study the sources in the case study on the previous page and answer the questions that follow.

1. There is some background information given about the authors of Sources A and B. What else would you need to know about the authors and the sources before evaluating their reliability?

2. Is Source A or Source B more memorable? Should historians write a good story?

3. Source C is a photo of Nasser. Do you think historians are influenced by such images? Is charisma a 20th-century concept? Does it make sense to ask if, for example, Napoleon was charismatic?

There is an interesting interplay between the arts and history. In one sense, the arts reflect the historical forces at play in society, but in another sense, the arts influence history. The next case study explores the complex relationship between them.

Case study: *Guerrillero Heroico*

The image below shows Cuban photographer Alberto 'Korda' Díaz holding his famous photograph of Ernesto 'Che' Guevara, known as *Guerrillero Heroico* or 'Heroic Guerrilla Fighter'.

Source A

▲ *Guerrillero Heroico* by Alberto 'Korda' Díaz, 1960.

At the time the photograph was taken, Guevara was listening to a speech by Fidel Castro. It became internationally popular after Guevara died in 1967. It is now considered the most reproduced image in the history of photography.

Some of the applications of the photograph include the three-peso Cuban banknote, the image of a vodka brand, tattoos worn by superstars, t-shirts, underwear, watches, cigar cases, and smartphone cases. It has also gone from being an image of protest to merchandising, not to mention appearing in museum exhibitions all over the world. This has certainly contributed to making people more aware of Che Guevara and events in Cuba.

'Heroic Guerrilla Fighter' has also been a source of inspiration to other artists. Study the images opposite.

Source B

▲ Portrait of Che by Jim Fitzpatrick, 1968.

Source C

▲ A Pop Art image of Che Guevara.

Activity 3

Study the sources in the case study on the previous page and answer the questions that follow.

1. Are you familiar with the image of Che Guevara in Source A? If you have seen it before, can you remember the context in which you have seen it? To what extent does your knowledge of the Cuban Revolution affect the way in which you interpret and appreciate the photograph in Source A?

2. How do you think the diffusion of the image of Che Guevara as shown in Source A has affected what is known and believed about the history of the Cuban Revolution?

3. At a 2006 photography exhibition that focused on the history of Korda's iconic portrait in the four and a half decades since it was taken, Jonathan Green, director of the UCR/California Museum of Photography, noted how 'Korda's image has worked its way into languages around the world... There isn't anything else in history that serves in this way.' Can you think of other examples where works of art have become symbols of events or people?

4. Consider the statement: 'A work of art is enlarged by its interpretation.' To what extent do these re-enactments (Sources B and C) of *Guerrillero Heroico* contribute to or change the interpretation of Korda's work? What light do they throw on how Guevara is perceived as a leading figure of the Cuban revolution?

Historical development

Historical development is one of the criteria on the knowledge framework that ToK uses to differentiate between the areas of knowledge. Historical development is part of all the areas of knowledge, recognizing that our knowledge and the way we approach that knowledge changes through time. For instance, the way we approach natural sciences and what we know about them today is quite different from a hundred years ago.

You can use this concept to explore how our approach to history changes, i.e. what subjects we study in history, how our views change as more information comes into the public domain, and how our current values influence our view of the past. Historians use reason to construct a logical interpretation of the past based upon the available information. Sometimes there is so much information that it is difficult to find a single thread of cause and effect in it. Sometimes there is too little information. Occasionally new information becomes known, as official documents are released or research is completed.

Historians are human beings with roots in their own time, place, and background. Their interpretations have an emotional and cultural context, so it is not surprising that the interpretations change over time as society's values change.

Here is a case study exploring how both history and our view of history can change.

Case study: Changing perceptions of Mussolini

The historical perspectives of Mussolini that seem to prevail nowadays are associated with the failure of the Fascist State and his incompetence in World War II. However, if you had lived before the invasion of Abyssinia (1935), you would probably have had a very different perspective.

Source A

Below are examples of what two of Mussolini's political contemporaries had to say about him during the 1920s and 30s: Mahatma Gandhi, for example, had called him

❝ one of the great statesmen of our time

Winston Churchill had said:

❝ If I had been Italian, I am sure I would have been with you from the beginning.

In 1934, a composer called Cole Porter mentioned Mussolini in the lyrics of his song 'You are the top'.

Source B

❝ You are the top
You are the great Houdini
You are the top
You are Mussolini

Cole Porter, 'You are the top', 1934

Source C

In 1933, President Roosevelt praised Mussolini in a letter to an American representative:

> ... I am much interested and deeply impressed by what he has accomplished and by his evidenced honest purpose of restoring Italy and seeking to prevent general European trouble.

However, in July 1943, upon hearing Mussolini's resignation, Roosevelt said,

> the first crack in the Axis has come. The criminal, corrupt Fascist regime in Italy is going to pieces.

Quotations from www.ihr.org/jhr/v15/v15n3p6_weber.html and www.azquotes.com/author/12604-Franklin_D_Roosevelt/tag/purpose

Activity 4

Study the sources in the case study above and answer the questions that follow.

1. What was the context in which the different perceptions of Mussolini were expressed in the sources? Think of specific policies and events of the interwar period that may help to explain why Mussolini's government was perceived as a successful example to follow at the time. How important do you consider the context to be in explaining why these perceptions of Mussolini changed dramatically after 1935? Do we understand things as *they* are or understand them as *we* are?

2. Did you react to Gandhi's statement about Mussolini (Source A) in the same way as to Cole Porter's song (Source B)? Explain your answer. To what extent is the 'messenger more important than the message'? How important is this when assessing the reliability of what we read?

3. Can history be written without appealing to value judgements, or do we get a more meaningful experience if we are exposed to them?

4. Why do the negative judgements of Mussolini seem to have prevailed? Is there such a thing as a 'more acceptable history'? If so, what contributes to it?

5. Are we considering the past in all its complexities if we dismiss the positive views as mistaken? How, if at all, do they enrich our understanding of Mussolini and his times?

Personal and shared knowledge

ToK is interested in the links between shared knowledge and personal knowledge as it relates to history. You can use this concept to explore the role of key historians in shaping our shared knowledge, but you can also use it to investigate how our shared knowledge helps shape our own identities. One of the key concepts of IB History is that multiple interpretations are possible, and one of the key concepts of ToK is that individuals should be encouraged to think critically for themselves.

You can use the ToK concept of memory as a way into this topic. On a personal level, memory is important in creating our personalities; on a cultural level, collective memory is important in uniting, but also in dividing, people. The next case study explores memory in history.

Case study: Collective memory of life in the Soviet Union

History is a dynamic subject and historians always look for new ways to interpret the past. They do this by studying new sources that become available or, depending on the political or economic circumstances in which they are working, by asking different questions of the past.

Authoritarian leaders used history to shape a collective memory for the state they ruled. For example, consider *The History of the All-Union Communist Party of the Soviet Union (Bolsheviks): Short Course*. Published in 1938, it was a piece of work commissioned by Stalin.

According to historian Robert Service,

Source A

 …the book was intended as the Bible of the regime. People were expected to read chapters at home after work … Attentive readers who wanted to believe in pronouncements issuing from Moscow persuaded themselves to put their trust in Stalin. And they had to suspend their doubting faculties at the same time.

From Robert Service, *Comrades: Communism: A World History*, Macmillan, 2007, p. 180

In the book, there was no mention of Trotsky or of the other Bolsheviks who had been purged by Stalin. Even if people had personal memories that were different from the official version of events, it was wise to forget those and to accept a different version of the past. Fundamental to the ability of leaders like Stalin to rewrite history was their power to determine what was true.

This next extract is taken from *Inside the Stalin Archives* by Jonathan Brent (2008). This book is an account of Brent's time in Russia in 1992, just after the end of the Soviet Union, when he was negotiating access to archive material for Yale University Press. Brent writes here of seeing a folder of documents on the Doctor's Plot of 1952. Inside was the testimony of Seymon Ignatiev, head of the MGB (later the KGB) at the time of the arrests.

Igantiev stated that Stalin had told him to pass all the 'confessions and testimony' directly to him because:

Source B

…we ourselves will be able to determine what is true and what is not true, what is important and what is not important … Stalin himself would determine the truth.

From Jonathan Brent, *Inside the Stalin Archives*, Atlas & Co., 2008, p. 231

The photograph below is taken in an Orthodox Church in Gori, Georgia. A man is seen holding an image of Stalin as if it were a religious icon. This service was held in 2005 to commemorate the 62nd anniversary of Stalin's death in March 1953.

Source C

▲ Photograph by Vano Shlamov.

Activity 5

Study the sources in the case study above and answer the questions that follow.

1. Sources A and B both give us some indication of how Stalin influenced collective memory in the Soviet Union. He decided what could be known and, once it was known, what was remembered. How 'true', do you think, are memories of people living in an authoritarian state?

2. In Source C, the commemoration of Stalin's death being part of a church service seems rather incongruous. What does this tell us about how societies 'manage' the act of remembering authoritarian leaders? Can you think of other examples where dead leaders are still revered, despite having been dictators responsible for the deaths of thousands (or millions) of their people?

3. In many countries today, the state decides what students should to be taught in history classes. Why, do you think, is this so? Work in groups to come up with specific examples from different countries.

4. Are there events that you remembered differently after you shared your memories with other people? Test this by discussing an event, perhaps from a year or more ago, with the class. Did someone else's memories remind you of something you had forgotten? How ready are we to accept that other people's memories of a shared experience may be more reliable than our own?

Conclusion

There is a considerable overlap between history and ToK. The concepts of change, continuity, significance, causation, consequence, and perspectives are included in the IB History syllabus and they fit well into the knowledge framework in ToK.

You can use skills you develop in history to add depth and meaning to your ToK presentations and essays. You can use skills developed in ToK to help you evaluate sources and to write the reflection section of your historical investigation. You can use the methodology of history to address the real-life issues that you discuss in ToK. By collecting evidence, weighing the value and limitations of sources, and building a logical, consistent interpretation of the facts you will be able to construct sound, well-supported arguments. History is one of the key areas of knowledge in ToK.

For further information about the ToK course, consult the *Pearson Baccalaureate: Theory of Knowledge, 2nd edition*.

FURTHER READING

Books and articles

Chapter 1: Fidel Castro and Cuba

Balfour, Sebastian, *Castro*, 3rd ed., Routledge, 2008

Baloyra, Enrique A. and James A. Morris (eds), *Conflict and Change in Cuba*, University of New Mexico Press, 1993

Batista, Fulgencio, *Cuba Betrayed*, Vantage Press, 1962

Benjamin, Jules, *The United States and the Origins of the Cuban Revolution*, Princeton University Press, 1990

Bethell, Leslie (ed.), *Cuba: A Short History*, Cambridge University Press, 1993

Bunck, J.M., *Fidel Castro and the Quest for a Revolutionary Culture in Cuba*, Pennsylvania University Press, 1994

Chomsky, Aviva (ed.), *The Cuba Reader: History, Culture, Politics*, Duke University Press, 2003

DePalma, Anthony, *The Man who Invented Fidel: Cuba, Castro and Herbert L. Matthews of the New York Times*, Public Affairs, 2006

Domínguez, Jorge I., *Cuba: Order and Revolution*, The Belknap Press of Harvard University Press, 1978

Farber, Samuel, *The Origins of the Cuban Revolution Reconsidered*, University of North Carolina Press, 2006

Fernández, Damián J. (ed.), *Cuban Studies since the Revolution*, University Press of Florida, 1992

Garcia, Luis M., *Child of the Revolution: Growing Up in Castro's Cuba*, Allen & Unwin, 2006

Goldstone, Jack A., *Revolutions: Theoretical, Comparative and Historical Studies*, Wadsworth Publishing, 2003

Guevara, Ernesto, *Episodes of the Cuban Revolutionary War 1956–58*, Pathfinder Press, 1996

Halperín Donghi, Tulio, *The Contemporary History of Latin America*, Duke University Press, 2003

Huberman, Leo and Paul Sweezy, *Cuba: Anatomy of a Revolution*, Monthly Review Press, 1960

Kapcia, Antoni, *Cuba in Revolution: A History Since the Fifties*, Reaktion Books, 2008

Kapcia, Antoni, *Cuba: Island of Dreams*, Berg, 2000

Kirk, John M., *Between God and the Party: Religion and Politics in Revolutionary Cuba*, University of South Florida Press, 1989

Lewis, Paul H., *Authoritarian Regimes in Latin America*, Rowman & Littlefield Publishers, 2006

Luis, William, *Culture and Customs of Cuba*, Greenwood Press, 2001

Pérez, Louis A., *Cuba: Between Reform and Revolution*, 5th ed., Oxford University Press, 2014

Pérez, Louis A., *On Becoming Cuban: Identity, Nationality and Culture*, HarperCollins, 1999

Pérez-Stable, Marifeli, *The Cuban Revolution: Origins, Course, and Legacy*, 3rd ed., Oxford University Press, 2011

Quirk, Robert E., *Fidel Castro*, W.W. Norton & Company, 1993

Rosendahl, Mona, *Inside the Revolution: Everyday Life in Socialist Cuba*, Cornell University Press, 1997

Selbin, Eric, *Modern Latin American Revolutions*, Westview Press, 1993

Smith, Lois M. and Alfred Padula, *Sex and Revolution: Women in Socialist Cuba*, Oxford University Press, 1996

Thomas, Hugh, *Cuba or the Pursuit of Freedom*, Da Capo Press, 1998

Chapter 2: Josef Stalin and the Soviet Union

Applebaum, Annie, *Iron Curtain*, Allen Lane, 2012

Brent, Jonathan, *Inside the Stalin Archives*, Atlas & Co, 2008

Brown, Archie, *The Rise and Fall of Communism*, HarperCollins, 2009

Corin, Chris and Terry Fiehn, *Communist Russia under Lenin and Stalin*, Hodder Murray, 2002

Deutscher, Isaac, *Stalin: A Political Biography*, 2nd ed., Penguin, 1966

Ferguson, Niall, *The War of the World: History's Age of Hatred*, Penguin, 2006

Figes, Orlando, *The Whisperers*, Penguin, 2008

Fischer, John, *The Scared Men in the Kremlin*, Hamish Hamilton, 1947

Fitzpatrick, Sheila (ed.), *Stalinism*, Routledge, 2000

Getty, J. Arch and Oleg V. Naumov, *The Road to Terror: Stalin and the Self-Destruction of the Bolsheviks, 1932–1939*, Yale University Press, 2010

Gill, Graeme, *Stalinism*, 2nd ed., Palgrave Macmillan, 1998

Hobsbawm, Eric, *Revolutionaries*, Abacus, 2007

Hosking, Geoffrey, *A History of the Soviet Union 1917–1991*, Fontana, 1992

Kershaw, Ian and Moshe Lewin (eds), *Stalinism and Nazism*, Cambridge, 1997

Lee, Stephen J., *Stalin and the Soviet Union*, Routledge, 1999

Lewin, Moshe, *The Soviet Century*, Verso, 2005

Lowe, Norman, *Mastering Twentieth Century Russian History*, Palgrave, 2002

McAuley, Mary, *Soviet Politics 1917–1991*, Oxford University Press, 1992

McCauley, Martin, *The Soviet Union 1917–1991*, 2nd ed., Routledge, 1993

Montefiore, Simon Sebag, *The Court of the Red Tsar*, Phoenix, 2003

Nove, Alec, *The Soviet Economic System*, 3rd ed., Routledge, 1987

Rappaport, Helen, *Conspirator, Lenin in Exile*, Windmill, 2010

Setter, David, *It was a Long Time Ago, and It Never Happened Anyway*, Yale University Press, 2002

Service, Robert, *A History of Modern Russia: From Nicholas II to Putin*, 2nd ed., Penguin, 2003

Service, Robert, *Comrades: Communism: A World History*, Macmillan, 2008

Volkogonov, Dmitri, *The Rise and Fall of the Soviet Empire*, HarperCollins, 1999

Chapter 3: Mao Zedong and China

Blaustein, Albert P. (ed.), *Fundamental Legal Documents of Communist China*, F.B. Rothman, 1962

Chang, Jung and John Halliday, *Mao: The Unknown Story*, Vintage, 2007

Chen, Jan: *Mao's China and the Cold War*, University of North Carolina Press, 2001

Chieng, Peikai and Michael Lestz, *The Search for Modern China: A Documentary History*, W.W. Norton & Company, 1999

Dikotter, Frank, *Mao's Great Famine*, Bloomsbury, 2010

Moïse, Edwin, *Modern China*, 3rd ed., Routledge, 2008

Feigon, Lee, *Mao: A Reinterpretation*, Ivan R. Dee, 2002

Fenby, Jonathan, *The Penguin History of Modern China*, 2nd Revised ed., Penguin, 2013

Gittings, John, *The Changing Face of China*, Oxford University Press, 2006

Green, James, *China*, Oxford, 1989

Hobsbawm, Eric, *Age of Extremes: The Short Twentieth Century, 1914–1991*, Michael Joseph, 1994

Houn, Franklin, *A Short History of Chinese Communism*, Prentice-Hall, 1973

Hsu, Immanuel, *China Without Mao*, Oxford University Press, 1982

Hsu, Immanuel, *The Rise of Modern China*, Oxford University Press, 2000

Kueh, Y.Y., 'The Maoist Legacy and China's New Industrialization Strategy', *The China Quarterly*, no. 119, September 1989

Lawrance, Alan, *China Since 1919*, Routledge, 2004

Li, D.J. (ed.), *The Road to Communism: China Since 1912*, Van Nostrand Reinhold, 1971

Li, Zhisui, *The Private Life of Chairman Mao*, Random House, 1994

'Long Live Mao Zedong's Thought', *Peking Review*, vol. 9, no. 27, 1 July 1966

Lynch, Michael, *The People's Republic of China 1949–1976*, Hodder Education, 2008

MacFarquhar, R., *The Origins of the Cultural Revolution*, Columbia University Press, 1983

Meisner, Maurice, *Mao's China and After*, The Free Press, 1999

Morcombe, Margot and Mark Fielding, *China in Revolution*, McGraw Hill, 2007

'Resolution on Certain Questions in the History of our Party Since the Founding of the People's Republic', *Beijing Review*, no. 27, 6 July 1981

Schoenhals, Michael, *China's Cultural Revolution, 1966–1969: Not a Dinner Party*, M.E. Sharpe, 1996

Schram, Stuart (ed.), *Mao's Road to Power: Revolutionary Writings 1912–1949*, vol. 3, M.E. Sharpe, 1995

Snow, Edgar, *Red Star over China*, Random House, 1968

Spence, Jonathan, *The Search for Modern China*, W.W. Norton & Company, 2001

Spence, Jonathan, *Mao*, Viking, 1999

Suyin, Han, *A Mortal Flower*, Jonathan Cape, 1966

Vohra, Ranbir, *China's Path to Modernization*, Prentice Hall, 2000

Chapter 4: Benito Mussolini and Italy

Di Scala, Spencer M., *Italy: From Revolution to Republic, 1700 to the Present*. 2nd ed. Westview Press, 1998

Fermi, Laura, *Mussolini*, University of Chicago Press, 1966

Gallo, Max, *Mussolini's Italy. Twenty Years of the Fascist Era*, MacMillan Publishing, 1973

Gentile, Emilio, '6: Fascism in Power: The Totalitarian Experiment' In *Liberal and Fascist Italy: 1900–1945*, edited by Adrian Lyttelton, 139–74. The Short Oxford History of Italy, Oxford University Press, 2002

Gruber, Helmut, and Pamela Graves (eds), *Women and Socialism, Socialism and Women: Europe between the Two World Wars*, Berghahn Books, 1998

Jensen, Richard, 'Futurism and Fascism' in *History Today*, November 1995

Kallis, Aristotle A., *Fascist Ideology: Territory and Expansionism in Italy and Germany, 1922–1945*, Routledge, 2000

Killinger, Charles L., *The History of Italy*, Greenwood Press, 2002

Lyttelton, Adrian (eds.), *Liberal and Fascist Italy: 1900–1945. The Short Oxford History of Italy*, Oxford University Press, 2002

Lyttelton, Adrian, *The Seizure of Power: Fascism in Italy, 1919–1929*, Revised ed., Routledge, 2004

Mack Smith, Denis, *Italy: A Modern History*, University of Michigan Press, 1959

Morgan, Philip, *Fascism in Europe, 1919–1945*, Routledge, 2002

Payne, Stanley G., *A History of Fascism 1914–1945*, University of Wisconsin, 1995

Pollard, John, *The Fascist Experience in Italy*, Routledge, 1998

Welch, David, *Modern European History, 1871–2000: A Documentary Reader*, 2nd ed., Routledge, 1999

Williamson, David G., *The Age of the Dictators: A Study of the European Dictatorships, 1918–53*, Pearson Education Limited, 2007

Chapter 5: Gamal Abdel Nasser and Egypt

Aburish, Said, *Nasser: The Last Arab*, Duckworth, 2004

Alexander, Anne, *Nasser*, Haus Publishing, 2005

Brown, Archie, *The Rise and Fall of Communism*, HarperCollins, 2009

Freedman, Lawrence, *A Choice of Enemies*, Phoenix, 2008

Hobsbawm, Eric, *Revolutionaries*, Abacus, 2007

Lucas, Scott W., *Divided We Stand*, Hodder and Stoughton, 1996

Mansfield, Peter, *A History of the Middle East*, Penguin, 1991

Mazrui, Ali and Michael Tidy, *Nationalism and New States in Africa*, Heinemann, 1984

Meredith, Martin, *The State of Africa*, The Free Press, 2006

Nutting, Anthony, *Nasser*, Constable, 1972

Rogan, Eugene, *The Arabs: A History*, Allen Lane, 2009

Stephens, Robert, *Nasser*, Simon & Schuster, 1971

Websites

To visit the following websites, go to www.pearsonhotlinks.com, enter the title or ISBN, and click on the relevant weblink.

Chapter 1: Fidel Castro and Cuba

The Economic History of Cuba

Documents relating to Cuba's economic and social history – click on Weblink 1.1.

Latin American Studies

Provides useful links to other websites. Links are classified by category – clink on Weblink 1.2.

The International Institute for the Study of Cuba

A London-based organization devoted to studying the 'social experience' of Cuba – click on Weblink 1.3.

Castro Speech Database

Includes some of the most important speeches and press conferences given by Castro between 1959 and 1996 – click on Weblink 1.4.

Magnum photos

Online exhibition of photographs to commemorate the revolution's 50th anniversary – click on Weblink 1.5.

Fidel Castro – PBS

Contains maps, timelines, original footage and articles on the history of Cuba under Fidel Castro – click on Weblink 1.6.

Propaganda posters

These posters will help you understand Cuba's view on many of the Cold War conflicts – click on Weblink 1.7.

Chapter 2: Josef Stalin and the Soviet Union

Old posters about Stalin and the Soviet people

A good site for propaganda posters published in the Soviet Union – click on Weblink 2.1.

Marxists website

A useful site to browse for more information on 'socialist realism' and with good links. Be a little wary of the source, however – click on Weblink 2.2.

Holocaust Research Project

Information on the German invasion of the Soviet Union – click on Weblink 2.3.

Cold War – National Archives

Useful archives or links to the role of Stalin in the Cold War – click on Weblink 2.4.

Soviet archives

A Library of Congress exhibition on the Soviet archives – click on Weblink 2.5.

Chapter 3: Mao Zedong and China

The Historical Experience of the Dictatorship of the Proletariat

Full text of the book by the Foreign Languages Press – click on Weblink 3.1.

Stefan Landsberger's Chinese Propaganda Poster Pages

Stefan Landsberger's book and website are invaluable sources for anyone studying China under Mao. The series showing how China's perception of the role of women changed over time is well worth viewing – click on Weblink 3.2.

Selected Works of Mao Zedong

Extensive collections of writings by Mao Zedong from Marxists.org – click on Weblink 3.3.

Chapter 4: Benito Mussolini and Italy

Propaganda Posters

An interesting collection of government propaganda posters – click on Weblink 4.1.

Mussolini Declares War in 1940

It's very useful to see Mussolini 'in action'. Also, to assess popular reaction to the declaration of war and the support for Mussolini – click on Weblink 4.2.

Political Speeches

This website contains all of Mussolini's speeches between 1914 and 1923 – click on Weblink 4.3.

Political Speeches

This website contains all of Mussolini's speeches between 1914 and 1923 – click on Weblink 4.3.

Chapter 5: Gamal Abdel Nasser and Egypt

Six-Day War

Website about the 1967 conflict, which includes some analysis of Nasser's handling of the situation – click on Weblink 5.1.

Mid East Web

A major website on Middle Eastern affairs. Search the website with the term 'Nasser' to bring up primary and secondary sources – click on Weblink 5.2.

Suez Crisis

In-depth BBC history of this episode in Egyptian history – click on Weblink 5.3.

The Other Side of Suez

A documentary on The Other Side of Suez – click on Weblink 5.4.

Glossary

abrogate: To revoke or do away with a law or formal agreement.

anschluss: The annexation of Austria by Germany in 1938.

apartheid: Meaning segregation, the term refers to a former policy of segregation as well as political and economic discrimination against non-whites in the Republic of South Africa between 1948 and 1994.

Arab League: Negotiations to set up a league of Arab states began in 1942. A meeting took place in Alexandria, Egypt, in 1943 but it was not until 1945 that the Arab League was officially established. It consisted of six Arab nations: Egypt, Transjordan, Iraq, Saudi Arabia, Syria, and Lebanon. Yemen joined soon after.

asylum: Granting a citizen of one country refuge in a foreign, sovereign state, or its territory.

autarky: Meaning economic independence or self-sufficiency.

Ba'athist Party: Meaning renaissance or resurrection, the first Ba'athist Party was founded in Syria in 1940 and began as a secular anti-imperialist political party that aimed to unite the Arab countries.

Baghdad Pact: In 1955, Britain, Iraq, Turkey, Iran, and Pakistan joined together in a NATO-style alliance with the aim of preventing the spread of Soviet influence into the Middle East.

barefoot doctors: Introduced into China in 1965, these were farmers who had received basic training in primary care services such as immunization and delivering births. The aim was to bring health care to rural areas using both traditional Chinese and modern Western methods.

batistianos: Supporters of Cuban president Fulgencio Batista (1940–1944). Batista was also a Cuban dictator from 1952 to 1959, before being overthrown during the Cuban Revolution.

blitzkrieg: The German term for 'lightning war'; an intense military campaign intended to bring about a swift victory.

Bolshevik: A member of the majority faction of the Russian Social Democratic Labour Party, which seized power in the October Revolution of 1917.

bond: A certificate issued by a government or a company promising to repay borrowed money at a fixed interest rate at a specified time.

capitalism: An economic system where a great deal of trade and industry is privately owned and runs to make a profit.

centrally planned economy: A system in which the state directs and controls all major economic areas and decides upon the distribution of resources and production, following a national plan.

class enemies: According to Karl Marx, class struggle lay at the heart of human interaction: conflict between classes, each one fighting for its own interests, lay within every society. For example, in China, the interests of the middle classes (or bourgeois including the GMD) would not be the same as those of the peasants or the proletariat whose interests were championed by the CPC.

Comintern: The abbreviation for the Communist International. This organization was set up in Moscow in March 1919 and its task was to coordinate communist parties all over the world, helping the spread of global communism.

communism: A political viewpoint in which all businesses and farms should be owned by the state on behalf of the people. Only one leader and party is needed, and goods will be distributed to individuals by the state. Everyone will thus get what is needed and everyone will be working for the collective good.

Communist Information Bureau (Cominform): Established in 1947, Cominform was, to some extent, a response to the development of the Marshall Plan or European Recovery Plan. Czechoslovakia and Poland had shown interest in taking part in the Marshall Plan, but Stalin wanted to ensure that there was a uniform (negative) response among the satellite states of the Eastern Bloc.

Communist Party of China (CPC): The ruling political party of the People's Republic of China, founded in 1921. In 1949 it defeated the Guomindang and has been in power since.

Confederación Nacional del Trabajo (CNT): Translated as the National Confederation of Labour, it was founded in 1911 but was banned at various times, it was the largest labour union in Spain and supported by the Comintern.

cooperative: An association managed by the people who work in it.

Council for Mutual Economic Assistance (Comecon): Established in 1949 as a kind of trade organization among communist states. It was not limited to the Eastern Bloc and, in time, included Mongolia, Cuba, and Vietnam.

coup: A violent or illegal seizure of power by a small group or clique.

democratic centralism: A decision-making system and disciplinary policy adopted by the Communist Party of the Soviet Union, subsequently followed by the Communist Party of China and by communist parties in other countries.

Democratic Movement for National Liberation (DMNL): This party united the Egyptian Movement for National Liberation with Iskra. Both parties had been set up in 1943 and both were communist. The DMNL was also known by its Arabic acronym, Haditu.

détente: The easing of hostility or strained relations between countries.

economies of scale: A term used by economists to convey the idea that an increase in the scale of production can increase total output and can reduce the average cost of each unit of output. In the case of Chinese agriculture, the bigger the farm, the more efficient the production, because of mechanization, cooperation, and specialized labour. This was supposed to lead to higher productivity.

embargo: An official ban on trade or other commercial activity with a specific country.

expropriation: Taking property out of an owner's hands by public authority.

fascism: A political ideology that favours limited freedom of people, nationalism, use of violence to achieve ends, and an aggressive foreign policy. Power is in the hands of an elite leader or leadership. Italian Fascism (Fascism for short) is the name given by Mussolini to his movement from 1922.

fedayeen: It means 'freedom fighters'. These were Palestinian refugees living in Gaza and Sinai who launched surprise attacks on Israeli border posts or settlements.

fellahin: The name given in Egypt to the poor peasant farmers who worked the land. The land reforms carried out after the 1952 revolution were intended to benefit the *fellahin*.

feudalism: In European history, the system of feudalism refers to a system of government whereby the King would parcel out land to his knights, who swore loyalty to him. They would be given ownership of both the land and the peasants who farmed it.

Gang of Four: This was the name given (as an insult) to the group that included Jiang Qing, Wang Hongwen, Zhang Chunqiao, and Yao Wenyuan. They behaved ruthlessly during the Cultural Revolution enforcing the purging of all opposition and readily condemning party officials as 'counter-revolutionaries'. It was said that Mao was the first to refer to them as a gang, when he warned them not to behave 'like a gang'.

Gosplan: Meaning the State Planning Commission, it was set up in February 1921 to coordinate and organize the Soviet economy. It was very important in gathering statistics and allocating resources for the Five-Year Plans. It continued to function until 1991.

Great Depression: The economic crises that began in the United States in 1929 with the collapse of the stock market, and which led to financial ruin of banks in Europe and the United States, and impacted on economies worldwide during the 1930s.

guerrilla: An irregular military force fighting small-scale, fast-moving actions against conventional military and police forces. Guerrilla tactics involve constantly shifting points of attack, sabotage, and terrorism. The strategy of the guerrilla is to wear down the enemy until he can be defeated in conventional battle or sues for peace. (The word guerrilla means 'little/small war' in Spanish.)

gulag: A network of forced labour camps in the Soviet Union, or a camp in this network.

Guomindang (GMD): This is the name of the Nationalist party led by Jiang Jieshi that fought against the Communists in the Chinese Civil War. After it lost to Mao Zedong's Communists in the Civil War, it set up Chinese Nationalist government on the island of Taiwan (also known as Republic of China).

historiography: The study of the writing of history and of written histories.

Holodomor A Ukrainian word that means to kill by starvation.

ideologue: A supporter of an ideology who is uncompromising in his or her belief.

Islamic Caliphate: An area ruled by a caliph or chief Muslim ruler.

kulak: The name given to many of the peasants in the Soviet Union who resisted attempts by Stalin to collectivize farms. These so-called 'richer peasants' were arrested and either deported or executed.

League of Nations: An international organization set up after World War I intended to maintain peace and encourage disarmament.

lictor: A Roman official who protected the magistrates of the city.

mandate: A commission from the League of Nations to a member state to administer a territory.

manifesto: A public declaration of a political party's or candidate's policy and aims, most likely to be issued before an election.

martial law: An extreme measure to control society during war or periods of civil unrest. Certain civil liberties are suspended and government military personnel have the authority to make and enforce civil and criminal laws.

Marxism: A political ideology based on the works of Karl Marx and Friedrich Engels, the main belief of which was that the workers would rise up against the middle and upper classes to create a society where all resources are shared.

mass line: A term used in communist literature to refer to the leadership of the masses (hence, mass line). In Maoist thought, the 'mass line' referred specifically to the leadership that came from the peasants. Mao often used the phrase 'to learn from the peasants', meaning to use them as a source of practical knowledge, as opposed to party ideology that was too theoretical.

monoculture economy: The agricultural practice of producing or growing one single crop over a wide area.

Muslim Brotherhood: This movement embodied anti-colonialism with a call for a rejection of 'modernity' and a return to a more fundamentalist Islamic state.

national liberation movement: A group that arises in a developing nation to gain independence from foreign rule.

nationhood: The status of being a nation or developing a national identity.

nomenklatura: The members of the *nomenklatura* formed the 'ruling class' of the Soviet Union. These were the senior officials of the Communist Party, the ones who made the policies. The name comes from the list of jobs that were available within the Party.

non-alignment: A term to describe the movement in which a group of countries pursued a neutral position in the Cold War. The Non-Alignment Movement was officially established in Belgrade, 1961.

Glossary

North Atlantic Treaty Organization (NATO): A military alliance founded in 1949 by European and North American states for the defence of Europe and the North Atlantic against the perceived threat of Soviet aggression.

Palestine Liberation Organization (PLO): Set up by the Arab League in 1964 to use armed struggle to secure the 'right of return' for all Palestinians. Yasser Arafat was appointed chairman of the PLO in 1969 when it broke away from the control of the Arab states after their resounding defeat in the Six-Day War.

paramilitary organizations: Groups organized along military lines that are not part of the regular armed forces of a country.

***Partido Obrero de Unificación Marxista* (POUM):** Translated as the Workers' Party of Marxist Unification, this organization was founded in 1935 and had its strongest base in Catalonia. Its ideology was linked to that of Trotsky rather than Stalin.

***Partito Socialista Italiano* (PSI):** Translated as the Italian Socialist Party, the PSI was founded in 1892. It was one of the first Italian parties to have national presence. During World War I it adopted a pacifist, neutral position towards the conflict.

plebiscite: A plebiscite means that voters are given the opportunity to express their support of or opposition to a single issue.

Popular Front for the Liberation of Palestine (PFLP): An organization founded in 1967 by George Habash, who became its first secretary-general. Its ideology was both secular and socialist, and it called for armed struggle for the recovery of the Palestinian state.

popular front: A term to describe governments composed of left and centre-left parties, including members of a communist party. Until 1935, communist parties outside the Soviet Union had been ordered not to take part in government. With the rise of anti-communism, this policy was now reversed.

positive neutralism: A term used to describe the policy of non-alignment in the Cold War.

proletariat: Meaning the working class, they are wage earners who must earn their living by working.

Qing dynasty: A dynasty established by the Manchus that ruled China from 1644 to 1911.

rapprochement: An establishment or resumption of harmonious relations between two parties in international affairs.

ras: A term for local and regional Italian Fascist party bosses, named after the Ethiopian chieftains that had defeated Italy in 1896.

Red Week: A period in June 1914 when large-scale strikes and protests took place across Italy against liberal government reforms.

Russian Social Democratic Labour Party (RSDLP): This political party was set up in Minsk in 1898 and focused on the role of the workers in the overthrow of the autocratic system in Russia. Almost immediately, the leaders were arrested and sent into exile. Lenin, among others, went abroad.

Salò Republic: The Italian Social Republic was named after the town of Salò, near Lake Garda in northern Italy where Mussolini initially located his government.

self-determination: The process that enables a country to determine its own statehood and form its own government.

socialism: A political theory of social organization stressing shared or state ownership of production, industry, land, etc.

Sovnarkom: Meaning the Council of People's Commissars. The overthrow of the Provisional Government after the October Revolution of 1917 meant that it had to be replaced by a temporary government until elections could be held. Sovnarkom was the name of the council made up of 15 commissars or ministers. Lenin was the chairman, Trotsky became the commissar for foreign affairs, and Stalin was appointed the commissar for nationalities.

Stresa Pact: An agreement between Italy, Britain, and France signed in April 1935 to act collectively to resist a German challenge to the Treaty of Versailles. It broke down two months later, when Britain and Germany signed the Anglo-German Naval Agreement.

terms of trade: The relationship between the prices at which a country sells its exports and the prices paid for its imports.

theocracy: A system of government in which officials rule in the name of a god, or by divine guidance.

total war: A term used to describe a war in which all the resources of the state are put at the disposal of the government to achieve victory. This will often entail the taking over of vital industries for the duration of the war; the rationing of food and other necessities; the conscription of men (and women in some cases) into the army or into factories; restrictions on access to information, on travel, and so on.

Treaty of London (1915): Also known as the London Pact, it was a secret pact signed in London on 26 April 1915 by the United Kingdom, France, Russia, and Italy.

Treaty of St Germain (1919): A peace treaty concluded in 1919 between the Allies and the Austrian Republic that ended the Austro Hungarian Empire, redistributed parts of its territory and forbade Austria to unite with Germany.

Tripartite Agreement (1950): An agreement made between Britain, the United States, and France in 1950 to defend the armistice line (as determined by Arab–Israeli armistice agreements) and to control the sale of arms to the Middle East.

Twenty-one Demands: These were a set of Japanese demands made in 1915 that would have given Japan significant control over China.

universal suffrage: The right of almost all adults to vote in a political election.

Upper and Lower Egypt: These are geographic terms to describe the Upper and Lower stages of River Nile. Upper Egypt refers to the south, where the Nile enters Egypt from Sudan, and Lower Egypt refers to the north, where the Nile flows into the Mediterranean Sea.

veil: This refers to the niqab or the short veil worn to cover the face. The hijab or headscarf was more common in the countryside than the cities where, during much of the 20th century, the middle classes especially were less likely to adopt either the hijab or the niqab.

Vesenkha: Meaning the Supreme Council of the National Economy, this institution was set up in December 1917 to control the newly nationalized industries of the Russian Socialist Federative Soviet Republic and later of the Soviet Union. It existed until 1932, when it was reorganized into different departments.

Wehrmacht: The term used for the German army between 1935 and 1946.

Zionist: A follower of the political movement originally created for the re-establishment of a Jewish nation; it now focuses on the development and protection of the Jewish nation in Israel.

Index

Italic page numbers indicate an illustration, be it a picture, table or map. Bold page numbers indicate an interesting fact box.

Improve your learning

Take a look at some of the interactive tools on your eText.
Note that the examples below may be from a different title, but you will find topic-appropriate resources on your eText.

Vocabulary lists

Complete vocabulary lists help support you to understand any unusual terms.

Theory of Knowledge

Aboriginal people the people who have been in a region since ancient times

abstract existing in thought as an idea without an actual existence

abstract ideas existing in thought as an idea without actual existence

abstractions things reduced to their most basic characteristics

acquired to have taken possession or ownership of

adopted legally made part of a family that someone was not born into

agnostics people who doubt that there is a God

agricultural purposes related to farming

algebra the part of mathematics that uses letters and other general symbols to represent numbers, and quantities in formulae and equations

Allah the Muslim name for God

altruistic unselfish, willing to make sacrifices

ambiguity confusion because words or sentences have more than one meaning

Amish a Christian group living in old-fashioned ways in Pennsylvania and Ohio

...rsing engaging in a detailed examination

... detailed examination

...metry the branch of algebra that ...tric objects such as points, lines,

atheists people who do not believe ... deities

atom the smallest component of an ... living thing

audience participation the ability of t... to take part, ask questions

authoritarian governments governme... concentrate power in the hands of o... small group; people are not given fre... rights

authority figures people in a position ... over someone else

authority right to be believed or hav...

autism a mental condition that beg... childhood and which causes diffi... human communication and lan...

awakening reaching a higher lev...

axioms basic rules in mathema... considered to be absolute ...

Babylon Noah's city in Ir... was the capital of a...

Behaviourists psyc... observable, ...

biases opi... ide...

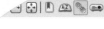

.gy

1.1 Introduction to cells

PDF

Main idea
In many celled organisms, individual cells take on specific tasks.
Individual cells may replace damaged or diseased cells when needed.

Understanding: According to the cell theory, living organisms are composed of cells.

Model sentence: **The** cell theory **states that** organisms **are made up of one or more cells.**

- Some living organisms are composed of only one cell, such as *Paramecium*. These organisms are referred to as unicellular.
- Multicellular organisms, such as trees and birds, are composed of many cells.

Hints for success: Whenever the term organism is used, think of cells and life.

Nature of science: In biology, there are often exceptions to theories and belief... There are exceptions to the cell theory statement that says all organisms ar... made up of cells.

...ntists recognize that exceptions to the cell theory include giant fun... ...ot have walls separating cells, and striated muscle cells i...

...ulary
...rtant cellular
... that all
... of one or
...e smallest
...ome from
... exist

...ng the

Audio

Audio versions of definitions and articulation sentences help you to understand and unlock key information.

Interactive glossary

A searchable audio glossary gives you a handy reference tool for any difficult words, with audio to support your learning. Select highlighted words in the text to hear the audio version of the term and definition.

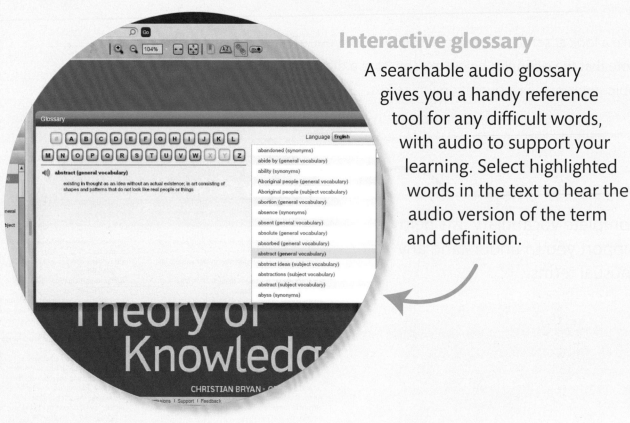

Notes

Add and save handy notes to help aid your revision.

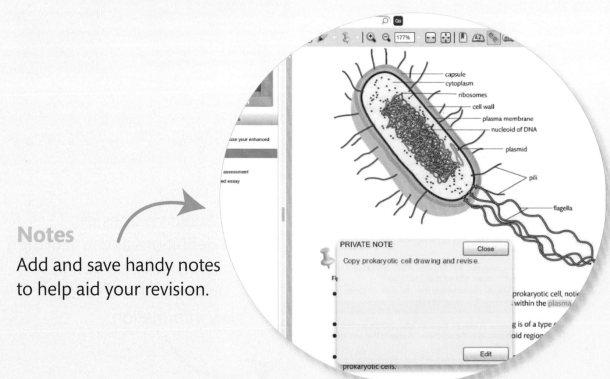